MW00812514

The Museum in the Cultural Sciences

BARD GRADUATE CENTER
CULTURAL HISTORIES OF THE
MATERIAL WORLD

Cultural Histories of the Material World is a series centered on the exploration of the material turn in the study of culture. Volumes in the series examine the ways human beings have shaped and interpreted the material world from a broad range of scholarly perspectives and show how attention to materiality can contribute to a more precise historical understanding of specific times, places, ways, and means.

Peter N. Miller, Series Editor

Other books in the series include:

Antiquarianism and Intellectual Life in Europe and China, 1500–1800
Peter N. Miller and François Louis, Editors

The Sea: Thalassography and Historiography
Peter N. Miller, Editor

Cultural Histories of the Material World
Peter N. Miller, Editor

Ways of Making and Knowing: The Material Culture of Empirical Knowledge
Pamela H. Smith, Amy R. W. Meyers, and Harold J. Cook, Editors

The Anthropology of Expeditions: Travel, Visualities, Afterlives
Joshua A. Bell and Erin L. Hasinoff, Editors

Ex Voto: Votive Giving Across Cultures
Ittai Weinryb, Editor

In Space We Read Time: On the History of Civilization and Geopolitics
Karl Schlögel

The Art of the Jewish Family: A History of Women in Early New York in Five Objects
Laura Arnold Leibman

The Museum in the Cultural Sciences

Collecting, Displaying, and Interpreting Material Culture in the Twentieth Century

Edited by Peter N. Miller

Bard Graduate Center

New York City

Peter N. Miller is dean and professor at Bard Graduate Center.

Distributed by the University of Chicago Press. This book may be purchased in quantity for educational, business, or promotional use. For information, please email marketing@press.uchicago.edu.

Designed by Laura Grey and Molly Haig
This book is set in New Baskerville ITC Pro.
Printed in the United States of America

Library of Congress Control Number: 2020942678
ISBN 978-1-941792-16-2

A catalogue record for this book is available from the British Library.

10 9 8 7 6 5 4 3 2 1

To my dear friends Béla Kapossy,
Joan-Pau Rubiés, Bill Sherman:
for years and years of talk and love

"Every beloved object is the center of a paradise."
—Novalis, *Miscellaneous Observations*

Contents

Series Editor's Preface

Very few people know, *really know*, their great-grandparents. Think about it. How many of you have been able—or really wanted—to find out about the world in which your great-grandparents grew up? *Their* family, *their* childhood influences. I certainly didn't. Yet it is indisputably true that those contexts influenced your great-grandparents' development and thus how they raised their children—your grandparents—and these, in turn, your parents. I don't have to go any further. The same is true among scholars. We usually have read all the works of our doctoral parents. Some of us will go on, motivated probably by curiosity though sometimes by necessity, to read the works of our teachers' teachers because we want to know why our teachers became what we knew them to be. But how many of us have made the effort to learn about the teachers of the teachers of our teachers? The trail goes cold.

Think of it: at a distance of four generations, almost like clockwork, a whole cohort of scholarship disappears into the abyss, not because of anything inherent in it but because of our own lack of interest or failure of curiosity or simple prioritizing of what is likely to interest our colleagues. I'm sure some of you are already formulating as an objection something we've all felt when browsing an open-stacks library collection, namely, how much old rubbish there is. But even if well more than half of what was produced in our great-grandparents' generation has earned its abyss, that means there is still a lot more to read than we generally read. Let's take one example. Is it really the case that from historians of the generation of Jacob Burckhardt we should today read only . . . Jacob

Burckhardt? There is so much interesting work that has been done in ferreting out facts and in posing questions. The virtue of these facts coming from a distant context allows us to see them in different and, inevitably, thought-provoking ways.

Burckhardt's young philosophical admirer Friedrich Nietzsche talked about how, in addition to the aspirational and preservational modes of thinking with the past, there was also the "critical" mode. He defined this as one's willingness "from time to time, to shatter and dissolve something to enable him to live: this he achieves by dragging it to the bar of judgment" (*On the Advantage and Disadvantage of History for Life*, §3). Our recuperation of a distant historiography is critical in just this way: it provides us with a platform from which to assault the self-confident redoubt of our own generation's received wisdom. As you can see from the reflections of the notable group of commentators we have corralled, the challenge of Otto Lauffer and Oswald Richter, although a century old, still rings loud and true. They have something important to tell us; they give us something important to think about.

In this, the year of the opening of the Humboldt Forum, it seems especially appropriate to bring Lauffer and Richter back into the conversation of the living, for it is something of their world that is being brought back to our attention in the center of Berlin. They might be as surprised to find their articles in the center of debate as to discover the old Berlin ethnographic collections brought back to the center of the city. But it was Richter, then a very young curator, who, while a confident supporter of the German "civilizing," imperial vision, also acknowledged more than a century ago that "until the seventeenth century ethnographic objects were looted items; in many ways they remain so today."

These texts have been lying in wait for us to catch up to them. A "critical historiography" recovers work of the scholarly past from its generational oblivion and uses it to sort out present-day problems. This book you are holding in your hands, then, like all books published in the series Cultural Histories of the Material World, works on two levels: it presents information that intervenes directly in our contemporary debates, and it makes an argument about ways to study the past.

Peter N. Miller
Bard Graduate Center
New York City

Acknowledgments

This has been a complicated project to bring into port. I want to thank the translators, first and foremost, Annika Fisher and Nils Schott, for their dedication to making nineteenth-century academic German accessible for twenty-first-century English readers. I want to thank Caspar Meyer for carefully reviewing the translations, and Christian Feest for putting his professional knowledge at the service of improving the translations. The copyeditor, Heidi Downey, persevered through the length of the project and the challenge of both the translated text and the submissions. This is the first book designed by Laura Grey since her return to Bard Graduate Center—it's great to have her back. Daniel Lee, as always, has made working on this project a thorough pleasure. Susan Weber read the introduction with her typical care and offered incisive and helpful comment. So did Marina Rustow. I thank them both. Andrew Abbott read the chapter on Max Weber and saved me from my ignorance in several instances. Of the contributors, to all of whom I am uniformly grateful, I want to single out Mariët Westermann, who, when she was at the Andrew W. Mellon Foundation, was responsible for teaching me about the importance of museums. My friendship with Béla Kapossy, Joan-Pau Rubiés, and Bill Sherman goes back to our time together in Cambridge. Looking back from today to the days of 7 North Terrace (of bad wine and good roses), I want to say how grateful I am, and how lucky.

P. N. M.

Introduction:
What Kind of Knowledge
Is Museum Knowledge?

Peter N. Miller

The two long, thoughtful articles translated and printed in this book are historical documents, telling us something of what was being thought in Germany in the first decade of the twentieth century. They are riveting in their intelligence, conceptual acuity, and range of reference. Because of this they are also provocations to us, right now, to think with them about how objects teach, how this teaching is activated through the objects' display, and how we should think of the museum within the cultural sciences.

Why are we doing it this way? Why try to answer a question about our present through our past? Because a "critical historiography," in the sense Nietzsche intended, gives more than answers to present questions. We want to see what a forgotten body of knowledge might tell us, but we also want to know why we have those questions to begin with. Indeed, questions themselves have a history. So, while in this book we return to the German museums journal *Museumskunde* and its world in the years 1905–10, by engaging in a critical history of scholarship we can discover ways to a new museum thinking—and change the future.

I

In 1904 the Kaiser-Friedrich-Museum, directed by Wilhelm Bode (he was not ennobled until 1913), was founded. In 1905 Adolf Bastian died. Bastian believed that ethnology museums constituted the material

1

archive of humanity. Their collections were to be research factories devoted to the production of new knowledge. He saw a sharp break between the wonder aimed at by the early modern cabinets of curiosities and the modern ethnological museum. Bode also saw a gulf between the idiosyncratic clutter of the *Wunderkammer* and the accessible aesthetics of the modern museum, leading him to characterize Bastian's museum-archive as an early modern dinosaur surviving into a later age. A generation later it was clear that Bode's vision had won out.[1]

Museumskunde began publishing in that same year, 1905. It was just a year after David Murray began his book *Museums: Their History and Their Use* by documenting the absence of a discussion of museums in the chief reference books of England, France, and Germany. At the time, museums did not even warrant a listing in the subject index of the British Museum.[2] The journal—edited by Karl Koetschau, who worked in the Dresden museums—has been the subject of new research, on both its attentiveness to questions of display and its cosmopolitanism, which was rare at the time.[3] In those early editions one sees the breadth of vision—the sense that the need of the moment was for tapping into a new and strong current of thought.

Museumskunde was, in fact, preceded by the *Zeitschrift für Museologie und Antiquitätenkunde*. It, too, had an editor associated with the Dresden museums—J. G. Theodor Grässe, who had headed the porcelain collection and then the Green Vault, with its *Wunderkammer*-like treasures. The publication was short-lived (1878–85), but observers have noted that it is "striking how contemporary many of the themes handled there are still today"—and this is true for *Museumskunde* as well.[4]

That the *Zeitschrift für Museologie* and *Museumskunde* were both based in Dresden reminds us how much innovative thinking there was outside Berlin. For example, the foundation in 1852 of the Römisch-Germanisch Museum in Mainz and the Germanisches Nationalmu-seum in Nürnberg had generated significant theoretical discussion.[5] Likewise, the two articles under review here are by scholars who were formed outside Berlin. From our perspective, the founding of *Museumskunde* may mark the last flowering of a provincial leadership in Germany's museum culture.

The lack of constraint that might characterize being outside Berlin could extend to the editorial process, as Koetschau was willing to publish two very long multipart articles by two men in their early thirties who were at the beginning of their careers.

The men are Otto Lauffer (1874–1949) and Oswald Richter (1873–1907). Lauffer was then assistant to the director of the Städtisches Historisches Museum in Frankfurt, and Richter had just arrived, in 1904, at the Museum für Völkerkunde in Berlin from the Royal Zoological and Anthropological-Ethnographic Museum in Dresden. Lauffer would go on to a glorious career as a museum director, professor, and university rector—and then an ignoble posterity as one of Hitler's willing professors.[6] Richter died at thirty-four, poisoned by an Indonesian arrow he had handled, a little too casually, in the course of his duties.[7]

It is unlikely the two knew each other, and yet, like Orion the hunter and Taurus the bull, their contributions to *Museumskunde* from 1906 and 1907 will never stop chasing each other. Lauffer's appreciation of his mentor, Moriz Heyne, "and the Archaeological Foundations of History Museums," appeared in *Museumskunde* in 1906 (page 153). Part 1 of Richter's ten-part "On the Ideal and Practical Tasks of Ethnographic Museums" followed on page 189. In 1907 the first of Lauffer's four-part "The Historical Museum: Its Character, Its Work, and How It Differs from Museums of Art and Applied Arts" was followed directly by part 2 of Richter (page 1 and page 14), and part 2 of Lauffer was followed by part 3 of Richter (page 78 and page 99). Lauffer's parts 3 and 4 had no echo, perhaps silently marking Richter's final collapse and death. The remaining parts of Richter's book-length essay appeared posthumously, in 1908 and 1909.

Readers would have swung from Lauffer's questioning of museum taxonomies to Richter's; from Lauffer's discussions of archaeology and history to Richter's of archaeology and ethnography; and from Lauffer's on the limits of collecting and collections to Richter's on the same limits. Their similarities and differences would have been hard to pinpoint in the flow of words. By publishing them as separate pieces here we give each his due: the scale of their argumentative effort is fully visible.

What I would like to do now, though, is to read them together again as a single argument about the kind of knowledge that is museum knowledge. This will enable us to see important connections to others working at the time on the philosophy of knowledge. Establishing this context not only will deepen our understanding of these two essays, and our appreciation of their authors, but will also enable us to find in these discussions materials for our own use as we continue to seek new roles for museums and museum knowledge within the cultural sciences and between the university and the wider public sphere.

II

The essays of Lauffer and Richter nest within the history of museums in Germany, and the history of museums in Germany is intricately bound up with the history of using objects as historical evidence.[8] Around 1900, the subject had become one of public debate. The historian Karl Lamprecht had challenged his colleagues to take seriously cultural history and material culture. They pushed back, accusing him of sloppiness and Marxism. Ethnologists like Bastian, for their part, argued for the importance of collecting and taxonomy but faced criticism from, among others, art historians, for collecting too many things and organizing them too poorly. These larger issues loom over the two essays we present here. The history of museum thinking in Germany should also be viewed in a still-broader, global perspective. In the United States, which was itself heavily dependent on German museum thinking—Gustav Friedrich Klemm's thinking about cultural history, for example, influenced Otis Mason's shaping of the Smithsonian's Bureau of American Ethnology— George Brown Goode, assistant secretary of the Smithsonian, articulated a strong theory of the role of museums. In a lecture delivered at the Brooklyn Institute (soon to be Museum) in February 1889, he proclaimed that "the museum of the future must stand side by side with the library and the laboratory, as a part of the teaching equipment of the college and university, and in the great cities co-operate with the public library as one of the principal agencies for the enlightenment of the people."[9]

Let us begin with Lauffer's key term. It is not Goode's "history museum" but the "historical museum," and there are many types of content, he implies, that fall under this category. For instance, it throws a bridge out to folklore and ethnology, which "history" would not. Richter's "ethnography," in parallel, throws a bridge out to the archive studies of the research historian.

Ironically, while Lauffer devotes himself to the "historical museum," and does so by comparing it with other kinds of museums, such as those devoted to archaeology, applied art, and ethnography, he is not interested in the history of these types of museums. Richter, by contrast, while ostensibly focused on the "ideal and practical," is attentive to its history. He takes us through its early modern origins in the *Kunst- und Wunderkammern* of the baroque in some detail, reminding us that when Richter began writing, Julius von Schlosser had not yet published his epochal *Art and Curiosity Cabinets of the Late Renaissance* (1908). Richter had to rely on much older works, Caspar F. Neickel's *Museographia* (1727) and Gustav Friedrich Klemm's *History of Collecting in Germany* (1837), which remained the standard reference works on the subject.

Instead of its history, Lauffer focuses on the idea of the historical museum and presents it as an *éloge* for Moriz Heyne. We include it in this volume as the prologue to his long essay because it introduces us to the essay's main theme: how to categorize material sources of the human past. For Heyne, all that survived of the past, literary or material, contributed to understanding the past in its fullness. Lauffer took his own broad commitment from Heyne.

Lauffer was also inspired by Hans von und zu Aufseß, the visionary founder of the Germanisches Nationalmuseum. Heyne, who was on the advisory board, brought Lauffer to work there just after he finished his doctorate (1896) and before he moved to Frankfurt (1902). The Nürnberg museum was important not just for its vision but also for that vision's vicissitudes: Aufseß was succeeded as director in 1863 by August von Essenwein, who shifted the museum's orientation from cultural history to applied arts. The same objects were displayed, but they were now interpreted in a different direction. Heyne, in turn, merited praise not just for his awareness of the power of display but for his resistance to the trend started in Nürnberg of turning objects collected for their evidentiary value into objects displayed for their exemplary value.

The change at the Germanisches Nationalmuseum seems to have sharpened Lauffer's thinking about the difference between the historical museum and the applied arts museum. The collections of the former were of heterogeneous origin, function, and content. If they belonged together, it was only because they spoke, however tangentially, to a place and its story. The applied arts museum, by contrast, had it easy: objects were collected, organized, and displayed according to very clear categories, such as technique, style, materials, and period. That clarity seemed to amplify the institution's claim to tell people how to think about things.

Moreover, Lauffer argued, whereas art museums could always fall back on the ideology of aesthetic quality, historical museums could not. Museums of applied arts had as their mandate the improvement of quality in the present, and thus had to be attuned to historical quality. But because the mandate of historical museums was to cover all periods, not only those of outstanding achievement, they were indifferent to questions of quality. When historical museums did collect works of high aesthetic intentionality, it had to be because those objects told something about the past that could not be ascertained otherwise—that is, where "art" functioned as evidence.

Lauffer saw the historical collection as existing in a direct relationship with place, and functioning, like a town archive, as a "vibrant and deserving protector of local historical research that presents varied educational materials to the townspeople" (65). This recalls Nietzsche's praise of what the locally minded antiquarian could do.

> The history of his city becomes for him the history of his self; he understands the wall, the turreted gate, the ordinance of the town council, the national festival like an illustrated diary of his youth and finds himself, his strength, his diligence, his pleasure, his judgment, his folly and rudeness, in all of them. Here one could live, he says to himself, for here one can live and will be able to live. . . . And so, with this "We," he looks beyond the ephemeral, curious, individual life and feels like the spirit of the house, the generation, and the city.[10]

Lauffer's discussion of the "problem of quality" in the historical museum was a problem for the ethnographic museum as well, and maybe more so. On the one hand, according to Richter, objects from South and East Asia were *too good* to belong in ethnography museums. Their home was the applied arts museum, both because the arts of Asia were highly developed and because they had had a "strong influence" on the development of European decorative arts. Guimet's collection in Paris was a reference point for Lauffer. On the other hand, Richter considered the products of the rest of the world to be of very low quality. "The rest of American art," Richter wrote, with its preference for the "monstrous and grotesquely distorted," tends to overload the individual object with intentionally fantastic or temperamental imagery, giving American art the impression of "barbarism and repugnant ugliness." Of the rest of the world, he concluded, only the Benin bronzes "approach the level of true portraiture." They deserved to be in a "museum for non-European art," he wrote, in an "eminent position that would, admittedly, be a struggle to fill" (116).

Thus, in the domain of ethnographic museums, the problem of "quality" was at the same time a problem of "place." One solution to the problem of the extreme variability of these museums' collections was to limit their geographical scope, sending the South and East Asian collections to art museums. Another was to remove European folklore and prehistoric materials from the ethnographic museum and into their own dedicated institutions, limiting the ethnographic to the non-European.

Where the ethnographic museum did have a clear identity was in its ability to serve the present, at least according to Richter. He advances imperial service as a "secondary" task of ethnographic museums. Colonial success, which for him does include paternalistic effort, required knowledge, and this could come only from ethnography, with museums diffusing knowledge through their public programming. Commercial and political actors could be educated in the ethnography museum before leaving the metropolis.

Reading Richter today means reencountering the racialist assumptions of 1900, when the essentializing of cultures and "league tables" of civilization were rarely discussed commonplaces. It also means acknowledging certain kinds of naiveté bordering on self-delusion— praise for the distinct, and beneficial, colonial mission of the cultured Germans, or uncritical genuflecting toward the Kaiser. And yet, and this is the complexity of historical realities that we seek in studying the past, Richter, like Adolf Bastian before him, was a cultural relativist whenever the point at issue was epistemological and not aesthetic or political.

He believed it unhistorical to consider European civilization as an absolute good, superior to all other cultures. And he believed it unhistorical to think that European civilization should be forced upon inhabitants of new colonies—displacing a locally evolved civilization that was not necessarily of intrinsically low value—and furthermore to believe that this force could employ any means necessary and require no plan for its acceptance. Richter quoted Felix von Luschan, one of Bastian's disciples and successors in the Ethnology Museum in Berlin— and also holder of the first chair in anthropology at the University of Berlin: "The culture of the so-called wild tribes is not worse than our own—merely different."

And Richter could also acknowledge that Germany's vast ethnographic holdings were stolen—as were, by extension, those in other European countries—an acknowledgment that remains highly charged. Yet here he was, a young man writing in the first decade of the twentieth century: "Incidentally, until the seventeenth century ethnographic objects were looted items; in many ways they remain so today" (97). This combination of attitudes that we find antithetical—support for colonial activity and uncomfortable awareness of the crime at the heart of collection histories—was not uncommon in the most intellectually sophisticated circles: Richter's views seem identical to those expressed by Luschan himself.[11]

For both Lauffer and Richter, "display" was the means by which museums created knowledge, though each had different leading principles. In the same way that the collecting policy of a historical museum had to follow the "purpose" of an artifact, its display policy could not, for Lauffer, emphasize style or material or aesthetics. As for the tendency to use cultural-historical modes of display for a decorative arts collection, Lauffer dismissed this as just another form of art history. Later he would identify the art historical mode of display as "stylistic-historical." He was very clear that display had to follow from first principles. For him, this meant establishing the purpose of an artifact.

> A military saber, a senator's rapier, and a hunting knife may resemble each other greatly, may stem from the same time period, may bear the same ornamentation, and may even have been created by the hand of the same master craftsman—but despite all this they may not be displayed together in a historical museum. The first is a weapon of war, the second is an antique communal artifact, and the third is a hunting weapon. Or, to provide another example: a silver drinking vessel, a communion chalice, and a guild goblet. In a historical museum they may not be grouped in the same showcase. (37–38)

Typology, which had served equally the ethnologist and the decorative arts specialist of the previous generation—Gustav Friedrich Klemm in Dresden was one, August von Essenwein in Nürnberg the other—was dropped in favor of purpose, or function. This, of course, demanded a familiarity with cultural context that the formal approach to shape or material did not. In other words, establishing "purpose" as the basis of display in the historical museum implied establishing historical scholarship as the basis of the historical museum. Self-conscious theorizing was a strategy of legitimation. "We must attempt," Lauffer wrote, "to articulate the inherent principles that should guide the historical museum" (40). Lauffer's quest for "inherent principles," or the theory behind the practice, is part of his project of reconstructing curatorial practice, and thus regrounding the historical museum, in the early 1900s.

For the museum whose purpose was not aesthetic education, Richter wrote, a "beautiful exhibition" was one that engaged its audience as education. More precisely, "a beautiful exhibition of a scientific collection," Richter continued, indicates a "well-ordered exhibition. Order means a methodical (or regulated) structure and visual clarity in the conceptualization." Objects were to be grouped not by their artistic merit, their decorative qualities, or their ability to arouse the sentiments (146). In this last category Richter had in mind the new innovation of the period room. If the historical museum could accommodate beautiful objects that were especially full of meaning, then, speaking for the ethnographic museum, Richter felt moved to remind his readers that "art should not strive to dominate science. Art becomes sterile and unenjoyable when science seeks to dominate rather than understand it" (146).

The "order" in an ethnographic museum was to be provided by space, not time or function. "The criteria for ordering the material should always be geographic in the first place and formal in the second: this principle must provide the firm structure for the collection" (155). By "formal," he referred to object types. Only within the subgroup of types was chronology to intervene as an organizing rule. Nor was Richter oblivious to the reality of display as an epistemological form. "Such an exhibit does not provide a factual cultural image of the way things actually were, but rather it creates images of cultures as they should be" (155).

Richter also analyzed the spaces in which objects were displayed—he disliked ornament and preferred a white box with nothing to distract the visitor. He argued that there should be an immediately recognizable organizing idea "that enables a narrower overview to group the objects easily and compare them within categories (such as sorcery and religion, weapons, clothing, jewelry, etc.), and a wider overview to instantly display the different ethnographic-geographic regions as self-contained entities" (149). Objects were not to interfere with other objects. Principles like symmetry were to be employed. The more art-historically interesting objects were to be placed closest to the visitor. The project of "visual explanation of objects" meant that objects, images, and copies could all be employed. Most important was the role of museum displays for providing an image of the character of different peoples.

Attention to display led Richter to insist on "the inalienable rights" (*Das gute Recht*) of a museum object. "After the extensive treatment an object undergoes to be ready for the museum, it earns . . . its place in a worthy, safe, tasteful, and scientifically appropriate exhibition as the subject of scholarly research." In the future, he wrote, "we must promote the idea that every object, no matter how insignificant its material or craftsmanship, deserves protection and careful treatment" (146). It is the ethnographer who defends the rights of the object regardless of its perceived significance, while it is the curator, or the curatorial side of the ethnographer—Richter does not distinctly separate the activities from the people—who presents them to the public. The curator had to know the collection and the space. He had to be willing to experiment and to fail. "He should not shy away from trying things. . . . He should deal with failures like a true artist and strive with patience and tenacity to achieve the desired outcome" (151).

Richter's extraordinary formulation in terms of the "rights of the object" actually echoes the language used by W. M. Flinders Petrie in his just recently published *Methods and Aims in Archaeology* (1904). There is no way to know whether Richter read this work; nevertheless, there are some clear parallels. First of all, Petrie also mixes the "ideal" and "practical" tasks. The latter take in chapters devoted to "the excavator," "the labourers," "recording in the field," "photographing," "preservation of objects" and "packing"; the former, "archaeological evidence," "ethics of archaeology," and "the fascination of history," with which he concludes.

And yet there is far more that resonates between the two short books. Petrie, like Richter, is engaged in defending the status of his field as a science. And, like Richter—and, indeed, as we have seen, Bastian—Petrie tries to uphold the value of material culture independently of aesthetics. Archaeology, he complains, "is still attracted by pretty things, rather than by real knowledge."[12] Like them, too, his description of his own new science is as the science of the human, and if Richter had replaced its first word with "Ethnology," no one would have found a thought out of place: "Archaeology,—the knowledge of how man has acquired his present position and powers—is one of the widest studies, best fitted to open the mind, and to produce that type of wide interests and toleration which is the highest result of education."[13]

But to come back to "the inalienable right of the museum object" (das gute Recht eines Museumsgegenstandes), Petrie frames his whole chapter "The Ethics of Archaeology" in terms of rights. He begins by contrasting the individual right of the individual excavator with those of the wider community that has a stake in the archaeological research. (Like Bastian, Petrie writes with an urgency born of seeing excavations ruin sites and objects, and excavations themselves be destroyed by others.) Then he turns to the objects. He rails against "show museums where display is thought of before knowledge." For the sake of a single specimen, he writes, an entire ancient ensemble will be wrecked. And once entering a collection, an object will frequently be mistreated:

> Stones will be built into walls, and ruined by the damp bringing salt out; objects are left to drop to pieces from lack of chemical knowledge, or from the official dread of the responsibility of doing right instead of allowing wrong. Information is deliberately destroyed; labels are thrown away or heaped together out of the way in a glass case where the objects are artistically displayed, with no more history than if they had come from a dealer.[14]

There are the rights of the community, the rights of the object, and, "in every direction," Petrie continues, "we unquestioningly assume that the future has its rights." And as we live in "past ages by insight and association," we understand that the past, too, has rights. "A work that has cost days, weeks, or years of toil has a right to existence." To let it be destroyed is "to destroy that portion of life solidified;—so much will, so much labour, so much living reality." The life of past men—and past things—"preserved to us has rights as veritably as the life of present men."[15]

Petrie's skepticism about the stability of things—he spoke of "the transitory stewardship of things"—led him to skepticism about museums as *the* solution to the problem of past things. He feared that the whole-sale gathering of objects would only "ensure that such things will perish in the course of time. A museum is only a temporary place."[16] In contrast, the Germans were enthusiastic supporters of the museum as a new place of research. Lauffer identified this move with Aufseß's vision for Nürn-berg. His transfer of objects from the material world to the museum's collection followed a taxonomic map that reflected an ambition to fur-ther research. And the museum's display, in turn, followed the contours of that map.[17] Lauffer saw the historical museum as best geared for this task because it collected both texts and objects—an institutional heir to early modern antiquarianism.[18]

Both Richter's and Lauffer's museums were places of knowledge. But what kind of knowledge was museum knowledge? This question takes us to the heart of these two essays, and why they can be read as one argument. Lauffer proposed getting around the confusion surrounding the historical museum by rebranding it as a "cultural history" museum.

But this was itself an ambiguous category, then as now. As Lauffer noted wryly: "With this terminology, however, we have jumped out of the frying pan and into the fire" (42).

Cultural history may have been invented in the nineteenth century, but it sat atop a major intellectual and political fault line. Its subject matter was often attested through nontextual remains, and its categories extended well beyond the familiar boundaries of the political. Moreover, in contemporary Germany its focus on the people, and on the material remains of how ordinary people lived, smacked of Marxism and of 1848 (and then of 1871 in Paris), too much for a society struggling with its sense of proper hierarchy. Furthermore, those who did this kind of history operated outside the university and so felt little external need to define exactly what they were doing. Nature, and academia, abhorring a vacuum, others rushed in to supply definitions, not always sympathetically. But the problem did not go away, for as late as the 1960s two of the greatest living historians, both connected to the very stream we are discussing, wrote about the "problem" of cultural history or went off "in search of" it.[19] A scholarly generation later believed it had identified a "new" cultural history—something which provoked another scholar to point to the existence of this "old" (nineteenth-century) cultural history.[20] Lauffer was right: relabeling the history museum as the cultural history museum solved nothing, as it merely swapped out one uncertain meaning for another.

Instead of giving up, however, Lauffer boldly tried his hand at defining cultural history. He split it into six parts: concepts and beliefs, which included inner life (ethics, aesthetics, and legal studies); words, or the history in language; sounds, or the history of music; customs and practices, including the history of conventions and rituals; economic history, which became a slightly different category focused not on content so much as type of sources; and objects. This, in turn, broke down into archaeology, technology, and art history. Lauffer wanted to focus on objects, both because they had largely been ignored by academics and because, to him as a museum person, objects were central.

Lauffer's effort to bend "cultural history" back toward the study of things more generally, including museum collections, represents a kind of resistance to the contemporary movement toward disciplinization. "The technological or stylistically oriented presentations favored by museums of art and applied art simply do not work in a historical museum. Only a cultural-historical—or, if another name is preferred, an archaeological—presentation is appropriate here" (37). By identifying archaeology with cultural history Lauffer was hitching together two terms of still-mobile meaning, both derived from early modern antiquarianism, in the hope of establishing some new, firm definition.

For Lauffer, "object study" was not one thing but three. Seeking an object's purpose was the task of archaeology; focusing on its material was the domain of technology; and studying its decoration was done by art history. Lauffer explained that he would have preferred to use the older term *Altertumskunde* rather than the newer "archaeology," but the older term had already become obscure.

> Archaeology involves all forms of external culture, regardless of material, technique, or style. The field studies the typical forms that objects took in order to fulfill a certain purpose at the time they were developed, as well as how these forms changed under the influence of new viewpoints, customs, and technical abilities, while still fulfilling their initial purpose. (46–47)

Archaeology also included those processes whereby "decoration may take over the form, so that objects no longer fulfill their intended purpose." It extended beyond the objects themselves to all the neighboring departments of cultural history. The pursuit of these ghostly traces, as well as the attentiveness to neighborly relations, suggests that the study of *Nachleben*, as in the contemporary work of Aby Warburg, could be considered part of the province of archaeology.

Like Lauffer, Richter was also thinking about what he termed the "archaeological idea." That this idea crossed the boundary between ethnography and cultural history is itself important to note, as Richter's intellectual forerunner Kristian Bahnson had kept the ethnographic museum clearly in the category of cultural history museum.[21] In his discussion of religion and religious artifacts he explained that "this material can be called archaeological in that it has sharply defined boundaries and is particularly well suited to become the specialized or even primary purpose of a museum of ethnographic objects."[22] The archaeological perspective meant emphasizing the cult's actual artifacts, and the art historical, its representations of religious figures and ritual objects.

Richter also describes the passage of time in archaeological terms as the laying down of strata. Unpacking the way an earlier layer of meaning was preserved in the art forms of a later one was what cultural history did—and this made its practice archaeological. Dating could be made precise by comparing artifacts and surviving texts. This had the effect of making cultural history heir to the antiquarians, who did the same thing for the same reasons, and not to the contemporary archaeologists, for whom prehistory had become the model. In fact, for Richter "prehistoric archaeology" was a "*contradictio in adjecto*" (127). It was simply, he thought, impossible to fully understand archaeological evidence that was not closely linked to written evidence.

Richter acknowledged that "the word 'archaeological' is not normally applied in this wider sense"—that is, as a method of cultural history or, in even more precise terms, "historical archaeology." Rather, it was used to address the "artistic value and character of (classical and ancient) monuments" (127). It came from those who were interested in the history of ancient art. This was the tradition that began with Winckelmann, who used the direct term *Geschichte*, and that continued into the nineteenth century under the banner of *Archäologie der Kunst*, an ambiguous term that pulled in two directions. Classical archaeology derived from art history and so primarily focused on the form of the object. Objects as part of lived life in the past constituted, rather, the task of *Altertumskunde*— the eighteenth-century German term for antiquarianism. When Lauffer used the term *Altertum* in the singular ("an antiquity"; "an antique [object]"), he was pointing to the antiquarian end of the spectrum of *Archäologie der Kunst*. The assessment and constellating of these interpretations was the job of still another discipline, history. But this tripartite division of labor between history, art history, and archaeology had been sketched out only for ancient things—no one had yet made clear how it all worked for more modern artifacts. As Richter put it, "Interestingly, we lack a word that describes archaeological objects, or ancient monuments, from the viewpoint of general cultural history" (127).

Lauffer tried to provide an answer to the question Richter was asking by turning, once again, to Aufseß and the Germanisches Nationalmuseum. Aufseß had used *Altertumskunde* to refer to material remains from any historical period, whether ancient or early modern (the collecting policy of the Germanisches Nationalmuseum extended up to 1648). "Antiquities" had been used since the Renaissance in a fairly straightforward way to denote things from the past. *Antiquitates* was the larger whole that those terms together illuminated: law, religion, calendar, ritual, government, games—the realm which, by the middle of the nineteenth century, was regularly being called "culture." The study of antiquities was antiquarianism, or *antiquarisch.* It was Germanized in the eighteenth century as *Altertumskunde,* and this term was being used as late as 1878 to signify "material culture" more generally (as in the *Zeitschrift für Museologie und Antiquitätenkunde*). Lauffer wanted to make a clean break with this complicated past and so turned to the new word of the day: "archaeology."

Lauffer's antiquities, or *Altertümer,* fell into defined categories—and the categories were laid down, more or less, by Marcus Terentius Varro in the forty-one books of his *Human and Divine Antiquities* (first century BCE). He identified four types: public, private, military, and sacred. Lauffer's narrower categories cut the same territory into eighths: family, domestic ("which, together with the first group, constitute the bulk of private antiquities"), civic and community, legal, ecclesiastical, profane art, scientific, and military (78).

Lauffer then used these categories to organize the display of objects in his "historical museum." Those relevant to the household might be grouped in one room, whereas those relevant to the military or church might appear in another. One room per category might be ideal, but Lauffer admitted that the needs of different buildings had to be respected. These antiquarian-origin categories he redescribed as "culture groups," following Otto Lehmann, director of the Mannheim and then Altona museums. That makes Franz Boas, in turn, into a disciple of Heyne and thus, more distantly, of the antiquarian origins of cultural presentation.

Archaeology as a window into past culture through things brought it very close to the meaning of ethnography. In fact, it was Lauffer who argued that "archaeology essentially is a part of ethnographic studies, limited to the past of its own people. Just as ethnography uses simple descriptions of external culture as the basis for deeper research into folklore, genealogy, customs, and conceptions—so too does archaeology use physical objects as the starting point for wider scientific research" (47). But this ethnographic aspect of the artifact did not depend on age-value. It is its "degree of difference" from the present that made something an "antiquity"—which is why folkloric objects could belong in a history museum. And to make this point Lauffer cites none other than Richter (88n4).

When Lauffer showed how "purpose" as a display principle was capable of discriminating between, in his example, a saber, a rapier, and a hunting knife, he was approaching material remains as a historian. But he was also approaching his own culture as something unfamiliar and capable of being grasped only from the outside in. In short, he was thinking like an ethnographer.

When Richter placed the ethnographic museum in a genealogy that descended from the age of the *Wunderkammer*, he was thinking like an archaeologist. He noted, however, that the study of the distant past through things and the study of the distant present through things were done by the same people: the antiquaries. In the twinning of Richter and Lauffer, with each describing his vision in the terms of the other, there is a silent but uncanny return to the antiquarian synthesis. Lauffer's recourse to a Varronian *Antiquitates-Altertumskunde* is the tip of this submerged continent.

When Richter, in turn, explained that he was using ethnography as a way of studying the "cultural lives" of peoples who developed outside the ancient Mediterranean in a "philological and historical-comparative way," he had one man in mind: the person he called "the old master." Out of the cosmos of Goethe's *West-östliche Divan*, Richter extracted a paradigmatic couplet.

> He who knows himself and others
> Here will also see:
> That the East and West, like brothers,
> Parted ne'er shall be.

> (Wer sich selbst und andre kennt,
> Wird auch hier erkennen:
> Orient und Occident
> Sind nicht mehr zu trennen.)[23]

Poetry in a museum taxonomy! Goethe had turned his research of the *Divan* years into the notion of *Weltliteratur*, or world literature. Citing Goethe was a way of making ethnography another kind of world literature. Richter actually saw the project of cultural contact between East and West as *the* fundamental subject of history, "already voiced by Herodotus, the father of history," and as the basis of his own work (133).

For Richter, this was a live issue, and not just because of the imperialist-colonialist dimension to the ethnographic museum addressed earlier. The question of archaeology and its relationship to ethnography spoke to the fundamental scientific purpose of museums. Having archaeological monuments amid ethnographic collections allowed for a conversation between the artifacts. The archaeological brought out the slow-changing element of time in the ethnographic; the ethnographic, the possibilities for use in the archaeological. Having them together allowed for the curating of exhibitions that enabled one to travel in time from present to past, or past to present. "In this way, an archaeological collection of exceptional scientific merit could be curated to offer not only a lively understanding of the monuments but also an instructive glimpse into aspects of wider cultural history" (132). Richter thought that even a study of those considered "primitive" in fact "leads to an understanding of the present in a similar way as the study of the past." Ethnographic museums worked like "museums of history and culture" inasmuch as they held up to view past ways of living or being which had "been fully or partly overcome." The objects from our own culture's past, as well as those from people who are "living testaments to our cultural past," all spoke to distance (102–3).

III

An introduction to Lauffer and Richter—one that aimed to interpret them for their most direct application to museum thinking as we know it—could stop here. These long-lost essays speak directly to today's concerns about collection, display, interpretation, and taxonomy, as well as about indigeneity and cultural property. For that reason alone they warrant disinterring, discussion, and incorporation into our own lumber room of ideas.

But they also, especially Richter's piece, aspire to something else and, with that, open museum thinking onto a deeper and broader landscape of epistemological reflection. What might appear from the perspective of the history of museums to be metatheory in fact offers, I would argue, a bridge to the wider humanities. In what follows, we will build that bridge and then cross it.

Richter's quotation from Goethe, significant in itself, is used to introduce a discussion of the "Ideal Tasks" of the museum. It begins with two sections devoted to what can only be described as a philosophical investigation.[24] These sections distinguish Richter's treatment from similar treatments of the topic, even those written not long after, such as Richard Thurnwald's "Über Völkerkundemuseen, ihre wissenschaftlichen Bedingungen und Ziele," published in *Museumskunde* in 1912. This suggests that the philosophical turn was Richter's interest, not the field's as a whole. It is the part of this essay that might still seem obscure. For example, he talks about a "comparative-genetic method," about "observational disciplines." He distinguishes between "causal analysis" and "logical analysis." He notes how ethnography tends to be associated with the "natural" rather than the "human" sciences, after identifying the former with "explanation" and the latter with "interpretation." It is "interpretation" and, connected to it, "criticism" that addresses the question of motivations that denominate the humanities (nature having no motives). But he also contrasts "understanding" and "knowledge." Linking these two registers, types of knowledge and their respective epistemologies, Richter concludes that ethnography defies identification with natural science both because of the "nature of its subject matter" and because of the "type of its research methods" (91–92). Richter's goal was to assert the place of ethnography amid the cultural sciences and to show how this mattered both internally to the history of science and externally to the history of ethnographic museums. Ethnography was to educate via the study of "material evidences" and use a museum's object holdings to illustrate "psychological" and "cultural-historical" truths (103).[25]

In reading these sentences one suspects that Richter is drawing on a conceptual vocabulary borrowed from elsewhere. For the practicing ethnographer, whether in the field or the museum, this part of Richter's account might have seemed superfluous, if not convoluted. For he was not intervening here in debates about objects or their display. If debates about an object's facticity are first order and theories of its presentation are second order, then Richter's interest in the conceptual foundations, or presuppositions, of those theories constitutes a third order and could be described as *metatheoretical.* In these sections Richter is inserting museum scholarship into the wider contemporary debate about the identity of the human, or "cultural," sciences. In fact, it is only by reading him in this context that we can glimpse, through the haze of his prose and in a project truncated by death, what he might have been aiming at and where his argument might have gone. But to fully understand this we will have to go outside the specific museums debate as it unfolded in the pages of *Museumskunde* and reach for the work of a thinker just then exploring the epistemological foundations of the cultural sciences: Max Weber.

In this section we will read Richter through the lens of Weber in order to better understand the terms he uses in this article. In the concluding essay we will read Weber through the lens of Richter. His exactly contemporary work on the philosophy of knowledge provided the kind of sharp-edged conceptual argumentation that Richter was seeking. By using Weber to elaborate what Richter only scaffolded, and then using Richter to draw Weber into an arena he ostensibly ignored, we can make the much bigger argument that Richter was never able to develop: that museum science is a cultural science.

When Richter begins by stating an opposition between the human and the natural sciences, he is nodding in the direction of the debate about the kind of knowledge that defined each of them. That debate was launched by Helmholtz's attack on Goethe qua poet doing science in his 1853 lectures at Königsberg and broadened in an 1862 lecture at Heidelberg devoted to explaining what was distinctive about the "sciences of investigation." Wilhelm Dilthey seems to have immediately responded. We have the early fragment "On the Study of Man and History" (ca. 1865) and then "On the Study of the History of the Sciences of Man, Society, and the State" (1875) leading to his *Introduction to the Human Sciences* (1883), which argued that the human sciences were a science, but a different kind of science. This was then rearticulated in the southwestern school of neo-Kantianism, first by Wilhelm Windelband in his so-called rectorial address, *Geschichte und Naturwissenschaft* (1894), and then by his student Heinrich Rickert, in his much more influential *Kulturwissenschaft und Naturwissenschaft* (1896). Rickert and Weber were close friends and intellectual partners.[26]

Richter first argues that the natural and human sciences are actually both sciences of the empirical. Yes, ethnography had been identified with the natural sciences because of a "comparative" approach, which he equated with "natural scientific method." But in the very next sentence he undercuts this by arguing that its terms, "causal" and "logical analysis," "induction," and "comparison," were used in both the human and natural sciences. He then refers to the "method of individual and general comparison," which he says was "actually" the method of all the observational sciences, not just the natural ones (91).

This shared commitment to the empirical was reflected through two lenses. Richter argued that the natural sciences worked toward "explanation," whereas the humanities relied on "interpretation and criticism." Nature could be explained but not interpreted; human subjects could be interpreted but not explained. The reasons for this difference were that, first, interpretation was about seeking internal motivation, while natural scientific explanation was about appearances. Second, interpretation was a function of understanding, and understanding of human beings was possible only by other human beings.

This whole paragraph of Richter comes straight out of Dilthey and Rickert. Schleiermacher put understanding, or *Verstehen*, at the heart of the biblical hermeneutic he developed. August Boeckh was his student and imported it into the philologist's toolkit. Johann Gustav Droysen sat in Boeckh's lectures in Berlin and then made it the theoretical center-piece of the lectures he gave on historical method at the University of Berlin from 1857 onward and published in summary form in 1882. It was Dilthey who claimed *Verstehen* as the cornerstone of the human sciences.[27]

Richter went out of his way to cast the mental furniture of the eth-nographer in the philosophical language of the day. "The ultimate objective of all ethnographic work, which is thus the general task of ethnographic museums, can only be this: to contribute to the knowl-edge and understanding of ourselves. Ethnography pursues such knowledge and understanding" (99–100). "Knowledge" (*Erkenntnis*) was important for the neo-Kantians, and "understanding," as we have seen, for the historians. We need not presume that Richter was quot-ing anyone so much as reflecting the mainstream of discussions of the human sciences circa 1900. But this attention to epistemology is so precise and unnecessary that it could not be there by accident.

Coming to know means differentiating and perceiving differ-ences. To understand means to grasp or apprehend the connec-tions through which something has come into being. Knowledge of ourselves implies, for the ethnographer, knowledge of our char-acter: that is, (1) knowledge of the general similarity of psycho-logical elements, above all the most common needs of all human communities and their historical effects—which is to say, their external psychological effects (Bastian's "elementary thoughts"); and (2) knowledge of the actual formal differences in the social psychology of different human communities among the histori-cal effects that depend on accidental, external stimulation, most notably the characteristic means which we as well as other people have developed in dealing with cultural pressures. An understand-ing of the present entails comprehension of how separate cultural traditions have evolved: be it the great expressions of cultural life—including language and literature, mythology and religion, laws and customs, and so forth—or an individual, very specific, cultural-historical fact. (100–101)

Richter even presents ethnography as the necessary last step in bringing understanding back to the self. It was in the ethnographic production and not in the highest or most finely developed forms of culture, such as religion and art, that real understanding of the human was to be found. Warburg's exactly contemporaneous search for the persistence of the antique, whether in Athens or Oraibi, can be seen as a similar form of self-therapy. It was Freud who was just then taking this the next step, drilling for *Verstehen* deeper than had ever been done before. Freud's own archaeological collection sits at the point of contact between these deep histories.

The approach chosen by Richter in trying to identify the theoretical concepts lying behind ethnographic practice seems entirely Weberian: metatheoretical critique is used to establish learning on sure foundations. In this case, it is the old notion of ethnography as a natural science that Richter wished to reappraise by showing the common conceptual arsenal of all the empirical sciences.

That things had come to this pass was the result of two contingencies. First, the nineteenth-century disciplinary "moment" was made by ethnographers who were natural scientists. That earlier ethnographers were travelers or missionaries who were trained in philology or history— or in more recent times psychology—had been lost. Second, the central term, "natural scientific method," emerged as a rebuke to positivist fact-mongering and as an encouragement "for empirical research to counter the speculative philosophy of Hegel."[28] Richter pushed back against "natural scientific method" out of a conviction that terminology could smuggle in all sorts of occluded meanings and thereby cause confusion.

Richter had high hopes for what ethnography could do for the cultural sciences. He believed that the advent of ethnography as a settled discipline "would initiate a new era for the entire field of the cultural sciences." Its use of "general comparison" as a method of studying objects extended beyond things to "religion (mythology) and customs." Its spread—"the new methodology"—replaced the older "historical and comparative studies in the humanities." Richter quoted Franz Boas proclaiming that anthropology had already become "a method applicable to all the mental sciences and indispensable to all of them" (93).[29]

Many of these sciences were already being studied alongside one another, Richter noted, in Karl Lamprecht's historical seminar at the University of Leipzig, titled "Exercises in Comparative Cultural History [*vergleichenden Kulturgeschichte*]."[30] If the ethnographic method was taking over the *Kulturwissenschaften*, then it was conceivable that ethnographic museums could set the tone for the other *kulturwissenschaftlich* museums. The museum was to show the "cultural-historical and psychological truths" arising out of its ethnographic material. To "research the intellectual results," as well as "to discover cultural-historical connections and the psychological laws of a people: these are the tasks of the field of ethnographic (and sociopsychological) science" (103). With this we can see that Richter, like Lauffer (though coming from ethnography rather than archaeology), was seeking to redefine how we understand the past through things.

Richter not only becomes less obscure when placed back into the wider contemporary discussion of the natural and human sciences, but he becomes a thinker with an argument. By 1900, Lamprecht's effort to make cultural history the cutting-edge interdisciplinary integrator had crashed upon the rocks of his own shortcomings. Lauffer and Richter pushed object-based history and ethnography into the gap left by Lamprecht's failure. This was a moment when it was possible to see the emergence of a new museums science within the new circle of the cultural sciences.[31] We might see Warburg, a former student of Lamprecht's who had planned to habilitate in anthropology in Berlin in 1896–97, doing this for his art historical cultural science.[32] And, in his essays of the first decade of the twentieth century, Weber was doing the same for the cultural science that he would not call sociology until 1910. We can read all these works, some famous and some forgotten, with enormous contemporary benefit, both for the creativity of their question posing and for the analytical incisiveness of their answer giving. We invite new readers of Lauffer and Richter to ponder how they might answer some of today's questions and, even more, how they might reframe and restate some of those questions. We present them to you here in the hope of enhancing the quality of our contemporary conversation with resources drawn from the past.

1.   For this contrast, see H. Glenn Penny, introduction to *In Humboldt's Shadow: A Tragic History of German Ethnology* (Princeton, NJ: Princeton University Press, 2021), 1–14.

2.   David Murray, *Museums: Their History and Their Use* (Glasgow, 1904), 1:v.

3.   Andrea Meyer, "The Journal *Museumskunde*: Another Link Between the Museums of the World," in *The Museum Is Open: Towards a Transnational History of Museums, 1750–1940*, ed. Andrea Meyer and Bénédicte Savoy (Berlin: De Gruyter, 2014), 179–90; Andrea Meyer, "Museums in Print: The Interplay of Texts and Images in the Journal *Museumskunde*," in *Images of the Art Museum: Connecting Gaze and Discourse in the History of Museology*, ed. Eva-Maria Troelenberg and Melania Savino (Berlin: De Gruyter, 2017), 93–110.

4.   Werner Hilgers, "100 Jahre–69 Jahrgänge: Zum Jubiläum der 'Museumskunde,'" *Museumskunde* 70 (2005): 7.

5.   See Peter N. Miller, *History and Its Objects: Antiquarianism and Material Culture Since 1500* (Ithaca, NY: Cornell University Press, 2017), chs. 6–8.

6.   On Lauffer, see Gudrun M. König and Elisabeth Timm, "'Deutsche' Dinge: Der Germanist Otto Lauffer zwischen Altertums- und Volkskunde," in *Schriftlose Vergangenheiten: Geschichtsschreibung an ihrer Grenze—von der Frühen Neuzeit bis in die Gegenwart*, ed. Lisa Regazzoni (Berlin: De Gruyter, 2019), 157–92.

7.   Richter tells us that he wrote the article in 1904 and published a condensed version, "Zum Verständnis der ethnographischen Museen," in the *Dresdner Anzeiger* on February 26, 1905. (Part of it was translated into Dutch as *Museum voor land- en volkenkunde en Maritiem museum "Prins Hendrik" te Rotterdam* [Rotterdam, 1906], 7–9.) Because we know little about Richter, I am extremely grateful to Christian Feest for the following information. Paul Oswald Richter was born on September 5, 1873, in Schneeberg/Saxony and studied Indo-European languages at the University of Leipzig under Karl Brugmann. His PhD dissertation, "Die unechten Nominalkomposita des Altindischen und Altiranischen" (1887), was published in *Indogermanische Forschungen* 9 (1898): 1–62, 183–252. (Part 1, an offprint of this article, was issued in book form in 1897, and both parts were published in 1898 by Truebner in Strassburg; both book versions include a CV that may provide some information on Richter's family and early years. There appears to be no copy in either Frankfurt or Vienna; Harvard and Yale have copies of the 1898 edition.) In 1898 he was hired as assistant for ethnography at the Royal Zoological and Anthropological-Ethnographic Museum Dresden, where his colleague as curator was Willy Foy, with whom he wrote "Zur Timor-Ornamentik" in the *Festschrift for A. B. Meyer* (*Abhandlungen und Berichte des Königl. Zoologischen und Anthropologisch-Ethnographischen Museums zu Dresden* 8, pt. 3 [1899]). In 1900 he published two articles in the *Zeitschrift für vergleichende Sprachforschung auf dem Gebiete der indogermanischen Sprachen* 36: "Griech. Δεσπότης," 111–23, and "Der Plural von gAw. mazdāh- hura-," 584–89. In 1901 he published (with Adolf Bernhard Meyer) "Die Helme aus Messingblech aus Celébes

und den Molukken: Die Bestattungsweisen der Minehassa in Nord Celébes," in *Ethnographische Miszellen* I (*Abhandlungen und Berichte des Königl. Zoologischen und Anthropologisch-Ethnographischen Museums zu Dresden* 9, pt. 6), 32–144; and in 1903, again with Meyer in *Ethnographische Miszellen* II (*Abhandlungen und Berichte des Königl. Zoologischen und Anthropologisch-Ethnographischen Museums zu Dresden* 10, pt. 6)—a number of essays on Indonesian ethnography based on the collection of Paul Sarasin. He moved to the Museum für Völkerkunde in Berlin in 1904 and died there in 1907.

8. For the full account presupposed in the paragraphs that follow, see Miller, *History and Its Objects*.

9. George Brown Goode, *The Museums of the Future* (Washington, DC: Government Printing Office, 1891) [From the *Report of the National Museum, 1888–89*, 427–45], 427. Goode also acknowledges Klemm's importance here (435) and in the parallel *Museum-History and Museums of History*, a lecture originally delivered to the American Historical Association annual meeting in 1888, in which he also explicitly discusses *Culturgeschichte* as an untranslatable German term and institution occupying the space between fine art and natural history (Goode, *Museum-History and Museums of History* [New York: Knickerbocker Press, 1889], 270, 268). And we know that Richter knew Goode's work: he cites him as the epigraph for his essay!

10. Friedrich Nietzsche, *On the Advantage and Disadvantage of History for Life*, §3.

11. See Perry, *In Humboldt's Shadow*, ch. 3.

12. W. M. Flinders Petrie, *Methods and Aims in Archaeology* (London: Macmillan, 1904), vii.

13. Petrie, *Methods and Aims*, viii.

14. Petrie, *Method and Aims*, 171.

15. Petrie, *Methods and Aims*, 176–77.

16. Petrie, *Methods and Aims*, 180.

17. For the wider German story, see Miller, *History and Its Objects*, ch. 8.

18. Comparison with studies of museum-based research a generation later underscores the intellectual sophistication of Lauffer's and Richter's youthful essays. See Fritz Drevermann, "Die Forschungsaufgabe der naturhistorischen Museen"; Max Sauerlandt, "Die Forschungsaufgaben der kunsthistorischen Museen"; and Wilhelm Pessler, "Die Forschungsaufgaben der kulturgeschichtlichen Museen," all in *Forschungsinstitute: Ihre Geschichte, Organisation und Ziele*, ed. Ludolph Brauer, Albrecht Mendelssohn Bartholdy, and Adolf Meyer, 2 vols. (Hamburg: Paul Hartung, 1930), 1:164–74, 209–26, 260–79.

19. Ernst Gombrich, *In Search of Cultural History* (London, 1970); Felix Gilbert, "Cultural History and Its Problems," *Comité International des Sciences Historiques: Rapports* 1 (1960): 40–58.

20. Lynn Hunt, ed., *The New Cultural History* (Berkeley: University of California Press, 1989); Donald R. Kelley, "The Old Cultural History," *History of the Human Sciences* 9 (1996): 101–26.

21. Kristian Bahnson, "Ueber die ethnographischen Museen: Mit besonderer Berücksichtigung der Sammlungen in Deutschland, Oesterreich und

Italien," *Mittheilungen der anthropologischen Gesellschaft in Wien* 18, n.s. 8 (1888): 113.

22. Bahnson, "Ueber ethnographischen Museen," 40.

23. Johann Wolfgang von Goethe, *Sämtliche Werke* (Frankfurt a.M.: Deutscher Klassiker, 1994), vol. 3/I· *Divan; Nachlaß-Stücke*, 614.

24. Notes include references to two works analyzing contemporary philosophical arguments: Erich Adickes, *Kant Contra Haeckel* (1901), and Oswald Külpe, *Die Philosophie der Gegenwart in Deutschland* (1902).

25. Richter buried these discussions deep in his very long footnotes, where their importance and implications were hidden. They have been disinterred in order to make Richter's vision more accessible.

26. See Guy Oakes, *Weber and Rickert: Concept Formation in the Cultural Sciences* (Cambridge, MA: MIT Press, 1988); Guy Oakes, "Rickert's Value Theory and the Foundations of Weber's Methodology," *Sociological Theory* 6 (1988): 38–51.

27. For a good summary, see Charles R. Bambach, *Heidegger, Dilthey, and the Crisis of Historicism* (Ithaca, NY: Cornell University Press, 1995), chs. 2–4.

28. Richter's bibliographical citation offers a window onto what the standard sources on the topic were ca. 1900: Franz Bopp, *Über das Conjugationssystem der Sanskritsprache in Vergleichung mit jenem der griechischen, lateinischen, persischen und germanischen Sprache* (Frankfurt a.M., 1816); Jacob Grimm, *Deutsche Grammatik*, vol. 1 (Göttingen, 1819), and *Deutsche Rechtsalterthümer* (Göttingen, 1828); Adalbert Kuhn, *Zur ältesten Geschichte der indogermanischen Völker: Osterprogamm des Berliner Real-Gymnasiums* (1845), and *Die Herabkunft des Feuers und des Gottertranks* (Berlin, 1859).

29. Franz Boas, "The History of Anthropology," *Science*, n.s. 20, 512 (October 21, 1904): 513–23. Was "mental" the American translator's way of reaching for the otherwise untranslatable *Geisteswissenschaften?*

30. Miller, *History and Its Objects*, ch. 2.

31. See Miller, "*Kulturwissenschaft* Before Warburg," in *Aby Warburg 150: Work, Legacy, and Promise*, ed. David Freedberg and Claudia Wedepohl (Berlin: De Gruyter, forthcoming).

32. See Horst Bredekamp, *Aby Warburg, der Indianer: Berliner Erkundungen einer liberalen Ethnologie* (Berlin: Wagenbach, 2019).

PART I

From the Pages of *Museumskunde*

A Note on the Text

The essays published here appeared in the journal *Museumskunde* over several numbers and several years. We have assembled them in order to present the full force of their argument. With that in mind, several editorial decisions were made.

The main body of Otto Lauffer's text is constituted by "Das historische Museum: Sein Wesen und Wirken und sein Unterschied von den Kunst- und Kunstgewerbe-Museen," *Museumskunde* 3 (1907). We have preceded it, by way of introduction, with Lauffer, "Moriz Heyne und die archäologischen Grundlagen der historischen Museen," *Museumskunde* 2 (1906), and appended to it, by way of conclusion, a few pages from "Herr Schwedeler-Meyer und die historischen Museen," *Museumskunde* 6 (1910).

Of the ten parts of Oswald Richter's "Über die idealen und praktischen Aufgaben der ethnographischen Museen" spread over *Museumskunde* 2 (1906), 3 (1907), 4 (1908), 5 (1909), and 6 (1910), we have omitted in its entirety the section published in *Museumskunde* 4 (1908), 156–68 (paragraphs 62–80). We decided to suppress more selectively other paragraphs that similarly dealt with technical issues of collections management and that led far from our main subject. In addition, especially in Richter's introductory sections, we moved material from the notes into the text. German academic writing ca. 1900 favored enormous footnotes, many of which were, in fact, mini bibliographical essays. Where Richter's references and his questions still seemed valuable, I have moved relevant content into the text. Where they have not, I have cut them. From the standpoint of the history of scholarship, Richter's bibliographical horizon lets us see into a moment just before the literatures on art and ethnographic collecting crystallized into the form they still retain. For ease of reference, we have included the original system of numbered paragraphs that Richter employed, though—as will be evident—there are gaps in the numbering where paragraphs or sections have been moved or omitted. For anyone interested in Richter's complete argument, copies of *Museumskunde* are easily accessed online through the Hathi Trust, among others.

My goal in all this has been to produce a clear, readable text that communicates to the present the force and intellectual clarity of these two texts, which are part of the history of the twentieth century and yet also, I believe, speak to us in the twenty-first.

P. N. M.

The Historical Museum:
Its Character, Its Work,
and How It Differs from Museums
of Art and Applied Arts

Otto Lauffer

Text translated by Annika Fisher and adapted from Otto Lauffer, "Das historische Museum: Sein Wesen und Wirken und sein Unterschied von den Kunst- und Kunstgewerbe-Museen," which appeared in *Museumskunde: Zeitschrift für Verwaltung und Technik öffentlicher und privater Sammlungen*, over the span of three volumes: 2 (1906): 153–62; 3 (1907): 1–14, 78–99, 179–88, 222–47; and 6 (1910): 32–40.

Prologue: Moriz Heyne and the Archaeological Foundations
of Historical Museums
1. Names and Terms
2. Artifacts as Archaeological Sources
3. Collections of Antiquities and the Localized Limit of Their Scope
4. Historical Museums and Collections of Art
5. On the Collecting Practices of Historical Museums
6. The Ordering of Historical-Archaeological Collections
7. The Scientific Obligations of Historical Museums
Coda: The Special Significance of the Historical Museum

**Prologue: Moriz Heyne and the Archaeological Foundations
of Historical Museums**[1]

Moriz Heyne died on the first of March, 1906, in Göttingen, and scholars of German philology as well as German museum studies mourn his passing in equal measure. He will be missed greatly by these

29

disciplines, since his devotion to both characterizes the nature of his work and constitutes the primary strength of his academic persona. Most distressingly, with his passing we have lost an intellectual force that has remained unique in Germany. In his area of specialization, he had no colleagues who could rival him, and none of his students have shown themselves to be his equals. He could hold forth just as well on topics of German language and intellectual culture as on German antiquities. He was equally knowledgeable about words and things. This was the most compelling facet of Heyne's intellect: he could work simultaneously within these two areas not as someone holding two irons in the same fire but rather as someone who could merge the fields together, forging a more exalted unity. It is for good reason that he attained such high academic acclaim in his rare subject.

Heyne's educational history reveals the road he traveled to his unique position. Fate had forced him early on to find his own path. He was born June 8, 1837, in Weißenfels, the son of a master rope maker. He was obliged to halt his studies shortly before graduating from high school. After he had worked for a number of years in the municipal offices, however, improved circumstances allowed him to enter university in the fall of 1860. In 1863, after earning an exemption from graduation exams by ministerial decree, he received his PhD. His diligence and unusual independence are evident in the fact that at this point he had already completed two extensive scholarly works, including an edition of *Beowulf.* His teacher Heinrich Leo was a lasting influence, but Heyne developed his true intellectual character on his own. After fighting for his independent academic convictions in his youth, he preserved them throughout his life. They are also what gave him the strength to pursue unwaveringly his own goals at a time when other practitioners of German philology were concerned with intellectual problems that barely piqued his curiosity. While some of his interests may have appeared outmoded, he was merely on his own autonomous trajectory.

To mention briefly the important dates of Heyne's career: he qualified as professor at Halle in December 1864, became associate professor in 1869, replaced Wackernagel as chair in Basel in 1870, and transferred to Göttingen in 1883, and he continued to be highly prolific until his death. We can barely touch on the extraordinary work he completed in his forty-two years of academic accomplishment: his critical editions of *Beowulf,* Ulfilas, *The Heliand,* etc., and his comprehensive lexical work, which earned him the role of principal editor of the Grimms' dictionary.

For our purposes, it is important to clarify his relationship to the study of German antiquity.

Let me begin by saying that Heyne cannot be blamed for the fact that the field of German antiquity is still not recognized as its own discipline. Its establishment was the guiding principle for all Heyne's scholarly pursuits, and he considered himself a German archaeologist in the same sense as classical archaeologists always have. Thus we should all pursue our disciplinary identity as archaeologists! He understood his mission as a Germanist to be the study of German cultural history from all periods and in all forms, and therefore did not limit his interests to grammar, literature, or even mythology. He was not satisfied with adducing other expressions of German culture as they pertain to those particular fields. His goal was to provide a big picture [*Gesamtbild*] in which all components were of equal value and merited equal consideration. For this reason he studied German ethnology, economic history, legal history, familial and domestic antiquities, warfare, ecclesiastical and civic antiquities, art history, and the history of science with the same passion as language, literature, and mythology. To be an expert in all these individual fields was not his objective. Rather, he wanted to show how these areas interpenetrated and how they should be examined holistically in order to provide a comprehensive picture of German culture.

Because Heyne's goal was to describe conditions and developments, he was primarily concerned with averages and types. The particular greatness of an individual person was of no significant interest to him. Similarly, while he respected masterpieces of literature and art, he was fundamentally interested only in what was typical—that is to say, he was mostly interested in how an artist was the product of his time and circumstances. From Heyne's perspective, cultural and historical factors were always the most essential, even if he was dealing with artworks of the highest order. This was my impression from his lectures and from our later personal relationship. For him, even the inconsequential could prove valuable, since he understood each expression of human life as a useful signifier of cultural history.

Heyne drew from a great variety of sources in order to form his intellectual conclusions, and he was astoundingly adept at employing them for his purposes. Written sources as well as oral accounts, verbal expressions as well as public monuments—Heyne understood these all as equally valid witnesses of the past, as long as there was no doubt as to their integrity. So it is for this reason that Heyne the Germanist also turned his attention—and, even more so, his passion—to the study of physical objects and their museological treatment. One can discern the same impulse that motivated the Baron von Aufseß to care for public monuments. The baron, despite his scholarly importance and his academically well-conceived plans, has been insufficiently appreciated as the founder of the Germanic National Museum.

The study of prehistoric physical culture must have played a part in Heyne's academic plans from the start. This is evident as early as 1864, when Heyne's studies on *Beowulf* were complemented by his booklet on the "Construction and Circumstance of Halle Heorot." Rarely considered at the time of publication, it has lately received the acclaim it deserves. I cannot say precisely when Heyne transitioned from a purely scholarly analysis of antiquity to practical museology. In any case, he was already devoting much of his attention and time to the collections in Basel, where he had been appointed, and the museum made significant improvements under his guidance. This museum work resulted in his publication *Kunst im Hause* [Art at home] (1880/82), and his involvement with the display of objects became in fact so committed as to suggest that he would devote himself completely to museology. The esteem which Heyne gained in museological circles is evident from the fact of his appointment in 1883 to the administrative board of the Germanic Museum, a role he treasured. At this time, however, considerable effort was expended on securing his energy for the *Grimm Encyclopedia*, which was largely why a chair was created for him in Göttingen.

When Heyne came to Göttingen, there was no museum to speak of. He assembled single-handedly the collection now held in the twenty-four partly overfilled rooms of the Civic Gallery of Antiquities. It was a sight to behold how he managed first to convince ever-widening circles of stakeholders that the founding and development of such a museum was possible and then showed how the cooperation of the townspeople and the farmers, of the poor and the rich, of the lower and the upper classes, could be engaged for this purpose.

The Civic Gallery of Antiquities in Göttingen emphasized its local character even more so than the museum in Basel. According to the "Short Guide" written by Heyne in June 1900, the objective of the institution in Göttingen was to collect and display, with scientific order, visual materials related to the political and cultural history of the city and the principality of Göttingen and Grubenhagen. Objects of extraordinary aesthetic value are not found there, nor should they be expected. The museum does not seek to pose as an art gallery but is rather a historical museum. And in that idea is the crux of Heyne's significance to the

study of German antiquities and German museology—an importance
that in the coming decades should and undoubtedly will be appreciated
much more than it was during Heyne's lifetime. Heyne laid out with
the necessary consistency which specialized subfields the study of
German archaeology should encompass as a discipline, and upon this
intellectual basis he helped to create a way of envisioning the historical
museum. Archaeological research and the historical museum, especially
in regard to German antiquity, are unthinkable without each other.
Heyne taught us this principle through his own work and through his
academic character. It constitutes his primary contribution to German
museology, and for this reason it is not only right but also necessary that
he henceforth be honored.

It is impossible to write Heyne's obituary without turning it into an
entire treatise, for to truly acknowledge his position and influence we
must examine the state of archaeology and historical museums in the
German homeland. As I have already said, "German Antiquity" as a field
of study does not really exist. At first sight, however, the opposite seems
to be the case, as there are a large number of associations dedicated to
history and prehistory throughout Germany. But a glimpse into their
publications makes plain that with few exceptions the only fields being
investigated are political and economic history.

No journal exists right now that specializes in German archaeology,
and we urgently need one. We did have one in the past: the Baron
von Aufseß's *Anzeiger für Kunde der deutschen Vorzeit* was such an
essential publication. But August Essenwein, whose importance as a
preeminent collector and administrator I do not wish to deny, allowed
the publication to fold and be replaced by the journal *Mitteilungen aus
dem germanischen Nationalmuseum*. This change had implications beyond
limiting the topics covered by the journal to objects in the museum's
own collection, although Essenwein himself may have been barely aware
of the ramifications. As a matter of principle, the change had drastic
significance. This was at the time when Essenwein severed the Germanic
Museum from its foundations in German studies, and whether this shift
is interpreted as a result of the reformatted journal or as a coincidental
occurrence, it remains a fact that, from Essenwein's time forward,
historical museums became increasingly akin to art galleries.

From this time on, scientific developments in the field of archaeology
were limited to a few select specialties: the studies of prehistoric and
Romano-Germanic antiquities, weaponry, heraldry, numismatics, seals,
and in some sense religious antiquities. Some of these areas—mostly

those furthest removed from the world of art collection—now have specialized museums that support active intellectual pursuits in their field. There are also societies and commissions devoted to promoting research in some of these subtopics, and even some local organizations interested in antiquity that have successfully encouraged scholarship.

Pursued by only a handful of scholars from each field, German archaeology as a science has not yet been established. It is also unfortunate that the academics who are pushed to publish their research about objects that intersect with their interests are cultural historians like Georg Steinhausen, linguists like Rudolf Meringer and Otto Schrader, or folklorists (as evidenced in the journals of the Berlin, Saxon, Bavarian, and Austrian societies). And the scholars who should be willing to tackle archaeological matters, namely the representatives of historical museums and the Germanists, seem to keep themselves far removed from the field of archaeology—at least that is how their academic work makes it appear. Foremost among these, particularly at the larger museums that we are mainly considering, are trained art historians, who are understandably drawn to the aesthetic and art historical issues involved. And we must state, although without reproach, that these scholars almost never make use of their background in German studies, which is essential for truly understanding historical collections. Among the Germanists, Moriz Heyne could until recently be counted as the only one who pursued German archaeology for its own sake. Awareness of his unique position was publicized by his most personal work, the *Fünf Bücher deutscher Hausaltertümer* [The five books of German antiquities of the home], of which the first three volumes, *Housing*, *Food*, and *Care of the Body and Clothing*, he completed with astounding speed in 1899, 1901, and 1903. These works alone make clear how much we will miss Heyne's scholarship. Today we gaze at these volumes and wonder who will complete the series.

When Heyne presented the preliminary lecture on *Antiquities of the Home* on August 22, 1899, he said it would be "wonderful to be able to greet a younger generation of Germanistic students who would wish to join in the work outlined in these books." Unfortunately, his wish remains unfulfilled. We doubt whether any appropriately educated disciples will emerge to complete the fourth volume, *Trade and Commerce*, which is, as far as we know, only half finished. It is with sorrow that we see Heyne's optimistic plans for his intended projects fade away. Heyne had planned, directly after the completion of the fourth volume, to write a monograph about the history of dance before returning to the final volume of

Antiquities of the Home, which was to deal with "the great subject of communal living." He was even hopeful that he could still commence work on a large dictionary of German antiquity, an urgently necessary work for the field of German archaeology.

These unfulfilled plans of Heyne's . . . how much food for thought they give us. "German archaeology has just begun with its labors!" he once proclaimed to me, indicating which fields still needed scholarly attention. He must have been cognizant that his work on the antiquities of the home addressed only a small fraction of German archaeology, leaving the vast remainder awaiting similar attention. Subsequent studies should address familial antiquities and every other aspect of private life, followed by examinations of the antiquities relating to the state, the community, war, punishment, the church, and finally science. We must pause to contemplate the meaning of these subcategories and the breadth of work implied by each—even when employing the treatment Heyne used for his study of the antiquities of the home that provided mere "baselines of the topic" instead of an "exhaustive treatment that covers the subject in adequate detail." Even from a distanced perspective it must be admitted that this labor can no longer be left to those who happen to possess a personal preference for it, as Heyne did. What is needed is an intellectual center to ensure the continued study of German archaeology.

There is indeed a German commission at the Royal Prussian Academy of the Sciences, and the names of its members—Konrad Burdach, Gustav Roethe, and Erich Schmidt—attest to the high level of its intellectual standing. But the work of this commission, documented in the minutes of the proceedings in Berlin, is largely oriented toward literature and linguistic history, aimed at illuminating the "study of our national intellectual history." The treatment of objects, which require their own specialized scientific methods, is beyond the scope of this commission. What is required for the study of German antiquity is a designated archaeological institute, which should be feasible. Just consider the amounts we receive every year from the state for the care of classical antiquities. In 1902, the budget for the Imperial German Archaeological Institute in Berlin was 172,010 Mark. A fifth of this sum would be enough to provide the study of German antiquities a safe location to expand. There can be no doubt that eventually a German archaeological commission will be deemed necessary, just as several years ago the Romano-Germanic commission was founded by the archaeological institute. As long as Moriz Heyne was alive, we still had hope that such an assembly would form, with him at its center. But now he lies buried, and his work has come to an end—far too soon, from our perspective. It therefore behooves us to at least preserve his intellectual inheritance. And that is why we are going house to house, knocking upon every door, to awaken the German conscience to recognize what we owe to the study of our national culture and the history of our people.

Having laid out Heyne's groundbreaking significance for scientific German archaeology, we must now consider his impact on the field of museology. The intellectual foundation upon which a collection is assembled determines the character of the museum—not the artifacts of the collection themselves. But now, as surely we all concur, we must begin to develop a substantial number of our public collections with an archaeological focus, namely the historical museums. Just as Heyne was the exemplar of a German archaeologist, so too his Göttingen gallery, despite its humble size, can be considered the model of an improved historical museum. This does not imply that Heyne amassed a great sum of extraordinarily precious individual objects. The field itself did not have a particularly rich external culture, and in addition, his extremely meager allotted budget would make this impossible in today's art market. But Heyne knew how to arrange what he did assemble, so that the individual pieces seemed almost able to speak to their viewers themselves. The vibrant power of the Göttingen Museum rests in this ability to make the past comprehensible, allowing the intellectual purpose of the collection to be clearly recognizable. Just mentioning this museum can squelch any derogatory chatter about historical museums giving off the whiff of the grave and the stench of decay.

The secret to Heyne's many successes is actually very simple. It consists of conscientiously identifying and fulfilling the mission of a local historical museum. Heyne, with full awareness and heedless of his own area of study, focused only on the geographic area of Göttingen and Grubenhagen, and his strength lay largely in this voluntary limitation of his scope. In this way his museum gained the unity and cohesion that has such a soothing effect on its visitors—an advantage shared by the Germanic Museum, which has limited its collection to German antiquities and will hopefully continue to do so in the future.

The second decisive aspect of Heyne's museological work concerns his consistent resistance to the strong influence of the applied arts museums, to which historical museums have increasingly fallen prey over the last decades owing to the leanings of several influential personalities. Heyne's archaeological training provided him with a protective shield.

He understood that historical museums have to create their collections through different means than do museums of applied arts, and that objects of interest to the decorative arts belonged in collections of historical museums only if they fulfilled a single condition: namely, that they originated in the craft production of their home region. For this reason, for example, Heyne assembled an impressive collection of glazed earthenware from Münden, which he was still interested in expanding at the time of his passing. In the meantime, however, he refused to add any other production of this ceramic technique to his collection because no other Fayence pottery besides that from Münden fell under the museum's remit. In this way he protected the collection from splintering, keeping it pure from accidental influences, which, despite the possibility of being valuable in and of themselves, in practice serve only to obscure to the public the true purpose of the museum.

On the other hand, he did begin collecting from an early date several object types of which other galleries possessed very few examples, both then and today. He was among the first to understand his museum's scope to include monuments that reflect the entire range of folk culture. For example, his collection of Jewish antiquities from the synagogues of Göttingen and its region counts as the first of its kind in Germany. And I doubt if any other German museum, even today, could boast a comparable assortment of craft instruments.

Heyne understood how best to display this comprehensive type of collection through expert museological presentation. In this regard, too, his guiding methodology was very simple. He looked to the archaeological basis of the historical exhibition to logically discern its controlling principle. Archaeology should guide this type of museum display just as it categorizes forms of cultural expression in its academic discipline. The technological or stylistically oriented presentations favored by museums of art and applied arts simply do not work in a historical museum. Only a cultural-historical—or, if another name is preferred, an archaeological— presentation is appropriate here. The grouping of artifacts on display is not determined by their formal characteristics or medium but rather, quite simply, by their purpose. Let us take just one example. A military saber, a senator's rapier, and a hunting knife may resemble each other greatly, may stem from the same time period, may bear the same ornamentation, and may even have been created by the hand of the same master craftsman—but despite all this they may not be displayed together in a historical museum. The first is a weapon of war, the second is a communal artifact, and the third is a hunting weapon. Or, to provide another example: a silver drinking vessel, a communion chalice, and a guild goblet. In a historical museum they may not be grouped in the same showcase of metalwork as they would be in a museum of decorative arts. Instead, the first must be placed among antiquities of the home, the second with ecclesiastical objects, and finally, the third with other guild antiquities. Their purpose alone is decisive. By itself, this theoretical stipulation seems very simple, but it is a pity it is not followed everywhere in practice. In more than one historical museum it is plainly evident that the model of applied arts museums is being emulated, allowing technological displays next to cultural-historical ones. Heyne never once fell prey to this error while designing the Göttingen Museum, and therein lies once again the exemplary nature of his collection. Display, as well as the individual objects themselves, carries significance. Both, however, are the result of one and the same thing: an archaeologically based plan for the museum. Accordingly, each exhibit reflects the premeditated and focused orientation of the museum itself, which should truly be regarded as exemplary.

In this way, with his undaunted vigor, Moriz Heyne also influenced the field of museology. And what were the resulting ramifications? I recall a conference in Mannheim on September 21 and 22, 1903, at which the idea of "museums as institutions of national education" was discussed. A wide selection of German authorities on museology attended this seminar, but the fact that historical museums also existed in Germany, which in their essence and effect differed completely from other types of galleries, was insufficiently addressed. Heyne did not participate at this conference, but even if he had attended, he would have barely entered the discussion. His practice at such gatherings was to speak up only when it was absolutely required. But this I know for certain: despite everything, he would have returned home with the conviction that the era of independent development was also coming for the field of German archaeology and for the historical museum—and that his role in this future could not be denied. Throughout his life the resolute certainty that he was pursuing the correct path with his intellectual and museological efforts never left him. May his work soon bear fruit, and may we all honor his memory.

1. Names and Terms[2]

In the following we aim to define the character and function of a historical museum. In so doing, we should be aware from the start that grappling with this topic is not always a welcome task, owing not only to internal difficulties but also to purely external considerations. Two very important points of view should be addressed in this light.

We must reflect on the prevailing trends of thought that generally—and specifically, for our large leading collections—define the character of museum studies. Aesthetic and art historical interests dominate the museum world, and the issues that arise from this milieu are undoubtedly appropriate for art museums and museums of applied arts. But to apply these formulations to the very different types of collections that feature antiquities causes such historical museums to be measured by entirely inappropriate standards. The result naturally casts these museums in an unfavorable light. At the same time we must admit that historical collections, as we will examine further, perhaps themselves have failed to outline a clearly defined mission. They vary greatly in their systems of organization and fail to demonstrate a well-developed and independent perspective to guide their methods of acquisition and display. These failings make it difficult to evaluate them correctly. For our purposes, none of this is of essential importance. We are concerned only with the purely external result: namely, the circumstance that from the vast majority of colleagues we cannot expect active engagement in the following debate.

We do not need to hide how painful we find this fact. But neither can we allow ourselves to be swayed to avoid a confrontation. It is, after all, up to us to bring about the changes necessary to improve the status of historical museums. The obvious inequality of the museums must be acknowledged for any new understanding to evolve. We are also motivated by a different issue that weighs on us even more, since it concerns our own colleagues. We fear that several of them will voice a snide criticism or even make an outright attack concerning the upcoming dialogue. This is not at all our intent, and fear of being misunderstood in this way is almost enough to silence us.

A brief reminder of the topic's history reveals that this particular worry is not entirely unfounded. On the whole, the field of museology has not been around for very long, and historical museums in particular have barely passed the initial phase of their development—excluding those that developed from courtly collections. The men who overcame great obstacles to establish and develop these museums are largely still at their labors today. They will recall the many concessions they were forced to make in the effort of furthering their museums—involving preexisting collections, too little space, or too little money, as well as the passions and occasional foolishness of their benefactors—and because of these practical experiences they may be somewhat wary of our more theoretical propositions.

Despite all this, we should not be discouraged. We must attempt to articulate the inherent principles that should guide the historical museum. Every museologist recognizes this necessity, and any museum visitor would agree after traveling from town to town, visiting and comparing the various institutions that bear the name "historical museum." It would become apparent in short order that this designation is applied to widely varied collections—collections that differ not only obviously on account of their individual holdings, but also on account of the range in philosophies that govern their collections, groupings, and methods of display. There are seemingly endless varieties of weapons, applied arts objects, war memorabilia, a few good and a very many average pictures, and practical artifacts from both public and private lives. To put it briefly, after touring a half dozen of these collections and standing before yet another historical museum in the next town, the visitor can draw no sure conclusions from his previous experiences about what will be found inside or how it will be ordered.

We do not wish to deny that some variation among collections is necessary, as the regions of our fatherland developed differently and accordingly have created different types of monuments. But such a perspective would once again focus on the individual objects of the collection, which cannot be our guiding determinants in the present context. Through their historical, aesthetic, or material value, individual items can determine the quality of an antiques store but not the museological character of a public collection. Let me just insert that the variety of the assembled artifacts is always welcome, since this diversity is stimulating and gives rise to increased pedagogical opportunities.

We, however, have entirely different concerns. The label "historical museum" is used by so many existing institutions, as well as new collections, that it must be considered a genus—which serves to signal from the start that the collection in question differs in a particular way from other types of collections. Since a commonly used name typically designates an agreed-upon meaning, we should be able to assume that all museums sharing this name also share principles of collection and organization. And this is precisely what is not the case.

The negative consequences of this confusion become clear when we consider the corresponding situation for museums of applied arts, which do much better at clarifying their objectives. When we enter a museum of applied arts, we know we can expect a collection of objects unified by generally recognized principles—namely, that the holdings will display a certain formal style or are prototypical of a certain modern form of creation. Among the stewards of these museums one can also discern, on average, a shared understanding as to what objects the institution should purchase, what they should include in their exhibits, and what they should reject on principle—in other words, an agreement on what is beneficial to their collections. This certainty does not exist to the same degree among historical museums. The difference in the ways these two types of museums assemble and organize their objects is even greater. In museums of applied arts, a shared foundational principle guides the methods of display. They arrange one part of their collection according to technique and the other according to style. In any of these museums a viewer can with confidence expect an exact answer to the questions "Where are the works made of iron?" "Where are textiles?" "Where are ceramics?" etc., and in most now also "Where is the room of Renaissance art?" and "Where is the baroque art?" etc. However, if visitors to a historical museum ask, "Where are the antiquities of private life? Where are ecclesiastical antiquities? Where are ancient items of warfare? Where are historical guild artifacts?" etc., they must fear evasive or partial responses, or perhaps even an uncomprehending smile.

It is evident that historical museums lack widely accepted basic guidelines to govern their acquisitions, and that they have also not reached any broad consensus on the question of arrangement. Thus, if a visitor stands before a museum today that is designated as historical, he can draw only negative conclusions about what can be expected inside—namely, that the artifacts on display have been assembled (to word it very carefully) *not* according to aesthetic considerations. If they were, then the collection would be labeled as an art or applied arts museum, and the historical aspect would not be emphasized. If we look for a positive definition, we can only guess at its content. We may at least be able to expect that a certain number of local artifacts will be present inside. But we are unable to get a firm grasp on how they will be displayed. In other words, despite the large number of historical museums in Germany, the name "historical museum" is not a clearly delineated term that expresses the character of the institution it labels.

We are by no means acknowledging anything new here. Many colleagues have long conceded this fact. It is indicative that the designation "historical museum" has been—and continues to be—avoided by many galleries. Many have settled upon the title "cultural-historical collections," which seems preferable, as it suggests a certain limiting tendency. With this terminology, however, we have jumped out of the frying pan and into the fire. I will not hesitate to claim that the fundamental agreement about the nature of archaeological collections that we seek is hindered by nothing as much as by this unlucky phrase: "cultural history."

Despite the frequency with which the term "cultural history" is employed in the museum world, it is rare that even two institutions are referencing the same concept with these words. It is nearly impossible to concisely define what the term is intended to designate. Let us look at just one of many examples. The "Official Guide" to the historical museum in Basel from the year 1906 lists the museum's goals on page iv: "First, all artifacts should be collected that are of historical significance in the widest sense of the word to the city of Basel and its surroundings; second, the museum should be a place of encouragement and education for the applied arts of today; and third, the museum should strive to convey the domestic life of our forefathers, so that the observant visitor can appreciate its cultural history as well as history and decorative arts." The unnamed author of this list differentiates between objects that are "historically significant in the widest sense of the word" and those that are "cultural historical." The text does not clearly indicate what precisely separates these two areas of interest, which is not a commonplace differentiation. If I understand the author correctly, then the artifacts of public life are deemed historic, while those of private life are considered cultural historical. Whether we accept or reject this distinction does not matter. It is only important to recognize that a veil obscures the way the author has chosen to express himself, so that the reader remains uncertain whether he understands the meaning correctly. This is not to blame the author. This case is typical, since we have all become accustomed to repeatedly using "cultural history" with the silent assumption that our readers will interpret the term just as we do. In reality, as we shall see, this is absolutely not the case.

So, what does cultural history even mean? The linguist speaks of a cultural-historical method to study the evolution of words; the economic historian uses it to designate different economic forms; the lawyer uses it for the history of legal concepts; the theologian uses it for the expression of cultural ethics; the art historian uses it for aesthetic or stylistic developments. After wading through myriad interpretations of this increasingly baffling term, we turn to professional historians, and specifically those who consider themselves devoted to the study of a scientific cultural history (such as Karl Gotthard Lamprecht and

Georg Steinhausen). Their conclusion is that the essence of all cultural-historical research concerns the history of the inner man—the mentality of a people. This view completely undermines the museum's claim to the terminology, since the history of the inner man can be illustrated by physical artifacts only to a very limited degree. And physical artifacts are what our cultural-historical collections have to work with. So, are we founding and furthering such collections only to nurture an inferior aspect of cultural history?

It is apparent that this is not the case. As is generally acknowledged, as well as evident in our discussion so far, these varied fields clearly view "cultural history" as an established term. The difficulty—or rather, we should say, the confusion—arises from the fact that an array of more or less related disciplines employ the term "cultural history" without evoking precisely the same idea, so that almost everyone who mentions cultural history really refers only to a specific part of the entire concept—one that is related to his own field. Other facets of the term are either completely disregarded or at best only partially considered.

Accordingly, the best way to make improvements in the future seems to be to create an overview of the entire topic of cultural history. Of course, mapping out a precise and analytical scientific system cannot be our task at the moment. It is, moreover, doubtful, given the wide range of historical factors at play, that any individual, regardless of his level of knowledge, would be able to lay out such a system in a completely satisfying manner. We would like to offer a few small suggestions.

If we are interpreting the situation correctly, then it is the task of cultural history to examine all manifestations of the human spirit, as it develops and transforms, while taking into consideration the individual, the family, the community, the country, and the people as a whole. And cultural history should focus on the manifestations that are typical and commonly repeated—not on extraordinary, atypical, or isolated phenomena. These typical expressions of human life may take many different forms, such as concepts, beliefs, words, sounds, customs, practices, economic systems, and ultimately physical objects. Cultural history as a scientific field seeks to investigate all these areas with equal zeal. However, scholars tend to focus on some of these expressions (which we hope have been listed comprehensively above) while engaging other expressions only as explanatory parallels. This results in a range of subdisciplines—or rather, associated areas of research. These are the very areas, as mentioned above, that like to assert that the term "cultural history" applies to their field alone.

If we organize the facets of cultural history by their subfield of historical research, we can generate the following list:

I.   Concepts and Beliefs: history of the inner life (ethics, aesthetics, and legal studies)
II. Words: linguistics
III. Sounds: history of music
IV. Customs and Practices: history of habits
V.   Economic Systems: economic history
VI. Objects:
     a) archaeology
     b) technology
     c) art history

From this outline we can trace in what way researchers in different fields interpret their own "cultural-historical mode of investigation." It is generally recognized that each specialist's work is supplemented and further elucidated by the research of related fields. The list shows us at the same time that what is considered the central focus may change from one field to the next and that the method of scientific inquiry must also change as a consequence of the given field's premises and differing points of view. It is for this reason that a true comprehension of the term "cultural history" remains so challenging whenever the term is invoked. Such difficulties are naturally compounded by the fact that the sources upon which all inquiry rests are not easily divided among the six categories, but rather fall within two broad types: written historical sources and physical objects. Most recently the burgeoning field of folklore studies has added the surviving manifestations of folklife as a new type of source.

Our discussion of the term "cultural history" has been somewhat lengthy. We needed to create a foundation for our investigations, and owing to the great prevalence of the term we could not disregard it. Even had we so desired, the frequent use in the museum world of the labels "Cultural Historical Collection" and "Exhibit of Cultural History" require explanation. In order to proceed we must once again underscore that we use the term "cultural history" to refer to the collective concept, not to one of its isolated parts. It follows that for the type of museum we are discussing here, the term "Cultural History Museum" is of as little use as "Historical Museum." If we could employ instead "Collection of Antiquities" or "Archaeological Collection," then we could hope to avoid the recurrent misunderstandings surrounding the terminology.

2. Artifacts as Archaeological Sources

> Everything that happens leaves traces: traces in the nature
> that surrounds us, traces in the minds of people. The traces in
> nature that are tangible and perceptible to the senses become
> monuments to what has happened. The traces in the minds of
> people become memories that account for what has happened. In
> interpreting monuments we depend on their materials, on visual
> training and natural aptitude for spatial and formal relationships.
> Research begins with observation and critical contemplation.
> Monuments include all types and techniques of art, pictures, tools
> of every quality, buildings of every use, houses, and castles, as well
> as streets, canals, walls, and border ramparts.

Alexander Cartellieri uttered these words in his inaugural academic
address "On the Nature and Classification of History" (Leipzig
[1905], 11) and thereby included physical artifacts among the array
of historical sources and promoted their scientific study as a form of
historical research. We see this statement as a good sign that today we
have overcome a one-sided view of historical research and historical
observation that gives no equal credence to the study of physical objects.
We hope also that the complaints which Rudolf Wackernagel in 1887
still urgently voiced in his highly regarded paper "The Preservation of
Antiquities from the Fatherland in Basel" can now be silenced. However,
in Cartellieri's words also lies a warning to all interested in the care of
physical monuments. If we want monuments to play an increasing role
in scientific research, as they deserve to, then we must also ensure that
the academic study of objects from all perspectives is undertaken in as
consistent and rigorous a manner as possible. Up to this point we have
primarily judged an object from antiquity on the aesthetic and stylistic
merits of its formal properties. We have in most cases also considered
the material out of which it is produced. But one issue has been far
too frequently neglected: the purpose that the object served. And yet,
as everyone knows, purpose determines the external appearance of
something just as much as its materials and artistic features do.

Under normal circumstances, purpose is always the initial motivating
factor for the creation of an object. Purpose determines an object's uses,
how it interacts with other phenomena of daily life, and what it is called.
Purpose is so essential to an object's usefulness, or lack thereof, that
it should be contemplated even when regarding the aesthetic value of

the object's exterior form. A viewer must consider whether the material chosen complements the object's purpose, and how the artistic design itself serves its use.

The appearance of an object is influenced by its purpose as well as by its material and decoration. These three aspects work in accord, and depending on the scholar, one or the other may be emphasized as the determining factor. Three possibilities can result, which can be satisfied by three different fields, namely art history, technology, and archaeology. Among these, art history (or style history, if the objects are functional) emphasizes issues of decoration and the development of aesthetically pleasing forms.[3] Art history is interested only in an object that expresses the inherent human desire for beauty and decoration, thereby gaining a particular value and higher meaning than is entailed in the purpose and materials of the object itself. In contrast, technology begins with the material. It notes the properties of an object's substance and how they are exhibited in different ways through different materials. Technology deals with the manner in which these attributes are manipulated by the craft of humans. It also seeks to establish the limits of artistic usability through the different properties of the materials and how they are emphasized by the technical means employed.

Finally, there is the scientific discipline that places the *use* of an object at the very center of its focus; for lack of a better name, we call this field archaeology. Obviously, we would greatly prefer the lovely German word *Altertumskunde*, but then we are faced with the same issues that plague the term "cultural history." The term *Altertumskunde* is employed by many camps and saddled with various connotations by different scientific interests that use it for their own purposes. Therefore we can barely use the term today without being misunderstood by one side or another. This author himself used to employ the term *Altertumskunde* in reference to archaeology. And he had not long ago written to the ethnographic sector of the Organization for Societies of German History and Antiquity to suggest that a short definition of the term would put to rest misunderstandings. To his chagrin, however, he learned that the term was understood to refer partly to related academic fields and partly to the realm of practical museology. For this reason we will avoid *Altertumskunde* as much as possible.

Archaeology involves all forms of external culture, regardless of material, technique, or style. The field studies the typical forms that objects took in order to fulfill a certain purpose at the time they were developed, as well as how these forms changed under the influence of new viewpoints, customs, and technical abilities, while still fulfilling their initial purpose. Archaeology further considers how decoration may take over the form, so that objects no longer fulfill their intended purpose in their natural manner. Other changes could come about because of increasingly complex economic pressures or the influence of new customs that complicated the objects' original purpose. Archaeology studies how such developments can cause a form to evolve into two or more related implements. The original designations can become insufficient, just as words can become antiquated and meanings too narrow, requiring that new terms be coined for related concepts.

Thus, archaeology does not merely focus on objects themselves but reaches far beyond to encompass nearly all adjacent fields of cultural history. By finding interrelationships, archaeology can interpret objects as spiritually and economically meaningful cultural artifacts. Furthermore, the discipline places its results in a causal relationship with those of ethnology and historical geography, providing these fields with rich material and inspiration. Archaeology essentially is a part of ethnographic studies, limited to the past of its own people. Just as ethnography uses simple descriptions of external culture as the basis for deeper research into folklore, genealogy, customs, and conceptions—so too does archaeology use physical objects as the starting point for wider scientific research. In this way, physical objects are primarily viewed in regard to their ascribed purpose as ethnographic objects of use. But this is not the only limitation to the materials appropriate for study. A second must be added: the only objects that are useful as archaeological source material are those that we have designated as "antiquities."

As in every field of cultural history, archaeology is limited to the study of the past. The field attempts to learn about the historical precursors of a culture and to examine each step along the way. This alone shows that the age of an object is not enough to characterize it as an antiquity. The determining factor is much more about the object's degree of difference from our culture of today. The object should embody the cultural trends of the past that were traversed to result in the cultural norms of today. Thus artifacts that are relatively recent but display these characteristics may be deemed "antiquities," while much older objects may not earn this designation. In practice, the result is that no archaeological museum is able to produce a scientifically sound justification for restricting its holdings to a specific time period, such as the empire style, for example.

The factor that determines whether an object is an archaeological resource is its degree of difference from objects of the present culture.

With this insight we have gained a secure footing for assessing the group of artifacts—objects of folklore and ethnic studies—that has increasingly found a place in our historical museums despite not being antiquities. Just like antiquities, however, these artifacts are ethnographic sources that aid in the study of national traditions. While their continuing production appears to distinguish them clearly from what we normally consider antiquities, it should be noted that their creation is associated only with specific regions. Furthermore, these objects are widely recognized as no longer representative of our modern-day cultural norms. With antiquities they share certain outmoded characteristics in relation to culture today, and thus they provide a rich source for study. Folkloric objects, excluding perhaps those that serve a specific agricultural purpose, can exemplify stagnating or slightly modified evocations of past cultural epochs. They are visible evidence of the cultural periods that defined much of their regions in earlier times. And they have retained their old forms, although they may have had new elements added or been altered somewhat to aid their purpose. Some of these objects that are still used in the present can provide invaluable insights about tools for which we would otherwise have only an inkling of their function, through written sources or old illustrations. The artifacts have also added to our understanding of antiquated language through their traditional names, providing vocabulary that is partly known through the objects and partly known as misunderstood expressions in written sources. The folkloric artifacts themselves help explicate such references and descriptions in the texts. In this way, such objects take their place among archaeological sources.[4]

Now that we have discussed how close to the present archaeological sources can date, the question poses itself as to how far back in time their domain extends. There can only be one answer. Just as classical archaeologists will study all artifacts dug up in the countries around the Mediterranean, so too must our archaeological work begin with the discovery of the earliest evidence of human activity. While so-called prehistoric studies, with their own practical and scientific methods, should remain a separate archaeological subfield, all archaeologists should familiarize themselves with this research as much as possible.

What is understood as prehistory no longer needs explanation. But since the term "prehistory" developed from a perspective that valued the written word as the only true historical source, perhaps a new designation should be considered. Given that we recognize in objects a documentary worth equivalent to that of written sources, we cannot conceive of a time period as existing "prior to history" for which archaeological excavations deliver year after year autonomous new evidence. Regardless, the dearth of any other fitting terminology gives us no choice but to continue to refer to "prehistory." But we must remain cognizant that this term rests on academic assumptions to which we object on principle.

The further back into the past our studies reach, the more frequently we will be unsure whether the artifact we are examining is typical in form—fulfilling archaeology's primary interest—or atypical, with random influences rendering its appearance unusual. Despite this uncertainty, we cannot ignore any ancient artifacts, since their rarity renders each one valuable to academics as well as to collectors. Even if an artifact of great age is an atypical sample, its archaeological significance remains unquestionable.

From more recent periods we of course have a richer collection of surviving artifacts, from which the typical forms and the anomalies are easily identifiable. Under such conditions the atypical forms are only rarely of particular interest to archaeologists. The pieces that are typical objects of use constitute the preferred source material for archaeology.

One special sort of source material deserving mention is memorabilia. Judged by their external appearance, objects in this category can seem meaningless—without clear archaeological, art historical, or technological merit. But like archaeological sources, they accrue their value through the purpose that they once served. Our interest in such sources does not lie with their generalized, typical use in the past, however—in contrast with archaeological sources—but with the very specific role that they played upon a single occasion of a historically important moment. Their value lies in aiding the recollection of a meaningful historical event or an extraordinary historical figure to which the object is connected (in a way not necessarily visible but evident in oral or written accounts). Clearly this value can be of a sentimental sort only, the strength of which is determined by the historical interest that we associate with the item. When memorabilia are linked to the history of the state or community, then a large group of interested parties have a stake in the memory that they preserve. In this case, we must view memorabilia as a type of public memento, bearing in mind that such items are merely accessories and lack independent documentary value. Memorabilia can serve to visualize only an occurrence that is documented by other means. In any case, the assessment of their value must be undertaken with caution. Their status is just a hair above that of curiosities, which are memorabilia that do not evoke a general interest and therefore have no role in historical research.

3. Collections of Antiquities and the Localized Limit of Their Scope[5]

Let us now turn away from a purely intellectual discussion of archaeology to address some practical questions in the field of museology. We should not delude ourselves into thinking that we have anything novel to say to the few great collections of antiquities in Germany. These institutions, through the individual perspectives of their founders and the course of their development, have acquired their unique character. Their right to existence is part of their very essence. But because they have attained this prominent position through the wealth of their holdings, they are, by their nature, exceptional examples. For this reason we will focus instead on small and middle-range museums. In addition to being more practical, this effort of looking initially at smaller institutions before moving on to larger ones will sharpen our perceptions as to what is typical for museums as a whole.

In the case that small archaeological museums and local collections even have firm annual funding, the sums available to expand their holdings are generally very small. For them, Wilhelm von Bode's words are apt: limited means necessitate—to an even greater extent—a clear understanding of an organization's aim.[6] It is paramount that these museums be free from the influence of other types of collections, particularly those specializing in the technical or applied arts. Owing to widely perceived obligations, archaeological museums frequently have to cede money and space to art museums. Since the small archaeological collections are unable to acquire ancient artwork, they need to be strengthened in their conviction that a museum can be made from pieces that have no artistic merit. To avoid being seen as junk storage rooms, these museums must fulfill their archaeological and academic mandates of presenting to the public the lifestyle of their ancestors.

Different issues affect museums of intermediate size, including some larger national collections. While they do have greater financial resources, these museums also have more demands placed upon them: they must be able to educate visitors in the areas of natural history, ethnography, high art, applied art, and archaeology—equally. This multifaceted set of obligations may be counted as an advantage, and indeed it is so long as it does not lead to the splintering of material into subfields in a scientifically unsatisfying manner. From another perspective, however, such a complex mission may be seen as detrimental. For in these museums there is generally not a desire to sharply divide the various departments from one another. Even if such a division were desirable from a technical standpoint, it would increase the risk of blurring how physical objects are examined in different subdisciplines. It is not always possible to strictly differentiate the historical-antiquarian perspective (which is of primary interest to us here) from that of the applied arts, as the museum directors Karl Lacher in Graz and Alfred Overmann in Erfurt have managed to do.[7] Nor is it always possible to clearly segregate an independently run zone of the museum, as in the portion of the Lübeck Museum designated the Museum of Art and Cultural History. Accordingly, we should take a moment to emphasize the fundamentally different ways that museums can function.

In the following discussion we will consider historical museums that are fortunate enough to be located alongside specialized art and applied arts museums, and are thus able to concentrate on their specialized academic and museological agendas. These are the museums that most purely retain the character of a collection of antiquities—an identity that is underscored by their very proximity to other types of collections. Because these museums can clearly articulate their own collecting and display practices, they can show the public that collections of art and collections of antiquities are not in competition with each other. Instead, each type strives for its own goals, which can work to the other's advantage.

Let us now consider what items belong in a historical museum. One could argue that no one is qualified to make such specifications, and that each museum should decide on its own what it should collect. This objection, however, is not valid. Only a private citizen can collect whatever he wants. A public institution, which has a specific role to fulfill, cannot. The individual can follow his personal tastes and purchase antiquities that correspond to his archaeological interests. A museum director, however, cannot shift the area of focus of his collection in accordance with his own interests. A museum must strive to fulfill the expectations of the public. Because only scholars can judge the value of these expectations, each museum must have a plan for its collecting practices. Each museum must have a program set up according to academically unimpeachable guidelines. The public should demand this, whether they are interested in the development of the institution simply as taxpayers or want to see it evolve into a superlative scientific and educational center.

This is the fundamental difference between a private collection and a museum. A private collection may be tailored to an individual personality. It can, but does not have to, follow the outlines of a predetermined program. In contrast, a museum must relate to the general public, and its collections must evolve according to a systematic program. This is true for every museum—including those dedicated to antiquity. Accordingly, there are certain obligations that pertain to every archaeological collection.

Let us look at some firm evidence to prove our conclusion. The public institution most closely related to the historical museum is the historical archive. Both work along the same lines. Historical museums and archives both focus their collection and acquisition efforts on amassing evidence of historical conditions, developments, and events. They divide this effort, with the archive preserving original written sources and the museum preserving physical artifacts that act as historical monuments and archaeological evidence. Certain disparities arise from the circumstance that written sources primarily exist only as a single original edition, whereas archaeological facts are generally corroborated by a range of testimonies, all of equal historical value. Owing to the variety of source materials, the archive acts, from an administrative point of view, more as a warehouse, while the museum acts more as a display case. But these differences are in essence just external. The internal mission and intellectual pursuits of historical museums and archives remain identical, and if anyone doubts the right of historical museums to exist, they might as well question that of historical archives.[8]

Historical archives, which are generally much older than museums, have in practice focused their entire efforts within the limited boundaries of their home location. Similarly, historical museums must learn to collect only the antiquities of their own towns and surrounding regions, depending on how far the cultural influence of their city has spread. This must and will be the first step for historical museums to attain their desired independence. The result will be apparent when museums adopt the only title we recommend: Collections of Civic Antiquities. At the very least, whatever designation they choose, the museum's sensibilities and practices should follow along these lines.

We should not disregard this local focus and fall prey to the suspicion that there is no point to it. We are too easily swayed by the allure of what is distant. While we believe that we study objects from the past objectively, as much as that is even possible, when dealing with examples of considerable age we are equally quick to assume that they are more interesting than our familiar local antiquities, as if they are imbued with exotic qualities arising from a distant provenance. We need to free ourselves from this tendency. By limiting the scope of our collection, in accordance with our means, to local antiquities, we are acting for the benefit particularly of the smaller museum.

In comparison to more international collections of art, historical museums imbued with local flavor can tap the principal source of their own power: their popularity. In addition, these museums possess an ethical importance that has been much lauded in recent years, since they can tangibly buttress the affection people feel for their hometowns. A historical museum that chooses to forget or neglect its local focus robs itself of its central purpose. "Through its local character, a collection creates a warm atmosphere for its visitors. They are drawn not only by an interest in the arts, but also by the chance to enjoy the creations of their ancestors, whose flesh and blood the visitors themselves share. They can witness their predecessors' achievements and their memorials, so many of which still shape their homeland. As they learn of ancient accomplishments from which they still benefit, modern visitors may sense a continuity in their people's thoughts and feelings within themselves, perhaps more than they ever realized." This is how Heyne verbalized the role of historical museums a generation ago, with particular reference to the collection in Basel. In the same way, Overmann recently defined the purpose of the Erfurt historical museum with special emphasis on its local identity. He claimed that the museum should awake, preserve, and deepen interest in the city's rich history, love of the homeland (both in a specific and a general sense), and justified pride in the city of one's birth.[9]

Apart from the ethical roles local collections play, consideration of historical museums' academic roles also makes a clear case for limiting their scope to local antiquities. Anyone running such a museum knows from experience how multifaceted the academic expectations placed upon him are. He must be sufficiently familiar with the general history of the area to which his collection belongs in order to correctly judge the worth of local artifacts. Above all, he must be able to value his antiquities as archaeological source material and employ them as such. For this reason he must be comfortable with the research methods and results of all cultural history's subfields, which we have enumerated above. Of course it is impossible to be a specialist in all areas. But the curator is expected to have a sufficient overview in order to correctly and scientifically evaluate the local character of the objects entrusted to his collection. If an archaeological collection should equally consider all artifacts of public as well as private life in their complex ramifications, then even the best-informed and most well-rounded curator is able to satisfy these demands only within certain confines. To define these constraints geographically

is an obvious approach. Whatever falls outside the abilities of the curator should not be included in the collection, since "a truly introductory
museum can only be developed upon a basis of the most extensive, scientific study," as Alfred Lichtwark once said.[10] His views are surely apt
for archaeological museums as well. Whoever believes himself capable
of running a historical museum up to today's academic standards and
covering, say, all Germany, either overestimates the capability of such a
museum or underestimates his scientific obligations.

Above all, we should recognize that a museum limited to a localized
area does not need to compromise its scholarly importance. What it may
lack in breadth it gains richly in depth. By fulfilling its goals in the most
complete means possible, even a small museum can produce remarkable
results. More important, such a museum can provide a unique experience
by presenting a geographically defined group of ethnographic artifacts
as a unified whole.[11]

These insights, however, are not applicable to the very small
collections or so-called village museums. In the last several years much
has been said about the merits of these small "museums," particularly in
connection with more rural charitable efforts. Robert Mielke has written
a small book about them.[12]

Nonetheless, we maintain our conviction that there are certain lower
limits in the museum world that cannot be crossed without harm to the
greater good. Every museum, if it wants to claim that designation, needs
to fulfill certain prerequisites. These include that the state or some other
community entity provide the necessary guarantees; that the collection
be methodically assembled, adequately preserved and displayed, and
made available to the public; and that it be useful for academic pursuits.
Such guarantees, however, are not available for very small collections.
Their future is uncertain, the effect they can have on their small
audience is doubtful, and they can produce no academic work on their
own. For these reasons such museums have more of a splintering effect
and therefore constitute a harmful influence.

Although our discussion here is about "small museums," by these we
mean only those collections that adhere to the accepted museological
standards mentioned above. These reservations concerning the necessary
size of the collection should always be kept in mind in assessing local
historical collections.

The conviction that a museum on a tight budget does best with a
scope limited to its local culture is rightfully becoming more widespread
and has found great success in practice. To consider a few examples,

let us look at the collections in Basel, Göttingen, and Jena. Their ties to their local universities should also be noted. The museum in Basel, founded in 1856, is of particular interest because its founder and first director, Wilhelm Wackernagel, had originally not intended to limit the collection to local artifacts.[13] Rather, its focus evolved gradually through Wackernagel's museum practice. When M. Heyne took charge of the institution in 1874, he could definitively state, "Local character: that was the motto of the collection's founder in the final years before his death, and as his successor, I will continue this practice."[14] His view remained steadfast in Basel, and Heyne used the same approach when he took over the collection of antiquities in Göttingen. He defines the collection's mission in his "Short Guide" (1900): "to collect the visual material for the political and cultural history of Göttingen and the principalities of Göttingen and Grubenhagen." Paul Weber, director of the collection in Jena, took this well-thought-out stance a step further, confining his area of interest to Jena itself, since, as he put it, "the Jena Museum will collect on principle only objects related to the city of Jena and its inhabitants." In regard to judging the scholarly worth of purely local historical collections, Weber states, "There are countless objects in every town or city that urgently need to be conserved for the public on artistic, historic, or other grounds, but which can gain recognition only within the framework of that specific site. In the museums of larger cities these items would be burdensome and seem meaningless, but in their original location they provide invaluable inspiration and manifold learning opportunities."[15]

A number of further examples may be cited, even if Bode's claim about the "sadly rare practice of limiting the collection to local antiquities" remains true today, ten years later.[16] The Museum of Art and Cultural History in Lübeck has declared its task to be the assemblage of "the most comprehensive and well-rounded collection of items that are related to the artistic and cultural history of Lübeck and its current, as well as former, territories."[17] Another example is the successful Museum of Altona, which collects artifacts only from the region of Schleswig-Holstein. But even beyond these local collections, which depend almost entirely on city government for support, is an array of state museums that have adopted this practice in increasing numbers, giving emphatic support to our claim. The Swiss National Museum has from the start focused on creating a preferably comprehensive picture of cultural and artistic development "from the area of today's Switzerland."[18] The results of this mission are visible to all. Similarly, the exemplary Landes-Museum nassauischer Altertümer in Wiesbaden boldly adopted a conscious and purposeful commitment to its locality. In addition, Ernst Wagner has recently (with particular emphasis on the collection in Karlsruhe), claimed that a state museum should provide an ideally seamless overview of the historical development of its country as a whole, and of its various principalities, both in and of themselves and how they relate to each other. He also said that local collections have a similar mandate but are restricted to the territory of their city, including at most the surrounding regions.[19] As far as we know, no one has endorsed geographic limitation as forcefully as Lacher. He not only followed this principle when he expanded the "cultural historical collection of Styria" in his Graz Museum, but he also recommended it to others. He argued that "a truly comprehensive museological representation of folk-life is possible only through the constriction of geographic scope."[20]

We have mentioned a number of experienced curators who follow policies like Lacher's to guide their programming. They all support the fundamental principle that we are advocating as well: that the scope of a collection be geographically limited. Determining how restrictive the geographical boundaries for each museum should be will depend on the funding available. Museums that are able to expand their scope beyond the narrowest borders of their city walls will have to negotiate with their neighboring museums to decide how the territory will be represented in each institution. Hand-in-hand collaboration between neighboring museums is encouraged and undoubtedly beneficial for archaeological research.

Our recommendation for geographical limitation gives rise to the important question of how it should be applied to individual artifacts. Should it be understood that, in practice, only objects created within the confines of the museum's local territory be included in the collection? The answer derives from our earlier statements about the role of objects as archaeological source material. Our aim was not to imply that such institutions should illustrate only the local lines of object production. For historical museums, local culture is the primary concern, and that is a somewhat broader term. The object production of an area obviously will form a large part of its culture. But we must acknowledge that, even in relatively primitive times, cultural exchange existed between territories and could influence the character and appearance of local items. For historical museums, the crux of the issue is the extent to which imported products were subsumed by typical local culture. If, for example, the armory of a town demonstrably and repeatedly acquired its equipment from foreign armorers, swordsmiths, and gunsmiths, should we expect the historical museum of this town to wait, perhaps in vain, until a weapon produced in the town itself was finally for sale? Even if there was no evidence that weapons were imported during this period, the museum would have the right to purchase weapons produced elsewhere as long as they fulfilled a single condition: the weapons adhered to the form that was typical within the collection's region of focus. Another example: because we know that the wealthy traders from Frankfurt am Main in the sixteenth century bought finely crafted cups and goblets made by goldsmiths in Augsburg and Nürnberg, can we blame the historical museum of Frankfurt, the Leinwandhaus, if it features some of these pieces in its richly furnished Renaissance Room? And who in a North Friesian museum would wonder whether strong Dutch cultural influences were evident in its holdings? Who would claim that the stoneware of the Westerwald should be displayed only in the nearest historical museums when it has been widely exported for generations and clearly has influenced domestic culture in distant German provinces? And finally, only a historical museum blinded by hindsight would allow its collection of ecclesiastical objects to exclude their forefathers' wax votives, devotional pictures, consecration coins, and pilgrimage souvenirs, all of which were produced elsewhere by foreign artists.

Thus we come to the conclusion that all historical museums—even those focused on local goals—will occasionally need to acquire pieces created outside the realm of their official scope. By admitting this we seem to be right back where we started. You may say that we should not have gone to all this effort to clarify the theoretical advantages of geographical limitations when, in practice, the principle is full of holes. However, this objection misses the fact that any exemption from the local focus remains bound by one particular condition. It is our opinion that a historical museum may include foreign items only when the artifacts assist in the presentation of local culture in its *typical* form. A purely historical museum can therefore reject the acquisition of any item that does not represent the cultural norms of its local past. Strong emphasis needs to be placed on the average and the typical. Let us look at several examples. Even if there was proof that once upon a time a rich gentleman in a town imported his furnishings from Italy or France, a true historical museum would not only have zero obligation to acquire furniture of this type but would be wrong to do so. The public would all too easily be led to believe that their own forefathers had sat in such chairs and dined at such tables. Although any city would be fortunate to possess good Italian or French pieces in the public art gallery, they simply do not belong in a historical collection that is locally defined. And this is of primary importance in our context: the question is not what items are worthy of collecting but rather what items belong in a historical collection. Anyone today purchasing fine Italian or French furniture for a German museum would never assume that such pieces could help portray the normal home life of an earlier epoch. Rather, such furnishings are appealing on the grounds of their artistic merit—an important consideration no one wishes to deny, but one that is of no importance to local history or German archaeology.

Let us look at a further example. The history of various techniques of production is undoubtedly very interesting and tempting as a theme for museum displays. However, a locally limited historical museum has no obligation to systematically include examples of each technique within its collection. A certain technique that was never employed in the region to which the historical museum is dedicated will always appear alien within the collection and would easily lead to misconceptions.

Nor can a historical museum have the task of representing the various formal changes that were applied to artifacts created elsewhere with local techniques. Ceramics provide a classic example in this regard. Certainly no one would deny the great service that a number of our leading curators have provided with their studies of ceramics and the corresponding expansions of their collections. But local historical museums can in no way follow this model. Even in their ceramic collections, curators should include only specimens that were typical of the home culture. In the great majority of cases, this implies products deriving from local or perhaps regional workshops.

4. Historical Museums and Collections of Art

Our discussion can now turn to an important topic for museological practice: the relationship between the historical museum and the museum of applied [or decorative] arts, and how these two types of collections should be differentiated. We urgently need fundamental agreement on this issue, since historical museums continue to be burdened by the belief that they should shoulder tasks that actually belong to museums of applied arts. The primary concern lies with the objects constituting the collections. As we have discussed, the archaeological focus of historical museums dictates that each artifact's typical purpose is of primary importance. The art museum, on the other hand, concerned with aesthetics, style, and technology, emphasizes form and material. But a single object can reflect the interests of each group and be of academic value to both. Since every object simultaneously possesses purpose, material, and form, a layperson cannot immediately say with certainty whether a certain piece belongs in a historical or a decorative arts museum. The vast majority of objects in applied arts collections could also have a place in the right historical museum, since they are also typically useful objects. It is essential to note, however, that they do not belong in just *any* historical museum, but only in the one representing the geographical area of their creation. Herein lies the first deep-seated difference between the museums: To adequately fulfill its mandate, a collection of antiquities must limit its holdings to a defined geographic area. In contrast, a museum of decorative arts may have an international collection; its holdings may include anything of exemplary style and anything that represents our tastes or our techniques, regardless of where it originated.

The second fundamental difference is best expressed by Alfred Lichtwark in the *Brinckmann-Festschrift* (42): "Historical museums lack an innate emphasis on quality. The artistic merits of an object are always of secondary interest. A museum of decorative arts—even one lacking a closely defined remit—concentrates a priori on the artistic validity of each of its acquisitions." This is, in effect, the most fundamental difference between the two types of collections. Unfortunately, we must admit that on the following page Lichtwark frames this difference as a failing of historical museums, since they refused to demonstrate from the very start "the determination and energy to collect only quality items." This condemnation by an experienced and knowledgeable man, who is rightly held in the highest regard in the world of German museology and beyond, reveals more than any theoretical statement how urgently we need to reach an agreement about the tasks of archaeological collections on an academically unimpeachable basis. Otherwise, it is too easy for the public to conclude that historical museums and decorative arts museums are in competition with each other and should be consolidated— particularly the many small museums under amateur leadership. The public needs to reach this conclusion before Lichtwark's prediction from a prior era proves prescient: that "museums of applied arts are conclusively considered historical collections under which historical museums must fall in line, a subjugation their current administrators have long foreseen."

Would it not be justified, after hearing such respected commentary, to dismiss the differences we have claimed between collections of antiquities and museums of decorative arts? We do not think so. Lichtwark's words should rather be seen as new proof for our assertion that the term "historical museum" has been applied loosely to a wide range of museums. Surely one cannot repudiate someone for wanting to describe museums of applied arts as "historical museums" if their holdings include ancient artifacts. This name would not place the collection on a par with an "archaeological collection," but rather just indicate the presence of works from earlier eras. The determining internal difference is that, despite sharing the designation, only the museum of decorative arts acquires objects based solely on their artistic form. An archaeological museum could never do that. We must cling to this essential difference, and if we fail to uphold this most important and incontrovertible perspective in practice, then we could have spared ourselves the task of this long written explanation.

If a collection of antiquities were to purchase only "quality things"— and by that we mean artistically valuable things—then such a museum would fail to fulfill its archaeological mandate. To present the lifestyle of our ancestors we must recognize that not every epoch was lucky enough to possess an aesthetic culture during every age. And an aesthetic culture does not mean that every area of life during that time was equally enhanced. Since the archaeological purpose of the historical museum is to exhibit the cultural circumstances and developments of all periods, it must give the same care and attention to artistically weak periods as to artistically strong ones. It follows then that a historical museum cannot acquire only items of artistic quality. Frequently, artistically lacking and even artistically poor pieces will bear sufficient archaeological import to justify their inclusion in a museum. Consider artifacts from the so-called prehistoric period. Coin collections provide further examples. No one doubts their scholarly importance or questions their inclusion in museums. Yet, if solely judged on artistic merit, scarcely any coin collection would make the cut. Nonetheless, there is widespread agreement that artistically mediocre or even poor objects merit collection. Their historical worth, and thus also their museological worth as memory items of local history, is not determined by their formal qualities.

So the core difference remains: the decorative arts museum of today is interested in items of artistic merit, while the historical museum is also interested in those of lesser to no artistic merit. This is not to say that the historical museum is insensitive to an artifact's formal qualities. The fact that a stylistic examination of an artifact helps to provide approximate dating should not be undervalued for archaeological research. Additionally, it is obvious that of two completely equal archaeological monuments, anyone given a choice would prefer the artistically superior one. Archaeological perspectives can be far more successfully conveyed to the public if they are illustrated by items that have benefited from an artistic hand skilled in ornamentation and with a flair for style.

In sum, a historical museum can acquire artwork if it fits within its scope—and it can constitute a true jewel of the collection—but not all a historical museum's acquisitions need to be artworks. A piece's appropriateness for a historical museum does not depend on its artistic form but entirely on its archaeological meaning for local history. William Evans Hoyle rightly expresses this condition by claiming that all historical pieces "must be required to further an understanding of archaeology" (*Museumskunde* 2:183). We need to cling to this basic principle. It is the only way to ultimately silence the accusations leveled against historical museums, as Ernst Grosse rightly reiterated: "It is a fact that sadly only few know. The greatest source of distress for our museums is that they are burdened by an unfortunate merging of incompatible scientific and artistic needs and tasks."[21]

The third major difference that separates historical museums from museums of applied arts is widely acknowledged by all sides: Historical collections, and the scholarly work they produce, are primarily focused on the dissemination of an understanding of history. In contrast, art museums exhibit the technological, stylistic, and aesthetic achievements of the past while simultaneously supporting the aesthetic culture of the present day. For this reason, art museums possess not only representative pictures by the old masters but also exemplary work from today. They thereby engage directly with the interests and labors of modern life, while historical museums are more contemplative and academic. The former type of institution provides examples of good taste; the latter is concerned with the conditions and developments of the past.

The museum of decorative arts is therefore geared toward a practical effectiveness, which seems like an obvious advantage. But with this advantage comes a disadvantage that grows ever more pronounced over time: the art museum is and will always be *dependent* on the tastes of its time, which affects, in particular, its practices of acquisition. The more an era has developed its own independent design style, and the more an object is imbued with this style (with all its attendant benefits as well as shortcomings), the more doubtful it becomes that in subsequent time periods, with their own differing fashions, this object will be seen as an exemplary prototype worthy of display. For example, we only need to recall how much observers in the seventeenth and eighteenth centuries disparaged Gothic art. Owing to such changes in taste, collections in art museums are prone to experiencing difficult upheavals. How individual institutions will weather these upheavals and how they will deal with their existing collections are issues for the future. It is enough for now to mention the situation and to determine that, in contrast, historical museums experience such disruptions to a far lesser extent—if at all. We are in a much more objective and impersonal relationship with monuments of the past. While our judgment of the artistic forms of historical artifacts may change in the future, the objects themselves remain evidence of historical truths. It is in this light that they entered the collections of antiquities, and they will remain respected as such into the future—even if the strong historical interests of our present time should wane in the coming decades.

In addition to the influence of current cultural tastes, the personal taste of the responsible curator of the decorative arts collection is by no means irrelevant. After all, the greater the curator's ability, the greater is his personal stamp. This is no doubt also the case for historical museums, but not to the same extent. The director of a historical museum is restrained by a much more closely defined strategy. Acquisition practices do not hinge on the interests of the director but depend on the state of the field of archaeology and how it treats antiquities. Academic developments in the field should ideally be represented in the museum's holdings and exhibitions. Acquisitions are determined by archaeological and local considerations, and only when both of these are fulfilled does the personal preference of the museum director become a factor. In its composition, a historical museum has a far less personal character than does an art museum.

We hope we have convinced the reader that the historical museum and the decorative arts museum represent two thoroughly different types of collections. And we hope that the public will grasp this divergence with increasing clarity. At present, however, the inverse appears to be the case. It is readily apparent that the public, and often also the elite, fail to see any difference between the two types of museums. When asked why, a certain topic is raised again and again: instead of recognizing that the two institutions correspond to separate and distinct fields that overlap only slightly, the public seems, oddly, to emphasize and prefer exactly this overlap, as well as the fact that similar interests arise from this overlap and result in a steady exchange of discoveries.

Let us quote from Heinrich Angst when considering the overlap between local historical/archaeological research and work in the decorative arts: on page 6 of the publication celebrating the opening of the Swiss National Museum, he writes, "In contrast to the factory-produced wares of today, items of daily use from earlier centuries often bear the stamps of their individual creators and even their patrons, and may thus be seen as prototypes of applied art. This is why it is impossible to draw a precise line between historical museums and museums of decorative local arts." Let us note with satisfaction that Angst here emphasizes, even if not directly, the difference between interest in a household object and interest in its artistic ornamentation—which serves to set historical museums and art museums in opposition. We also cite this text so that no one is tempted to turn a superficial observation into a hard and fast distinction. For it should not be overlooked that Angst's claim applies only to the border between historical and *local* art museums. There is no discussion of the general principles defining what the applied arts embrace. Rather, Angst stresses the importance of a local specialization. The applied arts of the homeland: this is in practice where the concerns of the historical museum intersect with those of the art museum in the same town.

It is obvious that a historical museum, in its attempts to represent the past culture of its own town and neighboring areas, must integrate the work of established craftsmen and artisans. It is also obvious that the higher the artistic quality of this work, the more it is likely to be favored. Historical museums, however, are rightly expected to present a comprehensive view of local arts and crafts production, giving the public a broad understanding of the visual world of their forefathers. In addition, they are expected to provide researchers with the most thorough access possible to local artistic culture, which the museums alone are able to provide. Just as historical museums are expected to collect the imprints of local coin issues as thoroughly as possible, the same holds for other forms of local items. To provide an example from this writer's own area of research: the Civic Historical Museum of Frankfurt's academic and museological obligations to the local Höchst Porcelain Factory can be considered fulfilled only when the museum possesses all known types of this factory's dishware (excluding minor variations in decoration, of course), as well as all the factory's figural work, all of it in impeccable condition. If the director of the applied arts museum in the same town states that he is likewise compelled to purchase multiple exemplary products from the Höchst Factory, then we have a case where the interests of the historical museum and those of the art museum overlap. Such a situation, as we have stated, can occur only within the realm of local art production, and potential conflicts that might arise can in practice easily be resolved if the director of the applied arts museum accommodates the existing arrangement between the two museums. He recognizes that for the sake of all the interested parties in the field of historical / applied arts research, a small, locally defined area of art production needs to have all its comprehensive evidence assembled in one place—a requirement that would extend far beyond the museological abilities of his own institution. He hands off the burden of caring for the history of local art wares to his sister institution and makes do with a few relevant pieces of very good quality. Historical museums and museums of decorative arts should work with and for each other, cognizant that they are both educators of the same audience, which they can best serve by combining forces.

With this, let us leave the question of the relationship between the historical museum and the decorative arts museum. The reader can decide whether we have grappled with this question for too long. We believe that in today's environment this museological topic is most deserving of discussion among specialists. If we accept the perspective put forth here as fundamentally correct, then we have gained a means of evaluating the relationship between historical museums and collections of fine art, painting galleries, and sculpture gardens. For these varied types of collections as well, the intersection of interests of two given institutions that work side by side is in our view valid only in the realm of local art production and local art preservation.

In a town that houses both a historical museum and an art gallery, it is widely considered the task of the art gallery to provide museum-level care for the fine art of the region, in the way A. Lichtwark expressed in his essay "The Nearest" (*Museumskunde* 1:40–43). Accordingly, the historical museum must be able to justify its own efforts to acquire paintings. The boundary dividing the institutions must remain fluid, however. This is more than an issue of fairness. It is imperative that we do not take a hard line on dividing art objects between the two museums in a "wheat from the chaff" kind of way, placing all work of artistic merit in the art gallery and the rest in the historical museum. Our previous assertion that even artistically inferior objects can be useful for historical museums should not be interpreted to mean that historical museums are undeserving of artistically valuable works in equal circumstances.

Every historical museum will seek to collect three types of representational imagery in all possible techniques: first, depictions of local historical events; second, representations of landscapes, places, buildings, and so forth in their town; and third, portraits of people associated with local history. In the latter category, sculpture as well as painting should be considered. The details in such portrayals, in dress, household objects, interior design, and so forth, speak to the historical museum's archaeological interests, as well as to local historical interests. And these interests apply equally to works of greater or lesser artistic merit, while, of course, acknowledging that pieces of higher artistic quality are more desirable. These are the objects that would be appropriate for both art galleries and historical museums. However, any potential conflict can be easily overcome through mutual understanding, with both institutions agreeing alternately to forgo acquisitions or through some similar arrangement.

The case is slightly different for artworks that have no essential objective link to a locality but have become meaningful locally through their own histories or through a purpose that they have long served. Ecclesiastical artworks constitute by far the largest group of this type of imagery. Pieces from local churches can have great importance to historical museums. An altarpiece, whether it was created in the town or not, may have stood for centuries at a consecrated site within a church of the town, and many generations of townspeople may have knelt, prayed, been married, or baptized their children before it. Such a rich history would make the altarpiece an essential element in a local collection of ecclesiastical antiquities if the altarpiece was no longer housed in the church itself. If such an altarpiece has particular artistic qualities, then that is so much the better for the museum. But it would be unreasonable and even damaging for historical museums if the finest works of this type were immediately redirected toward art museums, leaving only lesser works for the historical collections. This practice would reduce historical museums to warehouses of junk, as they are sometimes unjustly accused of being.

As we know from experience, a historical museum that has conscientiously restricted its scope and thereby attained the position, alongside the historical archive, of a vibrant and deserving protector of local historical research that presents varied educational materials to the townspeople can enjoy great popularity. Such a museum can rightly claim that, on account of its scientific and educational importance, it deserves the same level of respect as that received by other types of museums and that its acquisition efforts be judged accordingly. The desires of other institutions, no matter how justified, should play no part in deciding the holdings of historical museums. We must ensure that historical museums are not unfairly denied acquisitions to the benefit of art museums.

This much is certain: art museums do not enhance the artistic value of ecclesiastical antiquities. There is no reason to claim that a work's artistic merits would be underappreciated in a historical museum, unless the museum were of truly low quality. The decision to remove a piece from its archaeological milieu just because its quality is higher than that of similar pieces must be carefully weighed. By taking it out of its archaeological setting we sever connections to its original function. Such inappropriate transplantation can destroy a work's ethical and scientific worth, which would undoubtedly have been preserved in an archaeological collection.

Let us summarize our views. Equally substantial reasons can be cited for why a particularly artistic piece of church art or a work from a similarly entrenched location should go to an art museum or to a historical museum. However, a prudent decision should be easy to attain as long as the question is approached with a mutual recognition of equality by both institutions.

We have spent much time on this discussion. We have addressed in detail the principal foundations that we feel should guide the collection practices of historical museums, as well as the limits of their remit and their differences from related institutions. Expert consensus on these issues, which is necessary for the further development of historical museums, will require still more discussion.

5. On the Collecting Practices of Historical Museums[22]

The mission of historical museums, like that of all museums, is to acquire original objects, since only originals hold documentary value. This is why historical monuments are worthy of collection. We have seen how, in practice, historical museums are often essentially forced to purchase a certain piece. This is the case when an item is of singular meaning, is proven to be of local origin, and comes on the market at a reasonable price. For every purchase the curator needs to research anew the validity of the object's relationship to local history, as well as investigate whether there are any external associations that bestow local importance on it and whether the provenance claimed by the prior owner is reliable. "Questions such as: 'From where?' 'For what purpose?' and 'In what connection?' should be asked in each individual case," says Karl Lacher. His words cannot be restated too frequently or fervently.[23] We should also bear in mind Franz Weber's essay "Local Historical Associations and Museums of Upper Bavaria," in which he asserts, "Naturally, in all practices of collection, the guiding thought must be the common bond between the collected objects in that area."[24]

It is essential to determine an object's exact provenance if at all possible. If an object with an uncertain provenance is both newer and from a genre already well represented in the museum, then acquisition is usually not recommended. The exception would be if the piece represented a key link in a typological sequence. Obviously, occasional allowances have to be made for prehistoric or medieval artifacts owing to their scarcity.

Similarly, as we have noted above, historical museums must limit their collections to what is justified or even demanded by local history, despite curators' frequent and understandable preference for showpieces. A town that perhaps has never had a period of rich visual culture should not attempt to manufacture the appearance of one in its historical museum.

It must also be emphasized that a historical museum cannot acquire complete works only. Instead, it will repeatedly be forced to incorporate fragmentary pieces if they possess documentary value. As Friedrich Deneken has said, antiquarian museums should "remain quite aware that their holdings are study materials for scientific purposes"[25] and that fragments may provide significant evidence.

When an item suitable for the museum appears on the market, the museum's task is to strike quickly and decisively in order to preclude the object's being carried off. When possible, it is even better not to wait until the artifact is on the open market. There should generally be sufficient oversight of a specific field so that antiquities, if they are up for sale, can be acquired through firsthand transaction. With today's art market, it can be assumed that more than one appropriate piece, including artistically good specimens, will be on offer. But the market is always a matter of chance, and as August Essenwein once said about his new duties, "The new executive board does not have the intention of leaving to chance what the institution will amount to." The work of every director of a historical museum must, above all else, involve being on the lookout for suitable objects, not relying on the market to eventually ferry necessary materials to the museum's door.[26]

This collection method not only prevents the removal of artifacts and their resulting devaluation but also leads to some fine and interesting pieces being rescued from the dark corners where they hide, unseen and unused by the public. This practice does not imply some sort of systematic robbery that seeks to remove historically and artistically valuable objects from public buildings and institutions in order to quickly swell the holdings of historical museums. No one can deny that every object is best located at the site for which it was created, and a historical museum should offer shelter in its collection only when a piece's preservation is threatened. There are, however, rare occasions when an artistically exceptional work is so poorly located that its effect is severely diminished. Only in these exceptional cases would we consider it justified to remove such a piece, even if its preservation were not endangered, and display it in a museum, where it would be accessible to the public and could have its intended effect.

The museum should strive with equal zeal to acquire items of local historical importance from private collectors and put them on public view. In this light we share R. Wackernagel's opinion that "certain things are from the start too big and too potent to belong in private ownership." He elaborates: "Banners that were captured in victorious battle, the staff under which law was practiced for centuries—are artifacts whose venerableness gives them the right to be objects of public, shared heritage."[27] We hope that this sentiment will gain resonance and acceptance.

On the topic of the collection efforts of museums, we must warn against efforts to amass as much as possible in as short a time as possible. There is no offense perpetrated by a curator that is more damaging than collecting mania. No museological effort is more detrimental, particularly for exhibitions, than the desire to fill the space as quickly as possible. To acquire something rapidly and to acquire it hastily are two very different things. We should never forget that a museum is intended to last for longer than a single human lifespan, and for that reason collections need to be amassed with contemplation and calm. We should not purchase what we can quickly grab but should purchase only what is essential according to an objectively well-reasoned agenda. And if, for reasons beyond our control, one or another piece evades our grasp, we must not forget that the museum may be able to obtain it in the future.

Fortunately, museums do not assemble their collections of originals only through purchases. A great number of items are donated. In normal circumstances, among these many gifts will be an array of objects that can be integrated into the collection immediately. However, if experience is a guide, there will be many donated items that will not find a place in the scheme of the collection. The curator then ends up possessing pieces that are not in and of themselves desirable for the museum. In our view, since the community at large is the true owner of the museum, an individual has no right to refuse any gifts, regardless of their worth or even their material value. Nor, however, should the curator be obligated to place such gifts and bequests on display, just as he is not forced to display any of the existing inventory. Some museums that have done so have ended up with disastrous exhibitions. There is only one good solution, which is possible only if the donor is well intended and understanding and is not giving the gift simply to immortalize his name in the largest possible font on the exhibition wall.

While donated pieces many not be appropriate for a certain collection, they may be of value to a different museum or even have worth on the antiquities market. At the very least they can almost always be used as objects of exchange. This leads us to an appropriate way to expand a collection, which will, we believe, continue to play an increasing role for museums. Doubtless the museum world will soon wish to take a step back from the isolated ways that different institutions of the same type currently go about their work in order to gain an overview of the vast possessions our public collections have amassed over time. The more we emphasize the local focus of the historical museum, the more we will be able to exchange objects among museums in order to return artifacts to their homelands. Both parties will come out as winners; we will have switches and not swindles. . . .

Up to this point we have discussed the collection of original artifacts, since the bulk of a collection must consist of originals. But in every area of collection there will also be a range of pieces that museums will never be able to exhibit for reasons outside their control but which they are obligated to present to the public as part of their particular agenda. By this we mean pieces that in and of themselves are technically manageable for display in any museum, but since they exist only as unique examples which are already in firm possession elsewhere, no other collection can possess them in the original. There is always a range of pieces of this type that, because of the museum's focus, must be displayed to the public, be they valuable as memorials of local history or as a missing link in an archaeological sequence.

In these cases, there is no choice but to make do with reproductions. We believe that from the viewpoint of historical museums, such copies should not be regarded as lesser, makeshift solutions, as some may believe at this time. Perhaps in museums of decorative arts, where the material of the object carries particular weight, reproductions are of little value. But this situation is slightly different for historical museums.

Obviously, even here a reproduction cannot bestow the documentary value of an original, but it can serve a historical-archaeological purpose to make the appearance of the original clearly visible to the public. While the scientific work of historical museums must involve originals, the museums' popular educational mission may be significantly furthered by high-quality reproductions. In any case, a historical museum is aided more by a cast of a piece from its local geographic region than by an original from elsewhere.

Historical museums have recognized the prodigious educational function of reproductions for many years and made good use of them in practice, which is really the goal of all museological efforts. It may be sufficient to cite just a couple of examples here. Since nearly the start of its collecting practices, the Germanic National Museum has made active and successful use of its large collection of reproductions as teaching aids. At a similar early date, W. Wackernagel looked into procuring reproductions for the Basel collection,[28] and more recently the Swiss National Museum kept its copies on display alongside the originals. Currently, even A. Overmann rightly recommends procuring reproductions for the Erfurt collection. There are many more examples that we will not detail here, for our goal is to underscore the importance, not the current prevalence, of reproductions and to endorse their use in historical museums.

We also would like to advocate the use of another museological aid that greatly assists historical museums with their educational obligations: models. Every historical museum possesses a range of pieces that will, for the foreseeable future and perhaps forever, be accessible only as reproductions. Likewise, a certain number of archaeological monuments can never be part of a collection of antiquities by virtue of their size, which exceeds what is generally workable in an average museum building. These include traditional forms of housing, various transportation methods such as ships and wagons, bridges, and castles and the different systems of historical fortifications. If these myriad elements are to be displayed in a historical museum—and there can be no doubt that they should be—then the use of models is the most practical means to do so. Every collection with an instructive intent would be well served by their use. The model's graphic clarity and simultaneous visibility to a large number of museum patrons directly facilitate public understanding far more than does a long theoretical presentation. For this reason the model has attained a status in our museums that it will likely retain for some time. We need look only to the Germanic Museum in Nürnberg, the Museum of Folklore in Berlin, the Styrian Civic Museum in Graz, the

Museum of Lübeck, and the new city museum in Braunschweig, among others, to find successful models of buildings and tools. Or we can recall that the expanded department of sea fishery in the Altona Museum consists primarily of models. Nevertheless, it seems to us that the use of models, especially for historical museums, could still be expanded, even at this point in time. Any attempt to visualize the field of German archaeology represented within an arbitrary German landscape depends on help from models in multiple ways. This fact is equally important to all historical museums.

6. The Ordering of Historical-Archaeological Collections[29]

Any discussion of the ordering of a museum must clearly delineate between two points. The first is the question of how a large, unwieldy mass of individual objects can be divided into finite and systematically unified groups. The second is the question of how, within such an overview, the different groups can be displayed so that each artifact is properly accentuated and forms a pleasing arrangement with the adjacent pieces. Thus we have to distinguish between the objective grouping and the decorative presentation of a museum's holdings. Groupings can result only from a scientific understanding of the intrinsic worth of each piece. Accordingly, only specialists are qualified to make these decisions in a satisfying way. In contrast, decorative presentation is superficial, but it is valuable because it increases the interest of the public. Since it can be realized more or less tastefully, this aspect of display always remains purely decorative. While we must not undervalue presentation, it must be of secondary importance to a scientific collection. The specialist can disregard it completely, since it has no bearing at all on scientific pursuits.

Owing to the preeminence of scientific questions, it is essential that the museologist, first and foremost, systematically group the collected artifacts. Decorative considerations should have no influence on this effort, no matter how tempting. Nothing is more destructive to objective organization of a historical museum than the influence of decorative intentions that are present from the outset. Only when the groupings are complete can the curator take up the mantle of designer. The extent of what he can accomplish to benefit his institution and the viewing public in this regard is well-known.

In attempting to order a historical-archaeological collection, we must remember that these collections, in the way that they were created, already present a clear concept and a sharply defined scientific focus.

When individual artifacts are brought together on the basis of their common origins or their functions, then we obviously believe that any consideration of their grouping must also stem from this guiding principle. If this were not the case, then we would betray the values that caused us to consider a piece worthy of acquisition in the first place. The public would stand before it without a clue, forced to suspect the entire collection of being nothing more than a cluster of curios. So just as we should demand that a collection be acquired according to a clear program, so too should we insist that it be organized in a manner that clearly renders the program recognizable.

Agreement on the question of order will encounter some resistance, in that every museologist will naturally feel tempted to orient his groupings according to the holdings of his own collection. It will always be the case that certain fields amply represented in one museum will have a smaller presence in another. Thus, it is not always easy for smaller museums—we could say, museums that are starting out—to understand how to group their objects on the basis of prototypes of larger collections. Nevertheless, we believe that it is definitely possible to develop an organizational plan applicable to all local historical-archaeological collections. The question must first be approached from the purely theoretical side, and in order for a proposed system to be universally useful, it must necessarily encompass all imaginable types of objects and types of usage.

If the determination of use was decisive for the acquisition of individual artifacts, then it must also be so for the organizational schema of the entire collection. This is our guiding principle. Thus we believe that a collection of antiquities should be arranged according to an archaeological perspective. Undoubtedly, we will hear that the essential regulative force in museums should be art history, as was recently voiced by a man as greatly respected by this author as Peter Jessen.[30] But this remark was directed solely at art museums, which are not up for discussion here. A collection of antiquities aims neither to satisfy the simple desire for artistic pleasure from a purely aesthetic perspective, nor to inspire or educate artists and craftsmen from a practical perspective. While the application of an art historical order is appropriate for collections of art, as E. Grosse has shown in closer detail, this should have no bearing on the ordering of collections of antiquities.[31]

Surely the historical museum will gladly provide an opportunity for aesthetic pleasure, practical stimulation, or the theoretical study of art, but its main purpose must lie, as we have discussed, in a completely different direction. We procure many pieces, which may lack formal beauty, because they are of local archaeological or historical importance. Accordingly, we cannot consider a principle of organization that would emphasize exactly this lack that we are forced to accept while at the same time driving into the background the very traits we treasure most. We can imagine what would result if we were to organize a historical museum into stylistic-historical groups. We would have to place the rococo garments with all other items from the rococo, Biedermeier suits with all other artifacts of that period's aesthetic; the traditional farm costumes would go to yet another place; and so forth. There would be no chance to visualize the development of German dress because a thousand other items would disrupt any continuity between the examples. Just consider the attempt to disperse a numismatic collection throughout the museum according to art historical criteria, and consider whether doing so would enhance the study of coins and monetary history. To cite just one more example, consider splitting up the weapons collection according to each piece's art historical position and dispersing the items throughout the museum. The archaeological focus on weaponry would be entirely lost, and this would be the case for all other areas of a collection. An art historical grouping system is of no use for a collection of antiquities. With this acknowledgment, we must resist the influence of the art museum, to which we are today accustomed.

Having dismissed the art historical order for an archaeological collection, we also hope to put to rest another organizational issue that has cropped up again and again throughout the last decade. In line with similar statements made by Julius Lessing in 1889, Justus Brinckmann advocates in the introduction to his guide to the Hamburg Museum a future "cultural-historical" arrangement for museums of decorative arts. This view is cited so frequently we need not repeat it here. The most reputable museums have since then adhered to his viewpoint. Wilhelm von Bode spoke of his agreement: "The cultural-historical viewpoint must be the primary one for the organization of a museum of applied arts. Only in this way—by displaying the artistic products of one epoch and one people all together—can the objects be correctly understood."[32] Lessing voiced a similar view shortly thereafter.[33] A. Lichtwark agreed,[34] while Eduard v. Ubisch said that Brinckmann's fundamental view on the cultural-historical arrangement of the decorative arts museum was "generally recognized as [being as] valid as it is difficult to implement."[35] Since so many well-respected specialists agree on the validity of cultural-historical display, one can observe time and again that their views are also thought to be relevant to the grouping of objects in historical museums.

But after examining such observations more closely, it is apparent that the term "cultural-historical" is applied only to a single subarea, as we have discussed earlier. Overmann is therefore completely correct when, in recommending the cultural-historical display for good reason to the Erfurt Industrial Museum, he explains it with the words, "that the collection is displayed according to periods of style."[36] We notice that the art historical considerations form the guiding principle for the groupings recommended by Brinckmann. Yet with our archaeological interests they have—as expected—nothing in common. If Brinckmann were to have already reorganized his museum in the manner he espouses, then we could be convinced by a mere glance that the character of an art collection has been retained. The collection would remain unchanged by either its aesthetic or its practical inclinations. Rather, the collection would have gained a—shall we say—new accent solely from a theoretical and educational perspective. Unfortunately, as this reorganization has not yet occurred, we have had to dwell on this case to ensure that theoretical opinions intended for art collections are not seamlessly transplanted onto archaeological collections.

In Hamburg, by the way, Brinckmann has, along with his regular labor of collecting the decorative arts, also worked with admirable zeal to recover historical artifacts local to Hamburg and its surroundings. For this reason there must clearly be some areas in his cultural-historical exhibition where local domestic antiquities are displayed in exactly the same way they would have been within a purely historical-archaeological museum in Hamburg.

At the same time, we must recall that in Hamburg, in addition to the Museum für Kunst und Gewerbe, there is the Sammlung Hamburgischer Altertümer, where local historical and archaeological interests should be the primary focus.

To reiterate our conclusions: Brinckmann's words and the related expressions of support for the arrangement of an antiquities collection are neither justified nor applicable. Therefore, in order to garner scholarly approval for our decisions on organizational matters we must seek other educated opinions, specifically those directed at historical and archaeological concerns. Fortunately, there is no lack of these. To begin, we should reconsider K. Lacher, who emphasizes repeatedly— as again in the newest edition of his museum guide—that he holds to the foundational principle that "every object should be displayed so that its original purpose can be seen."[37] Thus, for him, the purpose of an artifact not only determines whether it is appropriate for acquisition in his local collection but also affects its display. And Lacher has found a highly valuable fellow believer in Otto Lehmann, whose discussions about Mannheim are useful here.

Lehmann explicitly states that the fundamental goal of his museum is that "even the ignorant viewer becomes immediately aware of the purpose of the objects." He allows all thoughts of the decorative arts and of the history of style to fade into the background. His perspective on this topic is well known. Nevertheless, we believe that it is helpful to reiterate one of his examples, which clearly expresses his stance. Lehmann wrote: "On a hike I stepped into a farmhouse. In the twilight of the great hall, the farmer's wife worked in her colorful folk dress between shimmering brass basins that reflected the flickering hearth fire—an unforgettable image! Today the colorful garb of the woman has become an object of interest, the basins are considered artistic hammered ware, a colorfully painted trunk is newly discovered, and the stonework is of a sought-after type. Suppose that a whole array of these objects can be procured through many nice words plus a little something more and find their way into a museum. Now the hammered basins stand in a cabinet with maybe twenty others. They are of high art historical value. The earthenware is displayed elsewhere. The trunk is set up somewhere else to fill a noticeable gap in the historical development of woodwork. Such a result is actually barbaric. The entire scene is rent apart and ruined, perhaps never to be reunited. Of course, the scientist must be allowed to dissect this intimate scene with a sharp, unforgiving blade. But no matter how charming the forms and colors may be, how valuable the knowledge may be of the use and combination of colors in the crockery, the fact remains that the artistic character of each form and color, and the artistic sense of the folk group that created or employed these forms and colors, can be comprehensible only when they stand together in the milieu in which they were alive." Lehmann argues for the museological installations of interiors so long as they retain the original relationships of the objects.[38] In this example he prioritizes the aesthetic reasons for his viewpoint while also emphasizing functional history, as we will discuss below. Ultimately, grouping according to purpose is what is essential to him, since even interiors are nothing other than assemblages of domestic antiquities brought together on the basis of their functions in daily life.

After everything that we have said about the scientific prerequisites and collecting practices of historical museums, it is obvious that we believe archaeological considerations alone should determine the grouping of artifacts. We have shown that a stylistic-historical system is not applicable to a collection of antiquities, and the same can be said about a technological system. Antiquities intended to illuminate an archaeological situation or development cannot be ordered according to their shared materials or similar external characteristics. Consider the example of coin-like issues. They have nothing in common with coins used as currency except for the methods of their creation and, in some cases, their material. They serve an entirely different purpose, and therefore, in historical museums, may not be displayed with actual coins, just as they were rightly excluded from Arnold Luschin von Ebengreuth's text "Allgemeine Münzkunde und Geldgeschichte des Mittelalters und der neueren Zeit."[39] In a historical museum, portrait medallions belong with familial antiquities; jetons belong with trade antiquities; event and occasion medallions, together with tokens, belong with civic or community antiquities; and pilgrimage and consecration coins belong with ecclesiastical antiquities. Thus we deem it correct that P. Weber placed the medallion commemorating the history of an upper school in the "room of the university."[40] To list a further example: Who could express the visual history of trade guilds, as did M. Heyne in Göttingen and O. Lehmann in Altona, without on principle displaying together such divergent items as welcome and trade chalices, guild chests and scepters, signs and craft emblems, flags, apprenticeship documents, ordinances, and so forth?[41] Or, even more dramatically, consider the field of weaponry. Weapons of war and weapons of the hunt are conventionally considered very different objects of use, a fact made abundantly—and absurdly—clear by the image of a modern hunter daring to take the newest model of our infantry rifle on the hunt. Thus, in order to avoid fundamental false impressions, one must not display the weapons of war and those of the hunt together in a historical museum. One final example! The models available in historical museums should not be combined in a so-called model room solely because they are all miniaturized images of real objects. The public would necessarily have to conclude that the purpose of such a room was to display the construction abilities of the model crafter. In our view, all such replicas belong in the area of the exhibition where the real objects they depict are displayed.

Thus we reiterate: a technological system, just like a stylistic one, is not only unsuitable for a collection of antiquities but also runs directly counter to the essence of such a museum. In fact, the technological system in particular would entirely mask the independent and essentially unique character of the collection of antiquities in the eyes of the public. Since, as we have seen, there are pieces relevant to both historical museums and museums of applied arts, the public must be in a position to recognize how each object is suited to this or that museum. The public must be able to distinguish which interests are primary: the decorative arts (material and form) or archaeology (function). The museologist alone controls how this is accomplished. It is the objective systematic arrangement, executed with utmost consequence, that makes this determination. It is now clear: an archaeological collection can be arranged according to an archaeological perspective only. Otherwise, viewers are confused, and their visit is unsatisfactory.

Before we consider further the individual groupings, it is necessary to touch on a ramification of the ordering of historical museums, which should actually be viewed as its essential guiding principle. It is known that throughout world history, cultural development did not progress steadily in one single direction, continuing without disruption. There are cultural periods of history that move in different directions. This separation results when a dominant culture is overrun by a different culture, shaking its foundations so that its intellectual achievements crumble under the influence of foreign conceptions and perspectives; finally, a different formal world overruns and dissolves its external manifestations as well. Briefly put, the different periods in global history are at the same time separated from each other by the deep-seated differences of their corresponding cultures. Their external manifestations may still have certain recognizable connections, but they can no longer be seen as branches of the same archaeological development. Thus it is obvious that all historical museums that display the monuments of different cultures alongside one another must feel compelled to firmly delineate between them. Cultural difference can come into its own only through such divisions of the entire group according to the consensus of all specialists in historical museums. Special collections, however, such as those of rings, weaponry, ceramic work, and so on, frequently elide cultural boundaries.

Accordingly, the central issue for the ordering of a historical museum must be the separation of objects by their cultural groups. Thus we display artifacts of the so-called prehistoric cultures separately, just as we do the Roman-Germanic artifacts in western and southwestern Germany. Additionally, there are separate sections of "medieval" and "modern" objects. These objects, of course, number far more than those from vanished cultural epochs, but they are by no means superior in scientific importance. "Medieval" and "modern," to use those ghastly yet indispensable terms, should obviously not be treated as separate groups, as our fathers may have done. We now understand that the period of European cultural history that began around the middle of the first millennium, despite all the changes that have occurred in the interim and remain evident today, continues on the same track—all part of a smooth, unified development. It is therefore absolutely indefensible to mark a sharp division in the previously preferred period, the turn of the fifteenth century. In the museum, we cannot trace the development of many individual cultural groups up to this time, then group them together and call them "medieval" in order to differentiate them from the "modern era," which is itself archaeologically subdivided. Just as Georg Steinhausen's book *Geschichte der deutschen Kultur* does not present the end of the "Middle Ages" as a particular rupture, so too should our museological organization let the artifacts smoothly transition from the early medieval archaeological groups into the most modern era. We may, in some departments, perhaps allow recognition of a new chapter starting at the turn of the fifteenth century, but there should be no indication of a major cultural division.

If at this point we see ourselves compelled to offer an outline for the arrangement of an antiquities collection, this can amount only to an attempt. We hope that the schema we propose will be tested on many fronts and that the terminology we use will not be disregarded. We hope that this schema, perhaps with some modifications, will prove applicable to all German archaeological collections. If our plans are implemented, then perhaps the country will take a significant step toward the desired greater unity of its historical museums. The author himself has for several years applied the following schema, with a couple of small changes, to the grouping of new acquisitions set out in the *Annual Report for the Historical Museum of Frankfurt a. M.*, and has thereby been convinced that the schema is well suited to the ordering of all types of historical artifacts. It is our pleasure, furthermore, to report that shortly before his death, M. Heyne wrote to us to express his approval and that Karl Koetschau has also voiced his accord.[42]

Thus, we propose eight large primary groups as follows: I. familial antiquities; II. domestic antiquities, which, together with the first group, constitute the bulk of private antiquities; III. civic and community antiquities; IV. legal antiquities; V. ecclesiastical antiquities; VI. profane art antiquities; VII. scientific antiquities; and VIII. military antiquities.

I. Among familial antiquities we include portraits of any type (in the form of paintings, etchings, sculptures, medallions, etc.), coats of arms and private seals, family trees, genealogical charts, epithalamia, honorary remembrances, *Tottenbretter*, or death inscriptions, sarcophagi, funerary wreaths, epitaphs, and so on.

II. Domestic antiquities, which tend to constitute the group with the widest scope in a historical museum, can be divided into four main subgroups: (1) housing and household items; (2) textiles, folk costumes, and jewelry; (3) artifacts from social life; and (4) artifacts of trade and industry. The individual archaeological artifacts can be sorted in the following way:

(1) Housing and household items: (a) housing construction and house fixtures, including those related to the hearth (oven and chimney); (b) furniture; (c) lighting; (d) items for the kitchen and cellar; (e) dishware from fired clay; (f) stoneware; (g) earthenware; (h) glazed earthenware; (i) porcelain; (k [*sic*]) glassware; (l) pewterware; (m) dishware of precious metals; (n) eating utensils; (o) smoking and tobacco products; (p) tools for cloth production, sewing, and ironing; and (q) towing and farming equipment.

(2) Textiles, folk costumes, and jewelry: (a) textiles and embroidery; (b) traditional urban dress; (c) traditional peasant costume; and (d) jewelry.

(3) Artifacts from social life: (a) toys; (b) musical instruments; and (c) hunting supplies.

(4) Artifacts of trade and industry: (a) means of transportation; (b) trade antiquities; and (c) artifacts of industry.

III. Civic and community antiquities naturally fall into two categories. Civic antiquities include national emblems, artifacts of coronation, representations of the imperial quaternion, medals and badges of honor, civic monuments of civil service, and civic coins. Community antiquities, in contrast, comprise the artifacts of town administration, as well as of civil associations and guilds. The remains of town militias are also in this category, unlike those of the regular armed forces, which we organize with the antiquities of warfare.

IV. Legal antiquities consist mainly of antiquities used for punishment, which we treat as a special museological group.

V. Ecclesiastical antiquities can be divided into Christian religious monuments and Jewish ritual objects.

Christian objects fall into these groups: (a) church construction and its painted or sculptural décor; (b) liturgical sites and artifacts; (c) containers and instruments; and (d) liturgical robes. Jewish ritual objects can be divided into the same categories.

VI. Profane art antiquities are divided into (1) painting and graphic art; (2) sculpture (in clay, glazed earthenware, porcelain, stone, or metal); and (3) local decorative arts.

VII. Scientific antiquities consist exclusively of those instruments our predecessors used to learn about nature and represent it or with which they sought to measure time and space. These are mathematical, physical, and astronomical instruments, including clocks, maps, atlases, globes of the earth and the heavens, tellurians, and so on, as well as chemical-pharmaceutical artifacts.

VIII. Military antiquities are divided into weapons and armor, instruments of war, and fortification structures.

Each museum must retain some freedom as to the order in which it displays these archaeological groups within the exhibition. A determining factor will be the type of rooms available. There is only one requirement: that each of the named groups be displayed as an enclosed whole, neither interrupted nor disrupted by artifacts from a different archaeological department. The order and clarity of a collection of antiquities can be maintained only through coherence in the main groups. An archaeologist who places antiquities of punishment or of some other group among household antiquities in a historical museum evokes the same feeling of disorder as an art historian who places rococo works among the Gothic section in a collection organized by style history.

With this perspective, we come to the same conclusion that P. Weber voiced in regard to his own museum: "The main principle in the Jena Museum is that each room portrays a unified and self-contained whole and contains only those items that directly correspond to the primary theme of that room. Thus the 'Room of the City' contains only general urban antiquities, the 'Room of the Guilds' only guild-related antiquities, the 'Room of the University' only things that relate to the history of the university, etc. In this way, it is possible to diminish the confusing and tiring multiplicity and chaos that makes most visits to museums of antiquities so unpleasant and gives them the character of a curiosity cabinet. On the flip side, even the object that is unimportant

in and of itself attains meaning by finding its place in the grand scheme
through a strict organizational system. After all, most of the objects in a
small town's collection are of little value artistically. It is their place in the
development of cultural history that gives them meaning and justifies
their inclusion in a museum."[43]

Let us now say a word about the display of re-created living spaces,
which most museums love to include. Although we also like this type
of exhibit very much, two considerations must always be kept in mind.
First, such interiors must be created with the local environment in mind,
so that they accurately portray local domestic culture. At the same time,
these rooms not only must be historically correct in terms of the stylistic
assembly of the individual pieces, but they must also reflect the domestic
economy of the time and the history of economics and customs. Accordingly, such rooms may not be used as museological "showrooms." We
must always be on guard against the awfulness of overfilling these so-
called historical rooms, as J. Lessing has warned us: "One will fill the
rooms much fuller than they were in real life; one will attempt a pictur-
esque effect, and through the very effort of providing a cultural-historical
scene, one will sow the seeds of fallacies that will be all the more dangerous the more convincingly a predisposed museum curator manages to
arrange the re-created room."[44] Fortunately, throughout the last decade
commercial artists and museological authorities have rejected this false
and comical studio style in museums, and today it is easy to eliminate this
practice from an archaeological standpoint as well.

Historical interiors help contextualize a selection of the domestic
antiquities to showcase their stylistic changes as well as changes resulting
from fluctuating economic conditions. They will typically form the core
of the department of "domestic antiquities" in historical museums.
And, since they pose considerable difficulties for the museological
administration, they will likely exert a strong influence on the disposition
of new museum buildings, as has been evident in Zurich and Graz, for
example.[45] But under normal circumstances such interiors should not be
unduly emphasized. Rather, they should be integrated into the museum's
holdings without affecting the independence of the other archaeological
groups and their relation to the domestic antiquities.

Concerning our sixth group, artifacts related to the profane arts, we
note the following. Works of local painting and sculpture, which were
acquired not because of their material interest but for their artistic
qualities, can be included in this section only if there is no art collection
nearby dedicated to local art and its study. Small sculptures reflecting

local culture, however, will be found in every historical museum, as they form the transition to the domain of applied arts. Thus the items considered profane art will in most cases be essentially local arts and crafts. Concurrently, a collection of local applied arts should also be set up in the technological department of the decorative arts museum. As long as the collection is not too vast, the advantages of a display organized according to technological criteria will be self-evident. In the overall plan of the museum, the profane art will usually be aligned with the domestic antiquities, although other types of arrangement may be considered as long as a clear separation between the groups is strictly maintained.

We now turn to a special, self-enclosed group that is essential to every historical museum. This group encompasses representations of local historical events, along with related memorabilia, as well as images of personalities important to local history and depictions of native places. No historical museum can do without such an exhibition.

Only when the museum's holdings are divided in this way is the museologist free to decide the correct archaeological and local-historical place for each individual piece in order to display it in the best aesthetic light. This is to say, the artifacts should be shown decoratively so that their educational value is emphasized to the public in the most pleasant possible way. It is up to the museologist alone to decide how this is best accomplished in each individual case. Because this is a matter of personal taste, general guidelines are difficult to provide. We stress, however, that the primary focus must remain on the educational mission of the museum; decorative efforts are secondary. This plea for the educational imperative imposes a perspective on our practical museological work that can scarcely be overstated. After all, it encapsulates the central mission of every museum: to provide to the public direct visual access to the largest possible amount of educational material in as comprehensible a way as possible. To that end, let us quickly consider how historical museums are best able to fulfill this instructive mandate.

This educational imperative is true for museums of decorative arts as well, as J. Lessing, for example, has emphasized.[46] O. Lehmann goes so far as to identify public education and improvement as the single mission of his museum, by "letting the vivid visual nature of the material have an educational effect."[47] Similarly, with our exhibitions in historical museums we must seek to provide the best possible educational focus and widest possible consideration of the public. All that could possibly hinder the instructive agenda must be strongly avoided. There are primarily two museological errors that have a damaging effect in every museum and can have a nearly disastrous effect within historical museums. The first is breaking up the systems of grouping, and the second is overcrowding. Let us briefly discuss them.

The effort to integrate new acquisitions into a collection can easily lead a museum astray in a range of ways, particularly when combined with a chronic lack of space. It is tempting to place an artifact somewhere it does not belong according to the system. However, abandoning the organizational system can have dire consequences, and a single instance can cause the dam to break. It does not matter how wonderful the piece may be, in and of itself. If it is displayed in the wrong spot, it causes more harm than good to the entire museum. There is only one answer in such a case. If, due to external reasons, a piece cannot be placed where it belongs organizationally, then it should for the time being be placed in storage. In these cases one will no doubt search for a solution such that the new piece, owing to its particular historical and archaeological meaning, can take the place of one or more less important works, which will go into storage instead.

Overcrowding is a prominent affliction of many exhibitions, one that inhibits the public's ability to calmly view the artifacts and glean an instructive overview of the museum's purpose. It is necessary only to take someone on a museum tour to be fully convinced that most historical museums are just too big for the public, with far too much on display. Or just observe the blankness on the faces of museum visitors and notice how briefly most of them look at the many items displayed—particularly when the vitally important labeling is somewhat lacking—and how they then search for guidance from the docents. Particularly in historical museums, the docents frequently become guides—rather questionable ones. Overcrowding alone is to blame for all this. We are not even talking about the endless, bleak rows of prehistoric pots, which frankly repel every impartial visitor to a historical exhibition. The same is true for modern objects in nearly all museological departments. That is why we are convinced that all historical museums, once they have passed the initial stages of development, will quickly arrive at a moment when they need to divide their collection into two large parts: the part on display and the part placed in storage.

The displayed exhibits, carefully selected and shown in spacious showcases that tastefully reveal the systematic groupings, reveal a part of the museum's holdings to the public—this includes the best and most impressive artifacts—so that the public can study and enjoy the exhibition to the greatest possible effect and garner the greatest amount of historical-archaeological information. The storage room should not become a melee of abandoned objects, however. Rather, specialists must conserve the pieces that are not on display and keep them organized so that they can quickly locate and study any object at any time. Pieces in storage are grouped according to the exact same system and with the exact same care as the pieces on display. They can, however, be placed much closer together and forgo decorative installations; those are the only differences.

Through this division between the works in the displayed collection and those in storage, the educational potential of the institution is, without a doubt, substantially expanded. At the same time, it may be possible for historical museums to have two rooms of their exhibition hall available for changing displays of selected items from storage—one dedicated to archaeology and one to the local decorative arts. These rooms invigorate visitors' interest through their changing displays. This approach requires considerable effort on the part of museum administrators, but their work benefits the public.

7. The Scientific Obligations of Historical Museums

Our examination began with the scientific basis of our collections of antiquities, and we conclude with a discussion of the museum's scientific obligations. In this way, the treatment of the practical-museological question will to some extent be embedded in a discussion of theoretical-scientific considerations, which is what generally elevates our historical and archaeological work above the level of coarse hackwork. It is what gives our work its higher purpose and its essential meaning in the promotion of education. Every collection of antiquities must support such scientific work. A museum that is not consistently cognizant of this obligation abases itself and our national museology. Furthermore, each individual museologist must meet scientific prerequisites and undertake scientific work. Unfortunately, the public at large is not yet fully convinced of this viewpoint. If everyone thinks that they are justified in speaking about museum issues, then the perception remains that any random private collector or pensioner can develop into an esteemed director of a historical museum with just a little bit of time and sufficient instincts. This opinion needs to be resoundingly rejected. And precisely because we hope that some understanding friends of museums who are outside the inner circle of specialists will occasionally read these words, we must speak sharply. A groom who truly cares for his horse will allow him to be ridden only by someone who really knows how to ride. Directing a museum is, after all, a demanding task.

Anyone can quickly acquire some ability in the technique of excavation. But a scientific education and a wide range of knowledge that cannot be attained in a day is necessary for one to fully assess each unearthed discovery. This evaluation is necessary so that the artifacts, after being buried for millennia, can take on a new role: living witness to the history of humankind. Attaining a picture of primitive human culture from the artifacts' forms, technical qualities, distribution, and the ways in which they were uncovered requires deep understanding of the fields of anthropology, ethnology, and comparative cultural history, along with critical reflection—to say nothing of the varied scientific, anatomical, and technological requirements of the researcher in prehistory. Furthermore, who would want to risk voicing an opinion on the intellectual questions of the Roman-Germanic field without possessing an expert classical and archaeological education? And it is exactly the same case with medieval and modern German archaeology. He who lacks a scientifically grounded overview of the field of national cultural history in the widest sense, as discussed above, is not fit to do much beyond simple cataloging. He remains stuck in the cruder and perhaps unintellectual half of literary museum work, which regards only the external factors of the objects and has a merely descriptive character. Someone like this can never grow into the more difficult, important, and finer aspects of the work—the scientific analysis of antiquities' role in the history of human development and customs—because he lacks the foundational knowledge. The immediate result of a museum without scientific guidance is that the public is poorly served, and the museum itself is hurt most of all. . . .

It is not enough for historical-archaeological museums simply to fulfill the task of making widely recognized material available to the public. Rather, the value, the reputation, and the honor of our museums rest in their ability to position themselves as independent centers of scientific work. A museum employee who does not himself participate in independent study or facilitate any local historical research would miss this attractive and noble task, which entails an unavoidable moral obligation borne by all museum staff and by the museum itself. This viewpoint has been accepted without question from the time of the first historical museums in Germany. The Baron of Aufseß emphasized the scientifically productive character of the Germanic National Museum even before its founding. According to his clearly expressed conviction, the collections should "act as aids to the institute rather than be devoted to their own purposes."[48] His most important goal for his institution was scientific historical-archaeological work. He expressed this idea in a letter to the *Frankfurter Germanistentag* in 1846: the museum should function "in very close accord with historical societies. The societies are the bearers; the museum is the heart into which the hot blood should stream so that it can return purified to the veins."[49] The Baron von Aufseß's plans came to a head in the much-discussed and, to a large extent, unjustly appraised general repertory for German history and antiquities. But his ideas were rooted in his unwavering conviction that the historical museum must, above all, be a means to accomplish scientifically productive work.

Even if the baron's attempts to put these perspectives and plans into practice turned out to be unworkable, we must keep one thing in mind: that from a purely theoretical standpoint, his intentions were built upon scientifically unimpeachable foundations. Their practical implementation failed only because the baron did not establish a local framework for their scope, which would have been impossible in his time. Today, as historical collections appear throughout all Germany, we are in a better situation. Now that museums accept their obligation to take over the scientific and archaeological maintenance of their own local area, the baron's hopeful vision is renewed.

We are now at the end of our discussion. Although our analysis grew considerably larger in scope than planned, we still were able to indicate only briefly the multitude of considerations that are up for debate. We do not pretend to have discovered a schema that is binding on all historical museums for all time. Putting theoretical principles into practice will prompt minimal modifications in more than one case, which is fully expected. In this way the individual museums can determine to what extent they want to exceed our recommendations in their local or objective pursuits—so long as they adhere to adequate scientific rigor. . . .

But there is one idea that we must reiterate: the historical museum is an independent type of museum that differs greatly from an art collection and must be formed according to its own developmental guidelines. This means that it should be evaluated according to its own criteria. To promote rapid and complete acceptance of this fundamental viewpoint, we hope that our colleagues will express their views on our discussion. If any convincing corrections arise as a result of this input, we would be nothing but pleased, since everything we have written is intended to serve historical museums to the best of our abilities.

Coda: The Special Significance of the Historical Museum[50]

Anyone who has considered the questions of museology must grasp that historical museums have their own obligations, separate from those of art museums. Myriad interests involving prehistorical and historical research; family history; the study of coins, seals, and arms; the study of costumes, weapons, and uniforms; and ultimately ethnology as a whole are mostly absent from art and decorative arts museums. If not for this lack, then historical associations and ethnological organizations would never have set up collections of local folklore, especially since this generally occurred under conditions that compared unfavorably to richly endowed art collections. And proactive communities would never have volunteered to expand these organizations' collections with public funds, as happened in Berlin, Bremen, Frankfurt am Main, Hamburg, Cologne, Leipzig, and other places.

The public finds something in historical museums that is rare in art collections: namely, the satisfaction of cultural-historical interests and a resulting increase of pride in their homeland. It is for this reason that visitor numbers at historical museums consistently exceed those at art museums, often by more than a factor of two, despite the museums' relative inaccessibility and lack of accommodations.

Ultimately, historical museums are the only collections in which we can hope to combine literary and object-based research, with the increasingly called-for unification of German studies and ethnology on one side and the knowledge of real objects on the other. When Moriz Heyne died, Edward Schröder praised him for bringing the connection between literary and object-based study to a new height. He was able to accomplish this through his willingness to direct the historical museum of Basel while holding his German studies professorship, as well as later founding and directing the Städtische Altertumssammlung in Göttingen. He merged the insights from both facets of his work into a greater whole. Fortunately, his legacy survives through the many Germanists and comparative linguists who are not letting his unification effort fall into decline. The journal *Wörter und Sachen*, founded by Meringer and his friends, has become essential in this area.

To support literary research by presenting objects related to the texts is one part of this goal. Another part is the further explanation of literary and cultural-historical textual primary sources through artifacts and images. The essential scientific obligations of historical museums consist of these missions and of overtly site-specific historical investigations.

All these special duties of historical museums, which give them an importance separate from that of art collections, are fundamental for anyone interested in the study of German antiquities. Even the general public has such expectations of the museums.

1.   The following passage is from Otto Lauffer, "Moriz Heyne und die archäologischen Grundlagen der historischen Museen," *Museumskunde* 2 (1906): 153–62.

2.   Lauffer, "Das historische Museum," *Museumskunde* 3 (1907): 1–14.

3.   For simplicity's sake, we ask the reader's forgiveness for not considering coloristic beauty in addition to formal beauty.

4.   This viewpoint is articulated by Richter, *Museumskunde* 2 (1906): 204, by his claim that museums for history and ethnographic studies "focus on elements from the historical past that have now been fully or partly overcome and on objects from isolated areas of our own culture that provide living testaments to our cultural past."

5.   Lauffer, "Das historische Museum," 78–99.

6.   Wilhelm von Bode, *Kunst und Kunstgewerbe am Ende des neunzehnten Jahrhunderts* (Berlin: Cassirer, 1901), 67.

7.   Compare Karl Lacher, *Führer durch das steiermärkische kulturhistorische und Kunstgewerbe-Museum zu Graz* (1906), 8; and Alfred Overmann, *Die Aufgaben und die zukünftige Gestaltung des Erfurter Museums, Vortrag vom 9. Febr. 1903* (Erfurt, 1903), 2.

8.   Overmann agrees: "The collection of a historical museum should to a certain extent provide a supplement to the city archives. The archive preserves only written monuments. All other historically important artifacts from our town's past belong in the historical museum" (*Die Aufgaben und die zukünftige Gestaltung*, 4).

9.   Moriz Heyne, *Über die mittelalterliche Sammlung zu Basel* (Basel, 1857). See also Overmann, *Die Aufgaben und die zukünftige Gestaltung*.

10.   Alfred Lichtwark, *Brinckmann-Festschrift* (1902), 56.

11.   For concurring thoughts, see Overmann, *Die Aufgaben und die zukünftige Gestaltung*, 15–16.

12.   Robert Mielke, *Museen und Sammlungen: Ein Beitrag zu ihrer weiteren Entwicklung* (Berlin: F. Wunder, 1903).

13.   Wilhelm Wackernagel, *Über die mittelalterliche Sammlung zu Basel.*

14.   Heyne, *Über die mittelalterliche Sammlung zu Basel*, 7; Wackernagel, *Über die mittelalterliche Sammlung zu Basel*, 9.

15.   Paul Weber, "Thüringische Ortsmuseen," in *Deutsche Geschichtsblätter*, ed. Armin Tille, 5:16–25.

16.   Bode, *Kunst und Kunstgewerbe*, 68.

17.   *Führer durch das Museum in Lübeck*, 2nd ed. (1896), 10.

18.   This is how it is stated in the commission development of September 18, 1888. See Heinrich Angst, in *Festgabe auf die Eröffnung des Schweizerischen Landesmuseums in Zürich* (1898), 17.

19.   Ernst Wagner, *Über Museen und über die Großh. Staatssammlungen für Altertums- und Völkerkunde in Karlsruhe* (1906), 29–30.

20. Karl Lacher, *Die Aufgaben der Kunstgewerbemuseen auf kulturhistorischem Gebiete* (Graz: Self-published, 1901), 4.
21. Ernst Grosse, *Aufgabe und Einrichtung einer städtischen Kunstsammlung* (Tübingen-Leipzig, 1902), 3.
22. Lauffer, "Das historische Museum," 179–85.
23. See Lacher, *Die Aufgaben der Kunstgewerbemuseen*, 10.
24. From *Altbayerische Monatsschrift*, 3:5.
25. Friedrich Deneken, *Erster Bericht des städtischen Kaiser Wilhelm-Museums in Krefeld* (1899), 47.
26. Theodor Hampe, *Das Germanische Nationalmuseum von 1832 bis 1902* (Leipzig: Weber, 1902), 88.
27. Rudolf Wackernagel, *Über Altertumssammlungen: Festrede, gehalten bei der Eröffnung des historischen Museums Basel* (1894), 19–20.
28. Wilhelm Wackernagel, *Über die mittelalterliche Sammlung zu Basel*, 1.
29. Lauffer, "Das historische Museum," 222–45.
30. Peter Jessen, "Die Kunstmuseen," in *Die Museen als Volksbildungsstätten: Ergebnisse der 12. Konferenz der Centralstelle für Arbeiter-Wohlfahrtseinrichtungen* (Berlin: Carl Heymann, 1904), 14.
31. Grosse, *Aufgabe und Einrichtung einer städtischen Kunstsammlung*, 2–3.
32. Bode, *Kunst und Kunstgewerbe*, 64, 65.
33. Lessing, *Kunstgewerbeblatt*, N. F. VIII.
34. Lichtwark, *Brinckmann-Festschrift*, 42–45.
35. Ubisch, *Brinckmann-Festschrift*, 402.
36. Overmann, *Die Aufgaben und die zukünftige Gestaltung des Erfurter Museums*, 7.
37. Lacher, *Führer durch das steiermärkische kulturhistorische und Kunstgewerbe-Museum zu Graz*, 10.
38. Otto Lehmann, "Das Altonaer Museum," in *Die Museen als Volksbildungsstätten: Ergebnisse der 12. Konferenz der Centralstelle für Arbeiter-Wohlfahrtseinrichtungen* (Berlin: Carl Heymann, 1904), 36–46.
39. Cf. Georg von Below and Friedrich Meinecke, "Handbuch der mittelalterlichen und neueren Geschichte," *Abteilung 5: Hilfswissenschaft und Altertümer* (Munich: R. Oldenbourg, 1904).
40. Weber, in Tille, *Deutsche Geschichtsblätter*, 5:24.
41. Lehmann, "Das Altonaer Museum," 38.
42. Cf. *Museumskunde* 1 (1905): 236.
43. Weber, in Tille, *Deutsche Geschichtsblätter*, 5:22.
44. Lessing, *Kunstgewerbeblatt*, N. F. VIII: 83.
45. Cf. Angst, in *Festgabe auf die Eröffnung*, 25, and Lacher, "Altsteirische Wohnräume im Landesmuseum zu Graz," 2.
46. Lessing, *Kunstgewerbeblatt*, N. F. VIII: 85.
47. Lehmann, "Das Altonaer Museum," 36.
48. Hampe, *Das Germanische Nationalmuseum von 1832 bis 1902*, 36.
49. Hampe, *Das Germanische Nationalmuseum von 1832 bis 1902*, 20.
50. The main body of the text was published in 1907; this section was published several years after: Otto Laufer, "Herr Schwedeler-Meyer und die historischen Museen," *Museumskunde* 6 (1910): 32–40; the paragraphs here are at 38–39.

On the Ideal and Practical Tasks of Ethnographic Museums

Oswald Richter

Text translated by Annika Fisher and adapted from Oswald Richter, "Über die idealen und praktischen Aufgaben der ethnographischen Museen," which appeared in *Museumskunde: Zeitschrift für Verwaltung und Technik öffentlicher und privater Sammlungen,* over the span of five volumes: 2 (1906): 189–218; 3 (1907): 14–24, 99–124; 4 (1908): 92–106, 156–72, 224–35; 5 (1909): 102–13, 166–74, 231–6; and 6 (1910): 40–60, 131–7.

> The degree of civilization to which any nation, city, or province has attained is best shown by the character of its Public Museums and the liberality with which they are maintained.

—George Brown Goode

Historical Preliminary Remarks

The history of ethnographic museums is not yet written, for its development has just begun.[1]

The word "ethnography" can be traced to at least the eighteenth century.[2] In contrast, the word "anthropology" is far older. It may have been first used by Magnus Hundt in *Antropologium de ho(min)is dignitate, natura et p(ro)prietatibus etc.* (1506).[3] Ethnography is a field in the humanities (a "cultural science"), specifically a historical and psychological discipline.

The defense of ethnography as a natural science is not based on an emphasis on objectivity—that is, a viewpoint based on objects. Instead, it is based on assumptions about the analytic, inductive, and comparative methods that ethnography employs. In particular, the "comparative-genetic method," a process of seeking general parameters and comparisons, is considered a natural-scientific method, and thus it aligns ethnography with natural science.[4] This premise is linked with the belief that "our era of natural science" needs to be furthered. In truth, however, the goal of elementary analysis is simply to determine a given state of facts to fulfill purely descriptive purposes. Additionally, the methods that are often used in concert—including causal analysis, which seeks to divide a composed whole into its various causes, and logical analysis, which represents a composed whole as a combined system of causal relationships—are used by both the natural sciences and the humanities, and are applicable to both. The same can be said for induction and comparison. The method of individual and general comparison is actually the method of all observational disciplines.

Particular to natural science, due largely to its characteristic of being focused on certain aspects of natural science (we are not talking about astronomy or meteorology here), is the experimental method. This is based on the random variation of conditions for the purpose of observation. Particular to the humanities is the method of interpretation and criticism, which can be relevant only when dealing with circumstances resulting from intellectual motives or products. The manifestations of nature can be explained but not interpreted. Explanation in a narrower sense is classification using parameters or laws that pertain to the exterior of the world and how it appears to our intellect. These parameters determine how all manifestations in the world are linked. Explanations in this sense dominate in the field of natural science.

Interpretation is a perception of phenomena that serves to transmit these phenomena to our understanding. However, we can understand only phenomena whose causes are directly observable or are analogous to motives accessible to our self-perception. Interpretation thus concerns the inner motives of mental processes—that is to say: their motivation—in contrast to the explanations of the natural sciences, which concern only the exterior of the world. Motivation dominates the humanities. To criticize nature is beyond our powers; or rather, nature is beyond our criticism: nature is given as it is. In contrast, intellectual products may be both interpreted and criticized. In addition, criticism is relevant only to intellectual products—meaning phenomena that arise from motives, which are directly accessible to our own observation. These may be both systematically instructed and methodically acquired, since the historical treatment of human intellectual productivity can employ interpretation and criticism in the study of the humanities, particularly in philology and linguistics, but not in the natural sciences. Theodor Benfey said that the linguist is best suited "to become an ethnologist or a cultural historian."[5]

Thus, the conception of ethnography as a natural science is justified neither by the nature of its subject matter nor by the type of its research methods. Seen from the outside, this conception was far more a consequence of ethnography being historically associated with the scientific work of natural scientists (anthropologists and doctors) rather than with philologists, historians, or psychologists. The association is due to a variety of circumstances, including the anthropological interests of those influenced by the works of Darwin, Wallace, Haeckel, and Vogt; the power of Virchow's authority; and the introduction of ethnographic collections mainly through traveling natural historians. Thus, when this connection with natural-scientific (or medical) research dissolved, or when the natural scientists (or doctors) pursuing ethnography began to work more independently, many of their scientific methods were adapted to the research methods of the humanities. In essence, however, the term "natural-scientific method" is (despite its circumstantial link to ethnography) nothing but an expression of the justified opposition of positivism and empirical research to the speculative philosophy of Hegel. In any case, the natural sciences can be credited with bringing a scientific method to the treatment of ethnographic facts. This is principally evident in the main methods used for general comparisons in linguistics, in legal history, and in the history of mythology.[6] The false assessment of ethnography's role in the scientific system that resulted from this history was further solidified through the suggestive power of the catchword *zoon politikon*, defining humans as political animals.

That the majority of directors of today's ethnographic museums are still natural scientists, on the other hand, does not seem to result (at least not directly) from the circumstance that the *Curiosa Artificialia* had been housed with the *Naturalia* in the old cabinets of curiosities. Even in earlier times there were some who knew that these classes of objects should be held separately.[7]

In part because of the integration of ethnography and the natural sciences, terminology from the latter was introduced into ethnography, as it was in the three main areas of social psychology (the study of language, of myth, and of customs). This adoption of expressions borrowed from older forms of the natural sciences was originally intended in a metaphorical sense and occurred particularly within linguistics. (For example, language was called an organism. This expression was intended to impart only that language was not a random creation. It did not mean that language was alive in the way that organisms are material objects, living and existent. Rather, language is on a path of continual restructuring and development.) This terminology has cast the discipline in a bleak light. If ethnography wishes to correctly assess its manifestations, it must also free itself in the manner that linguistics did in the 1870s.

Once it was said, and believed, that the foundation of ethnography ("ethnology") would initiate a new era for the entire field of cultural studies. And for good reason. As a result of introducing methods of general comparison to the treatment of ethnographic objects, the data related to religion (mythology) and customs in the lives of the "primitive and uncivilized tribes," and the results supposedly attained via "comparative ethnography" or "ethnology," were taken into consideration in older fields of comparative humanities. This was done so successfully in the area of mythology, for example, that comparison in the Kuhn-Müller sense has been completely discredited. Furthermore, the new methodology is making inroads into the methods used in older historical and comparative studies in the humanities, which recently accepted ethnography into its circle. This reveals in the history of science the multifaceted applicability of ethnography also to the external history of ethnographic museums. Among the humanities fields greatly impacted are national economics, art history, and more recently and in a more limited sense, history. As Franz Boas wrote, "We cannot overestimate the influence of the bold generalizations made by the pioneers of modern anthropology. . . . Anthropology, which was hardly beginning to be a science, ceased at the same time to lose its character of being a single science, but became a method applicable to all the mental sciences and indispensable to all of them. We are still in the midst of this development."[8]

In fact, the establishment of ethnology, with a focus on the religions and customs of the people whom ethnography studies—and of humanity overall—was expected but has not occurred, just as a general study of linguistics has not developed. The once heralded study of the "primitive and uncivilized tribes" today remains largely discredited. Participation in its more solid research has never really taken off in the way it was expected to a generation or so ago.

First, this is likely due to natural scientists, who (also) deal with ethnographic objects and questions, because of their tendency to integrate historical issues with matters of natural science, as Boas noted. Second, the minimization of interest in ethnography, which was only passingly lively but has now awakened for entirely different reasons, is less the fault of scientific dilettantes (of which there are plenty around in ethnography) than of unscientific ones who employ ethnographic facts in a clumsy manner to reach sociological and sociopolitical conclusions and motivations [purposes].[9] The measured, critical ethos of research, as it is evoked by Haeckel's philosophy, must feel repelled by such research and literary production. The unscientific dilettantes, and not the specialists, are to blame for the idea that ethnographers are attempting to obfuscate—perhaps successfully—the fundamentals of Christianity through their study of religious history. This accusation is also leveled at the study of Buddhism. However, this preoccupation with Buddhism, as is seldom acknowledged, does not concern the unclouded study of the Buddha's teachings but rather characterizes what is known as the northern church of Buddhism, which involves many Brahmin elements, resulting in a philosophically and ethically less sympathetic version of the religion.

Since Ernst Grosse's essay in the *Festschrift für Adolf Bastian*, circumstances have improved somewhat. Today there are professorships in ethnography at the Universities of Berlin and Leipzig. In December 1899, the German Colonial Society resolved that it must urgently request that the government establish ethnological professorships at German universities. As has already been rightly bemoaned by Karl Weule, there are still no professorships at the university and military academy of Kiel, which are important for German interests overseas.[10] Nor are there any in Bonn, despite its location and dominance in the history of the humanities. This lack prevents Bonn from becoming a site of intellectual development in the field. Thus, it remains the case that an education in ethnography is attainable only through painstaking and time-consuming private study; the systematic education for the profession remains a dream for the future. Recently, in addition to Grosse and Weule, others have called for more professorships. Johann Gottfried von Herder already wondered how it was possible that there are professorships dedicated to stones, plants, and animals, but not to people themselves.[11]

Other countries have surpassed Germany in this regard, particularly France and the United States.[12] The Bureau of Ethnology in Washington, DC, is an agency dedicated to the field, and so is L'École et le Laboratoire d'Anthropologie in Paris. British scientists in Bristol in 1898 took up the call: "It is of urgent importance to press upon the Government the necessity of establishing a 'bureau of ethnology.'" In Germany, Wilhelm Waldeyer urged that a "great central research institute in connection with the biggest museum in the land (Berlin)" be established. He contin ued: "This central institute should be linked with the university, not only for its own benefit, but for anthropology itself. There is surely no field with such numerous connections to all other disciplines than anthropology in its widest sense."[13]

1. The ethnographic collections of Europe in general and of Germany in particular, insofar as they are today relatively independent institutions, developed accidentally and incidentally. The majority of the museums today, even if housed in separate departments, remain appendices of other museums that largely lack their own leadership. The links between the ethnographic departments and their attached museums vary widely. In Berlin, the ethnographic material was merged previously with the collections from the ancient Mediterranean, as is still the case in the Museo Archeologico [*sic*] in Madrid, which combines prehistoric and ancient artifacts.[14] In the civic Museum für Länder- und Völkerkunde in Rotterdam, the ethnographic material was combined with the collection of a naval museum, while in the Museum of La Porte de Hal in Brussels it was combined with a weapons collection (the museum retained this name until 1905, when it was renamed Musée du Cinquantenaire). It is probable that even in Dresden the ethnographic material would have been combined with the historical museum's collection had the director of the zoological museum not advocated for separation.

The link between ethnographic and zoological museums that persists today (in Bremen, Dresden, Hamburg, Vienna, etc.) and above all the fact that the directors of the ethnographic collections are still primarily natural scientists are based in general on the older conception of ethnography as a natural science, justifying its link to zoology.

The current younger generation has resisted this conception. Even though our tools, devices, and weapons are in some sense nothing but "projections" or completions of our organs, ethnography must consider them nevertheless as intellectual, rather than natural, products. Intellectual products can be understood only if they are considered in light of history and psychology. Very few ethnographic museums grew out of practical educational needs. An example of a collection that did is that of the Dutch Mission Organization in Rotterdam, which educates missionaries heading to the Dutch East Indies and is now attached to the Museum of

Geography and Ethnography. A second example is the collection in Delft of the former organization of colonial officers preparing to deploy to India, which is now dissolved. Some other museums, including the Dutch National Museum of Ethnography in Leiden, the Leipzig Museum, and the Dresden Museum, came into being as the result of public interest in the preservation of larger collections amassed by travelers or private citizens. However, the idea of creating a designated ethnographic museum as such, as is planned for Breslau, is thoroughly modern.[15]

The origin of the majority of today's independent ethnographic museums is the cabinets of curiosities, which were widespread in the previous century and included art objects and items from natural science. These collections were not the property of the state, which took the form of an absolute monarchy in those times. Rather, a few belonged to charitable organizations, such as the original collection of the Lübeck Museum, which belonged to a group founded in 1789.[16] The majority were from the treasuries of aristocratic houses. The owners of these noble houses loved the beautiful, the artful, the valuable, the uncommon, and the wonderful, as well as strange objects and things from the "wild" tribes. They kept such objects under their personal care, motivated by a sense of pleasure and wonder, and sometimes mystification and disgust—but always by a sense of interest.

Cabinets of curiosities and art cabinets were considered a standard part of home décor from the sixteenth through the eighteenth centuries and were thought to elevate a residence to the status of a royal court. (When interest in the curious and antiquarian phenomena of nature and of the intellect deepened enough to be considered scholarly, the term "museum" came into favor, reflecting the popularization of the sciences at the start of the eighteenth century. In the second half of the eighteenth century the term "collection" also became common.)[17] The cabinets held the first "ethnographic rarities" from the newly discovered eastern and western lands (East India and America), imported through Nürnberg, Augsburg, and the Hanseatic towns. The first nonaristocratic art and curiosity cabinets were in the art-minded trade centers of southern Germany: Augsburg (collectors included Anton and Raimund von Fugger, who had agents in Lisbon, as did the Welsers, which monopolized trade with India and the Spice Islands, in particular; both pursued trade with America) and Nürnberg.[18]

The most comprehensive nonaristocratic "art cabinet" (more precisely, rarity cabinet) in Bavaria was the Urban collection, which was called the Urbansche Saal (first located in Landshut, then in Ingolstadt,

Fig. 1. Engraving of the Museum Wormianum (or Ole Worm's cabinet
of curiosities), 1655.

and finally divided).[19] One of the oldest collections of this type belonged
to D. Lorenz Hofmann in Halle, of which a detailed description survives
from 1625 that includes many ethnographic objects.[20] One of the most
famous cabinets of natural items and rarities belonged to the Danish
doctor Olaus Wormius [Ole Worm] in 1655 (fig. 1).

Even older than the rarity cabinets and art chambers that appeared
in the time of the Renaissance and alongside the silver cabinets of the
wealthy dynasties were the *Schatzkammern*, the treasuries held by churches,
cathedral chapters, and favored cloisters (the cloisters, as islands which
preserved the remains of older culture, are still a type of museum).[21]
Since the church also displayed the commemorations of victories, such
as trophies looted from enemies "ideally near to the graves of the conquerors," these occasionally would have included ethnographic objects
(such as oriental or Mongolian).[22] The oldest museums of all are the
treasure houses of pagan temples.[23] Incidentally, until the seventeenth
century ethnographic objects were looted items; in many ways they
remain so today.

The oldest ethnographic collections in Germany were probably the private collections of the Roman villa owners in the German provinces on the Danube and the Rhine. Chinese (and Indian) antiquities, or at least antiquities with a true Chinese character, were known to have been in the Rhineland during the Roman epoch.[24] The oldest exotic items to reach France about which the chroniclers write are those of Harun al-Rashid, which he offered to Charlemagne as gifts in the years 801 and 802.[25] Any number of oriental objects may have reached ancient Gaul and ancient Germania (and Gallic or Germanic objects were sent to the East) through the travels of the Roman legions and the Mithras cult (including, along with objects, the lasting influences on medieval central Europe brought by the Huns and Mongols!). An aware, lively, and more general desire to own ethnographic objects developed in Germany only in the seventeenth century, particularly following Dutch colonization and trade. Since the start of the eighteenth century (that is, the provisional end of colonial advancement), the collections reveal that "the ethnographic and technical elements became less popular, ushering in a period of healthy and appropriate limitation." In contrast, a private luxury market developed, in particular through the increasing wealth of Holland and France, originally consisting of the merely occasional imports of individual East Asian artworks, especially Japanese lacquerware and Chinese and Japanese porcelain. This trend expanded to the massive import of East Asian porcelain, including the type made to order for Europe and in the European style, which resulted in the imitations of these decorative arts in Europe. The increase of interest in ethnographic objects that was introduced by Cook's travels has yet to subside.[26]

Thus, ethnographic collections were originally objects of aristocratic protection and goodwill or they were in the care of private societies. Later, following the great revolutions, the altered circumstances transferred the care of these items from private hands to the public. Under civic care, these collections expanded, fostered by an era of peace and unhindered by foreign obstruction.[27] The mobility among people stimulated the rapid and determined growth. In fact, many collections today have insufficient space, and visiting them can endanger body and soul. They urgently require more adequate housing, space for their beauty to shine.

2. When looking at the purely external developments of ethnographic museums and the field of ethnographic science, one can conclude that the former have outpaced the discipline, which has only just begun to gain academic acclaim and is not yet in possession of a rich and entrenched academic representation. Not only are the museums

numerous, but they have also become so all-encompassing that they are now challenges for their public authorities. In contrast, the internal development of ethnographic museums, generally speaking, which centers on their fruitful service to public education, is as backward as the field itself in regard to internal scientific development.[28] Ethnography still lacks a unifying and firmly grounded methodology and a developed professional criticism, as well as a general foundation of empirical insights.[29] The few valuable achievements that are actually relevant to the realm of popular education have not been put into service by the ethnographic museums. This is largely due to the directors of the museums themselves, who often have no inkling of the general research questions of their field because they do not belong to it themselves.

And yet, we cannot blame the directors entirely for this. The fact that ethnographic museums have no root in the consciousness of the people—or even in the consciousness of a specific discipline—means that there is simply no general public understanding of the museums' content and purpose. Museum administrators have not managed to make people more familiar with the institutions entrusted to their care. To some extent this can also be blamed on the lack of "ethnographic instruction" and on the authorities, who need to find the means to popularize ethnographic museums.[30]

We will next explore how museums can fulfill their general ideal requirements. But first, these ideal tasks must be established.

The Ideal Tasks

> He who knows himself and others
> Here will also see:
> That the East and West, like brothers,
> Parted ne'er shall be.

—Goethe

The Ultimate Objective of Ethnographic Work and the General Tasks of Ethnographic Museums

3. The ultimate objective of all ethnographic work, which is thus the general task of ethnographic museums, can only be this: to contribute

to the knowledge and understanding of ourselves. Ethnography pursues such knowledge and understanding by studying the current and former cultures of people whose ancestors were "not included in the framework of world history that revolved around the ancient cultures of the Mediterranean" and which remain in some way accessible today.[31]

The definition of the term "ethnography" adopted in this study is based on actual conditions in ethnographic museums and how people who work in these museums use the word. We must bear in mind that our use of the term may differ from others' use, such as, for example, the Japanese or Siamese (cf. the labeling in a museum for European culture, which Adolf Bastian saw in 1861 in the palace of King Mongkut in Bangkok[32]). Ethnography concerns the scientific inquiry into the cultural lives of peoples who developed for the most part independently of the culture of the ancient Mediterranean, specifically in a philological and historical-comparative way.[33] In contrast to the British and the Americans, the French have a marked preference for the unassuming expression "ethnography," particularly for their museums' empirical-historical, nonspeculative type of research, a term now favored by German museum staff as well. Its use consciously rejects the term "ethnology."[34] The given definition demonstrates that we, at least in general, have moved beyond the term *barbaroi* in our thinking as well as our terminology, if not in our practice.

The lack of clarity and inconsistency of meaning attendant on using the terms "ethnography," "ethnology," *Völkerkunde* (comparative ethnology), and *Völkerpsychologie* (ethnic, or folk, psychology) is so great that no solution seems feasible. The field requires a leading mind to give a permanent structure to the muddled schemas.[35] This lamentable situation can be partly blamed on the fact that the definitions are not *actual* definitions based on how the term is used but rather *ideal* definitions, outlining what the term should mean according to the interests and methodologies of individual practitioners. One almost wants to believe that the confusion surrounding these terms is an example of the increased deficit in our time of thought energy, as it is manifest in the tumult of common concepts produced by overspecialization.[36]

4. Coming to know means differentiating and perceiving differences. To understand means to grasp or apprehend the connections through which something has come into being. Knowledge of ourselves implies, for the ethnographer, knowledge of our character: that is, (1) knowledge of the general similarity of psychological elements, above all the most common needs of all human communities and their historical

effects—which is to say, their external psychological effects (Bastian's "elementary thoughts"); and (2) knowledge of the actual formal differences in the social psychology of different human communities among the historical effects that depend on accidental, external stimulation, most notably the characteristic means which we as well as other people have developed in dealing with cultural pressures. An understanding of the present entails comprehension of how separate cultural traditions have evolved: be it the great expressions of cultural life—including language and literature, mythology and religion, laws and customs, and so forth—or an individual, very specific cultural-historical fact.

We do not learn about our own manner only by comparing our culture with the cultures of antiquity or with those of our modern European brothers. Rather, we can understand it better when measured against the traits of cultures that do not stem from the ancient civilizations of the Mediterranean, even if they were influenced by them.[37] The comparison can also provide a living conception of our most ancient past, as well as some subsequent—and even contemporary—manifestations of our culture. Additionally, insight into the earliest stages in the development of cultural assets more broadly can be gleaned by comparing the individual possessions and circumstances of our mostly high culture with those of peoples from lower cultures, who remain in a more or less backward state.

5. In order to illustrate how ethnography can help us to attain awareness and understanding of ourselves, we should not draw on examples from the realms of religion or art, the highest and—for us, at least—most finely developed forms of our culture. Examples from the realm of technology would be able to fulfill this purpose as well, albeit not necessarily examples from our own modern and highly praised industries and technology. For in the example that we will discuss, it turns out that our industries and technology are neither sufficiently varied to encompass all possibilities in a given context—especially with respect to the irreplaceable artistic processes—nor do they always result in the highest achievements.

6. A comparison between the modern German textile industry and that in Java today illustrates that our method of printing patterns on finished plain fabric has similar results to the Javanese method called batik.[38] However, this comparison also reveals that our modern textile industry has not made use of all possible dyeing processes;[39] in addition, our dyeing methods accomplish far less than the Javanese batik method, which can quickly create a fully developed pattern on both sides of the

fabric, a pattern that, furthermore, matches up on each side. Another comparison in this medium also teaches us that our mechanical process of producing *chiné* is, from a purely formal and historically traceable perspective, nothing but a shortcut and mechanical coarsening of a protracted form of the oriental handicraft ikat, which produces far finer colors than *chiné*.[40] The history of *chiné* involves the procurement of the procedure from its original form in the East, which was later modified in Europe.[41]

7. A different example from the realm of material culture teaches that analogy, as much as the confirmation or hypothesis of direct borrowing (or indeed inheritance), can explain phenomena historically. Our dishware has a rimmed base along the bottom. This was surely not always the case. The oldest vessel undoubtedly was the cupped hand (leaving aside the pan-shaped tongue) or both hands cupped together. The first primitive improvements to this elemental vessel were seashells, nutshells, gourd rinds, or calvarias. Ethnography teaches us that these vessels are still widely used, even in places where pottery is practiced.[42] It is surely no coincidence that the primitive pottery vessels possessed neither a handle nor a rimmed base. Rather, their base was formed to resemble the natural vessels that were simultaneously in use: rounded like nutshells, bulbous like gourds, or pointed like some types of cucumber-y squash or nuts. Thus, it seems likely that the clay vessels did not overtake the natural vessels in development but rather were continuously aligned with them, at least initially echoing their shape. A high vessel with a pointed base did not have its own stand. It had to be placed in loose soil or sand to remain vertical. A vessel with curved bottom could be kept passably upright through amassed supports, such as stones. In Celebes and other places in the East Indian Archipelago, woven bases are employed; these have a shape that resembles the rims on our dishware.[43] In these examples, the vessel was divided into separate parts: the container and the base. Thus, the vessel with base appears to be a very late achievement, which, at least in parts of the world, developed as a unification of the original form of a container with a rounded (or pointed) base with a stand that supported it. The development of the handle, coincidentally, progressed similarly. It also resulted, at least in part, from the unification of what were originally two separate elements: the container and the tongs used to hold it after it was heated.[44]

8. The study of what have been called primitive tribes leads to an understanding of the present in a similar way as the study of the past.

Ethnographic museums provide services similar to the museums of history and culture, which focus on elements from the historical past that have now been fully or partly overcome and on objects from isolated areas of our own culture that provide living testaments to our cultural past. They are also similar to museums of archaeology and prehistory, which deal with objects from antiquity from cultures around the Mediterranean and their prehistory. This is the reason for the close kinship between the science of ethnography and the sciences of history, folk studies, archaeology, and prehistory. As far as the author knows, all these sciences are addressed in Karl Lamprecht's historical seminar at the University of Leipzig, titled "Exercises in Comparative Cultural History [*Übungen zur vergleichenden Kulturgeschichte*]."[45] The awareness of the close connection between the ethnography of primitive tribes and prehistory particularly merits more practical examination—a point to which we shall return.

The Primary Task

9. One aspect of the primary task of ethnographic museums is to provide an introduction to foreign cultures via their "material evidences," which, in its full breadth and with a systematically founded expansion of all its individual parts, would be possible only in a museum like the one in Berlin (cf. §58), and furthermore (at least within the borders of the empire) only desirable at one location (cf. §31).[46] The other aspect is not to reach specific cultural-historical or psychological findings on the basis of the intellectual creations of mankind that are the usual preserve of the field of ethnography. Rather, it is much more to establish an awareness of cultural-historical and psychological truths from the discipline's allotted ethnographic material through critical sorting and clear organization, and to transmit to further circles cultural-historical and psychological truths that are already acknowledged, insofar as they apply to concrete ethnographic material. In this way ethnographic museums can make use of their material ethically and educationally. To research the intellectual results, the general psychological conditions of which are the function of language, as well as to discover cultural-historical connections and the psychological laws of a people: these are the tasks of the field of ethnographic (and sociopsychological) science, which we must separate from the practical and educational work of ethnographic museums. Clearly, the actual scientific, practical, and educational demands of the ethno-

graphic field are currently more or less combined in a single person: the museum ethnographer, who is simultaneously the appointed representative of ethnographic science. Accordingly, since it is his job to determine the educational value of the field's findings, and since he must first independently produce these findings, ethnographic museums will be able to flourish only when they are associated with places of instruction and science, meaning universities. In general, the stimuli and didactic sense for choosing the material on display appropriately derive from academic teaching. Only in such a setting can the museums become a source of learning and stop confronting their visitors as an overwhelming sum of riddles.[47]

The Secondary Tasks

Along with this primary task, ethnographic museums also have certain national, political, and commercial tasks.

10. *The national task.* As the Great Elector Frederick William of Brandenburg said, "The . . . wealth and the status of a country are derived from commerce; seafaring and trade are the most noble pillars of a state, providing nourishment and sustenance through both water and manufacture." In addition, the words of Kaiser Wilhelm II: "Our future (or as we would like to say today, our present) lies on the water!" The Kaiser's words were surely not influenced by thoughts of colonial expansion but were rather (1) in consideration of the general worldwide expansion of German national interests; (2) in consideration of the need for protection, which every part of our population requires and today includes those representing German interests abroad; and (3) in consideration of a firm bond between all Germans who have emigrated as bearers and propagators of European civilization, and who are linked both to each other and to their fatherland.

Wherever he goes, the trader is the pioneer of civilization and colonial development; the priest and the soldier follow his lead. The trader founds new cultural centers and represents a (higher) level of cultural development that is layered atop a different or lower one. Through trade, he helps accelerate the spread of civilization, and cultural development follows quickly. He has a high mission in cultural history and will play a large role in world history. At the same time, the trader, as Kurt Hassert has correctly emphasized, "is capable of providing a great service to science. Everyone, whether an officer or a civil servant, a missionary, a

planter, or a trader, who goes into unknown territory has the duty to contribute to our knowledge. A regular clerk, Gustav Conrau, who sadly died
much too early, contributed more to our knowledge of the geography of
Cameroon than many travelers more widely known by the public. The
contributions of the Hamburg trade house Cesar Godeffroy to the scien
tific discovery of the South Seas will never be forgotten. . . . In this way, the
trader is a representative of commerce, a precursor of politics, a cultural
pioneer, and a scientific researcher—combined in a single person."[48]

The missionary can play a similar role. Recently, his obligations to
science have not only been acknowledged from a Catholic perspective
but have even been notably emphasized. Wilhelm Schmidt-Mödling,
who is known from his studies of language, edits a new journal "for
ethnology and linguistics" that is titled *Anthropos* (the first issue
appeared in 1906), in which missionaries are encouraged to contribute
to science in more intensive and systematic ways than heretofore. "And
not only for the [future missionaries], ethnographers, and linguists,
but also for the geographers, the sociologists, the psychologists, the
friends of the colonies, the merchants, and generally any educated
people who are interested in the lives and customs of foreign peoples
will *Anthropos* provide," as the prospectus advertises, "a wealth of
reliable material relating to different interests and areas of research."
Among the missionary organizations that have provided for the benefit
of ethnographic science, the most notable are the older, Protestant
"Nederlandsche Zendelinggenootschap" in Rotterdam, with the long
series of volumes of their rewarding *Mededeelingen* (since 1857), and
the "Gesellschaft der Missionare des Hl. Herzens Jesu" in Hiltrup near
Münster in Westfalia, with their *Marien-Monatsheften*.[49]

The idea behind the great words of the Kaiser, quoted above, logically
leads to the request for a fleet. The words remind us to think differently
about ourselves so that "our grandchildren can have free rein to conquer
the globe" (Lamprecht), and also to defend and retain our colonial possessions so that no one will one day take our crown. We must recognize
that we have a national obligation to expand our trade horizon, which
encompasses—as a result of the great discoveries of the eighteenth century, and modern transportation and technology—the entire globe. As
the Kaiser said to the German people, "Just look around. How the face
of the world has changed in the last several years! The old-world empires
have passed, and new ones are nascent. Nations suddenly appear on the
horizon and enter into competition with other peoples, although we
scarcely took note of them a moment ago. In the span of several moons,

incidents can occur that are revolutionary to international relations and impact the economic life of the people, which in old times needed centuries to play out. Accordingly, the tasks for our German Empire and people have grown to a mighty scale."[50]

Our great history obligates us to participate in the second, still unfinished, fearsome, and final expansion of the economic horizon, if we do not want to lose our economic standing and drift toward decline. We have already experienced such a setback in Germany: we need only think of the fall of the Hansa and our failure to participate in the initial expansion of the horizon along the coastal lands of the Indian and Atlantic Oceans during the Age of Discovery. Furthermore, we still do not know what purpose our present colonies will serve in this period of world history, which is wiping away all borders and transforming the cosmopolitan fantasy of a skyward-raging idealism into a practical cosmopolitanism. Thus we must not only protect and maintain our colonies; we must also lift, advance, and develop them. Both present circumstances—the need to participate in economic expansion and to protect our colonies—demand our systematic attention to the peoples of the globe and to our colonies in particular. Yes, we must make a certain degree of ethnographic and colonial knowledge part of the public domain of our nation. We should praise the organizations dedicated to elevating our knowledge of the colonies. However, the role of imparting a lively and impressive perspective on the cultures of many peoples of the globe, particularly in our colonies, will be played by our ethnographic museums. These museums should become places to cultivate knowledge through lectures, discussions, and other means.

11. *The political task.* The two additional secondary tasks of ethnographic museums, recently emphasized by Adolf Bastian and Felix von Luschan, are also linked to overseas politics and trade.[51] First: the political. Ethnographic museums should enable an understanding of the characteristics of people abroad in the light of modern European culture, particularly for the diplomat, the officer, and the mariner, who are all in charge of colonial politics and administration of the colonial state overseas, as well as for the missionary, who works in the service of Christian civilization. The museums should provide education so that political errors and unfortunate circumstances can be avoided and so that irregularities in the course of colonial relationships can be resolved swiftly. In particular, "the colonial administration should be made aware of customs and practices, as well as legal institutions and religious perspectives."[52] On the other hand, the state, as a colonial power, has certain

obligations to the ethnographic museums, which have been emphasized of late in the Netherlands. Notably, the German imperial government has been urged to address ethnographic tasks in regard to protectorates in Africa and Oceana.[53]

In this connection, two facts must be recalled.

The first is that ethnography as a science developed not only as a curious interest in the colonial territories.[54] It is much more attributable to *Development of Humankind* (1780), written in Europe "in the glimmer of the library's study lamp," spurring dilettantes from Jean-Jacques Rousseau's school to fantasize about "what civilization could learn from savagery." The actual experiences in the colonies gave rise to practical needs within societies that already had ethnographic interests; for example: in Batavia (Bataviaasch Genootschap voor Kunsten en Wetenschappen, begun on April 24, 1778), and in Calcutta (Asiatic Society of Bengal, founded by Sir William Jones in 1784). All this occurred before the word "ethnography" (or "ethnology") was even coined.[55]

Second, we should recall the successes achieved by the Portuguese Jesuits in the sixteenth to seventeenth centuries in Japan and China. They recorded precise observations of local customs in intelligent detail. Their achievements were overcome by the jealousy and the careless, wanton arrival of the Spanish Franciscan and Dominican monks, and by the slander of Buddhist priests.

And what is the state today?

It is a fact that the murder of the most commendable Father Rascher in New Pomerania may be explained by a lack of wisdom on the part of Catholic missionaries, who interfered in the traditional ways of life and exhibited arrogance in their use of an unreasonably harsh penal power, which was difficult to justify and drove the natives to the brink of despair. Only a lack of historical awareness would lead one to consider European civilization as an absolute good, superior to all other cultures. By the same token, it would be irresponsible to believe that European civilization should be forced upon inhabitants of new colonies, displacing a locally evolved civilization that is not intrinsically of low value—and to furthermore believe that it can be forced upon them without methodical preparation toward the acceptance of its benefits. "The culture of the so-called savages," writes Felix von Luschan, "is not worse than our own—merely different."[56]

Insight perhaps could have averted the Herero uprising. The Hereros are a warlike shepherd folk—herdsmen who indulge in thievery along with other peoples of the steppes and desert. It would be difficult to condition them in a lasting way to an ordered cultural development such as arboriculture, as that would change their nomadic culture. Victor Hehn, in his book *Kulturpflanzen und Haustiere*, indicated the slowness of the transition from a herdsman lifestyle to one settled in permanent housing. He recalled the experiences of the French in Algeria: their conquest of the Arabs extended only as far as the cultivation of the date palm.[57] Hehn's characterization of the behavior of the Arabs in regard to European colonists can be applied to our experience with the Hereros. The classic case in point is the south and east of Palestine, as well as Arabia itself. If prosperity or a more comfortable life were achieved in a city, then the sons of the desert would attack, and rob the happy townspeople or relocate to their settlements. And then others would come and do the same to them. It was a period of constant conquering and being conquered, in which, strangely enough, a cultural flowering could develop in Arabia (the Minaean, the Sabaean, and the Nabataean Empires) as well as Palestine (the Hebrew kingdom).[58]

Notable in this regard are two further events outside Germany, which should help avert this type of lamentable political experience. Consider the report of a committee of the National Academy of Sciences from the newest colonial power, North America, about scientific research in the Philippines in the interest of politics. The report (printed in *Science* in 1905) was attached to a dispatch which President Roosevelt addressed to the Senate and the House of Representatives in February 1905. The report from the academic committee assumes that the first motive for a scientific investigation of the Philippines is to further the trade and commercial activity of the locals—a goal, by the way, that today, after centuries of usufruct of colonial possessions, is still followed in certain Dutch circles in regard to its colonies in the East Indies. Experience has shown that the goal is best reached through a comprehensive study of the facts and conditions in a true intellectual spirit. The text reads: "The honor of the United States demands that every means be employed in attempts to avoid errors from occurring out of ignorance in the treatment of the large and relatively helpless population of this island. This initial attempt of the United States to bring foreign tropical races under the wing of Anglo-Saxon civilization should be led by strong scientific findings and principles." In truth, these are noble and proud words, worthy of the American nation as it surges forward in the path of humanity.

Second, consider the administrative reform of England's tropical colony that was planned by the colonial secretary Alfred Lyttelton (who stepped down in December 1905). Prior to this point, the governor of the colony was required to serve eighteen months in the colony before receiving a six-month vacation. According to the reform, the governor would serve six months in the colony and then six months in the office of colonial affairs in London (during which, of course, the post would be retained and business continue). This policy, which seems practical in many ways but still requires a trial period, is based on the idea that it would assure that the governors were prepared to provide the most competent advice to all interested bodies and persons in the colony, spanning scientific, missionary, industrial, and commercial concerns. In this way, the prosperity of the colony may be significantly improved.[59]

To be welcomed as a positive development in Germany are the trips by members of Parliament to the (African) colonies, which one hopes will become a standing arrangement.

We still need to determine how far the efforts of colonial societies in Germany have contributed to the initiation of a transition in the treatment of colonial peoples according to the ethnographic viewpoint.

12. *The commercial task.* While daily life brings each of us into contact with geographical, colonial, and ethnographic terms, a thorough commercial capability requires more: the systematic acquisition of knowledge that has practical value for global trade. Such a commercial education should be aided by ethnographic museums, which must be available to businessmen who do business with foreign peoples, trading surplus local products for foreign (colonial) ones. Of interest in this regard, and characteristic of the pragmatic disposition of a real trading people, is the "Informatie" (November 1603), written shortly after the Dutch had begun to colonize the East Indian Archipelago in 1599. In the text, which is today considered by ethnographers and commercial geographers as an immensely valuable source, the salesman thoroughly and knowledgeably compiled a list of what wares could be exchanged in the Far East, what wares were desired, what the traditional trade routes were, and how trade could be conducted most advantageously.[60] Museums should not only provide instruction and advice but also share information on the foreign peoples' particularities, commodities, and desires, which may assist in trade. . . .

The justification of "ethnological instruction." The greatness—or even dignity—of ethnography's task emerges from its relationship with economics, which we detailed above. Although this has been stressed before, it has not been generally noticed, let alone recognized. And, in light of the importance of ethnography to the advancement of our nation,[61] we should consider the practical suggestion for "ethnological instruction," of which Bastian, Grosse, von Luschan, and Ratzel have recently spoken.[62] The general scope of such instruction encompasses the following specialized foci: (1) an expansion of the geographic education in schools through the inclusion of ethnographic, and principally colonial, information,[63] (2) the provision of ethnographic training for teachers in schools and universities,[64] (3) ethnographic preparation for diplomats and colonial officers,[65] and (4) the cultivation of ethnography, above all in trade schools and trade universities.

Owing to the fact that "the lively increase of our populace, the peerless upswing of our industry, the competence of our businessmen, in short, the vivid vitality of the German people has tied and integrated us to the global commerce" (from the speech of the state secretary of the interior in the Reichstag, December 1899), "it is a self-evident consequence that the younger, growing generation must be introduced to the factual knowledge of the questions and tasks they will have to engage in their lifetime: they must be ethnologically educated with appropriate instruction."[66] "The further that commerce expands," says Hassert, "the more closely it will be involved with the political and social relationships of the people; and the more involved the business dealings become, the greater will grow the demands on the knowledge and ability of its agents and businessmen, the merchants. . . . If commerce is to maintain its glowing development, a respected businessman who is on top of the latest developments is a definite requirement." Hassert also justifies the necessity of a geographic and ethnographic education for the businessman, for "he must know the lands where we want to obtain raw products and sell our fabricated items." He continues: "It is interesting for him to learn about . . . diverse parts of the world and the different types of people who live in them. He will get familiar with the conditions of the various political, social, and economic lives of the people." One would not object if the governments of other lands, for whom external trade has become one of the main factors of their economic and thus political lives, would seek systematic geographic and ethnographic education for their merchants. But under normal circumstances such instruction by the state is of far less importance than are the traditions of a centuries-long practical experience in trade.[67] It is precisely this wealth of practical experience that we lack and which we must try to replace with education. Traditionally, the German merchant is aware of the commodities of his local and neighboring regions, which form the borders of his distribution area. To a certain extent he may also be familiar with exotic products, which he might encounter in his intermediary trades. Today, however, completely new economic problems have arisen, linked with sales to, and imports from, overseas regions. These new problems require new solutions.

In general, geographic instruction in Germany is not on the same level as the instruction offered in other fields, apart from the trade universities and perhaps also trade schools.[68] In the field of ethnography only trade universities have undertaken initial steps for its instruction. If the young businessman of today, the future leader of trade, were cognizant of his great need for deeper geographic understanding in light of production capabilities and the potential market capacity of peoples, as well as for general ethnographic knowledge, then he would realize how much he needs to learn (if he was not among the lucky few who attended a trade university). In addition to prior training, he will frequently also lack access to literature tailored to his needs, and even where such literature is available he will still require appropriate guidance. If we leave aside the difficulty of being introduced to "ethnological instruction," the businessman's need for knowledge of the colonies could be achieved through a publication similar to the British *Census of India* or the Dutch *Koloniaal-Verslag*.

This type of publication, issued by the imperial government, would serve as a useful handbook or reference work for all who are preparing themselves for work involving the colonies. But it would not replace the need to systematically educate colonial administrators as well as diplomats, and to fulfill this purpose ethnography would need to be divided into officially accepted disciplines for those preparing to work in the colonies and those pursuing diplomatic efforts, with the aim that these representatives of the government in the colonies would quickly be able to understand the spirit and living circumstances of the natives. The publication must include a thorough survey of the pragmatically conceived history of colonization and imperialism of all eras and peoples. The establishment of general "ethnological" professorships at universities (as was demanded of the German government in 1900 by the German Colonial Society) has scarcely achieved all it should in this regard. Far more expedient is an innovation that is limited in its obligations and focused on a delineated practical goal, for which we can thank the wide perspective and generosity of an Englishman. At the University of Oxford at the start of 1906, a new subject was offered that focused on the scientific representation of history and the development of colonialism. Germany should strongly consider such an arrangement.[69] We recommend such education not because we wish to "strive for a bleak world domination" but so that we can learn from history. We will always need to keep learning, so that a German global empire can flower and so "that all sides can enjoy the absolute trust of tranquil, honest, and peaceful neighbors."[70] It is perhaps asking too much to demand "that ethnology be given the primary role in the education of colonial officers on the basis of what is right and sensible." However, it is justified to claim: "The introduction of ethnological instruction is a demand not only in the interest of science but also in the interest of morality and national prosperity."[71]

From the image of the past, which is the real truth and from which we obtain our ideals, we gain an awareness of the necessity for "ethnological instruction." Bastian was committed to this idea, and his discussion of it seems prescient: "Error in judgment stems from error in understanding. Heads become heated, heads are beaten bloody, and this can easily lead to . . . insubordination, to rebelliousness, and so forth, so that finally we must appeal to some 'ultima ratio.' . . . At this point, expeditions will have to be accoutered or armored ships will have to be sent in order to control further barbarization. Everything is in danger of being engulfed . . . it will all cost much in blood and gold. . . . The teacher can offer resolutions at far less expense than the apparatus of a military demonstration."[72] We might add: brutal colonial wars, which have made other nations vast and rich, do not fit with our *Furor teutonicus*. Brutal egotism in colonial matters is not the German way.

The Side Effects

13. In addition to their secondary tasks, ethnographic museums have an array of valuable and wide-ranging side effects. The most prominent of these are artistic pleasure and creative inspiration. Ethnographic museums should care about both of these deeply, even though they are neither institutes of technical education nor art collections.

14. *Artistic pleasure.* The joy of art present in ethnographic museums and in the objects they collect has not been sufficiently noted. Visual arts, like poetry, religion, and music, are "a gift to the world and to the people, not a private inheritance of fine, educated men." Even tribes that we call primitive, wild, or cannibalistic have produced art with a degree of development that is beyond what we know today and that, as the author affirms through his own experience, can garner praise from recognized artists of today. Examples include the exquisite carvings of the Hervey Islands and New Zealand, which feature, respectively, delicate, net-like

linear ornamentation and massive, dominating spiral patterns. These works are masterpieces, and we have produced nothing comparable in our culture, since woodcarving has lost its preeminence among our folk art. The carvings from these two regions are examples of high art that developed independently of outside experience, and perhaps exactly for this reason artists implemented forms that may belong to the same branch of art found elsewhere but possess an entirely different character. And all this in worlds that are untouched by the marble beauty of Greece; that have no inkling of the monumental, symbol-laden artworks of West and South Asia; and that are unaffected by the "decorative arts and meditative art" of East Asia.[73] Significant value has also long been recognized in the artistic expressions of Asia, particularly the decorative art objects of its eastern region,[74] and in the bronzes from Benin in West Africa since the moment of their discovery.[75] But in recent years, particularly as a result of the lively activity of the Dutch Colonial Society "Oost en West," our awareness has spread to other areas. Examples include the minor arts and artistic handicraft of the Malay Islands, such as artists' accomplished carving in wood, ivory, horn, and so forth, for the hilts of krises in Java, Bali, and Madura.[76] Additionally, there are many masterpieces of textile art: the aristocratic gold- and silver-threaded silk weavings from Atjeh, with their magical allure; the *tjindes* (ikat-patterned fabric) of the Grissee; the cloths of Sumba, including the batiks of Solo, Preanger, and Madura, with their noble gravitas and fantastical patterns; and the evocative sarongs of Bentenan. Other examples are Javanese copperwares, with their fine chisel work, and the bamboo boxes, with clean and stylistic ornamentation, from the Bataks of North Sumatra, from Borneo and Timor.[77]

15. Today, art is increasingly recognized as a necessary correlative to worthwhile human existence and as a means of betterment for the masses. This is to say, it is no longer considered an expensive luxury for those of privilege. We need to reckon with this trend toward the aesthetic formation of the human subject, a factor that underlies the multifaceted obligations of our museums. The public's ever-growing interest in the arts has a twofold influence on museums' transformation: first, on the acquisition of inventory, and second, on the spaces and ways in which art is displayed. In recognizing the enduring value of all forms of beauty—for all people and in all times—ethnographic museums cannot ignore the highest artistic desires of the public. To keep up with the times, museums must become more cognizant of the aesthetic secondary effect of the ethnographic objects to increasingly facilitate the objects' aesthetic

reception (cf. §90). The issue of artistic quality has not been given its due because of the zeal for collecting (spurred by the suggestive force of the idea that primitive peoples are facing extinction) and because of the general dependence of fruitful scientific research on the quantity of objects. Only a few museums consider this factor within the parameters they have set for themselves (see §32). Among the ethnographic museums, the Dresden Museum is a widely recognized exception, as is the Hamburg Museum among the museums of applied arts.

16. *The creative inspiration.* The consideration of creative inspiration is similar to that of artistic pleasure: if it has been emphasized at all, it has not been emphasized enough. The ornamentation of the so-called primitive tribes, which developed independently of European tradition, is not only a rich source of new forms for European decorative arts but a way to introduce European culture to certain new technical skills or even applicable tools.[78] The influence of Asia in artistic and technical realms has been felt in the West in recent times; superficial knowledge of East Asia dates back to the seventeenth and eighteenth centuries.[79] Japanese art objects and painting, as well as Chinese (and Japanese) ceramics, have provided European arts and art-making techniques with new materials and new directions. Asia is also the source, as we have seen above, of the *chiné* technique used in making modern textiles. It may well transpire that the Dutch East Indies and even certain areas in the South Seas will play a role similar to Asia's, providing a source for new styles of ornamentation.[80] Furthermore, when our culture once again prioritizes love and sentiment over reason and knowledge, and when artistic sense is a greater guide than the taste of the parvenu, then we will witness new textile techniques (such as batik) and the rebirth of old art forms (such as wood carving), which have been devalued through mechanization.

The author would also like to express his hope that museums of ethnology will gain in educational importance. Moral achievements, not intellectual ones, are of utmost importance to the world. They allow us to move into the realm of ideals, which, in turn, elevate us and encourage us to devote our will to the service of a practical fulfillment of the known Good. The museum ethnographer should not be primarily interested in the discovery of new truths. Rather, he should be devoted to furthering an education that deepens our understanding of the world. This education should guide and prepare individuals to focus their efforts on service to the nation. Ethnographic museums should emphasize this final point in particular. The Germany of the future will be increasingly oriented toward foreign countries, and ethnographic museums should strive to awaken interest in and understanding of their character!

The Special Purposes of Ethnographic Museums[81]

When we review our previous discussions, we see a gamut of obligations and requirements that ethnographic museums ideally should fulfill. Obviously, no ethnographic museum can do so in complete measure, for reasons simply beyond their control. Rather, the individual ethnographic museums whose directors are aware of these overall demands and see the role of museums as more than the mere compiling and housing of ethnographic artifacts will always emphasize one or another aspect of their duties. They may at the outset see one responsibility as their main, or even only, goal. In the future, this tendency may become more pronounced.

The Independence of Secondary Duties

18. This is the case with colonial museums—for example, in Berlin (next to the Museum of Folklore) and in Haarlem (in the Netherlands)—or trade museums—for example, in Bremen (in connection with the Museum of Ethnology).[82] In these museums, the national-colonial and commercial subfields, previously deemed secondary, have become independent. This shift also brings out the more specific conception of the trade museum as an instructive collection of raw materials and imported products, with scientifically ordered samples of stock for export.

Kurt Hassert has correctly emphasized the broader significance of ethnography for the trade museum: "Trade museums are among the best means for furthering an education in business. Today, many assume that these museums are nothing but a display of sample items destined for export. There is, however, a fundamental difference between the two. Whereas the trade display deals with sales and changes in response to industrial production and fashion, the museum seeks permanence— an exhibition chiefly of the people's labor via a display of their particular products. An example of such a museum is the Museum of Ethnology in Bremen."[83] The display of export samples would be cast in an ethnographic light inasmuch as it focuses on reproductions of ethnographic originals that were intended for export. Such a sample stock could be combined with a collection of the original artworks that were reproduced for export (though this would not be desirable from an ethnographic perspective). The sample of stock for export might also be combined with the artistic elements that may be used in trade, such as local ornamentation, and so on.

The Independence of Side Effects

19. To date, no effort has been made to bring out the artistic value of ethnographic objects, which are considered secondary effects in ethnological collections, or to erect a museum of ethnographic objects devoted to art or creative inspiration. In spite of this omission, the aesthetic delight which many ethnographic objects offer is obvious and would render the creation of such a museum fitting.

20. *A museum of ethnographic artworks.* As has been postulated above (§14), more attention should be paid to the aesthetic qualities of the objects in ethnographic museums (cf. §58). And below we discuss the museums' obligation to provide an aesthetically appropriate home for the collected objects (§90ff.). For now, let us consider the idea of a museum composed of artistically valuable ethnographic objects exhibited in a tranquil atmosphere that allows time for their appreciation. One can expect that wherever this idea might first be implemented, the majority of artifacts will come from the cultures of the Near East, South Asia, and East Asia.[84] Pre-Columbian art, with its underdeveloped, perspectiveless painting and its stiff and squared-off sculptural forms, could play no role in such a museum. Only in Peruvian ceramics—with their skillful representations verging on humor and brilliant portraiture—are these qualities superseded. The rest of American art derives its value and coherence from rich symbolism and allusions to the superhuman. It brings to mind oriental art but lacks its softer and rounder forms and its better-observed proportions. Neither arbitrary nor wayward, the predilection in individual works for the monstrous and grotesquely distorted nevertheless impresses with its barbarism and repugnant ugliness.[85] Only the splendid bronze art (lost-wax casting) from Benin in western Africa, together with Asian art from which it was possibly derived, can fill us with wonder and joy and speak to us intelligibly. With their vivid and advanced naturalism, the Beninese heads approach the level of true portraiture, able to capture and re-create what is seen.[86] This art is especially adept for reenvisioning the Negro and the European man but also is excellently suited for animals, especially the rooster and the leopard. In a museum for non-European art, the bronzes from Benin would deserve an eminent position that would, admittedly, be a struggle to fill.

21. *An ethnographic-technical museum.* While the technical or formal properties of at least some ethnographic objects would offer creative inspiration, the idea of dedicating a museum to this urge is less likely

to be up for discussion than the idea of elevating artistic pleasure to a primary purpose. Currently, all care for ethnographic material that could inspire our art, and especially our handicrafts, is left to collections of prints and drawings and to museums of applied arts. If the creative inspiration issuing from ethnographic artifacts were to become the primary focus of a museum, then these collections would likely form the starting point.

Limiting the General Mission Through Exclusion of Certain Types of Objects

22. The specialized goals that collections of ethnographic materials may set as their primary foci relate not only to the secondary tasks and secondary effects of ethnographic museums. Rather, their principal goal can bring about fragmentation into a great range of special tasks set independently as ends in their own right. It is tempting to assert that there is currently even an inclination toward emphasizing just any aspect of the museum's primary task. In this way, the act of collecting can be guided by the preference for one of the general forms of cultural expression, such as clothing, housing, art, music, or religion; or by the predilection for certain types of objects, such as vessels, containers, money, arms, or weavings; or from the viewpoint of the materials or the cultural period.

23. This movement toward the development of certain aspects of the general task of ethnographic museums has initially been evident among private collections, where it bears the character of a collection of rarities and curiosities. What elevates these collections above the cabinets of curiosities of prior centuries is that they no longer consist of a wild, colorful mix of objects of all types. Rather, they are planned out, guided by an idea, and ultimately limited to a particular group of objects of a certain type. This group is then developed further—possibly by broadening the geographic scope as far as possible or extending the chronological range. In this way it is conceivable, although not certain, to attain the basis for a study of the interrelation of different material forms and, finally, the representation of their history. Thus, there are collections, for example, of bows, of pipes, of spoons, of shoes, of cowries, as well as of porcelain, of jade objects, and of stone tools. Even a collection of straw hats is planned. The greatest and most significant example of this type of collection is that devoted to religious history in

the Musée Guimet, which has been state property since 1888 when it was moved to Paris from Lyon.

24. But this increasing desire to develop a particular aspect of the broader field occurs not only in private collections. Ethnographic museums themselves are unquestionably tending toward restrictions, either by deaccessioning certain categories of their holdings or discontinuing the expansion of certain areas of ethnography, or through a decision to concentrate on specific aspects of cultural life, geographic areas, or periods of cultural history.

25. *The exclusion of the applied arts from South and East Asia.* In the field of South and East Asian minor arts, the exclusion of certain types of objects from active collecting has allowed museums of decorative arts and cabinets of prints and drawings to challenge the status of ethnographic museums, despite the fact that relevant works from Japan attained in some respects the pinnacle of artistic achievement. In effect, ethnographic museums have voluntarily relinquished the cultivation of this field, accepting items only if their form, their antiquity, or the content of their representation is exceptionally valuable. Examples of Asian minor arts already possess a general relationship with European minor arts: in both places, artistic sensibility revealed itself in the same categories of small objects. Asian minor arts appear to have had a strong influence on European minor arts, and hopefully these exemplary prototypes can also offer stimuli in the future. The refusal of ethnographic museums to provide special care for these types of works is therefore well founded, and its justification is generally acknowledged.[87]

26. *The separation of the European collections.* In Germany there is general agreement at least in principle about the permissibility (or necessity) of separating parts of the European collection—except those concerned with the European Ural-Altaic peoples, such as the Lapps, Finns, and possibly the Magyars—and placing them in the newly established museums of folklore. This practice, however, has yet to be implemented everywhere; it has not yet happened in Dresden, for example. Although the European ethnographic collections in Berlin are still held in the Museum of Ethnology, they are not on display. In the Paris Trocadéro such collections are displayed alongside those from Africa, Asia, Oceania, and America, reflecting the fact that museological issues are generally lagging in France. In this case, the ethnographic museum's process of self-limitation has not yet made perceivable progress.

27. *The possible separation of prehistoric materials.* Next, we come to the question, scarcely raised and already answered, of whether prehistoric

materials from outside Europe should be part of the prehistoric collections or the ethnographic ones.

Since clarity about the terminology involved is vital to comprehending any controversy, we must first determine what we mean by the term "prehistoric" in this context. When the word "prehistoric" is applied to ethnographic objects of primitive people, its meaning appears to be narrower than the word implies in the literal sense or in relation to the phenomena it originally designated. Obviously, the term is employed in a general sense for a period of the past that is preserved today in material remains only, without a contemporaneous written record (or interpretation). The choice of designating this period "prehistoric" is premised on an understanding of the word "history" that foregrounds not the development of culture or general intellectual movements but the idea that the history of a people starts when it begins to develop a fixed, written literature. This interpretation of history is clearly not applicable to primitive people. When, for example, would "history" begin on the islands of the South Seas? With the exception of a few, possibly indigenous examples of pictograms that are incomprehensible to us, history seems to survive only in oral forms. There is no literary transmission recorded by the indigenous people themselves that gives, or rather gave, their "history." If it is claimed that "these people entered history when the first Europeans stepped upon their islands," then the definition of history is apparently different from the one given above, based on textual tradition. The contradiction between this understanding of the term and that in the word "prehistoric" becomes even clearer if we consider the latter simply as synonymous with happening "prior" to history and without recalling the meaning with which the word "history" was imbued. We generally just assume a meaning for "history" that works with our understanding of "prehistory." Wooden objects in New Zealand, for example, would be deemed prehistoric objects, since they existed prior to the Europeans' arrival and prior to written history. If so, what about the status of the wooden objects that were created *after* the Europeans' arrival but are unquestionably similar and of equal value to those made previously? Must these objects then count as historic works and be separated from the older versions? The answer is indisputably that New Zealanders were, like all islanders in the South Seas before the appearance of Europeans, "prehistoric" in the sense that they existed at a cultural level similar to what we imagine for people in European prehistory. With the arrival of the Europeans, the character of their conditions, which is labeled prehistoric in the context of general cultural history, was propelled toward an image of our modern cultural standing. This may have begun quietly, but it continues unbroken and with increasing speed. This influence irredeemably overcame the old, forcing it directly toward the new, with destructive effects. But there was no sudden, dramatic transition. With the arrival of the Europeans, the New Zealanders did not abruptly become something different. There was also no development of written literature. The concept of history that presupposes the foundation of fixed literary production or even the emergence of a historical sensibility—which is implied in the conventional coinage of the word "prehistoric"—is inadequate.[88] The history of a people in a narrower sense begins not when they start to develop written communication but when they come into contact with a foreign people.[89] This contact causes one of the two cultures (or a third one) to produce a reliable account, so that we know about it today (ἱστορία οἶδα "I know," ἵστωρ "witness"). In this sense, everything that occurred in Germany prior to the Roman invasion was prehistoric. Such contact between the outside world and a culturally or politically backward region need not result in its permanent expansion in cultural constitution or habitus or of political horizons.[90] How Japan experienced the renewed contact with European foreigners in the middle of the previous century can be gleaned from the history of Japan and the history of ancient Britain. "Following the period of the Roman invasion of Britannia, which is documented in the clear light of historical writing, there occurred a second, mythical, and, in a certain sense, prehistoric time after the Romans departed."[91] Thus there are also cases in which a period, preserved by history clear as day, once again descends into the darkness of a prehistoric time—until day breaks again.[92]

28. In relation to ethnographic artifacts, "prehistoric" or "prior to history" cannot be applied in the sense of occurring before the time when a people began to develop coherent, continuous, and fixed traditions, or in the sense of occurring prior to contact with a foreign people who then provided an account of the contact.[93] Instead, the term in our ethnographic context is used more narrowly to indicate objects from previous eras, belonging to cultural periods more or less lost from memory (the Stone Age or Bronze Age) and bearing evidence of monuments that are comparable to the prehistory of the Mediterranean and northern Europe. In this narrower sense, the (Paleolithic) artifacts, for example, of the so-called Moa hunters of New Zealand are considered prehistoric in comparison with the Neolithic culture of the Maori that continues into the present. Or, to put it more generally, prehistoric

can describe any archaeological evidence from a cultural period that is comparable to one of the three prehistoric epochs of the Mediterranean and northern Europe (the Old Stone Age, the New Stone Age, and the Bronze Age).

29. Overall, ethnographic museums of today will have little inclination to remove those pieces in their collection that are deemed prehistoric according to our narrow definition. By this we refer, in particular, to the prehistoric collection originating in America.[94] Pieces from today's primitive tribes from Asia, the South Seas and the Americas[95] are of course not even in question. This is the case despite the fact that at least the Paleolithic pieces from prehistoric Africa and Asia are likely to be understood only in relation to those from Europe.[96] The existence of a Stone Age in Africa, of which we have Paleolithic evidence from all parts of the continent, has disappeared just as comprehensively from the memory of the indigenous peoples as from our own. Additionally, the Iron Age predominating in Africa today is not connected to its Paleolithic past by an intermediate Bronze Age of the type that occurred in Europe and South Asia.[97] In this respect Africa resembles America and northern Asia.

Thus, in light of our current understanding of African prehistory and its suspected connections to the oldest prehistory of Europe, nothing stops us from removing the Paleolithic materials from ethnographic collections and placing them in prehistoric ones instead. However, deeper insight into ethnographic relationships is likely to show other ways in which aspects of prehistory can extend into the present. For example, there are sites where (Neolithic) stone tools are found together with contemporaneous artifacts of a different sort, such as pottery fragments or bone tools. Such survivals can also be identified in South Asia, where a true bronze culture superseded the Neolithic period. And this continuation goes beyond the way that prehistoric elements such as stone axes or bronze spear tips are today regarded as fetishes—a fact that could scarcely form a successful argument for leaving prehistoric materials in ethnographic collections.[98] Such insight links prehistory even more tightly to ethnography. But, on the other side, quite apart from the attitude of ethnographic museums toward non-European prehistory, there is already a plausible theory that the Paleolithic-prehistoric cultures of Europe, Asia, and Africa are widely separated provinces of an originally united culture.

Fundamentally, the result of such comparisons between the prehistory of the ancient peoples of the Mediterranean and northern Europe and that in other regions is generally to broaden the horizon of the prehistoric collections beyond the prehistory of their own fatherland to include the prehistory of greater Europe and beyond. In the future, over time, following the comprehensive study of similar materials, the scope of prehistoric collections will expand to include the prehistory of at least the Mediterranean people and northern Europe. Currently, if we examine the actual prehistoric collections of today, we see that non-European prehistory is exhibited with European prehistory (seen, for example, in the biggest prehistoric departments such as the British Museum in London, but also in small ones, like the Basel Museum of Ethnography).[99] Accordingly, pieces from North America, Egypt, and southern India can all be found together in the "prehistoric cabinet" in Basel.[100] Similarly, in the Galeries d'Anatomie in the Jardin des Plantes in Paris, there is an exhibition of the Stone Age that includes some of the most ancient artifacts from the time when cavemen were first differentiated from the animal world. Here, stone tools from all areas and epochs on earth are exhibited together, including finds from prehistoric Europe and Africa, as well as America and Asia, where remnants of the Stone Age continue today, and even the South Seas, where the Stone Age is largely still existent among the Melanesians. Thus we can conclude that, in realizing the proposed expansion of the horizons of prehistoric collections, the displays may invigorate exhibits of items from prehistoric Mediterranean and northern European areas through a comparative analysis with the very recently supplanted "prehistoric" cultures of certain tribes in much more remote regions.[101] These include the people of New Zealand and the cultures that are currently experiencing the transition to the Iron Age, such as the "prehistoric" people of central New Guinea and certain regions of Melanesia, as well as some Brazilian jungle Indians.[102]

Limiting the General Mission Through Emphasis on Certain Aspects (Specialization)[103]

So far we have discussed the exclusion of entire groups of objects from ethnographic collections as a means of limiting their purview. The subject has distracted us somewhat from our inquiry into the specialized tasks that ethnographic museums can set for themselves. More important to achieving this goal is the emphasis on the specific areas of research that remain within the realm of ethnography,[104] as well as the emphasis on specific geographic regions, aspects of cultural life, or periods of cultural history. By focusing on this shift in emphasis, we return to our original train of thought.

31. It is in any case an obvious advantage to emphasize a positive method as opposed to a negative decision. Here as elsewhere, specialization would allow institutions to become leaders in their chosen field. Specialization would diversify the currently uniform appearance of ethnographic museums. Furthermore, the process would distribute among different collections the overarching responsibility shared by all ethnographic museums.[105]

32. *The preference for specific geographic areas.* The lowest level of specialization that an ethnographic museum can set for itself while still fulfilling the general mission of ethnographic museums is to focus on a specific geographic area. It remains the lowest level even if the concentration concerns a region where the highest achievements of the human mind found their first manifestation in material culture. A case in point is the Dresden Museum, which was able to develop first-rate collections—on a par, in some respects, with those in the largest museums—by focusing on Indonesia and the Pacific. Recently the Hamburg Museum decided to focus on Melanesia. The large Berlin Museum was initially intended as a collection devoted to the so-called *Naturvölker* (primitive people), whereas the collections of Indian, Chinese, and Japanese artifacts attained their vast extent in contravention of the original plans.[106] Adolf Bastian, who was unable to curtail this expansion, perhaps entertained the idea of establishing separate oriental museums of art—Chinese, Japanese, Indian, etc.—as soon as financial conditions would allow it. Such an intention seems to be implied in his essay "Die wechselnden Phasen im geschichtlichen Sehkreis (II) auf asiatischem Kontinent," in which he speaks of separating art "from the existing ethnological museums . . . whereas the 'bulk' of the material (on a broadly defined foundation) has to remain in these institutions . . . associated with the diverse human races populating the globe."[107]

33. Among the more advanced specialized purposes that aim to foster a particular cultural aspect or period of cultural history, two merit closer attention. They include religious history and archaeology, both eminently suited as organizing principles (possibly in connection with a geographical limitation) for the creation of independent collections of ethnographic materials.

34. *The notion of religious history.* As mentioned, the history of religion was the exclusive guiding principle of the Musée Guimet (previously in Lyon, now in Paris; see §23 above) when it was still a private collection of

ethnographic objects. Guimet's plan was originally for a general museum of comparative religion, but it was later restricted to Asian religions and in turn expanded to Asian ethnography in general. Today, the history of religion is but one of several foci of the collection. A department of "Religious Collections of Oriental Cults of the Early Christian Period" has also been separated from the other ethnographic and historical materials in the large complex of the British Museum.

35. The Musée Guimet departs from a straightforward presentation of the religions of primitive people—which is justified for three reasons. First, primitive religious objects consist largely of amulets and fetishes which are produced in great numbers by all primitive tribes—peoples who intuitively perceived the natural world to be teeming with demons. Such religious items also include unaltered natural objects that were not manipulated by human hands, as well as artifacts of a foreign world: that is, objects with peculiar or unusual forms or objects that had attained their meaning under some strange and exceptional conditions. Such items were originally viewed with a devout gaze and played a part in cults practiced in private.[108] It would be a worthless endeavor to collect such indifferent objects—be it a stone, a shell, a mole's pelt, a bird's beak, a tooth, a foreign coin, or even a stone axe from previous inhabitants found in the ground. Second, as a consequence of our formerly prominent prejudicial view, which was based more on naiveté than prudishness, all these surviving objects of the "wild" tribes were understood as being related either to "blood" (or war) or "service to the devil" (religion). Thus a large number of items have been identified as religious objects, while they may, in truth, have only had profane and unholy purposes. Third—and most crucially—at present our knowledge about the use and purpose of true religious items by the so-called primitive tribes is entirely insufficient. Most explanations we have today are either interpretations by outsiders or the opinions of natives answering the leading questions of inquiring strangers. The critical curator or researcher of religious studies should be wary about both kinds of explanation. Only a native religious tradition can be a valid source, and this exists only in exceptional cases. Even if such sources are available, we are still far from having achieved a true comprehension of the religious history of primitive tribes.

Indisputably, representations of mythological material and religious figures, just like mythology and religion in general, can be understood and studied best where they are accompanied by religious literature produced by well-versed individuals belonging to that culture and writing for their own people. In the field of ethnography, the only source material we have of this sort concerns oriental religions.[109]

36. Although this situation seems to call for the study of religious history to be limited to the cultural groups of Asia in ancient and modern times, this would not be the right approach. Whatever the source of the burgeoning of religious reasoning—be it the pre-Columbian tribes or other primitive peoples—it would be wrong to exclude it from study. The undertaking should instead be broadened so as to illuminate all forms of religious life. Time and again we are reminded that in preliterary times the civilizations of Asia (indeed, like the peoples of northern Europe and the Mediterranean, especially the Greeks) exhibited customs and concepts relating to magic, fetishism, and ghost and ancestor worship, which find their closest analogies among the contemporary primitive people.[110] In some social circles in Asia, in fact, remnants of such customs persist to this day. In addition, ethnography, and religious studies in particular, already has a number of trusted sources in the form of critical observers of religious practices among primitive peoples. We have exact and well-founded knowledge of pre-Columbian cultural groups, particularly of the ancient Mexicans and their offshoots—the Pueblo Indians, who are eagerly studied today—as well as groups in other areas of Central America.[111]

37. Looking beyond the religions of Asia, the next important areas of collection concern demonstrably religious objects that express an idea. And, if possible, these objects should give a reliable indication of their origin and possess meaning that is accessible through literary research. A verifiably religious object should be identified as such by several observers who independently agree with each other and attest to its status. Alternatively, it must be comparable to a similar item from a related culture that is itself a verifiably religious object. Certain attributes that have a definite religious meaning can also serve to authenticate the religious status of an object. A large percentage of objects, however, will have to be accepted as being religious on good faith, based on the judgment of an authority who has proved to be a well-regarded, conscientious collector, observer, and researcher.

38. By deciding to no longer limit the historical study of religious thought to the ancient and modern civilizations of Asia, ethnographic museums dedicated to religion will lose their art historical character. If, however, such a restriction is left in place, the museum will inevitably become art historical, as we can see in the Musée Guimet. While one cannot say that all Asian art is religious, the inverse is true to a large extent: all religious representations from the major faiths of Asia are art. The art historical character of a religious collection would gain further in prominence—to the detriment of the pursuit of the history of religion—if collections dispensed with the systematic pursuit of a cult's

artifacts and emphasized instead only representations of religious figures and subjects.

39. *The archaeological idea.* A collection devoted to the history of
religion in the limited sense and one broadened to include its wider
conception would share the following: in both cases the collection
would include material that we could describe as archaeological. This
material is defined by clear boundaries and is well suited to become
the specialized or even primary purpose of a museum of ethnographic
objects. In at least one respect, however, the scientific interests of an
institute dedicated to such materials, as well as the aesthetic and art
historical interests of institutes with general art historical or primarily
artistic purposes, can pose a much greater danger to ethnographic
museums than the scientific interests of prehistoric collections pose
to their "prehistoric" materials. For example, the artworks of Benin,
despite having reached their height only a couple of centuries ago, are
rightly called antiquities. Yet today, much of this material is housed in
museums of decorative arts, such as that in Hamburg. Similarly, the
wonderful stone sculptures of the palace of M'schatta (east of Jordan
at the gateway to the Syrian desert, as yet of indeterminate date) are
found—at least at this point—in the Kaiser-Friedrich-Museum in Berlin rather than the Museum of Ethnography or the collection of Near
Eastern antiquities.[112]

Berlin newspapers repeatedly discussed the creation of a "Museum
of Asian Monuments [*Altertümer*]" in the foreseeable future (cf., for
example, the entertainment section in the *Tägliche Rundschau* of March
15 and the *Morgenausgabe* of April 6, 1905). This designation probably
stems from a mistreatment of the term "Asian Art Museum" by Wilhelm
Bode. If not, then the term *Altertümer* was used in the sense of *Antiq-
uitäten* (given that artistically valuable objects are almost always works of
a past era) and not in the sense of *archäologische Denkmäler.* This usage
would be in keeping with the suggestion in Bode's essay that the Persian-
Islamic collection of the Kaiser-Friedrich-Museum also be made into a
separate museum. In general, there is much uncertainty about the remit
of the proposed imperial institute of Asian art.[113]

40. In the course of history, new layers are continually being laid upon
older ones. In the field of cultural history, we can "archaeologically"
identify layers or periods of the past that seem to have disappeared
but are, in fact, preserved in art objects of a recognizable style. Such
monuments, in contrast to those of prehistoric epochs, can be given
absolute or at least relative chronological dates by reference to (possibly
contemporaneous) literary sources. These sources convey information

and other details about the objects' origins and purposes. By using this information we can situate artifacts within history in the narrower sense defined above, or we can associate them with facts that lie within our understanding of history. Accordingly, "prehistoric archaeology" is a *contradictio in adjecto*.[114] Only through written sources can we make sense of the subjects in archaeological monuments that derive from history, religion, life, and poetry. Archaeological evidence, on the other hand, is indispensable for understanding the literary sources that are not directly related to it.

The word "archaeological" is not normally applied in this wider sense. Nothing, however, stands in the way of using it in this way. We can compare the relationship between "archaeological" and "archaeology" (denoting a science and the embodiment of all archaeological artifacts) with that of "prehistoric" and "prehistory" and their usage. Owing to the primarily artistic value and character of (classical and ancient) monuments, "archaeological" is commonly employed to approach the subject from the point of view of art, just as the term "Ancient World" [*Altertum*] approaches it from that of a preoccupation with history. When archaeology was still primarily concerned with classical antiquity, archaeology regarded the objects of study from the perspective of art: that is, with a focus on formal characteristics. To analyze the meaning of the artifacts as part of the multifaceted requirements of life in the past to this day is left to classical studies [*Altertumslehre*], while the evaluation of these interpretations is left to history. This division of labor is easily explained and implemented in the field of classical archaeology, with its numerous subdisciplines calling for specialists. However, this division is neither possible nor desirable for archaeology beyond the classical world. Interestingly, we lack a word that describes archaeological objects, or ancient monuments, from the viewpoint of general cultural history.

Among the cultural periods that are preserved through artistic monuments and possibly inscriptions, we can identify the following within the area of cultural history that is currently classified as part of ethnography.

41. To begin with Asia:

1. *Ancient Indian art and its offshoots*, specifically in India.
   (a) The older, national Indian art, including Buddhist and Brahmin art with a Persian influence. The ancient Persian style itself was inherited from Near Eastern forms.[115]

(b) The art of the Gandhara monasteries, so-called Greco-Buddhist art: that is, the Buddhist art of India influenced by ancient Roman imperial art. The types and compositions of the Gandharan school became fundamental to the religious art of central Asia and the Far East (Tibet, China, Korea, Japan) and remain in evidence there today.[116]

(c) The art of Jainism, represented best in the structure built on Mount Abu (in the eleventh to thirteenth centuries under the Chalukya Dynasty). Its figurative content is dependent on Buddhism,[117] and its fine décor, omitting the figural, was prototypical for the marble filigree featured in the Islamic art of Ahmadabad in India, among other places.[118]

(d) The medicval Brahmin art (from the sixth to the thirteenth/fourteenth century). The Vishnu art of this type rests upon the translation of meaning from older Buddhist imagery. In contrast, the Shaivite art was more independent and contemporaneous with the last centuries of Buddhism in India. It was part of a national movement that created types of nature gods and developed a rich mythology.[119]

And further, outside India:

(e) The Indonesian art, the art of ancient Burma (Pegu, the Mon Empire, Dravidic cultivations of southern India, ancient Siam), and above all, ancient Cambodia (the empire of the Khmer, similarly under rulers of Indonesian heritage), which possessed grandiose and architectonic ruins of equal art historical importance to the temple of Angkor Wat, the temple of the Brahmin (Vishnu) cult.[120]

(f) The Indian art of the Malaysian Archipelago, especially from Java and Bali, whose most meaningful creation—and perhaps the greatest construction of the Buddhist cultural world overall—the temple of Borobudur in the Javanese province of Kedu, belonged to the northern school of the cult of Buddhism.[121]

2. *The (Arsacid) Sassanid art of Persia.* Although more in-depth research has only just begun, we can at least say that it, chronologically and artistically, forms one of the mediating links between the Hellenistic and Roman art of antiquity and the Arabic art of the Islamic world. Meanwhile, more research is necessary to investigate its relationship

with the older art of the Near East as well as with contemporaneous Asian art from the regions farther to the east and with Byzantine art.

3. *The newly discovered art of central Asia and Turkistan*,[122] which conveys a predominantly Iranian and northwest Indian character. On the one hand, this art forms the link between ancient and Christian Byzantine art, while on the other, it links Indian art to that of China and Japan.

Thus, so far as regions of Asia are concerned, this is a complete list of the archaeological cultures that are currently known to us and that ethnography is obligated to study.[123]

The archaeology of western Asia in the last centuries before Christ, namely the Hellenistic period and imperial Rome,[124] is best considered in its traditional connection together with the earlier archaeological stages of the Middle East and the classical world (as well as early Christianity), even though the boundaries of these regions with the Far East become increasingly blurred. The Islamic art of Persia and its neighboring areas—including India—will have to be excluded too from our list, for it cannot be considered in isolation from that of the areas to the west of the Euphrates all the way to Spain, where its legacy is still alive.

42. In Africa we exclude from the outset the entire North, particularly Egypt and the kingdom of Meroë in Ethiopia, with its peculiar blend of oriental and Greek art even prior to the Roman imperial era.[125] Meroë received no mention in ancient Egyptian sources but was known to the Greeks through Cambyses' campaign to Egypt and survived until the Ptolemaic era.[126] The only remaining areas that fall under the scope of ethnographic study are therefore:

4. *The remains of ancient Benin* (coast of Guinea, western Africa). As we have established above, these remains are rightly deemed antiquities.

5. *The enigmatic ruins of Zimbabwe in Rhodesia* (southeastern Africa). Owing to the lack of any conclusive information from documents—such as inscriptions—these finds must for the time being remain "prehistoric." Richard Nicklin Hall has pursued successful excavations there in recent years.[127]

43. By far the richest treasures of archaeological character in ethnographic museums are in the New World: America. They belong to various cultures that may be organized into three larger groupings.[128]

They may be designated as follows:

6. *In the Mexican cultural area*, the Nahuas, the Maya, and the Zapotec/Mixtec presented three coequal tribal groups. Each developed its particular cultural attributes, in accordance with its particular character.[129]

7. *The Isthmus cultural area*, with Costa Rica and Nicaragua on one side and Colombia on the other. The Greater Antilles may also be included here. This cultural area is idiosyncratic. As a whole, it functions as a divide between the culminating points of North and South America, with relationships in both directions. There is no lack of exchange and influence.[130]

8. *The Peruvian cultural area.* In Peru, the Quechua and the Kolya (Colla, also known as the Aymará) of the highlands and the Incan Peruvian tribes of the coast subsumed under the name Yunka (from the north to the south: Chimú, Mochika, or Tsintsha, etc.) are "according to their languages and heritage from very diverse nations, which obviously have influenced one another for a long time. Later, during the Inca conquest, these tribes were combined into a unified state. Their individual cultures, however, have retained their particular characteristics into the present day with no one group being the dominant source for the others."[131]

44. Glancing at this list of archaeological cultures, a layman unacquainted with the current status of our ethnographic museums' holdings may well assume that we are dealing with a massive amount of material. He may think that a museum dedicated to this material is necessary. Leaving aside the vast amount of pre-Columbian treasures that have been accumulated, the facts do not support this impression. In the best possible case, a fortunate museum may possess a couple of hundred relevant pieces, as is the case, for instance, with the objects from Benin. In general, however, we are dealing with nothing more than accidental beginnings or barely conscious additions to collections of archaeological character. A speedy and large-scale expansion of these collections is hindered by expenditures being required for other purposes. It should be emphasized that only museums that have identified one or more of these periods as an area of specialization—periods that are high points in the history of human intellectual development and

immensely important for the comprehension of cultures today—would be capable of collecting material in an organized, comprehensive, and large-scale way. While much of the material has not yet been excavated, it is nevertheless exposed to the destructive influences of time, human greed, and ignorance. One hopes that insight into these circumstances will lead to determined intervention before it is too late.[132]

45. The removal of archaeological monuments from ethnographic museums would encounter, apart from the purely external difficulties, serious intellectual reservations. The separation would result either in museums that contain only material from contemporary Asian civilizations and primitive tribes or in new ethnographic museums devoted to archaeological ends. Either solution would obscure the connection between the artifacts of past eras and cultural situations of the present. A few examples suffice to illustrate the potential impact. Albert Grünwedel, for instance, discusses the relationship between ancient Buddhist monuments and modern Buddhist art in Tibet, China, and Japan: "Most monuments from the first heyday under King Ashoka have largely vanished. Isolated groups of huge rubble heaps attest to a time when central India was covered with Buddhist structures. The traditional forms still thriving in the churches outside India are powerful sources to help us understand the ancient lost monuments. Thus Buddhist archaeology must start with research in the modern pantheon, especially with the religious manifestations of the northern school in Tibet, China, and Japan. Here individual artistic types may be recognized and parallels sought with the art of ancient India."[133] Felix von Luschan speaks about the connections between bronze art in ancient Benin and the lost-wax brass casting techniques of today's Guinea in *Zeitschrift für Ethnologie* (Verh. 30 [1898]: 152): "The art of ancient Benin sees its last remnants doubtlessly in the modern creations of the Ashanti and in Dahomey. Since transitional pieces have also been identified, we may recognize an unbroken connection that spans several centuries." Finally, in the New World, as we have mentioned above, the Pueblo Indians are in many ways the continuation of the cultural groups of Mexico and Central America.

46. Therefore we must grant that cultural connections are a fact. And yet we would be hard pressed to affirm that the link between archaeological materials and other artifacts in ethnographic museums carries sufficient weight to always require attention. In the first place, archaeological cultures are self-contained manifestations that have to be emphasized in their own right, unaffected by material that is either directly or not at all related. As a group, their closest relationships are among themselves,

as is evident in Asian and, to some extent, American regions (see §§41 and 43). The coherence of such archaeological cultures is, however, obscured if masses of contemporary ethnographic material are included in the display. For example, even when Hindu antiquities from Java are grouped together, they are not exhibited in connection with India— specifically, ancient India. Instead, they are exhibited according to the principle best suited for ethnographic collections, namely geographic location (see §100). Thus Hindu antiquities from Java are exhibited with ethnographic artifacts from modern Java, and Hindu antiquities of southern Sulawesi are exhibited with ethnographic artifacts from southern Sulawesi, and so forth. In ethnographic museums where an independent collection of archaeological antiquities is not considered feasible, we recommend segregating those holdings to a designated space (such as a special room) away from the general ethnographic material and arranging them according to temporal and geographic criteria.

The fact that archaeological cultures are phenomena of the past that cohere internally and, in part, with each other means that their connections with the ethnographic situation of the present become less important in the organization of ethnographic museums. Their significance also diminishes because the relevant archaeological material explains only limited aspects of the ethnographic present, not its entire peculiarity. By the same token, the cultural situation of the past never permits complete explanation by that of the present. This realization at the same time suggests that an exhibition could include certain *selected* objects of contemporary ethnography that assist with the understanding and explanation of archaeological monuments. In this way, an archaeological collection of exceptional scientific merit could be curated to offer not only a lively understanding of the monuments but also an instructive glimpse into aspects of wider cultural history.[134]

Of course, a curator who wishes to secure the viewer's impression that archaeological monuments are serenely self-contained and unencumbered by surrounding clutter will have the following questions about our proposals. Above all, what pieces from the separated material should be left together or reassembled for the sake of historical consistency? For instance, should the prototypical Greek sculptures not be displayed with sculptures from the Gandharan monastery to illustrate their influence?[135] Is a collection of modern sculpture intellectually plausible only in connection with Greek sculptural works, which influenced them and provided their very spirit? Is the connection between a group of phenomena in some scientific area not from the same moment of time more or less the result of unseen beginnings and a traditional retention of formational conditions beyond their own time?[136] Does not the course of science dictate that certain aspects of the comprehensive body of knowledge that constitutes a scientific discipline will ultimately develop and grow to such an extent that they can no longer feasibly be considered elements of the original body of knowledge? It cannot be denied that this does occur. Indian archaeology, at least, is about to expand beyond the scope of general ethnography to become an independent academic field. But since we are dealing with an area in which the understanding of the represented object or form is not readily apparent to the viewer, we should recognize that the isolating detachment of the archaeological material from its relationships with the present (and, we could even add, the past) aids neither the academic discipline nor the desire of the laity to reach a true understanding.[137] A separation of the collections therefore would be academically useful and educational to the public only if archaeology retained some of the ethnographic material that explains it.

There is no internal criterion that determines the moment to elevate an evolving field of study and its material to a higher level of autonomous importance. Only the external perspective of the accumulated material can indicate when the time is right. And yet no one can doubt that the separation of the material has its internal justification, even if it appears to be due to purely external reasons: it will be implemented—as is currently the case with archaeological cultures, at least those of Asia (India)—because sensitivity to the special value of the separated field has grown.[138]

47. The highest aim for such a more or less independent department of archaeological-ethnographic monuments concerns research into the connections between East and West in the widest sense: to work toward the solution of the main problems in world history, which were already voiced by Herodotus, the father of history, and which today's great battles in the Far East have brought to our attention in distressing ways. Otto Gruppe discussed this connection nearly twenty years ago in his critical, educational, and stimulating book *Greek Culture and Myth and Its Relation to Oriental Religions* [*Die griechischen Culte und Mythen in ihren Beziehungen zu den orientalischen Religionen*], vol. 1 (1887). He claimed that the similarities between the myths and cults of European and oriental peoples can be explained by the presence of an inclusive and universal cultural community that transcends linguistic and national barriers. He even speculated about a past link of some kind between East Asia and

America. Similarly, Albert Grünwedel's comprehensive study *Buddhist Art in India* [*Buddhistische Kunst in Indien*] (1st ed. 1893, 2nd ed. 1900), which was free of romantic fantasy and rested squarely on astute and thorough research, once and for all eliminated the perceived barriers dividing the art of the ancient Mediterranean and the Near East, on the one hand, and the art of central, southern, and eastern Asia, on the other. He also demonstrated that the Gandharan art of northwestern India transmitted ancient ideals of Apollonian beauty all the way to the hierarchic art of East Asia. And just as in all important cultural areas the Occident had demonstrably been the recipient of influences in ancient times—"the stimuli spread from Babylon, the Middle East, Egypt, through the barbaric tribes of Greece to found European culture"[139]—influence also spread in the opposite direction. Following the routes blazed by the passions of ancient conquerors, the spirit of Greek sculpture, theater, and many other cultural domains was transmitted to the East (with Greek words even penetrating into central and southern Asia, including China and Japan). In far higher measure, however, Asia influenced the West, with unparalleled and long-lasting repercussions, reaching well beyond trade (as, for instance, in the Silk Road). Its true depth and breadth is just beginning to be recognized,[140] as is the awareness of its likely wide-ranging importance for religious thought, far exceeding that of the Bible and Babel movement. In addition, more precise research into the artistic influences on the Occident through the Orient is still necessary. Although largely speculation, certainty is growing that the dominant role Asia played, along with Egypt, in cultural history is not limited to its influence on the ancient Mediterranean and Europe. It has been conjectured that the bronze art of Benin was dependent upon the bronze work of the Asian Orient—a theory to which the author hopes to return later. And, just as there has never been a lack of speculation about possible links between the religious worldviews of the New World and those of the Old in previous times, so the hypothesis has reappeared today suggesting a connection between pre-Columbian and ancient Asian artistic practices.[141] Perhaps in the future we will gain clarity about these theories by uncovering proof that the manifestations which currently stand side by side without clear links in fact reveal demonstrable connections. In this pursuit we should consider the New World, the Western world, by examining not only the primitive tribes, like those of the Northwest, but also the older cultural peoples, such as those of Central America. They may constitute the furthest Eastern point. In any case, the old master is correct when he says:

He who knows himself and others
Here will also see:
That the East and West, like brothers,
Parted ne'er shall be.

Retrospect and Prospect

48. In casting one concluding glance over our debate, we can see that in their current conception the ideal general purpose of ethnographic museums has been subject to a restriction—a double restriction in fact, one involuntary, the other voluntary.

The involuntary restriction they suffer insofar as outside forces took over materials that ethnographic museums believed was their due. In previous eras, and up to the present in many cases, ethnographic museums were, owing to the multifaceted relevance of the material, often combined with other museums. They became "appendices" under a single administration. Thus it seems that in the future other collections of cultural objects will become mortal competitors by deflecting objects of a certain type that fit their particular, specialized purpose. As a result, ethnographic museums are vying—to their own detriment—with collections of art that will take anything touched by a hint of beauty, as well as with collections of folklore, prehistoric collections, archaeological museums, collections of weapons, naval museums, libraries of written materials, and so on. At this point in time, ethnographic material tends to become increasingly dislodged and dispersed.

A voluntary restriction is specialization upon a certain field. There are some particular cases: the Musée Guimet developed from a private collection; the Congo Museum in Tervuren near Brussels belongs to the Congolese state and has a civic agenda; and a number of colonial museums similarly serve civic purposes and are therefore classified differently. Apart from these outliers, there is currently no public museum in Europe that has planned from its conception to dedicate itself to a subfield—such as the ones we detailed above—separate from the general ethnographic mission. In our discussion thus far, we have concluded that such a development would not be an impossibility. Why shouldn't there be museums supported by the German Empire that specialize in Asian religions, Asian archaeology, or Asian art? See §57 on the idea to erect a museum of casts of ancient Javanese stone sculptures, which was called for in Dutch ethnographic circles several years ago.

49. In light of the involuntary dislocation and the anticipated and increasing limitation of the materials collected, the scope of the ethnographic museums' general mission is changing. These developments seem to indicate that the term "ethnographic museums" in its current usage will become obsolete. There is a call for a *new* understanding of museums of general ethnography, which contrasts them with collections of ethnographic materials with a specialized purpose. It is as if these ethnographic museums that have failed to focus on one of the specializations which we have detailed here are required to identify a new purpose and a new task to justify their existence. Should a new conceptualization of the ethnographic museum and its role indeed appear, then there can be little doubt that the job of ethnographic museums must be implemented on a large scale, and above all, on a solid, scientific basis (historically or psychologically). They should follow the precocious example of the outstanding museum in Oxford, which derived from the private collection of Pitt Rivers (Augustus Lane Fox). The museums must provide instructive presentations of the general developmental history of the human intellect, insofar as it is manifest in individual genres of objects.[142] The question of whether such a change is already apparent in how ethnographic materials are dealt with today is a concern not for the ideal but for the practical obligations of the ethnographic museums (cf. §99).

Obituary of Oswald Richter[143]

At the young age of barely thirty-four, Oswald Richter has been taken from us.

Readers of this journal know him as the author of the present large-scale project, which attests to his comprehensive knowledge and his piercing visionary acumen. This work will outlast its author.

After initial studies in linguistics, Richter began to concentrate on the ethnography of Indonesia. The fruits of his research are preserved in a number of formidable essays in the *Festschrift* for Adolf Bernhard Meyer, in *Ethnographische Miszellen* I and II (Abhandlungen und Berichte des Königlichen Zoologischen und Anthropologisch-Ethnographischen Museums zu Dresden, III–X, 1899–1903) and in the exemplary work *Celebes* I (Publikationen aus dem Kgl. Ethnographischen Museum zu Dresden, XIV, 1903). The first paper was written with W. Foy, the other with Meyer. His later works, in part based on decades of projected research, have unfortunately remained unfinished.

Richter did superb work as a museum curator. After training in Meyer's school and engaging in educational travel, Richter focused his ambition and his extraordinary work ethic on the task of preserving the high distinction and character of the ethnographic museum of Dresden. He helped to methodically expand the world-famous Indonesian and Oceanic collection of the museum and to enrich it through the addition of exquisite pieces. He took care of each object, displaying it elegantly in the appropriate setting and employing all possible technological advances to aid in its presentation—a task that grew more difficult every year due to the increasing dearth of space.

Richter's strength lay in the details of museum work. He was a valuable asset to the Dresden Museum for seven years. The seed of his passing was planted while serving the museum. Near the close of 1902, he contracted blood poisoning while examining poisoned darts from the Samang people of Malaysia. After he refused medical attention for far too long, he became gravely ill. Impatient to resume his interrupted work, he refused to take the necessary and urgently recommended rest period; he returned to work too soon, and his body never had the chance to regain its vigor.

When Richter joined the Berlin Museum of Ethnology in 1904, his strength was already gone. It did not take long for signs of his creeping illness to manifest themselves. From that point on, his professional duties were a heroic martyrdom. We are told how he struggled to work, day after day, in pain, unmindful of any advice offered by doctors or friends. He wished to die while laboring in service to the museum. His lonely and serious life knew no pleasure—none at all—save for work and the fulfillment of duty. Oswald Richter's passing marked the end of a pure man and a true scholar.

Oskar Nuoffer
Dresden

The Practical Tasks

50. Our discussion assumes that we are dealing with modern museums of general ethnography: in other words, scientific collections. Museums of ethnographic materials that focus on a specialized purpose, particularly

one that is to some degree nonacademic (such as practical, aesthetic, etc.), should naturally also have specialized practical agendas and particular facilities, as would be the case, for instance, in museums of Asian archaeology or Asian art.

For an archaeological museum, the appropriateness of a geographic-historical display is self-evident. A museum for the art of a people or a cultural complex, by contrast, can establish a wide variety of purposes, each of which would require the collection to be treated in a particular way (cf. Ernst Grosse, "Über den Ausbau und die Aufstellung öffentlicher Sammlungen von ostasiastischen Kunstwerken," *Museumskunde* 1 [1905]: 123–39; and Woldemar von Seidlitz, "Ein deutsches Museum für asiatische Kunst," ibid., 181–97). Exhibited pieces could serve artistic pleasure or scientific awareness. Grosse writes: "These two uses are so widely divergent that any attempt to do justice to both is likely to satisfy the needs of neither the art lover nor the researcher" (123; cf. Seidlitz, 186ff.). "To serve the purpose of aesthetic pleasure," Grosse writes, "it would be absurd to constrict the exhibit to a historical or any other academic schema; in this case the only important issue is to select pieces that are able to impart the greatest and most lasting artistic impression. This goal is more likely to be achieved the less one allows oneself to be distracted by scientific considerations and interests" (131f.). Grosse's latter thought about the selection of materials is no doubt correct. However, we cannot ignore that, as Grosse himself emphasizes, "different artworks from the same period [and we may add, of the same culture] go together very well, as a rule" (133). Thus a historical-geographic display should not a priori be considered mutually exclusive with one that aims at aesthetic effect. A similar view is expressed by Seidlitz: "To combine varied artworks from the same period and same region to create a comprehensive picture of a culture means to not shy away from, for example, displaying etching and woodcuts by Dürer and his followers next to German pictures of the sixteenth century, in addition to other German woodcuts, gold metalwork, weapons, and more works from the same era, all unified in a single space. Only in this way can each artifact, born from the spirit of its time, be correctly seen and clearly understood."[144]

Wilhelm Bode also opted for the combination of paintings with sculpture, furniture, and tapestries of the same time and school: "Attempts in museums themselves show, however, that such a mixture can be realized only to a limited extent in public collections. Even a fairly regular distribution of paintings and sculptures along the walls can give an extremely agitated impression. As a rule, the pieces are liable to compromise each other, not to mention that except for the Louvre's collection of French art of the seventeenth and eighteenth centuries and Munich's collection of German art from the Middle Ages and the Renaissance, no other museums possess a sufficient array of artworks to provide a well-balanced combination of different media. Italian art must already be excluded owing to the architectonic combination of most of their large paintings. For German art, by contrast, such exhibitions are possible, and indeed preferable, since painters and sculptors usually worked together in creating German altarpieces."[145] Without a doubt, it would take special sensitivity and skill to wed beauty with truth. For some general comments on aesthetic displays, see §92 below.

We do not wish to imply that the practical issues faced by museums are new. There were already concerns in the time of the cabinets of curiosities. In his treatise *Inscriptiones vel tituli Theatri amplissimi . . .* , published in Munich in 1565, Samuel von Quiccheberg detailed a remarkably prudent classification of the material for a collection. A classification of ethnographic objects may be gleaned from it as well.[146] Later, during the time of art and natural history cabinets, Johann Daniel Major, in his *Unvorgreiflichen Bedenken von Kunst- und Naturalienkammern* of 1674, advocated not only a separation of the *Naturalia* from the *Artificialia*—or at least a *ratione materiae* arrangement—but also a clear order for each of the two groups, as well as their careful housing. He spoke for "small, open drawers of metal, painted with oil paint," in addition to boxes filled with sand "if some examples of the species were too small." This method recalls Adolf Bernhard Meyer's exhibition in the Zoological Museum in Dresden, which displayed bird's eggs in black metal boxes filled with sawdust that had been dyed black. Major called for light, clean, well-labeled storage, akin to a supply room.[147] Caspar F. Neickel (Jenckel) sharply criticized the exhibition of the Hamburg Collection, which was private at that time, in his *Museographia oder Anleitung zum rechten Begriff und nützlicher Anlegung der Museorum oder Raritäten-Kammern* (1772). He also presented his own views on the best circumstances and form of a museum space: "Because of the comfortable air . . . this chamber of rarities I imagine" is oriented "toward the southeast" and "is about twice as long as it is wide." It "lies toward the light of day for even the smallest thing in it to be perceived." About the display of the "Curiosa Artificialia" he notes that they are to be "set up in such a way . . . that both the artfulness [*Kunst*] of the objects and their intention may be perceived." Neickel also writes about the necessity of a library, consisting of "books placed on graceful shelves or on *repositorii* made for that purpose," discusses "museums or containers for rarities," and speaks of his desire to work in the room with the collections, at a long, narrow table, and to have access to the museum catalogue as well as to files such as the museum's chronicles. He even broaches the idea of a "universal rarity cabinet," which would not unify all existing "rarities" in their original form but rather "drawings and reproductions [*Abrisse und Bildungen*] of the pieces I am lacking." He goes on to say that in these drawings, "everything should be sketched in vivid colors or at least in ink for me to experience the original, natural color." The museum in the Richterianum was elegantly designed, containing "graceful glass pyramids with exhibits [*Schaustücke*] and pretty cabinets."[148]

Tasks with Respect to the Objects

If all vice is born of idleness, then all virtue is born of work.

—Fritz Schultze, *Psychologie der Naturvölker* (1900), 243

Collecting

52. *The urgency of collection.* As for every museum, the central task of the ethnographic museum is to collect. And for an ethnographic museum in particular, the emphasis on collecting should be stressed to the highest degree. Adolf Bastian issued a last-minute exhortation and alarm call to collect artifacts from primitive tribes while they are still in existence.[149] The priority of collecting at German museums has for some time drawn the attention of England and the United States, kindling in them the desire to make up for lost ground. From an academic standpoint, competition between museums can only be regarded favorably, since a healthy rivalry promises the richest and most energetically pursued propagation of the materials for collection. In recent years the cost of artifacts from nearly all locales has risen. We are nearing a time when ethnographic artifacts will become objects of speculation in the world marketplace and demand exorbitant sums. Prices are already so high for certain regions, including East Asia and New Zealand, that it is no longer possible to amass a collection, either piecemeal or as a whole, without extraordinary means—if at all. Any collecting from New Zealand

will soon be impossible. In East Asia, "where the practice of collecting necessitates thorough reform,"[150] the focus has up to this point been on commodities more than art. Even with vast means readily available, it would be possible to rectify this missed opportunity on a large scale only through truly fortuitous connections.[151] In any case, the money earmarked for acquisitions by museum administrations is generally already on the meager side and will be increasingly unable to fulfill even modest ambitions. Thus museums are more or less dependent on the generosity of friends and donors, who either bequeath or lend their own collections to the museums or provide assistance when exceptional opportunities occur. Museums that receive aid put up honorary plaques bearing a not insignificant number of names. In some cases, as in Berlin, aid committees that can raise funds if necessary take the place of individual donors.[152]

53. *Research trips.* Purchase, donation, or loan are not the only means of expanding a collection. Recently, spurred by Bastian's call to action and motivated by his example, ethnographic museums have repeatedly employed travelers or sent their own staffers on collection and research trips to unexplored territories.[153] Captain A. Jacobsen's missions for the Berlin Museum to northwestern America, the East Indian Archipelago, and the Amur are well known. Recently a great number of the Berlin Museum's own employees have undertaken such trips, earning the museum its exalted place in the history of ethnography. The director of the Vienna Museum, among others, has followed suit. In America, Morris Ketchum Jesup provided the staff of the American Museum of Natural History in New York with the means for such research trips. In a similar vein, Arthur Baessler recently contributed a great sum to the Berlin Museum to fund ethnographic fieldwork in the South Seas. Through trips like these it is possible to attain large, well-rounded collections representing specific areas. The biggest advantage is that the travelers are themselves academically trained and can critically assess and collect material that is far more useful to science than are the inventories assembled by varied and potentially less trustworthy sources.[154] Today, general classifications such as "Indian" and "Oceanic," and descriptors redolent of "devil's work" and bloodshed, which were still common in the first half of the previous century, no longer meet our standards. Today we demand to know the precise find spot of an object. This find spot needs to be distinguished from the provenance of an object, which must be given greater prominence in the descriptions of objects by those collecting the artifacts. Objects that arrive at a museum without information on

their find spot and without an identifiable provenance should not even be accepted. In addition to the provenance, the indigenous name of the object should be noted, as well as the purpose of its ornamentation, its use, its method of creation, and its material. For objects obtained either through sales from dealers or through gifts from donors, these specifications are, as a rule, rarely and insufficiently met. The missing information can be uncovered only through a comparative or arduous and time-consuming literary study. However, a critical traveler, such as one trained by a museum, can obtain the necessary information prior to acquisition with far greater ease. Greater systematic organization of this kind of collecting by academically trained travelers is, in the interest of science, much desired. The preparation must also include the study of the prehistory of the region in question, as it is preserved in old sources (travel accounts, etc.). We are approaching a point in time when many cultures that fall under the scope of ethnography will have vanished, if indeed they have not done so already. It will no longer be possible to verify the infinite number of details that cannot be gleaned from archival sources and literature. For the cultures that have already died out, experts are urgently needed to engage in research at the locations where they once flourished. And this needs to occur before their last vestiges fall prey to forces of nature and lack of understanding. The threat can come from charlatans, vain journalists, globetrotters, or even soldiers on new military expeditions, who can endanger scientific knowledge in a senseless or even vandalistic way by removing components or remains from these sites.[155] Such disruption of the artifacts' original context destroys much of the evidence that could have been interpreted by specialists. Work must be done before it is too late to preserve data for educated observers. Ethnographic museums provide safe houses for both the beginnings and the culminations of human culture, as well as its manifestations in the present and the past—in particular, where cultures that do not rest upon a Mediterranean heritage are concerned. The museums offer stalwart protection for what would otherwise be irretrievably exposed to eradication.

54. *Supplementing inventory through casts, photographs, etc.* A valuable supplemental aid to research and public education is the systematic augmentation of a museum's inventory through casts and photographs (as well as drawings and rubbings). Generally, all ethnographic museums employ these means, although their procurement is often more sporadic and accidental than intentional. Casts and images are able to round out

a collection of objects and render the museum more complete. Every collection has some gaps in its holdings, and, barring some unforeseen windfall, will always have those gaps. For example, most museums have insufficient examples of masterpieces of ancient East Asian art, Javanese antiquities, and Polynesian artifacts.[156] In addition to casts, a museum exhibition could also include pictures of important artworks that it does not possess as either originals or casts. The Dresden Museum, which currently possesses one of the world's foremost collections of artifacts from New Zealand, included a large number of casts in its exhibitions, despite its many riches. Also, in its display dedicated to the Minahasa region of North Celebes, the Dresden Museum includes photographs of pictographic writing, the originals of which are in the Wereldmuseum in Rotterdam.

55. Such an augmentation of the holdings of a collection through casts, photographs, and so forth will be possible on a large scale only if ethnographic museums agree to help each other out more willingly than has been the case thus far—as Augustin Krämer has pointed out.[157] Most museums now fulfill the basic prerequisite of having their own photographic studios.[158] However, most institutions do not yet have on their staff specialized photographers or molders trained to make casts, although the Berlin Museum does have a caster.[159] This deficit should be overcome in the future, rendering ethnographic collections independent in this regard, just as most sculptural galleries are today.

56. A special source to aid in the completion of the inventory along these lines is casts or images of objects for sale in the art market that are for whatever reason unobtainable. The use of these materials in reproductions should not engender any moralistic concerns. If I am correctly informed, archaeological museums have long made use of this practice. Dealers themselves are increasingly forthcoming with museum administrations by providing them drawings or photographs of objects or collections that are for sale. Notably, W. D. Webster in London was always most willing to offer to those who were interested splendid drawings, rubbings, or photographs he himself had made of objects that entered the market through him. His catalogues, which date to 1895, also provide an enduring benefit for the academic field. His example was followed by the companies of J. F. G. Umlauff in Hamburg, who issued a sumptuous catalogue detailing his entire inventory, as well as W. O. Oldman in London. The catalogues of Webster, Umlauff, and Oldman may also be purchased at booksellers.

57. *Specialization by applying all methods of completing a collection.* There are cultures, such as East Asian, pre-Columbian Mexican, all the ancient American, ancient Javanese, and Hindu, and even that of New Zealand, which inspire such high artistic and historic interest that every photograph or cast provides a significant enrichment of an ethnographic collection that does not already own a similar work. Given these circumstances, it is probable that in the near future a centralized special museum will be founded to assemble casts or illustrations of every object that is well-known generally or at least within its own artistic field. Several years ago the wonderful idea was voiced in Dutch ethnographic circles to open a museum of casts of ancient Javanese stone sculptures. Unfortunately, as far as this author knows, no concrete steps have been taken to realize this proposal. One hopes the present lines—in addition to the example recently set by the French government in Phnom Penh, Cambodia[160]—will motivate a reengagement with the plans!

58. *Quality and quantity* (cf. §15 above, as well as §14). In addition to specializing its collection in certain geographic or cultural historical areas, an ethnographic museum may secure a special advantage and status by concentrating on quality. Some museums strive for breadth, seeking to present individual cultures as comprehensively as possible by acquiring all types of their cultural manifestations. (To present all cultures with the same systematic development is possible only for a museum on the scale of Berlin's.) However, a museum could emphasize instead the quality of individual pieces—that is, the collection of "good, old pieces." By good, old pieces we mean ancient, well-crafted artifacts that have been in use for a long time, that remain unaffected by the forces of history, and above all, are free of European interference. They should be of a local style, created with special love or special meaning to fulfill their purpose for their creators—and not for Europeans. These objects should be solid, with the patina of use and time, and of a pure type in the local style. In this regard, the Dresden Museum is noteworthy because it has been successful in acquiring a great number of artifacts from the South Seas. This institute is the only one of the ethnographic museums at this time to be fully committed to quality as its guiding principle. Its motto recalls Hans Dedekam's praise for the museum of decorative arts in Leipzig and the reputation of the Hamburg Museum for Arts and Crafts under the direction of Justus Brinckmann: "Just a little, but good, if not indeed the best, even if it's expensive."[161]

59. An emphasis on quality as defined here should not, however, be confused with the attempt to acquire rare, mysterious, materially valuable,

or particularly artistic objects. These desires motivated the majority of collections of roughly a quarter of a century ago and occasionally still characterize the acquisitions of several ethnographic museums today. Motivations like these are nothing other than the continuation of the pre-museological style of collecting that resulted in the amassing of rarities in cabinets of curiosities. In connection with the widening of the geographic horizon and a general strengthening of pragmatism, a younger, more scientifically oriented generation of ethnographers has overcome this manner of collection. Today, an interest in rarities seems like a transitional step from pre-museological collecting practices to the current methods based on the principle of quality in the sense we have defined above.

60. This qualitative focus, however, directly contradicts the emphasis on quantity demanded by scientific interests. Quantity may be defined not only as we have delineated in §58 as a comprehensive and systematic representation of all individual cultural expressions of a region, but also in a far broader sense. As scientists of a particular region, ethnographers strive for academic understanding not by acquiring a great variety of items in a haphazard manner but rather by acquiring a limited series of similar artifacts from the same place of creation. Thus, from an academic perspective, collections should possess many duplicates, since the scientific research of objects has shown that series of artifacts are required for full comprehension.

No clear-cut rule can resolve the conflict between the demands of collecting quality and quantity. There is, however, a warning for both camps: be on guard against acquiring pieces that too clearly bear the traces of European meddling or the character of something newly created, superficial, or hastily fashioned as an export product. In general, the decision to acquire based on quality or quantity will come from the particular relationship that the ethnographic museum and its specific milieu has with the public and its expectations of the museum. The preference for quality may dominate at an ethnographic museum in a city with a strong artistic character. The preference for quantity may reign at a museum in a city with a brisk academic spirit, particularly when the museum itself has direct connections with a university. Of course, the funds available for acquisition and the business connections of the museum, among other factors, will also be decisive.

61. As we have suggested in §9, ethnographic museums will most likely experience a similar fate as archaeological museums: they will become more or less closely aligned with educational centers and

universities, since they will flourish only in association with such academic institutions. In attempts to combat this trend of subjugating museums to universities, perhaps the museums best suited to preserving their independence will be those with a longer tradition of emphasizing quality, as well as emphasizing the secondary effects and secondary tasks (see §§18–21).

The Display[162]

81. *The inalienable rights of a museum object.* After the extensive treatment an object undergoes to be ready for the museum, it earns first and foremost the benefit which such an institution can offer: that is, its place in a worthy, safe, tasteful, and scientifically appropriate exhibition as the subject of scholarly research. We must promote the idea that every object, no matter how insignificant its material or craftsmanship, deserves protection and careful treatment. It has the right to be easily accessed for study and to be objectively and pleasingly arranged when on display.

The Tasteful Exhibition

90. *The term "a beautiful exhibition."* A tastefully presented exhibition of an ethnographic—scientific—collection need not imply that the objects are grouped primarily with a view to their artistic merit. Nor does it entail arrangements based on gradations of artistic value or decorative and formal qualities, or subtle arrangements in interiors evoking sentimental, intimate, or imposing feelings.[163] Certainly the tasks of ethnographic museums include the effective display of objects of artistic quality (see §15 above). This obligation must be fulfilled, however, without the display itself becoming unscientific (fig. 2). Art should not strive to dominate science. Art becomes sterile and unenjoyable when science seeks to dominate rather than understand it. By the same token, if beauty is allowed to overshadow truth and historical reality, science is suffocated and fantastical fallacies given victory for the sake of an illusory gratification. A beautiful exhibition of a scientific collection indicates in the first place nothing but a well-ordered exhibition. Order means a methodical (or regulated) structure and visual clarity in the conceptualization of the exhibition's layout. A tasteful exhibition accordingly demands (1) a wide-ranging display of tasteful cabinets in several large, well-lit, uncluttered, serious, and dignified rooms with

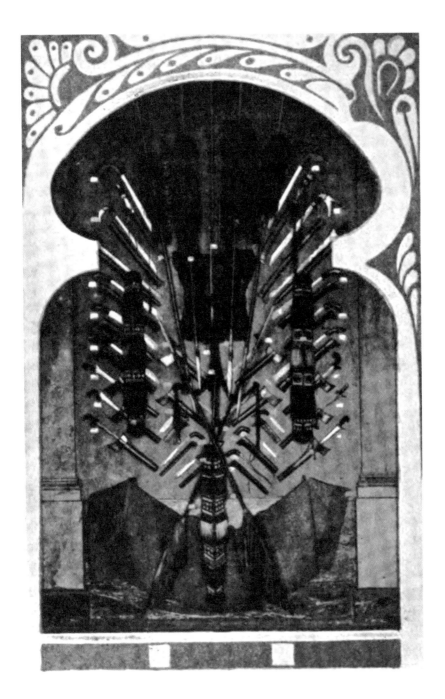

Fig. 2. A counterexample.

wide and open passageways; (2) a clear, topical ordering of the materials; (3) a formally open and clean arrangement of the individual objects presented in ways that please the eye.[164]

91. *The avoidance of distracting decoration within the exhibition space.* With respect to the furnishing and tasteful décor of the rooms as well as the cabinets, the tasks of ethnographic museums coincide with those of museums in general: to enable serene pleasure. While these shared goals fall outside the specific themes of this discussion, we can briefly touch on how the exhibition space and cabinets should appear. It is important to note that the types of decoration that are generally considered enhancements are in fact greatly disruptive and distracting in the museum context. A wall painting in the modern style is already a distraction. The ceiling and walls of the main hall of the zoological department of the Civic Museum in Altona is painted in such a way. The Congo Museum in Brussels has several cabinets in its entry hall in the modern furniture style. Downright repellent is the effect of the painting on the wide and ungainly framework of several cabinets in the Bremen Museum of Ethnology, which uses the pattern and colors of the objects contained within the furniture. Similarly distasteful but slightly more bearable are the decorative reliefs frequently seen in collections of natural history, such as in the Natural History Museum in London and the zoological department of the Civic Museum in Altona. In the former museum, terracotta bricks on the interior as well as the exterior of the building (such as the large, churchlike exhibition hall through which the structure is entered) depict a lofty frieze of animals and fish;[165] in the latter, one gallery is supported by columns with sea creatures on their bases. The decorum of the construction and décor in the elegant Galeries d'Anatomie in the Jardin des Plantes in Paris seems so restrained by contrast! The reliefs and sculptures by Frémiet and others, despite being very closely associated with the contents of the building, are mounted outside the collection, namely, around the area that leads to the gardens, at the narrow side by the entrance, and in the white entrance hall. Unfortunately, even this largely exemplary museum has an element we need to criticize. At the stairs to the gallery of the anthropological collection and surrounding the gallery ramp itself is a wrought iron trellis depicting a leafy vine.[166] Although it is artistic, the trellis is too massive and eye-catching. Any such ornamentation, regardless of how tasteful it may be, should be avoided in exhibition halls, since it draws attention away from the exhibited materials. The objects must be allowed to have a pure and undisturbed effect on their own.

92. *Some guiding principles for the aesthetically acceptable exhibition of objects.* Obviously, the formal aspects guiding the display of objects will depend on the type of materials involved and will differ from museum to museum. Certain guiding principles, however, may be identified as generally valid regardless of the types of materials exhibited. We will identify and discuss a number of these principles below.[167]

(a) *The installation should be focused around an immediately recognizable organizing idea.* An aesthetically correct installation of ethnographic objects is one that enables a narrower overview to group the objects easily and compare them within categories (such as sorcery and religion, weapons, clothing, jewelry, etc.), and a wider overview to instantly display the different ethnographic-geographic regions as self-contained entities. Creating such an installation is an art and requires a breadth of understanding. An exhibition of this sort can provide a clear and concise picture even within a moderate space. Its installation involves many objects and so necessitates many shelves of varying widths placed in a more or less tiered display.

(b) *No object may block another, even to a small degree.* Obviously this stipulation for a spacious, airy installation will always remain an unattainable aspiration. It is possible and desirable, however, to avoid a jam-packed display. In direct contradiction to its generally worthy ideal, the lack of space has often invited the warehousing of objects within the collection on display. In addition to the compartmentalizing of space, this constraint makes a reasonably sensible and accessible exhibition far more difficult, if not impossible. The warehousing of the exhibited collection suffocates the objects. Similarly dangerous is the clutter that continually grows with the addition of further objects. The most distressing example of such a situation is the Rijks Ethnographic Museum in Leiden. This museum's previous director did not hesitate to publicly critique this shortcoming of his own institution. To warehouse objects within the exhibited collection is in no way tolerable and is, in fact, hardly ever defensible, since it is almost always avoidable. If warehousing objects is necessary, it should occur outside the exhibition space.

(c) *Symmetry can be justified if it places focus on an item or aspect that nonspecialists could easily miss or if it encourages comparison among objects of the same type.* However, it should not be employed to emphasize artistically superior objects, since that would deflect interest from the less artistically stimulating objects surrounding them. Generally, the attainable goal of symmetrical displays is the equilateral, balanced distribution of abundance in relation to emptiness within the cabinet; but symmetry should equally be attendant on the organization of the object categories if the display is to give the impression of an elegant and measured sense of calm.

(d) *Objects that are distinguished from similar items by their artistic details (such as ornamentation) should generally be positioned in the foreground.* This applies also to objects that are considered particularly precious within their category for whatever reason.[168] Krämer's directive should be followed: "No fine object that is worth seeing should be placed deeper than 80 cm or higher than 160 cm."[169] And it is right to emphasize independent and authentic artistic creations that possess an enduring and accessible artistic efficacy. As Ernst Grosse stressed, even in a scientifically oriented collection the display should ensure that "each individual piece is able to produce its aesthetic effect fully and purely." It matters "to the researcher no less than the art lover that the art object is positioned in the way that the artist would have wanted it to be seen . . . since even science studies the artwork as such, and its artistic essence is recognizable only if its artistic effect is acknowledged."[170]

Of course, we should recognize that at least in the case of religious art, a part of the power these objects had over their viewers—perhaps the most meaningful part, which their creators meant for them to possess—is now lost forever. It is not only a matter of our current inability to understand these objects' full meanings, save for a precious few exceptions known to specialists. And it is not only a matter of these objects now being removed from the temples in which they once stood, no longer surrounded by the muted light of holy zeal sparkling with splendor or terrifying with horror in the half-night. We need to keep in mind that cult images developed out of their environments and can be correctly understood only as a part of their culture. They were created by their artists to function artistically in this context. And, of course, this is not only the case for the Asian cult image.

(e) *Finally, in terms of the formal aspects of an installation, we should stress that the organization of a collection must be all the more visually pleasing when it must counter any shortcomings, such as a smaller scope or a deficient exhibition space.* This is not to say that greater disorderliness or uncleanliness is permissible in a larger museum with more imposing rooms. Such forms of unpleasantness are not excusable in a grander context just because more effort is required to eradicate them. Regardless of size, museums must maintain clean and orderly appearances. The objects are owed this, as well as the public. Museums should stimulate a desire for order in their visiting public, as well as affirm and increase the public's appreciation for the protection of all objects that are entrusted to their care. Such respect is particularly important in the case of foreign objects that are threatened today by widespread barbarism and acts of unbridled destruction. Above all, museums must be free of unappealing dirt and clutter, which is regrettably found in more than one ethnographic museum. Ethnographic museums are not junk shops or storage rooms. The indolent viewpoint that the initial treatment of an ethnographic object is sufficient, regardless of whether it provides sufficient protection or fulfills the demands for orderliness and cleanliness, is wrong. The belief that the manner of presentation is inconsequential if the object receives a halfway scientifically correct method of storage must be recognized as a delinquency—bordering on extreme neglect—on the part of the museum.

93. *The difficulties of implementing an aesthetically appropriate exhibition of the objects.* The exhortation for an exhibition of objects that is satisfying from an aesthetic perspective may pose some difficulties for the museum administration but can prove worthwhile and enjoyable. Many may not know today how gratifying it is to organize and present an innately unimpressive ethnographic collection in a way that is scientifically correct as well as aesthetically pleasing. It is an art that is not universally understood and is, as a rule, quite undervalued. In the interest of creating an elegant and artistic impression that makes the museum a place for the public to enjoy, no exhibition should be installed only by low-level employees after the curator has determined its location. Instead, the curator himself should take up the task with love and care. He should guide the installation from start to finish himself. Even if he lacks the necessary experience to gain quick command of the material earmarked for display and of the room at his disposal, he should not shy away from trying things in order to create an artistically pleasant display. He should deal with failures like a true artist and strive with patience and tenacity to achieve the desired outcome.

The objective organization of a collection demands specialized and specific consideration for each type of museum. The only sensible principle appropriate for ethnographic museums will be discussed in §100ff.

The Internal Structure of an Exhibition (Scientific-Geographical, Not Fantastical-Systematic)[171]

99. *The unscientific nature of a systematic exhibition.* As discussed in §46, the internal schema to be adopted for organizing exhibited objects is geographical. Ethnographic collections should not be ordered systematically—that is to say, according to object categories. Exhibits should not, for example, feature string instruments, baskets, spoons, spears, and so on as separate groups. The role of museum displays is not to present series of objects from varied places of origin but rather to provide an image of the character of different peoples. An organization according to object categories intended to "illustrate the history of man" is worthless.[172] Placing objects of the same sort together even if they do not come from historically or linguistically related groups of people (or even if they do derive from related people, only part of the objects come into consideration) leads to the assumption that they are closely connected when that is not actually in evidence.

Really, only two types of correlation should be considered: (1) the external, historical connection, which is either the inheritance from a time before the separation of peoples (or to put it more precisely, the inheritance of some shared developmental experience from this time) or the borrowing by one people from another; (2) the internal, psychological connection provided by the identity, if it is possible to corroborate it, of two or more developmental phenomena assumed on the basis of a documented observation or of the same calculated intention. These two types of connection, however, do not exhaust the possible explanations for similar cultural manifestations, such as the same ornamentation or identically formed objects that serve the same purpose. The conclusion that a psychological connection must be present if one of the two types of historical connection is absent would reveal a limited inquiry, one that is unaware of the fact that the same results (i.e., the same effects) can arise from very different causes, and, above all, in very different ways.

The belief that our instruments, tools, and weapons are nothing but projections of our organs, or the completion or refinement of our organs, refers only to their general origin, not their specific beginnings, which could have been different in each case. Furthermore, this belief shows only that they present themselves to us today in this way, but not that they consciously were created out of that conception. It is much more likely the case that they unconsciously came into being in this way. It is verifiable that different beginnings can have the same final results in the area of ornamentation: geometric patterns have developed through completely different processes in various places on earth independently of each other.[173]

As discussed above, the handles on vessels may have a variety of origins. Earthen vessels do not appear to have universally arisen from the accident—that was later repeated on purpose—of sealing a basket with clay and then placing it, first accidentally and later purposefully, near the fire to harden the clay. The European high (shaft) boot did not necessarily develop in the same way as the fur boot of the Hyperboreans. One may be thought of as a unification of the sole with the leg encasing (sock, pants), as is argued by Heinrich Schurtz; the other, Schurtz continues, may have developed from a sandal (elevated slipper) with the shoe as an intermediary step, in that the sandal first was given a wider breadth than the foot and then tied to the leg with the bands coming up to cover the sides of the foot, with the foot covering later expanded to include the leg.[174] Furthermore, in the case of the cuffed boot the form of the shaft can depend on the shape of the shinbone that it touches. A comparison of the spear-tipped blowpipe from Borneo with our modern bayonet rifles (both types of implement involve a tube-shaped firing weapon combined with a spearing weapon) shows enough similarities to suggest that the same intended function inspired both designs—namely, the idea of using a firearm simultaneously as a thrusting weapon. But is this really the case? The spear-tipped blowpipe is likely a simplification of two weapons that were originally used side by side: the spear and the blowpipe. Its purpose was therefore not the one just outlined but rather a different one—not the actualization of a firearm but rather, to put it in vulgar psychological terms, a freeing from discomfort. Our rifle with an attached bayonet cannot be explained as a similar simplification. Since the bayonet was first used by the Dutch regiments in East India, it has been assumed that the idea was taken over from the Malays, who attached a dagger, their kris, onto a gun and thereby constructed the kind of spear with which they were familiar.[175] The uncertainty and care given to weighing the external or internal connections of the last two examples show to what extent, particularly for this type of research, "a sure result can only be attained through an inductive path, and the examination of countless details is called for before the total comprehension desired by ethnology can be attained." "There has never been a lack of theories about the development of humankind's material and intellectual achievements, about progress and regress among primitive peoples."[176]

That a museum must serve the truth has recently also been emphasized by Augustus Pitt. He deems it the "justification of existence" of a museum, as a museum is itself "a place from which we may at any time attain irrefutable and trustworthy answers."[177] This is the reason for his stance against the "interieurs" in art and applied art museums. The character of the premature, the hasty, and the biased and fantastical, which typifies a museum such as the one in Oxford, is clearly evident from what William Henry Holmes writes about a group displayed with the intent of explaining the history of sculpture: "In the first stages of the art only simple, useful articles were made; later these were elaborated aesthetically and personal ornaments were added; then gradually the processes were applied to working out the rude, block-like imperfectly proportioned figures of animals and men; these were totems, fetishes, and idols, and illustrate a third stage in our progressive series. Later still portraiture was attempted; and a kind of rigid, formal likeness was worked out, marking a fourth step. Then, in the higher nations, correct form and expression came into being, and finally the realistic and ideal work, represented by the highest Greek art, was developed."[178]

The grouping of objects according to typological rather than geographical criteria is naive, uncritical, and gives rise to misconceptions that a public institution must avoid in the interest of truth. A display based on object categories also makes it more difficult to attain a true cultural overview and deprives the researcher of any opportunity of using the collection for critical study. Such displays are rooted in the cult of the primitive, in the idea of a museum as a place to envision the primitive stages of human development in all areas of social life. They are a function of the pleasure of curiosities for which fantastical explanations can be invented, of the pleasure of imagination as a pursuit in its own right. These myriad missteps can be encapsulated by a single word: unscientific. In truth, there has never been a public ethnographic collection of a state or town run by an exemplary intellectual director that was arranged systematically throughout.[179] There are two collections that are today (still) systematically organized: namely, the Pitt Rivers Museum in Oxford (which used to be the private collection of Lane-Fox Pitt Rivers and has belonged to the Oxford University museums since 1884) and the Horniman Museum in London (belonging to Mr. F. J. Horniman). These institutions are essentially the creations of enthusiastic private citizens.[180] Just as misguided as exhibitions organized according to object types are exhibitions organized according to material. In the British Museum in London, for example, objects are to a great extent organized according to the categories of stone, bronze, gold, and pottery.[181]

100. *The sole justification for a geographic-ethnic exhibition.* A strictly scientific exhibition that enables an overview must be geographically and ethnically focused. More precisely, the objects must first be ordered into geographically distinct areas of production, and second, within these areas, according to clear object groups (weaponry, clothing, jewelry, hygienic items, objects for enjoyment, household items, weavings, travel and transportation items, hunting, fishing, trade and exchange, music, decorative arts, art creation, magic and religion, etc.), which ideally should appear in the same order within each geographic section of the display.[182] Within each section, there may also be a temporal order. This means, for example, that prehistoric and archaeological objects are displayed separately,[183] or that native styles are shown to be the lasting effect of the influence of previous, foreign cultures.[184] The criteria for ordering the material should always be geographic in the first place and formal in the second: this principle must provide the firm structure for the collection.

101. *The concept of a "geographic display."* A geographic display is organized according to the places where the objects were created, not the places where they were discovered. Objects are arranged according to where they were made and not where they were found. The places where the objects were created do not coincide with places where they were distributed. Such an exhibit does not provide a factual cultural image of the way things actually were, but rather it creates images of cultures as they should be. People, after all, do not sit hermetically confined in bell jars. The movements and migrations of people intermingle their products. An exhibition based on places of creation is therefore also not objective, but it is an absolute necessity in the interest of truth and scientific research. First, all older museums own a very high number of objects (in some departments of older museums, this number is certainly more than half) that were collected at a time when no weight was placed on the specific indication of the place of origin. Even today in all museums there are a great number of objects without any indication of their origin

or with scant and completely unreliable information. From the outset, the administration can put such objects on display only according to where they probably originated or where some final ingredients were added. Second, only the pressure of providing a plausible place of creation for each object allows us to ascertain what traits are indigenous to certain peoples, and thereby to recognize the connections among the tribes and the history behind the cultures.

102. *The term "area of creation."* How precisely should we understand the term "area of creation"? The answer is: as precisely as possible. This plea for precision is not a result of academic pedantry but is instead based on two facts that have been ascertained through experience.

First, the cultural expressions of so-called native people can vary greatly from one another, despite their being located on unbroken terrain without geographic barriers. This is primarily the result of generally meager or one-sided communication. The general cultural output of the cove of Geelvink in Dutch New Guinea differs completely from that of Humboldt Bay (Yos Sudarso Bay). And still new characteristics are found a short distance away from Humboldt Bay, at Lake Sentani, whence the Dresden Museum attained a small but very interesting collection. Further to the east of German New Guinea, new cultural landscapes continually come into view along the coast: the cultures of the Berlin Harbor area, of the estuary of the Ramu and the Empress Augusta River, of Astrolabe Bay, and of the Finschhafen region. The cultural landscape found in British New Guinea is just as diverse. New Guinea in particular, where currently only the coastal areas are known in the West, forms a prime example of the marked diversity in cultural styles (rather than stages). Although certain characteristic cultural manifestations can be widespread, such as the headrest, the tapioca mallet, and certain forms of clubs, it is possible for the expert to glance at a piece before him and to know immediately without effort precisely from where it came. A headrest from Geelvink Bay looks entirely different from one from the Humboldt Bay region, the area of Finschhafen, or Tami Island. Despite their proximity, the indigenous people have imprinted their cultural creations with their own specific, idiosyncratic character—a style that developed organically and differs consistently from that of their neighbors. Naturally, the multiplicity of cultural forms is particularly noticeable on islands with limited movement and interregional contact, such as in large swaths of Polynesia. There is more of a shared cultural landscape in the East Indian Archipelago, since trade fostered some degree of uniform distribution of cultural goods, at least along the coasts. An ethnographic museum must be able to express this multiplicity of cultural styles that depend on their geographic sites of creation.

Second, close proximity of multiple distinct styles does not imply an absolute rejection of outside influences. For example, the people from Tami Island in German New Guinea create V-shaped bowls decorated in a style found nowhere else in the world. But they create these bowls less for themselves than for export. The people are sailors and trade their bowls far into Kaiser Wilhelmsland.[185] Similarly, the people from Bilibili and from Teste Island at the eastern tip of British New Guinea make pottery in a very specific style that is primarily used for trade with their neighbors.[186] The people from East Celebes (Sulawesi), through a type of industrial enterprise, created a distinctive sword with a wide blade. These swords, long referred to as *tambokschen*, are found widely throughout the eastern area of the East Indian Archipelago, all the way to New Guinea.[187] Thus, certain areas can both have their own individual style *and* be centers of industry and trade, purposefully distributing their products over a wide area beyond the borders of their local style. In order to represent the purity of a specific local culture in the museum, foreign objects should be omitted from the region that possessed them and displayed with material from the region that created them, unless they have been altered in a way that is characteristic of the region to which they were exported. It might seem a better solution to leave the objects among other items found in the same region and label them as imports. This, however, cannot be permitted, on account of the resulting fragmentation of the holdings from the places where the imported objects were created. Frequently, a representative example of a given type of exported object may be lacking in the collection of its place of creation, and its inclusion is therefore essential to offer a complete picture of that area's culture.

103. *The creation of a display arranged according to places of creation.* A prerequisite of an exhibition organized according to places of creation is a thorough, critical analysis of the collection. The current general lack of knowledge and widespread lack of resources for research in museums have two obvious results: unconscious errors are unavoidable, and a number of objects of indeterminate origin cannot be ordered. In the last decade, the Dresden Museum attempted to install an exhibition organized by place of creation.[188] The objects from individual sites of creation were divided from each other by matte glass "partitions" set on trestles, which are also used in the Leipzig Museum. In addition, a separate cabinet was devoted to objects of an indeterminate origin. One should not expect this to be a particularly large group. The origins of these

objects are continually being identified through various means: newly acquired collections, notes in older works stumbled upon accidentally, new publications, written questionnaires, and verbal inquiries made in conversation with experts. These same means can help rectify errors in existing displays.

In the interest of a unified execution of the exhibition's principles the museum administration should if possible refuse the wish that is frequently and precisely expressed by donors: that their collection be exhibited separately in its entirety. Such a display should be allowed only under the condition that it will be for a limited duration. Separate displays of complete collections that have been bequeathed to a museum end up segregating objects that should be exhibited together and imposing upon the academic and administrative tasks of the institution.

Tasks with Respect to the Public

The Description of the History of Discovery[189]

124. The description of the object's geographic discovery can be presented in conjunction with geographic information. The discovery of territory can be of national interest (in the case of the Bismarck Archipelago), as well as of general interest (in the case of Indonesia and the South Seas, which had important historical results, or in the case of Benin, which significantly shifted our cultural understanding of the abilities of Negroes). In the case of Benin, reference to the sources can also point out that the kingdom and its culture were already known in the sixteenth and seventeenth centuries. However, since knowledge of the region was lost and the old accounts were disregarded, the rediscovery of 1897 came as a great surprise. Explanations of this sort have hardly ever been included in ethnographic museums. Equally rare have been explanations relating to the following two areas.

Discussion of the Study of Race

125. Laypeople must be made aware of the racial distinctions within humankind—or at least of the assumed affiliation of a certain people with a certain race. With circumspection, they can also learn of assumptions about racial correlations and about racial stratification of the population

in a certain area, as well as the reasons behind these assumptions. Above all, these viewpoints must be supported by visual representation, since a vibrant understanding of a culture necessitates a conceptualization of what its indigenous members looked like.

Discussion of Commerce

On the question of whether ethnographic collections via their labels and maps should also impart information about economically important events to the extent that they fall within their domain, see §12 above.

Pictures and Figures

126. *Visual depictions of indigenous people.* The primary task of explanatory images, as with three-dimensional figures, is to make museum visitors familiar with the indigenous people, supplying a visual understanding beyond that of the textual label. The most general and basic level of such explanatory material includes images of racial types like those of Rudolf Martin and Hölzel,[190] which offer an array of sketched heads with indigenous jewelry in more or less authentic detail. Photographic portraits of native peoples are, of course, more accurate, although they are less appealing owing to the lack of color. Prints of these subjects enlarged to life size are available for purchase. Especially valuable are photographs depicting indigenous people in their native dress and engaged in characteristic activities, since such representations offer a more complete and educational vantage point. The National Archive for Ethnography makes available a variety of colored illustrations of this type. While not as accurate as photographs, these pictures can be used for display in copies or originals, as in the Dresden Museum. Drawings and paintings by natives themselves can also be used in this manner. For example, Schurtz employed drawings by Eskimos, Japanese people, and Korean people in his *Urgeschichte der Kultur* of 1900.

127. *The visual explanations of objects.*

(a) *Methods of production and use.* Aside from helping to visualize the bearers of a given culture, images of the type discussed in the preceding paragraphs also depict how objects are used, how clothes are worn, and so forth. Special pictures in which people either do not appear at all or are a part of the background can help explain the purpose of objects by illustrating their use, production, and so forth. In this regard, the existing literature provides a wealth of material that can be reproduced and presented to the public in conjunction with the objects. For example, the use of fire-making equipment, the production of Paleolithic stone tools, the arm bands of *Tridacna gigas*, and the pounding of rice have been understood only through images. Here, too, material of historical value can be used. The way pectorals made from sperm whale tooth were worn (a very rare example is found in the Dresden Museum) or the way a military boat was navigated in New Zealand can be illustrated with pictures from Cook's travel accounts. The use of a lance with a lasso in deer hunts in South Celebes and southern Borneo is depicted in Salomon Müller, *Land- en Volkenkunde*. Edifying images can also be created from descriptions, such as the illustration in the Dresden Museum of the dance boards worn on high hats by the Baining (in the Gazelle Peninsula, New Pomerania).

(b) *External and internal relationships*. Apart from production and use practices, images can also depict objects that have an external or internal relationship with the exhibited object. For example, it is far easier to understand the specific form of the bird-head mace from New Caledonia when it is displayed next to an image of the bird on which it is based (the *kagu, Rhinochetus jabatus*). Bronze depictions of houses from Benin can be displayed next to Drapper's engraving of the city of Benin. The borrowing of the Tumpal pattern in Javanese batik from India can be proven by comparing the depiction of the king of Candy in Ceylon, who is dressed in Indian garb with the Tumpal pattern. This derivation is discussed in the work on Indian batik art by Gerret Pieter Rouffaer and Hendrik Herman Juynboll. And there are countless further examples.

(c) *Parallel examples of rare objects*. Rare pieces can be emphasized in several ways. As has been discussed above (cf. §92), a special object can be given prominent placement among the items in its display, the guidebook can make particular mention of the object, and its rarity can be stressed on its label, which can note its limited presence in other collections throughout the world. A further means of emphasis is to display images of well-known parallels alongside the object for comparative purposes. In the Dresden Museum, for example, this method was implemented to highlight the feathered cloaks, collars, and headgear from Hawaii. On three tableaus the viewer can see side-by-side images of all the well-known feather pieces of this type to the extent that pictures are available. These images allow the unique status of the Dresden cloak with its green feathers and the extreme rarity of the feather helmet with the same feathers to be effectively communicated. The same could be done for the Dresden Museum's two large wooden bowls from New Zealand in the shape of dogs(?). The only other places where pieces of this kind are found is in the Museum of Cambridge in England and in the Peabody Museum in Cambridge, Massachusetts, in the United States.

(d) *Reconstruction attempts.* We recommend the retention of incomplete objects in their partial form, while simultaneously suggesting that hypotheses or mere assumptions of their complete appearance could be indicated via sketches on their adjacent labels.

Other depictions of objects not present in the museum can also serve this purpose, including photographs (particularly of large panels) and plaster casts; see §54 above.

To put it succinctly, comparative images in an exhibition can function just as they do in books. The Dresden Museum has employed them in these aforementioned cases and is inclined to implement their use on a larger scale in the future.

128. *The figural depictions of indigenous peoples.* It is worth recalling the idealized representations of foreign peoples, which must first of all be considered as artistic creations—as works of monumental or small sculpture. Among the few eras of art history whose works are of ethnographic interest, the Hellenistic epoch takes a prominent place, above all the Pergamene sculptures, with their figures of Gauls and other statues which Attalos I consecrated to the cult of Athena. Pergamon itself was a kind of ethnographic museum where sculptures were set up to commemorate victories. We should also recall the head of an African maiden from Priene, as well as the smaller Alexandrian bronzes that portrayed figures from the street life of Alexandria and are comparable to our Viennese bronzes, such as the Nubian street singer and the market seller who crouches in front of his fruit with a monkey on his shoulder. These images demonstrate a loving immersion in the character and nature of the barbarian, for which we can search in vain in the days of Phidias and Praxiteles, before the rise of Alexander the Great. Pergamene art in

particular combines ethnographic representation with a high degree of anatomical knowledge, as is shown by the Borghese Warrior, while also demonstrating, for instance in the statues of the Gauls, an unreserved acknowledgment of the heroic grandeur of the barbarians and a sense of the staggering drama of their untamed pride. In the Alexandrian era, there was already too much barbarian blood in Greece for the old prejudice of Hellenic superiority to retain its validity. We cannot claim that subsequent eras, including our own, have ever again attained such a deep understanding of foreign barbarian peoples. In some instances the image and soul of the barbaric and primitive nature has drawn on fantastical inferences as much as scholarly sources—recall the sculptures in the Galeries d'Anatomie Comparée et d'Anthropologie in the Jardin des Plantes in Paris. We cannot speak of a creation based on observation or an understanding among wider circles of such types of subjects in the arts. A statue like Walter Sintenis's proud Negro still seems surprising and foreign—even in a time when the most remote tribes are threatened by matches, gunpowder, alcoholic spirits, and dangerous illnesses, and even in a city that boasts the largest ethnographic museum on earth. Accordingly, the thought of a (colonial) art gallery with reliefs in the style of the panels showing weapons as booty from the temple of Athena in Pergamon and with statues of foreign (colonial) people as they used to appear in the temple, has scarcely more value than the lovely dream of an idealist enthusing about the ennoblement of humanity through artistic contemplation—even at a time that is characterized by global exchange. The barbarian still stands far removed from our human experience. For an understanding of the characteristic customs of foreign blood cannot be deemed a self-evident property among a broad audience. Neither has some brotherly love born from an awareness that all humankind are children of God succeeded in forming bonds among people and uniting them in Christ, nor have the "increasingly dense ties embracing the globe [brought] the white man in such close community and contact . . . with the colored, lesser races" that "crossbreeding became the mother of many bestial products."[191]

(a) *Facial casts.* Three-dimensional facial casts are similarly rare but offer accurate information about indigenous people's physiognomy, much like the sketches and photographs of racial types by Martin, Hölzel, and Forbes. Casts by Finsch can be acquired from the Berlin Museum, and others are in the Schlagintweit Collection in the anthropological department of the Galeries d'Anatomie in Paris.[192]

(b) *Mannequins in costume*. Without a doubt, the most complete and impressive means of visualizing ethnographic objects are through life-sized mannequins, wearing authentic indigenous dress and, if possible, posing in realistic and characteristic situations.[193] In the words of Paul Sarasin: "All ethnographic objects appear as if alive when it is possible to glimpse them in use; merely propping them up in exhibitions makes them appear useless, as if dead."[194] For this reason, most museums today include mannequins or groups of such figures, including Berlin (where a large number feature in the Indian section), Leipzig, Bremen, and Rotterdam. However, while the stuffed animal displays in zoological museums (including the British Museum, the Horniman Museum in London, the Städtisches Museum in Bremen, and the Museum of the Artis Natura Magistra in Amsterdam) aim for both beauty and realistic accuracy,[195] the same cannot be said for the ethnographic mannequins in European museums.[196] The current lingering curiosity about the "wild" peoples of the world impresses on them the character of wax figure cabinets. Either the mannequins' facial types, body positions, and skin colors are more or less wildly unrealistic, or the display itself is a pastiche of objects that would never have been seen together in real life. In the interest of truth, only body casts should be used as the foundations of mannequins, in the same way that photographs are preferable over other pictures. This method has been employed at least partly in the Indian collection in the Berlin Museum, and less so in the Field Columbian Museum in Chicago.[197] If necessary, mannequin displays (possibly in conjunction with Finsch facial casts) could also be modeled after good-quality photographs. Errors in dress (the crassest examples are in the Musée d'Artillerie in Paris) are largely due to the creator not having at his disposal all the elements that the figure should be wearing. Mistakes of this type can be lessened by refusing to purchase mannequins from dealers who tend to be indifferent to scientific precision and veracity. Instead, mannequins should be produced at the museums under critical scientific observation. Several years ago, the Dresden Museum employed a weaver from Java for this purpose.

The production of wax figure displays is very expensive, in part because the conservation of the ethnographic accoutrements usually necessitates a protective glass case. The grave damage that dust and flies can inflict over time was evident several years ago with the "Javanese Family Group" display in the Wereldmuseum in Rotterdam. The current, more industrious director has recently undertaken a thorough cleaning of the group.[198]

(c) *Models, or modeled figurines.* Representations of indigenous peoples made of painted clay, papier-mâché, and similar materials cannot replace life-size costumed mannequins, but they do offer their own advantages. They are relatively inexpensive and therefore lend themselves to widespread use. When they are produced on location (such as Indian tribal groups manufactured in India), we have affirmation that the figurines combine items that were worn in real life and thus truly make the indigenous life visible. Without requiring a great deal of space, they allow for the representation of complete and large scenes of everyday life.[199] The Indian department of the Berlin Museum displays a great number of these figurines, some of them of very fine and accurate quality. Obviously there will also be figurines modeled in a lumpy, crude way from clay or other materials. In general, figurines are still dressed dolls, but they differ notably from actual ethnographic objects such as the dolls made by indigenous cultures as toys and so forth, which as a rule render reality in a very rough manner.

129. *Costumes on painted casts of body parts.* Museum administrations may also use casts of body parts to allow for a partial effect of the mannequin figure without the great expense. For example, head ornamentation can be displayed in an impressive way using busts, such as the painted Finsch types. In the Dresden Museum these were used to great effect for displaying the feather and forehead ornamentation from British New Guinea. Incidentally, since busts may include the full chest or just the upper portion of the chest, they are also able to display pectoral and neck ornamentations. Arm decoration can be displayed on painted arm casts. These examples not only serve to illustrate how the jewelry was worn, but also provide an image of how the ornamentation would have appeared against the skin tone of its intended wearers.

130. *Models and copies.* Some ethnographic objects that may be available are rarely acquired by museums owing to their great size and the difficulties of transporting them either as originals or in casts. Such items, whether as originals or casts, can also be difficult to display in the museum space. Examples include functional objects such as buildings, boats, ships, stone funerary structures, large wooden carvings, and large traps to catch wild animals, as well as artworks such as cast work, carvings, and paintings. In such cases, a model—a miniature sculptural reproduction—can serve as a welcome stand-in for the original. In some

cases, however, dependable photographs would perhaps provide an even better option. As is the case with the figurines discussed above, a sharp distinction has to be drawn between models that are made for export (particularly after repeated advance requests by foreign visitors) and models made by the indigenous people themselves for whatever internal reason linked to local lifestyles and artistic relationships. Work of this latter sort includes models of houses or ships as playthings, boat models as spirit vessels, sarcophagi models as containers (as on the island of Bali), and so forth, but primarily the Chinese and Japanese copies of works of older East Asian art.[200] These objects are ethnographic objects in the fullest sense of the word and can serve the museum's purpose of visualizing the objects that they reproduce in miniature. There is no value to models that represent objects in a rough, ad hoc manner, such as tools (knives, axes, etc.) or games, which are surely obtainable in the original and are not at all difficult to display in museum interiors, and they especially do not belong in larger collections.[201] Models of this type are frequently brought back by travelers who have made a cursory visit abroad and lacked the opportunity or desire to pursue acquisitions more carefully. The models are created by opportunistic natives using European means of production with the intent of selling to foreigners. They constitute the dregs of ethnography, since they provide no glimpse into the abilities of the people and instead offer up a false or sadly altered one. Museums should obviously not purchase such items and should furthermore refuse all donations of this sort.

The Provision of Explanatory Material

131. As we have discussed, the means that need to be harnessed to explain a scientifically ordered collection are vast—almost overly so.[202] But the explanatory material should not become excessive or too intrusive. Labels should not choke the collection, and the attention of the viewer should not be directed away from the objects to the educational aids instead. The right proportion must be maintained so that the amount of explanatory material satisfies a pedagogical maxim: all means should help but must be applied with tact to the right degree.

Furthermore, the production of explanatory material as it is suggested above not only demands a great deal from the scientific staff of the museum but also requires the existence of an adequate technical apparatus in order to prevent it from becoming excessively expensive and time-consuming.

1.   In the meantime, we can compare Kristian Bahnson, "Über ethno-
     graphische Museen" (*Mitteilungen der Anthropologischen Gesellschaft Wien*
     XVIII = N. F. VIII) (Vienna, 1888). The discussion above developed from
     an essay (begun in 1904) by the author, published in *Dresdner Anzeiger*
     (February 26, 1905), titled "Zum Verständnis der ethnographischen
     Museen." A Dutch translation of the essay's main points appeared in
     the *Koloniaal Weekblad "Oost en West"* (March 30, 1905). See also *Museum
     voor land- en volkenkunde en Maritiem museum "Prins Hendrik," te Rotterdam:
     Verslag over het jaar 1905* (= Jaarverslag 22) (Rotterdam: Museum voor lan-
     den volkenkunde, 1906), 7–9. Franz Heger's discussion of the history of
     ethnographic museums is not quite accurate in *Festschrift für Adolf Bastian*
     (1896), 585, 586f.
2.   Cf. "Ethnographische Bildergallerie: Eine Reihe von Sittenbildern aus
     der neuesten Völkerkunde, in *Beytrag zu einer redenden Naturlehre und
     Phsyiognomik der Menschheit*, 2 vols. (Nürnberg, 1791).
3.   Back in the classical period, we see the term *anthropologos*, meaning "to talk
     about other people," in Aristotle, *Ethics* 4.8. Formulating a thorough his-
     tory of this word would be a task equally difficult and interesting, and a sig-
     nificant contribution to the history of the intellectual currents of humanity.
4.   For example, Adolf Bastian, *Die Vorstellungen von der Seele* (1875), 4, 6,
     and "Über Methoden in der Ethnologie," *Petermanns Mittheilungen* 3
     (1893): 6: "the . . . natural-scientific method of induction, which is based
     on comparisons."
5.   Theodor Benfey in *Kleinere Schriften*, ed. Adalbert Bezzenberger, vol. 2,
     pt. 4 (1892), 52.
6.   Franz Bopp, *Über das Conjugationssystem der Sanskritsprache in Vergleichung
     mit jenem der griechischen, lateinischen, persischen und germanischen
     Sprache* (Frankfurt a. M., 1816); and particularly Jacob Grimm, *Deutsche
     Grammatik*, vol. 1 (Göttingen, 1819), and *Deutsche Rechtsalterthümer*
     (Göttingen, 1828). See also Adalbert Kuhn, *Zur ältesten Geschichte der
     indogermanischen Völker: Osterprogramm des Berliner Real-Gymnasiums* (1845),
     and *Die Herabkunft des Feuers und des Gottertranks* (Berlin, 1859).
7.   See Gustav Friedrich Klemm, *Zur Geschichte der Sammlungen für Wissenschaft
     und Kunst* (1837), 233. According to Klemm, it was not until the eigh-
     teenth century that natural items were systematically separated from art
     objects and historical monuments, though he cites Johann Daniel Major as
     having advocated for this earlier in *Unvorgreiffliches Bedenken von Kunst- und
     Naturalien-Kammern* (Kiel, 1674).
8.   Franz Boas, "Address at the International Congress of Arts and Sciences,
     St. Louis, September 1904," *Science*, n.s. 20, no. 512 (October 21, 1904).
9.   Boas, "Address." The minimization of interest in ethnography has been
     correctly stressed by Ernst Grosse in *Festschrift für Adolf Bastian* (1896),
     601; cf. Rudolf Martin, *Anthropologie als Wissenschaft und Lehrfach* (1901),
     17, 18; and Edouard De Jonghe, *La place de l'ethnographie dans les études
     universitaires* (Congrès International d'Expansion Économique Mondiale,
     Mons 1905, section 5: Expansion civilisatrice vers les pays neufs), 3.
10. Karl Weule, *Völkerkunde und Urgeschichte im 20. Jahrhundert* (1902), 30, as
     urged by Georg Buschan, ibid., 71.

11. According to Adolf Bastian, *Die wechselnden Phasen im geschichtlichen Sehkreis* (*IV*) (1900), 29.

12. Cf. De Jonghe, *La place de l'ethnographie dans les études universitaires*, 2.

13. Wilhelm Waldeyer, "Universitäten und anthropologischer Unterricht," *Correspondenz-blatt der Deutschen Gesellschaft für Anthropologie* 30 (1899): 74b; see also his obituary for Adolf Bastian, *Zeitschrift für Ethnologie* 37(1905): 256.

14. Paul Ehrenreich, "Reise durch die iberische Halbinsel," *Zeitschrift für Ethnologie* 28 (1886): *Verhandlungen der berliner Gesellschaft für Anthropologie, Ethnologie und Urgeschichte*, 50f.

15. Leiden has the honor of possessing the first systematically assembled ethnographic collection: the (second) Japanese collection of Franz von Siebold, which was acquired by the Dutch state in 1838. It was a collection that "fulfilled all the criteria for comprehensive cultural-historical material from a single location" (Bahnson, "Über ethnographische Museen," 2). It was due only to a lack of space that the collection was "temporarily" not housed in the Koninklijk Kabinet van Zeldzaamheden in Gravenhagen, where ethnographic material had been placed earlier, but instead in Leiden, where von Siebold resided. On July 1, 1864, the collection was named the Rijks Ethnographisch Museum. In 1883 the remaining ethnographic materials from the Koninklijk Kabinet van Zeldzaamheden were also moved to Leiden. Thus, this "temporary" ("in afwachtig," ca. 1839) museum became "in perpetuum." See Gerret Pieter Rouffaer, *Nieuwe wegen voor indische Volkenkunde* (De Gids, February 1904), 20f.

16. Through 1903 the ethnographic museum in Leipzig that developed from the purchase of the cultural-historical collections of Gustav Friedrich Klemm was the property of a private society. On January 1, 1904, the collection came under civic administration.

17. See Klemm, *Zur Geschichte der Sammlungen*, 144ff.

18. See Karl Lamprecht, *Deutsche Geschichte* 3, v. 2 (1904): 491f.; and Karl Wilhelm Hiersemann, *Antiquariat und Buchhandlung in Leipzig*, cat. 321, p. 15, no. 171, and pp. 148ff., no. 1481.

19. See Oskar Münsterberg, *Zeitschrift des Münchner Alterthumsverein*, N. F. VI (1894): 21ff.

20. See Klemm, *Zur Geschichte der Sammlungen*, 213ff.

21. See Klemm, *Zur Geschichte der Sammlungen*, 135ff.

22. See Klemm, *Zur Geschichte der Sammlungen*, 142.

23. As fittingly mentioned by Richard Fritzsche, *Neue Jahrbücher für das klassische Altertum*, vol. 1, pt. 13 (1904), 625 (cf. Adolf Bastian, *Zur heutigen Sachlage der Ethnologie* [Berlin, 1899], 25).

24. See Berthold Laufer, *Globus* 88 (1905): 45ff.

25. Ernest-Théodore Hamy, *Les origines du Musée d'Ethnographie* (Paris, 1890), 5n1.

26. See Klemm, *Zur Geschichte der Sammlungen*, 148, 254.

27. The case of the Leipzig Museum, where the administrative costs of the ethnographic collection became too much for even its wealthy society, was an exception.

28. Possible exceptions are the large North American museums, above all the

Field Columbian Museum in Chicago and the US National Museum in Washington, DC. A newer addition is the American Museum of Natural History in New York.

29. In the vast majority of cases of ethnographic scientific activity, a researcher cannot consult a nearby specialist with knowledge similar to his own who could offer meticulous criticism of his work.

30. On the necessity and practical form of such a field of study, see below, §§9–12.

31. *Führer durch das Königlichen Museum für Völkerkunde zu Berlin*, 12th ed. (1905), 3.

32. See Adolf Bastian, *Die wechselnden Phasen im geschichtlichen Sehkreis (IV) und ihre Rückwirkungen auf die Völkerkunde* (1900), 11.

33. For a similar definition of "ethnology," see Grosse, *Festschrift für Adolf Bastian*, 597.

34. See also De Jonghe, *La place de l'ethnographie dans les études universitaires*, 4.

35. This "lack of clarity and consensus in relation to the terms 'anthropology,' 'ethnology,' 'Völkerkunde,' and 'Volkskunde,' etc." was discussed by M. Winternitz in *Globus* 78 (1900): 345–50, 370–77, with reference to "some of the best-known handbooks and most prominent members of the field." The subsequent literature on these terms has found as little agreement as the prior literature: Rudolf Martin, *Anthropologie als Wissenschaft und Lehrfach* (Jena, 1901); Weule, *Völkerkunde und Urgeschichte*; Heinrich Schurtz, *Völkerkunde: Die Erdkunde*, ed. M. Klar, pt. XVI (Leipzig, 1903), 1–3; S. R. Steinmetz, "Die Aufgaben der Sozial-Ethnologie," *Korrespondenzblatt der deutschen Gesellschaft für Anthropologie, Ethnologie und Urgeschichte* 34 (1903, 1904): 139–43; Siegmund Günther, *Ziele, Richtpunkte und Methoden der modernen Völkerkunde* (Stuttgart, 1904); De Jonghe, *La place de l'ethnographie dans les études universitaires* 2f., 4.

36. This has recently also been highlighted by philosophers, among them Erich Adickes, *Kant contra Haeckel* (1901), 121f., and Oswald Külpe, *Die Philosophie der Gegenwart in Deutschland* (1902), 2f.

37. Above all, the art of (South and East) Asia is not independent of the cultural circle that blossomed from the peoples of the Mediterranean.

38. "Batik refers to the painting of [European] cotton on both sides with [bees'] wax, in order to prevent those areas covered by the wax from picking up the dye in a cold or lukewarm dye bath. After being dipped in the dye, the cloth is placed in hot water. This liquefies the wax, which rises to the surface owing to its lighter specific gravity. This procedure can be repeated with different colors and changing patterns of wax coverage. In this way, differences in pattern, color tonality, and colorfastness can be obtained, similar to the effect of fabric that is woven from colored yarns." *Ethnographische Miszellen* II (1903): 24n4.

39. Although the Netherlands has practiced batik for a long time (cf. the introduction to the great works of Gerret Pieter Rouffaer and Hendrik Herman Juynboll, *Die indische Batikkunst* [1900], and Herman Ambrosius Jan Baanders, *Over nieuwe proeven van batik-technick in Nederland* [Amsterdam, 1901]), the technique was newly introduced in Germany (Berlin and Munich). But one cannot say that the process is in the public domain of the

European textile industry, or that its results have been fully introduced to European fashion. In Holland, where batik is also practiced on velvet and where batik fabric is occasionally seen being worn (as on decorative vests), the term *Batikken* is universally known. German (Javanese) batiks are advertised in fashion magazines. On German batik technique, see Robert Breuer, *Batiks: Kunst und Handwerk* 54, no. 12 (1904): 333ff. See also Johannes Aarnout Loeber in *Koloniaal Weekblad "Oost en West"* (November 2, 1905): 1, sp. 4. According to *Koloniaal Weekblad*, a course in batik will also be offered in Paris ([March 8, 1904]: 1, sp. 3).

40.   "Ikat is a method of coloring cloth in which the warp threads, the weft threads, or both are partly dyed, once or multiple times, with the goal of creating a certain pattern through the weaving. In this process, specific sections of the thread are bound up so that they remain undyed while the rest is placed in a color bath." *Ethnographische Miszellen* II (1903): 24ff. Ikat comes from central Asia (Turkistan). It was introduced to Europe under the name *chiné-technique* in France via Siamese prototypes between 1684 and 1750 using silk cloth (the term *chiné* is of unknown origin; possibly it indicates Chinese [Indian], or possibly it comes from the French *chaine*). Later, in place of the binding, the print on the warp or weft thread was introduced. See Gerret Pieter Rouffaer, *Over Ikat's, Tjine's, Patola's en Chiné's* (1902), 3ff., 21ff.

41.   This is surely one of the very rare cases of transmission of a superior element from a generally inferior culture into a higher culture. It is "one of the best known historical facts that people with a very low culture tend to go under after the import of a very high culture" and that "people of a very high culture have difficulty taking up even individual elements of a lower culture." See Karl Lamprecht, *Moderne Geschichtswissenschaft* (1905), 115.

42.   By the way, ornamental gourd flasks are still found in Europe today (as in the Balkans).

43.   See *Publikationen aus dem Königlich Ethnographischen Museum zu Dresden* 14 (1903): 48a. From the sixth level in Troy, clay bases for vessels were found: cf. Hubert Schmidt in Wilhelm Dörpfeld, *Troja und Ilion* 1 (1902): 293 and supplement 40 II and III.

44.   For a different theory on the development of the handle, see *Publikationen aus dem Kgl. Ethnographischen Museum zu Dresden*, 31a.

45.   On the relationship between "Volkskunde" and "Völkerkunde," see Raimund Friedrich Kaindl, *Völkerkunde, Volkskunde und Völkerwissenschaft: Österreichische Rundschau* (Vienna) IV (1905): 143–50, and Georg Thilenius, *Mitteilungen das Verbandes deutscher Vereine für Volkskunde* (*Korrespondenzblatt*), no. 3 (January 1906): 14–17. On the relationship between prehistory and ethnography, see the author's work in *Globus* 88 (1905): 154f., §27ff., §176.

46.   William Henry Holmes, *Annual Report of the United States National Museum for 1901* (1903), 256f.: "The material evidences of culture are . . . seen to be of vast extent and importance, but it should be observed that, notwithstanding this fact, all culture cannot be illustrated in the museum, for in it we can utilize material things only. We cannot show by its collections the social, moral, religious, and intellectual traits of man save in an

indirect way. We can do little to illustrate language save by displaying the methods of its expression to the eye in pictures and letters. We can tell little of religion save by assembling the idols and devices that represent its symbolism and the paraphernalia which pertain to the practice of its rites. We can tell nothing of music save by a display of the curious array of instruments used in producing sound, and society and government are even less within the sphere of the museum."

47. Recently, Waldeyer's closing words on the celebration of Adolf Bastian on March 11, 1905 (see Bastian, *Gedächtnisfeier, am 11. März, 1905, Berlin,* 26), have made it known that Bastian was working to affiliate the Berlin Museum with the University of Berlin: "Bastian strove with all his energy to develop this museum and the anthropological society into a large institute that would work under the auspices of a university. Such an institute would offer systematic instruction in all the anthropological and ethnological disciplines, as well as further independent research through means and space in all the encompassed fields. Such a big plan cannot be realized quickly and with one stroke, but it must be brought to fruition. Germany is unfortunately already behind other cultures in this regard." Cf. Adolf Bastian, *Die wechselnden Phasen im geschichtlichen Sehkreis (I) occidentalischer Cultur* (1900), 28.

48. Kurt Hassert, *Zu Friedrich Ratzels Gedächtnis* (Leipzig: Seele, 1904), 167ff.

49. On a practical formulation of the scientific efforts in conjunction with missionaries (and with colonial administration), see also Max Müller, *Essays* (German ed.) IV (1876), 148ff.

50. Cf. Karl Lamprecht, *Deutsche Geschichte* 3, v. 2 (1904): 496.

51. Adolf Bastian, *Tijdschr. voor Ind. Taal-, Land-, en Vokenk* 40 (1898): 203, 208; *Zur heutigen Sachlage der Ethnologie*; *Die wechselnden Phasen im geschichtlichen Sehkreis (I) occidentalischer Cultur* (1900); *Die wechselnden Phasen im geschichtlichen Sehkreis (III) hier und da* (1900); *Die wechselnden Phasen im geschichtlichen Sehkreis (IV) und ihre Rückwirkungen auf die Völkerkunde* (1900), esp. 21ff.; Felix von Luschan, *Verh. 7. Internationale Geographisches Kongress* (Berlin, 1899), 611f.; *Zeitschrift für Ethnologie Verh.* 35 (1903): 1037, and *Anleitung für ethnographische Beobachtungen und Sammlungen in Afrika und Oceanien* (1904), 6; cf. also Oskar. Münsterberg, *Nation und Welt (weltwirtschaftliche Beilage zu "National-Zeitung")*, April 27, 1904, 1. Fitting with the intellectualism of his psychology, Bastian emphasizes the exploration of mental life in his discussions of the political treatment of the "wild"; cf. *Zur heutigen Sachlage der Ethnologie*, 44.

52. Bastian, *Zur heutigen Sachlage der Ethnologie*, 40.

53. See Felix von Luschan, *Anleitung zu wissenschaftlichen Beobachtungen auf Reisen*, ed. Georg von Neumayer, 3 (1905), 46f., of the *Separatabzug*. Recently, Hermann Klaatsch, in *Weltall und Menschheit* 2 (1903): 320, also reminded the state of its obligations to physical anthropology: "Perhaps an awareness will awake among the deciding powers in the final hour that our colonial efforts must also assist our scientific endeavors and that it is the duty of cultured nations to preserve documentation that can aid our understanding of the prehistory of our own people."

54. Karl Weule's words in *Völkerkunde und Urgeschichte*, 2 (cf. *Meyers Konversations-Lexikon* 5, 17 [1897], 383b) are misleading: "Ethnography and ethnology, as fields of modern science, may be traced back to the year 1829. At that time, the natural scientist Milne-Edwards (on page 43, the name was corrected to W. F. Edwards) wrote a letter to Thierry, which initiated the foundation of the Société ethnologique, the first of its type."

55. On this, see Bastian, *Zur heutigen Sachlage der Ethnologie*, 10, notes; cf. also 40.

56. Luschan, *Verh. 7. Internationale Geographisches Kongress*, 612. On the unfairness of a contemptuous valuation of "natural man," see Karl Bücher, *Entstehung der Volkswirtschaft*, 3rd ed. (1901), 97.

57. Victor Hehn, *Kulturpflanzen und Haustiere* (1894), 120, 129.

58. On Hebraic herdsmen of the desert and their occupation of Canaan, see the brief but apt remarks of Hermann Guthe, *Geschichte des Volkes Israel* (1899), 10, 27f., 44, 55f., 61–63. On nomadic Arabs as tradespeople and later as a settled and highly cultured society, see Eduard Meyer, *Geschichte des Alterthums*, vol. 3 (Suttgart: Cotta, 1901), §86, 142–47. For two further examples of an unfortunate political structure that resulted from ethnographic or geographic mistakes, see Kurt Hassert, "Die geographische Bildung des Kaufmanns," in *Zu Friedrich Ratzels Gedächtnis*, 155. Georg Buschan recounts examples of personal errors in judgment in the treatment of natives in the colonies that were used to diminish the standing of the government. Buschan, *Centralbibliothek für Anthropologie*, V (1900), 70.

59. See Paul Walther, *Deutsche Kolonialzeitung* 22, no. 51 (December 23, 1905): 528b.

60. This "Informatie van Diverse Landen etc." is published in Rouffaer and Juynboll, *Die indische Batikkunst*. The manuscript from which this print was made (it is located in the Dutch Imperial Archives; an excerpt previously published by Edouard De Jonge, *Opkomst* III [1865], 149–63), is itself an old copy, which excluded the illustrations that were part of the original. Thus the text that was most valuable to the salesman was copied.

61. Bastian once said (in *Die wechselnden Phasen im geschichtlichen Sehkreis* [*IV*], *und ihre Rückwirkungen auf die Völkerkunde* [1900], 18f.): "The causal link between ethnological collections and the most extensive questions about life in today's social world (considering human and world affairs) has remained obscure . . . just as the link between industrial technology (with its promotion of international prosperity) and chemical laboratories was obscure when (fifty years ago) the first such institutions could arise only with the help of charitable contributions, as the government showed itself to be reluctant. Now (as we have learned from experiences accumulated in the meanwhile), the government understands its advantage better: namely, to equip institutes of chemistry and physics with their necessary funding and accrue abundant interest on the invested capital in the form of increased tax income (through the retroactive effect of technology on industry and, furthermore, on trade)."

62. Except for Bastian's writings (*Die wechselnden Phasen im geschichtlichen Sehkreis: I and III* [1900]), compare also no. II, 5f. and 14; and no. IV,

iv ff., 1, 3, 8f., 20, 21f., in the same text. Furthermore: Grosse, "Ueber den Ethnologischen Unterricht," *Festschrift für Adolf Bastian* (Berlin, 1896), 595–604; Luschan, *Verh. 7. Internationale Geographisches Kongress,* 611, 612; and F. Ratzel, in a paper presented in January 1902 in Leipzig titled "Die geographische Bildung des Kaufmanns." Kurt Hassert published a very worthwhile paper with the same title in *Zu Ratzels Gedächtnis,* 131–68, which includes further literature.

63.   In Bremen, school trips to the Städtisches Museum für Natur-, Völker- und Handelskunde are obligatory, twice in the summer semester.

64.   On the necessity of a representative for ethnography at universities for theoretical reasons, see above. On the structure of academic "ethnological instruction," see above all Grosse, "Ueber den ethnologischen Unterricht," and De Jonghe, *La place de l'ethnographie dans les études universitaires,* 7ff.; on the creation of a relevant collection of educational materials, see Felix von Luschan, *Globus* 88 (1905): 239ff.

65.   This has been suggested by Wilhelm Waldeyer, *Correspondenz-Blatt der Deutschen Gesellschaft für Anthropologie* 30 (1899): 74a.

66.   Adolf Bastian, *Die wechselnden Phasen im geschichtlichen Sehkreis (I),* 7. In ibid., 17, Bastian presents the following logical chain ("causal link") between the welfare of the people and ethnographic museums: today, the welfare of the people depends in a large part on the universal ("cosmopolitan") movements of the people, which, to be successful, depends on knowledge about different peoples, which is gained in turn through "ethnologic" instruction. And for this "ethnologic" instruction ethnographic collections are an essential foundation.

67.   Hassert, *Zu Friedrich Ratzels Gedächtnis,* 153–54. Obviously, the accurate and continually increasing wealth of experience of such nations does not fail to include state measures to increase colonial trade and the promotion of the understanding of the colonial state.

68.   "It is particularly indicative for our German educational system that the vocational school provides a better geographic foundation than the high school. The high school student usually knows everything about the old Greek colonies; in contrast, he knows next to nothing about the much closer German colonies. This explains, to a large part, the indifference many Germans have for our territories overseas." Hassert, *Zu Friedrich Ratzels Gedächtnis,* 155f. Recently (on February 12, 1906), the Prussian culture minister distributed a circular to colleagues in Prussian provincial schools, through which the editors and publishers of textbooks were encouraged to replace the misleading, paltry, or out-of-date accounts of the German colonies in elementary school textbooks with excerpts of the best-known works of colonial literature from the compilation made by the German Colonial Society in new editions. This measure was certainly widely well received.

69.   England can thank the generosity of the well-known South African millionaire Beit for the establishment of the professorship. Mr. Beit increased the yearly wages of the docents by £900. An instructor previously of Corpus Christi College, Mr. H. E. Egerton, was the first to become a colonial professor.

70. Frequently, however, our historical instruction of today does not regard
the ethical or practical sense at all, instead completely favoring the
intellectual sense. Thus very little is achieved except the creation of
academic discoveries and the acquisition of so-called useful knowledge—
that is to say, a scholarly education.

71 Luschan, *Verh. 7. Internationale Geographisches Kongress*, 612.

72. Bastian, *Zur heutigen Sachlage der Ethnologie*, 12; cf. ibid., 44, which says
nearly the same thing. Clairvoyance about world politics seems to have
been one of Bastian's qualities in general. In his readable small text *Der
Völkerverkehr und seine Verständigungsmittel im Hinblick auf China* (Berlin,
1900), written prior to the Chinese-European wars, he identified in China
not only a "terrifying premonition of an ominous and disastrous approaching catastrophe" but predicted the "growth of a superpower from
those wars, that appears determined to dominate the destiny of East Asia
in the future" (Japan, not Russia).

73. Traditionally, for example, all long and staff-shaped objects in New
Zealand, such as chiefs' staffs, oars, axe handles, and lances, had an
overarching decorative schema that is sparse and admirably precise. The
barbaric decoration on the entire surface of these objects is a newer
development. The sparse and precise decorative schema can hardly be
explained by good taste. Rather, the source is something else: it reflects
the replacement of some former attribute of each object that was
precisely located and served a practical purpose, which was replaced by
artistic decoration when the attribute was no longer necessary.

74. As Ernst Grosse recently discussed in *Museumskunde* 1 (1905): 123ff., the
actual art of East Asia is still barely known and is scarcely represented in
museums. On p. 124, he writes, "In smaller museums, objects that have
obvious Chinese origin are displayed in cabinets full of colorful porcelain, laborious carvings in ivory and hard stone, and showy silk fabrics.
But, unfortunately, nearly all these so-called artworks demonstrate less
of the art and more of the trade of their home country. Chinese art has
never just been handicraft, even during the period of its deepest disinte-
gration to which the majority of the industrial products in those collections belong. The best and most powerful art of China was free artwork
in the form of independent works of sculpture and, above all, painting."
"Chinese art is therefore terribly represented in European museums: of
its essence, its development, and its meaning, our collections give us not
only an inadequate impression, but also a misleading one" (127). "The
Japanese collections in our museums are better and richer than the Chinese and the Korean, but are still neither good nor complete. The exact
same error is being perpetrated here: precisely the most important
branches and the best time periods of art are neglected. In the wealthi-
est institutions, one can at least gain the impression of the decorative
arts from the latest and weakest period, the waning Tokugawa period,
but these overly fine and feminine decorative pieces of a generation that
possessed an excess of leisure and very little freedom demonstrate none
of the simple and elevated masculine beauty of the great free art that
ennobled prior generations" (128). On the importance of Asian artistic

production in general, in relation to aesthetics and taste, Woldemar von Seidlitz (*Museumskunde* 1 [1905]: 189, 197) wrote: "In this regard, the peoples of Asia—the Chinese, the Japanese, the Muslims, and to a lesser extent, the Indians—have brought art to a level of design and perfection that affects our awareness and perspective more and more. It is becoming an integral aspect of our culture. We must expect that the Oriental viewpoint, which places particular importance not only on the purity of form but also on the beauty of color, will, over time, be considered equal to the art of antiquity with its predilection for form. . . . From the artistic side, we recognize a manifestation of Asian culture in particular directions, namely, in consideration of the taste and construction of form evident in the color use and ornamentation of building elements, furniture, and instruments, which has reached a peak that far exceeds all our achievements to date. Therefore, as soon as Asian art is recognized as a new cultural element on our horizon, it cannot long be overlooked if we do not want to concede our creative power to other people."

75.   For many years the author has been convinced that the bronzes of Benin did not develop independently in West Africa, come from Egypt, or result from the influence or learning of European casting methods. Rather, the Benin bronzes were creations of a cultural mix between West African and different oriental elements. While there may have been an older, inherited tradition of wood or ivory carving, the bronzes were made either under the influence of the true bronze artists of South India or were, apart from a few exceptions, the actual work of those artists themselves.

76.   The richest and definitely the most magnificent collections of these items currently are in the Dresden Museum and the Berlin museums.

77.   Cf. primarily Gerret Pieter Rouffaer's article "(Beeldende) Kunst" in the *Encyclopaedie van Nederlandsch-Indië*, ed. Pieter Antonie van der Lith, II (o. J.), 324ff.

78.   Karl Koetschau expresses this well (*Dresdner Jahrbuch* [1905], 97) in his view that skilled artists do not need to copy elements of ornamentation but should rather study the work in order to understand the decorative mastery from its technical and artistic sides: "When an artist or craftsman really understands a piece, such as the distribution of ornamentation on a surface, then he has learned more than if he had made hundreds of sketches in a notebook."

79.   Only the more recent episodes of influence should be considered in our future outlook. The further we go back in history, the stronger the impression grows that the culture in Europe, especially with regard to material culture, was very similar to Asia, or that Europe may even have been a cultural-historical province of Asia. Europe would have likely remained so, or increasingly become so, if our small tribe of people did not produce such intellectual heroes as Homer, Euripides, Phidias, Socrates, and Thucydides, who, we hope, have ultimately freed our higher intellectual spirit from orientalism.

80. The author has heard that the ornamentation of the "Dàyak" of Borneo has already been used on a modern poster. Recently, Paul and Fritz Sarasin have employed border patterns of Celebes origin on the original bindings of their two-part travelogue "Reisen in Celebes" (1905). The author permits himself to remark that the ornamentation of the bamboo boxes of West Timor apparently makes excellent lace patterns; see *Abhandlungen und Berichte des Königlichen Zoologischen und Anthropologisch-Ethnographischen Museums zu Dresden: Festschrift* (1899), no. 3; and Johannes Aarnout Loeber, *Timoreesch Snijwerk en Ornament* ('s-Gravenhage, 1904).

81. From Richter, *Museumskunde* 3 (1907): 14ff.

82. Another ethnographic collection "devoted to trade purposes" ("Commercial Museum") is in Philadelphia, next to the University Collection and the museum of the Academy of Natural Sciences. See Ehrenreich, *Zeitschrift für Ethnologie* 32 (1900): 11. According to *Kolonial Weekblad* 2, no. 30, Bijblad 1 (October 9, 1902), another colonial museum was intended for Paris, modeled on the Haarlem Colonial Museum and the Brussels Trade Museum.

83. Hassert, *Zu Friedrich Ratzels Gedächtnis*, 164.

84. See Woldemar von Seidlitz, "Ein deutsches Museum für asiatische Kunst," *Museumskunde* 1 (1905): 181–97. With respect to its material, one of the main tasks of such a museum would be the expansion of the East Asian collection. Obviously, at least in principle, Ernst Grosse is correct in *Museumskunde* 1 (1905): 131, when he states that this task alone "is so great and difficult that its full realization necessitates the foundation of a dedicated institute endowed with extraordinary resources. Only a large national museum of East Asian art would be able to amass a collection to display the entirety of Eastern artistic production with all its multifaceted ramifications, as well as its organic and historical connections." For a comment about the formal structure of a museum of Asian art, see the note in §50.

85. For some time, writers have used the term *zusammengebüffelte Häßlichkeit* (crammed-together hideousness) for the art of ancient Mexico.

86. Who would doubt, for example, that a master of the art of portraiture created some of the female bronze heads?

87. For Adolf Bastian's thoughts on the removal of Asian artworks from ethnographic museums in general, see §32.

88. Compare also Sophus Müller, *Urgeschichte Europas*, trans. Otto Luitpold Jiriczek (Strasbourg: Trübner, 1905), 1.

89. To enter world history implies achieving continual contact with European history.

90. This situation is often associated with undertakings that result in a general interest and national awareness of cohesion. The mood is expressed in religious terms as a hero cult.

91. Richard Fritzsche, "Zur Geschichte der mythologischen Wissenschaft," *Festschrift des Königlichen Gymnasiums zu Schneeberg* (Schneeberg, 1891), 5.

92. Another example of this type is from Benin in western Africa. Its unusual

high culture for Africa was well-known in Europe in the sixteenth and seventeenth centuries. After that point, however, Beninese art completely faded from European consciousness, until it was rediscovered in 1897.

93.   By the way, numerous accounts of contact between cultures, such as ancient Asian peoples meeting the primitive tribes from the surrounding regions, are either not yet known, or if they are known, are not (generally) accessible or acknowledged as valuable.

94.   It should be noted here that today the mounds of the Mississippi region and the multitude of artifacts that were retrieved from there are no longer ascribed to some mysterious "Moundbuilder" people. Instead, they likely originated from the predecessors of the Indian tribes encountered in the region during the era of European discovery. "And anyone who has had the opportunity to compare the antiquities and modern ethnographic materials of this region would acknowledge that the culture of the cliff dwellers and the abandoned Pueblos of New Mexico and Arizona are similar to that of the agricultural, village-dwelling tribes which still live in this region"; see Eduard Seler, *Gesammelte Abhandlungen zur amerikanischen Sprach- und Altertumskunde* II (1904), 14.

95.   In the upper Xingu region (Brazil), the expedition of von den Steinen found Cariban-speaking tribes that were still living in Neolithic conditions. See K. von den Steinen, *Unter den Naturvölkern Zentral-Brasiliens* (1894), 202ff.

96.   Compare Müller, *Urgeschichte Europas*, 3.

97.   There is evidence that the Eskimos cold-processed meteor iron (with stone tools). North and Middle American civilizations apparently did not know iron. Copper was used, particularly for hand tools and for the typical, coin-like objects in the form of three- to four-finger-wide T-shaped pieces of copper. This copper was not only processed cold, it was also cast and tempered. Nevertheless, the use of copper and "bronze" had barely any influence on the long-standing use of stone instruments, especially of obsidian. In ancient Mexico, the processing of precious metals was known and highly developed. See M. Wichmann, *Über die Metalle bei den altmexikanischen Kulturvölkern* (Halle, 1885). Recently in South America (southern Peru, Bolivia), club-shaped weapons made of lodestone have been found. In some alloys iron is found as well. The ancient Peruvians were also familiar with casting techniques of precious metals and copper alloys, although with the latter only to a minor extent. In any case, copper and iron were of little importance for culture in America. In Africa, brass casting was known only in the west. Its origin is obscure.

98.   The attempt has been made to connect the newly discovered Bronze Age in the Malaysian Archipelago to the bronze-casting techniques currently existing in the region; see *Ethnographische Miszellen* II (1903): 72ff. For an example of how elements of a Stone Age extend into an Iron Age, consider the hafted stone axe found among the Gilyak alongside an iron axe hafted in the old manner.

99.   As may be expected because of the institution's limitations of space, in Basel the prehistoric collection, just like the "European collection," is combined with the ethnographic one.

100. Fritz Sarasin, "Bericht über die Sammlung für Völkerkunde des Basler Museums für das Jahr 1904," *Verhandlungen der Naturforschenden Gesellschaft zu Basel* 18 (1906): 33–47. See also Paul Sarasin, *Zur Einführung in das Prähistorische Kabinett der Sammlung für Völkerkunde im Basler Museum* (Basel, 1906).

101. In general, it is justified to call prehistoric people the *Naturvolker* (primitive people) of pre- and early history. They are also described in this way by some contemporary prehistorians (such as Moritz Hoernes, *Urgeschichte der bildenden Kunst in Europa* [1898]).

102. The combination of prehistoric exhibits with a collection relating to at least one contemporary "Stone Age" people would also make apparent the mistaken way that the laity uses the term. Even though specialists define the term differently, laymen usually take Stone Age to mean that the culture in question used exclusively—or at least primarily—stone implements (in addition to pottery). In fact, however, stone only happened to be the material that was—owing to the dearth of metal—used for the production of weapons and cutting tools, and that survived on account of the durability of the substance. Central Brazilian Indians and inhabitants of Humboldt Bay in Dutch New Guinea exemplify how some tribes that still live in the "Stone Age" do not even produce their own stone axes, but rather know them only as imported goods. Cf. Karl von den Steinen, *Unter den Naturvölkern Zentral-Brasiliens* (1894), 203; and D. A. P. Koning, *Bijdragen Taal-, Land- en Volkenkunde van Nederlandsch.-Indië* (7), I (1903), 278. Ormu in the north of the Cyclops Mountains "is bekend doordat het de omgeving voorziet van steenen voor bijlen"; see also Adolf Bernhard Meyer, *Abhandlungen und Berichte des Königlichen Zoologischen und Anthropologisch-Ethnographischen Museums zu Dresden* 10, no. 4 (1902/3): 5, 6.

103. [What follows is taken from Richter, *Museumskunde* 3 (1907): 99ff.]

104. It goes without saying that the museums which have adopted a specialized purpose could reduce their scope even further by prioritizing specific types of object in their collections. For example, a colonial museum could limit its remit from the outset to the German colonies in the South Seas, a museum of non-European art on the arts of Asia, and a museum aiming to inspire through ethnographic displays of ornaments, woodcarving, or indeed technology.

105. Ernst Grosse, in *Museumskunde* 1 (1905): 131, has recently suggested that the leaders of ethnographic museums create a museum of East Asian art collaboratively by sharing the task: "While up to now individual institutions tended to stretch themselves too far, it would be better for each museum to specialize its activity in coordination with others. In this way, the different collections, despite their spatial separation, would coalesce into a significant unity, and we could attain, even without a central museum, a comprehensive collection of East Asian art."

106. Cf. *Führer durch die ethnographischen Abteilung der Königl. Museen* (1877), 6f., 25f. In this light, Albert Grünwedel wrote in his obituary of Bastian (*Jahrbücher d. kgl. Preuß. Museen* 26, no. 2 [1905]: 7ff.): "He has done great things, especially for ancient American cultures and for the ethnography of Africa and Oceania" (111).

107. Adolf Bastian, *Die wechselnden Phasen im geschichtlichen Sehkreis (II) auf asiatischem Kontinent* (1900), 9.

108. To understand the psychological processes involved in the sudden transformation of an object into an amulet (as opposed to an amulet produced according to traditional norms), we can compare the accounts of two indigenous people from the Middle Celebes describing how they came into possession of flint axe amulets: *Ethnographische Miszellen* II, nos. 16 and 17 (1903). On the term "fetishism," see Richard Fritzsche, *Anfänge der Poesie* (Chemnitz, 1885), 31n1. The fundamental difference between a fetish and an amulet (a word which does not derive from the Arabic "ha-malet," meaning "attachment"; cf. Alois Walde, *Lateinisches etymologisches Wörterbuch* [1906], 27) is that the amulet has an inherently closer and more intimate relationship with its devout wearer than does the fetish. The amulet's magical power is unceasing, while the fetish, which lacks a close external link to the believer, "can easily have its poetic relationship dissolved and thus be regarded again with a prosaic gaze." For the terms "fetish," "amulet," and "talisman," see also Wilhelm Wundt, *Völkerpsychologie*, 2 vols. (Leipzig, 1906), 2:199ff.

109. The most solid research in religious studies will always deal with people who possess religious literature and a relatively advanced religious art, and in particular with those whose literature spans a long period during which their religious perspectives developed with relatively little interference from external missionary activity, intent on producing proselytes. There are only a few cases of such well-documented, continued religious formation, among them India, where religious writing existed in an unbroken chain from the most distant past into the present. Religious art emerges somewhat later among the Greeks, who compensated for the near absence of a strictly religious literature with their rich aesthetic-poetic and mythological writings and aesthetic-religious artworks. Among the Hebrews, on the other hand, religious art was almost completely absent.

110. Compare, for example, on Vedic religions: Hermann Oldenberg, *Religion des Veda* (1894), 58 (lower demons), 163ff. (maya), 400ff. (diksha and tapas), 476ff. (magic); and on Greek religions: E. Rohde, *Psyche*, 3rd ed. (1903); Theodor Gomperz, *Griechische Denker*, 2 vols. (Leipzig, 1896), 1:12ff.; and especially Otto Gruppe, *Griechische Mythologie und Religionsgeschichte* (1897), starting on 758. On the Hebrews, see Wilhelm Nowack, *Entstehung der israelitischen Religion* (1895), 6ff., and Rudolf Smend, *Alttestamentliche Religionsgeschichte* (1899), 131ff. (tree and stone cults), 145ff. (demon cults, sanctity, and impurity), and 151ff. (death and ancestor cults).

111. We need recall the only following names: Schrenck (eastern Iberia), Schimkewitsch (Sierra Leone), Bogoras and Jochelson (northeastern Asia), Skeat (Malaka), Adriani and Kruigt (Middle Celebes), Haddon (New Guinea), Spencer and Gillen (Australia), and Seler (pre-Columbian Mexico), among others.

112. But precisely for these artifacts a different accommodation is now intended: see Wilhelm Bode, *Museumskunde* 1 (1905): 14f., and

Ostasiatische Lloyd 19, no. 15 (April 14, 1905): 676f. ("Die Begründung eines Museums für asiatische Kunst in Berlin").

113. The idea, in a very general sense, was initially voiced by Seidlitz (cf. now *Museumskunde* 1 (1905): 181–97 ["Ein deutsches Museum für asiatische Kunst"]). Ernst Grosse, in *Museumskunde* 1 (1905): 123ff. (cf. esp. 131), for example, desired an imperial museum dedicated to East Asian art, while Wilhelm Bode, as we have seen, wanted to include Persian and Islamic art as well. (Cf. Bode, *Denkschrift, betreffend Erweiterungs- and Neubauten bei den kgl. Museen*, Berlin, February 1907, printed as ms.) Adolf Bastian, as outlined above in §32, even considered the creation of multiple museums of Asian art: one each for Indian, Chinese, and Japanese. This idea of an Asian art museum as expressed by Bode, von Seidlitz, and others has nothing to do with the concept discussed above about more or less independent archaeological departments within ethnographic museums, possibly even a museum of Asian archaeology.

114. Augustin Krämer suggests a definition for the terms that is neither precise nor reconcilable with the facts ("Der Neubau des Berliner Museums für Völkerkunde im Lichte der ethnographischen Forschung," *Globus* 86, no. 2 [July 7, 1904]: 21–24, here 22b). According to him, artifacts are archaeological if they belong to a disappeared civilization, and prehistoric if they belong to a primitive tribe before the development of the written word.

115. Cf. Albert Grünwedel, *Buddhistische Kunst in Indien* (1893; Berlin: Spemann, 1900), 28ff.

116. The monuments of Gandaharan art have been brought to new life by Grünwedel in the work cited above.

117. Grünwedel, *Buddhistische Kunst in Indien*, 185n1. For a differing conclusion, see Georg Bühler, *Transactions of the Ninth International Congress of Orientalists* (London, 1893), 1:221; and Joseph Dahlmann, *Das Mahabharata als Epos und Rechtsbuch* (1895), 171ff.

118. Grünwedel, *Buddhistische Kunst in Indien*, 29.

119. Grünwedel, *Buddhistische Kunst in Indien*, 185n1.

120. The ruins of Angkor Wat have recently been visited by H. Stönner: see *Zeitschrift für Ethnologie* 35 (1903): 631ff.

121. The temple of Borobudur is also the work of northern Buddhist artists.

122. On this point, see Albert Grünwedel, "Bericht über archäologische Arbeiten in Idikutschari und Umgebung," *Abhandlung der I. Klasse der Königlich Bayerischen Akademie der Wissenschaften* 24, div. I (1900), and the older literature cited there in the introduction. Manichean painting, especially, belongs to this category as well; see Friedrich W. K. Müller, "Handschriften-Reste in Estrangelo-Schrift aus Turfan, Chinesisch-Turkistan," *Sitzungsberichte der Königlich Preußischen Akademie der Wissenschaften zu Berlin*, session of February 11, 1904, 348–52, and "Handschriften-Reste in Estrangelo-Schrift aus Turfan, Chinesisch-Turkistan, II. Theil," *Abhandlungen der Königlich Preußischen Akademie der Wissenschaften aus dem Jahre 1904*, app., 1–117; K. Keßler, "Mani, Manichäer," in *Realencyklopädie für protestantische Theologie*, 3rd ed., ed. Albert Hauck, vol. 12, 193–228 (Leipzig: Hinrichs, 1903), 222; and thus Grünwedel, *Buddhistische Kunst in Indien*, 184.

123.   We might add certain remains of older culture, which in part have a
"prehistoric" character, first of the Malayan Archipelago, whose origin
has at present not been determined with certainty, such as the dolmen
and other funereal constructions on Java. See H. E. Steinmetz, "Oudheid-
kundige beschrijving van de Afdeeling Bandawasa (Residentie Besoeki),"
Tijdschrift voor Indische Taal-, Land- en Volkenkunde XL (1898): 1–60. On
Sumba, see Johannes Elias Teysmann, "Verslag eener botanische Reis
over Timor en de daaronder ressorteerende eilanden Samauw, Alor,
Solor, Floris en Soemba," *Natuurkundig Tijdschrift voor Nederlandsch-Indië*
34, ser. 7, pt. 4 (1874): 348–517, here 433; Herman Frederik Carel ten
Kate, "Verslag eener reis in de Timor-groep en Polynésie," *Tijdschrift
van het koninklijk nederlandsch aardrijkskundig Genootschap,* 2nd ser., 9
(1894): 195–246, 333–90, 541–638, 659–700, and 765–823; and "Notiz
über Deformation des Schädels (Araukanien und Tahiti)," *Internationales
Archiv für Ethnographie* 7 (1894): 90; as well as W. C. Muller, "Soemba,
Tjendana of Sandelhout-Eiland," in *Encyclopaedie van Nederlandsch-Indië,*
ed. Joh. F. Snelleman, vol. 4, 5–9a ('s Gravenhage: Nijhoff, 1905), 5a. And
on the Minahasa peninsula of North Celebes, see Adolf Bernhard Meyer
and Oswald Richter, "'Bronze'-Zeit in Celebes," *Ethnographische Miszellen*
II, vol. 10, no. 6 of *Abhandlungen und Berichte des Königlichen Zoologischen
und Anthropologisch-Ethnographischen Museums zu Dresden* (1903): 72–91,
here 89–91. In the South Seas, too, we find "megalithic" structures, for
example on the Mariana island Tinian and the Caroline island Ponape;
see Louis de Freycinet, *Voyage autour du monde* [etc.], vol. 2 of *Historique*
(Paris: Pillet, 1829), 159, and the *Atlas historique* of that work (Paris: Pillet,
1825), 74–75; as well as Georg Fritz, "Die Chamorro: Eine Geschichte
und Ethnographie der Marianen," *Ethnologisches Notizblatt* 3, no. 3 (1904):
25–100, here 42–44, and Rudolf Hermann's [explanation of] pl. I, figs.
2–5, on page 103; and as is well known, on Easter Island. ·

124.   To this group belong:

(1) *The Seleucid art of Mesopotamia,* with which we are as little familiar as we
are with Hellenistic art on the Orontes River (Antiocheia), and for that
matter, on the Nile (Alexandreia).

(2) *Mithraic art* (see Franz Cumont, *Textes et monuments figurés relatifs
aux mystères de Mithra* [Brussels: Lamertin, 1896–99], and *The Mysteries
of Mithra,* trans. Thomas J. McCormack [Chicago: Open Court, 1903],
209–28), which, although it presents itself as an episode of Roman-Hellenistic art, is a truly Asian art, despite its loans from the treasure of types
created by Greek sculpture (it probably resulted from Roman-Hellenistic
influence on the oriental cult of Mithras)—for it does not seek to delight,
as Hellenic art does, but like oriental art, to narrate and instruct; it is not
confined to the purely human but weighs its figures down with meaningful attributes, with symbols that fill the observer with awe for the sublime
mystery of the latent; and although it was never and nowhere, at least not
in Asia, artistically centralized but rather dislocated. It is a mobile, itiner-
ant art, not tended by a cultured and noble class that loves art and whose

power comes from holding on to the inherited land but carried to and fro, all the way to the Iberian Peninsula, by the voluntarily or involuntarily mobile lower strata of the population of an empire.

The most susceptible to being treated ethnographically, at least in part, namely, where there are remnants of older cultures, are.

(3) *The monuments of the pre-Islamic–Arabic ruin sites* in the stony Arabian-Syrian desert. The Arabs developed an advanced culture early on in the south, already in antiquity but especially in the last centuries before and the first after Christ, and pushed north from the central Arabian lands, so that it was possible, for example, to call the province lying to the northeast of Palestine "Arabia." Recently, inscriptions in southern Arabic characters have even been found in northern Arabia—Albert Socin, "Araber, Arabia," in *Kurzes Bibelwörterbuch*, ed. Hermann Guthe, 37–38 (Tübingen: Mohr-Siebeck, 1903), 38; Otto Weber, *Arabien vor dem Islam*, vol. 3, no. 1 of *Der alte Orient*, 2nd ed. (Leipzig: Hinrichs, 1904), 26; and Fritz Hommel, *Grundriss der Geographie und Geschichte des alten Orients* (Munich: Beck, 1904), 135—indeed, even in Babylonia (see Hommel, *Grundriss*, 136). Of course we do not currently have a palpable sense of the fabulous magnificence of the ancient culture and art of this area, while in some of the more recent creations the basic forms of Western art shine through so obviously that [these works] belong in the context of Western art rather than in the context of the buildings whose study ethnography is more likely to undertake. These latter pertain above all to the culture and art of:

(a) *The South-Arabian empire of the Minaeans.* They had advance posts located in north(west)ern Arabia—in the oasis of Higr in the domain of the Thamud (Eduard Meyer, *Geschichte des Alterthums*, 3.86:144) and even further north, in areas bordering on Canaan (for example, Ma'on, today Ma'an, southeast of Petra; see Georg Beer, "Meunim," in Guthe, *Kurzes Bibelwörterbuch*, 433; Hermann Guthe, "Maon," in *Realencyclopädie* 12, 243–44; and generally, Fritz Hommel, *Die altisraelitische Überlieferung in inschriftlicher Beleuchtung: Ein Einspruch gegen die Aufstellungen der modernen Pentateuchkritik* [Munich: Lukaschik, 1897], 273–77; Hugo Winckler, "Musri, Meluhha, Ma'în," *Mitteilungen der Vorderasiatischen Gesellschaft* 3 (1898): no. 1, 1–56, and no. 4, 169–226; and Otto Weber, "Studien zur südarabischen Altertumskunde," *Mitteilungen der Vorderasiatischen Gesellschaft* 6 [1901]: 1–60, here 27), a "trade colony" (following Alfred Jeremias, *Das Alte Testament im Lichte des Alten Orients: Handbuch zur Biblisch-Orientalischen Altertumskunde* [Leipzig: Hinrichs, 1904], 156 and 241, the Old Testament's "Midianites"; see also Weber, *Arabien vor dem Islam*, 24 and 28–29; and Hommel, *Grundriss*, 133n4 and 142) that later probably became independent (see Weber, *Arabien vor dem Islam*, 29).

The oldest Mosaic cult entertained relationships with Minaic cultic forms—there was a Minaic shrine at Mount Horeb–Sinai, in the area of Edom (see Hommel, *Die altisraelitische Überlieferung*, 278–81; Weber, "Studien zur südarabischen Altertumskunde," 29–30, and *Arabien vor dem Islam*, 21–22 and 26; Jeremias, *Das Alte Testament im Lichte des Alten Orients*;

and Ditlef Nielsen, *Die altarabische Mondreligion und die mosaische Überlieferung* [Strasbourg: Trübner, 1904]).

(b) *The Southern Arabian country Hadhramaut,* which in Minaic times was closely connected (as a dependent part of the realm) to the (tribally related) Minaeans, but later, when the Sabaeans had replaced them, sought in the fight against Saba to use the turn of events to gain independence (Weber, "Studien zur südarabischen Altertumskunde," 38). Like the neighboring Katabania (on this point, see Weber, *Arabien vor dem Islam,* 23, and Hommel, *Grundriss,* 139–45), the land was rich in valuable agricultural goods and must have flourished in antiquity (on the Hadhramautic inscriptions, see Hommel, *Grundriss,* 136–39). Its ruins have recently been visited and examined several times (see the literature in Socin-Guthe, 244).

(c) *The area south of the Dead Sea to the Red Sea,* in antiquity steeped in Minaic culture, where formerly the Idumaeans reigned and later the Nabataeans dwelled, with a capital (situated about halfway between the Dead Sea and the Gulf of Aila) whose original name, as the Greek translation "Petra" instructs us, meant "rock." The Nabateans had settled in Petra by about 300 BC. Their realm stretched north all the way to Damascus and Palmyra; they had adopted Syriac and Greco-Roman culture (see Georg Beer, "Nabataeer," in Guthe, *Kurzes Bibelwörterbuch,* 458). The art of the cultural domain of Petra in particular was provincially Roman-Hellenistic.

(4) *The Hauran and of Syria east and northeast of the River Jordan generally.* The ruins in this area are from entirely different epochs, partly, for example, from Roman but partly perhaps from older Islamic times (see Josef Strzygowski, "Mschatta II: Kunstwissenschaftliche Untersuchung," *Jahrbuch der Königlich Preußischen Kunstsammlungen* 25 [1904]: 225–373). Possible architects are, in antiquity, the Nabataean Arabs who ruled the Hauran and, insofar as the ruins belong to the time after the middle of the third century AD, among others the (monophysitist-Christian) Ghassanids, a princely family of southern Arabian origin (from the house of Gafna) who entertained relations with Byzantium and Persia.

The scope of a museum for Asian art, if it is to promote an understanding of historical context at all, would have to be staked out differently, that is, much wider than that of a museum for Asian archaeology, for instance. In such a museum, it would be hard to do without ancient Persian art because of its influence on ancient Indian and Chinese-Turkestan art, and including Persian art would by itself lead to including the products of ancient Egyptian and other extra-Persian art. On the Persian influence on ancient Indian art, see Grünwedel, *Buddhistische Kunst in Indien* and elsewhere; on the character and origin of ancient Persian art, the brief but splendid presentation in Meyer, *Geschichte des Alterthums,* 3.75:121.

125. See Ferdinand Justi, *Grundriss der Iranischen Philologie* (1897), 2:425.

126. The ruins of Meroë are published in Frédéric Cailliaud, *Voyage à Méroé* [etc.], 4 vols., incl. an atlas (Paris: Imprimerie royale, 1826–27). On

the Meroitic Kingdom, where a genuinely African character is con-
cealed by an Egyptian envelope, see Meyer, *Geschichte des Alterthums*,
3.98–102:160–66, and Adolf Erman, *A Handbook of Egyptian Religion*, trans.
Agnes Sophia Griffith (London: Constable, 1907), 198–200.

127. See his *Great Zimbabwe, Mashonaland, Rhodesia* of 1905, and Richard
Nicklin Hall and W. G. Neal, *The Ancient Ruins of Rhodesia: Monomotapae
Imperium* (1902). The first printed description of these ruins appeared in
Barros, *Da Asia Dec.*, bk. 1, ch. 10 (1552). In 1871 the ruins were newly
discovered by Karl Mauch, just as Benin was rediscovered in 1897 despite
having been known to Europeans as early as the sixteenth century. Recently, MacIver discussed the high altar of the Rhodesia ruins with Felix von
Luschan at the meeting of the Berliner Gesellschaft für Anthropologie,
Ethnologie und Urgeschichte of February 17, 1906; see *Globus* 89 (1905):
34. MacIver dates the ruined city no earlier than the fifteenth or sixteenth
century. Cf. David Randall-MacIver, *Mediaeval Rhodesia* (1906), and Felix
von Luschan, *Zeitschrift für Ethnologie* 38 (1906): 872ff. The author main-
tains that the city originates in an earlier period.

128. What follows may be linked largely to the great exhibit of American
antiquities in the Königliches Museum für Völkerkunde in Berlin. Cf. the
guide to the exhibit, 12th ed. (1905), 127ff. (13th ed. [1906], 138ff.). In
addition, see Seler, *Gesammelte Abhandlungen* II, 13, 14, 24.

129. See Seler, *Gesammelte Abhandlungen* II, 13. The tribes that consider
themselves related by blood and language to the ancient inhabitants of
Mexico City are subsumed under the name Nahua (*Nauatlaca*). Mexicans
in a narrower sense, who are based in the area of Popocatépetl, particularly around the two large lakes—Chalco and Texcoco—spread as
tradesmen and conquerors throughout the Yucatán. At the time of the
conquistadors, they remained in compact groups in Guatemala, where
today the Pipil still speak an Aztec language, and in San Salvador, as
well as around the large freshwater sea in Nicaragua; see Seler, *Gesammelte Abhandlungen* II, 24. A special, unique culture developed among
the Mexicans that dwelt along the edges of the Mixteca and Zapoteca,
in the area around Teotitlán del Camino, as the result of their contact
with tribes that spoke other languages. The Mayan people are found
in many regions throughout Central America. Their primary seat was
in the Yucatán. Related groups live largely in Guatemala and in northwestern Honduras. The Huasteca were a scattered branch of the Mayan
family that actually remained closely tied to Mayan culture. They were
located near the Panuco, somewhat north of the primary Mexican area.
They were renowned for their artistic, colorful weavings and conducted
a flourishing trade in these products with Mexico. The Mixteca and the
Zapoteca, who spoke their own languages, were culturally related to
the Mexicans, bordering their empire to the south and east. Apart from
the three primary groups, several further elements were in the Mexican
cultural circle. The Tarasca lived to the west of Mexico and possessed
their own language. Their houses were carved of wood and painted,
and featured a stone-built pyramid at their apex. Like the Mexicans, the
Tarasca excelled at feather mosaics. The Totonaca and the Olmecs had

their seat to the north and southeast of Mexico, on the Gulf of Mexico stretching from the Laguna de Tamiahua to the Laguna de Términos (that is, from the southern border of the Huasteca to the northern border of the Mayan tribes). Tribes of Mexican origin spread from the highlands throughout this region.

130. People of Mexican heritage lived around Lake Nicaragua. They had a fairly similar culture to the Mankeme, who lived between northern Nicaragua and the Departements Nicoya in Costa Rica. Further south, toward the higher inland of Costa Rica, lived the Huetar, whose antiquities resemble those from the isthmus of Panama and whose culture seems to be aligned with that of the Colombian tribes. The gold work of the Panamanian tribes that spoke Cueva reveals a relationship with the antiquities of northeastern Colombia (Kimbaya). The Chibcha were the primary people in Colombia. As a result of successful military campaigns, they founded a great empire in the highlands around Bogotá. Compare Seler, *Gesammelte Abhandlungen* II, 13.

131. Seler, *Gesammelte Abhandlungen* II, 14. The Quechua's homeland spanned from Quito in Ecuador to south of Cuzco and into western Bolivia. Their nation was part of the Inca dynasty. To the south of the Quechua live to this day the Kalya in the highlands around Lake Titicaca. Their ancestors likely built what became the ruins of Tiahuanaco. Alongside the three primary tribes of the Quechua, the Kolya, and the Yunka, in areas in the highlands and along the coast, lived other tribes that spoke different languages and have ethnographically uncertain roots, such as the Cañari in southern Ecuador. The Inca did not attempt to suppress the cultures of the lands they conquered. Instead, they established colonies of their own people with elements of their own culture throughout these acquired territories, in an attempt to replace the indigenous traditions with their own. Thus we must distinguish an older, pre-Incan period from a younger layer that carries the imprint of Inca culture. Older cultural centers that attest to special characteristics are Trujillo, Huaraz, and Ica, as well as the area of the Kolya. The artistic assets and technical capabilities in these areas were, at least in part, further developed than in the Incan-Peruvian highlands of Cuzco itself. Their dominion later expanded northward to Quito. Ancient Peruvian culture also influenced the west of Gran Chaco, northern Chile, and northwestern Argentina.

132. We can compare, for example, what Josef Strzygowski, *Kleinasien: Ein Neuland der Kunstgeschichte* (1903), says about works from Syria and Asia Minor, and Albert Grünwedel, *Bericht über archäologische Arbeiten in Idikutschari* (1906), 179, about those from central Asia.

133. Grünwedel, *Buddhistische Kunst in Indien*, 3.

134. A connection of this type between archaeological monuments and the present-day ethnographic material that helps elucidate these monuments can be compared with an exhibition of sketches alongside paintings. Wilhelm Bode discusses such an attempt, in which sketches are displayed on desks beneath the paintings in *Museumskunde* 1 (1905): 9. "As advantageous as an exhibition may seem in theory that combines the blueprints and studies with the paintings of the same schools and

masters—if possible, even matching the sketch with its painting—in practice its execution turned out to be difficult. The material and treatment of the sketches, just like engravings or other reproductions, differ too greatly from those of the paintings and compromise the effect of the paintings."

135. "As far as its form is concerned, the art produced by the school of the Gandharan monastery is a mere appendage to ancient art. However, since it represents exclusively Indian subject matter, like the saints and legends of an Indian religion, it absolutely is a part of Indian life" (Grünwedel, *Buddhistische Kunst in Indien*, 81). Due to the Greek influence on Gandharan forms, Seidlitz (*Museumskunde* 1 [1905]: 182) also wants Gandharan art, along with a number of other artworks that straddle the border of different eras, to be represented in current museums of antiquity.

136. We can compare Gustav Pauli's fitting words about the modern gallery of paintings (*Museumskunde* 1 [1905]: 149): "The large galleries have already surpassed this measure [of a desirable maximum size]. . . . The galleries are already bewildering, and if they continue to grow at the current pace they will become veritable *megatheria* of urban construction. Dividing them would be the easiest solution. Why shouldn't a world city . . . contain a separate art museum of the Italian Renaissance, a gallery of Dutch painting, and a museum for graphic art? We are stuck in the age of the chamber of curiosities, more so than we realize."

137. Consider, for example, in this context the relationship between the art of Gandhara and antiquity.

138. Museums of decorative arts demonstrate how, once awakened, the awareness of the special value of a type of object can lead to the creation of a new type of museum. These museums were founded at a time when the minor arts were regarded as a special type of artistic activity (initially as a first step of sorts leading to true art). We can also recall other types of museums, like the pathological, the anatomical, etc.

139. Richard Fritzsche, "Der Anfang des Hellenentums," *Neue Jahrbücher für das klassische Altertum, Geschichte und deutsche Literatur* 13 (1904), div. I, no. 8, 545–65, and no. 9, 609–34, here no. 8, 553. The relationships of the Occident with the Orient may date back even much further. "It is . . . at least a very appealing and plausible idea that the broad cultural current from the Orient that has poured over Europe in all the older times of the current period of the earth and that most recently spread Christianity across all countries has come from the same direction in the time of the oldest recognizable human works that lies even further back. The first culture that confronts us in the small area of Europe likely came from the Orient," Sophus Müller writes in his new book, *Urgeschichte Europas*, 3; see also 8, 14, 17, and elsewhere.

140. Cf. the general comments in Grünwedel, *Buddhistische Kunst*, 76; Richard Pischel, "Antrittsrede," *Sitzungsberichte der Königlich Preußischen Akademie der Wissenschaften zu Berlin* (1903): 709–12, here 711; Konrad Burdach, "Die älteste Gestalt des West-östlichen Divans," *Sitzungsberichte der Königlich Preußischen Akademie der Wissenschaften zu Berlin* (1904): 858–900, here 900; and Strzygowski, "Mschatta II," 372–73.

141. Otto Gruppe has listed "religious concordances" of America and the
      ancient world under the aspect of a borrowing from the Far East in *Die
      griechischen Culte und Mythen in ihren Beziehungen zu den orientalischen Reli-
      gionen,* vol. 1 (Leipzig: Teubner, 1887), 226n13; among more recent work,
      see Jeremias, *Das Alte Testament im Lichte des alten Orients,* 111–12, 121n2,
      and 135n2; and above all, Paul Ehrenreich, *Die Mythen und Legenden der
      südamerikanischen Urvölker und ihre Beziehungen zu denen Nordamerikas und
      der alten Welt* (Berlin: Asher, 1905). A comprehensive, more enthusiastic
      than critical attempt at deriving ancient American customs generally,
      including artistic ideas, from ancient Asian culture, has been undertaken
      by Zelia Nuttall in her great book, *The Fundamental Principles of Old and
      New World Civilization* (Cambridge, MA: Peabody Museum, 1901). The
      most uncritical among the numerous writings of this kind, where only
      the effort expended by the author can make the reader believe that the
      work is intended to be taken seriously and not as a wild joke—a work in
      which, incidentally, we find similarly unscientific comparisons of words
      as in Nuttall's book—is Albert Eichhorn, *Naual oder die hohe Wissenschaft
      (Scientia mirabilis) der architectonischen und künstlerischen Composition bei den
      Maya-Völkern, deren Descendenten und Schülern* (Berlin: Spielmeyer, 1896).
      Objections to such endeavors have come from Eduard Seler, "Über den
      Ursprung der altamerikanischen Kulturen" and "Über den Ursprung
      der mittelamerikanischen Kulturen," in *Gesammelte Abhandlungen zur
      amerikanischen Sprach- und Alterthumskunde,* vol. 2, 3–15 and 16–30 (Berlin:
      Asher, 1904), as well as Konrad Theodor Preuss, "Phantasieen über die
      Grundlagen der Kultur," *Globus* 80, no. 1 (July 5, 1901): 9–12. See also
      Paul Ehrenreich, "Zur Frage der Beurtheilung und Bewerthung ethnolo-
      gischer Analogien," *Correspondenz-Blatt der Deutschen Gesellschaft für Anthro-
      pologie, Ethnologie und Urgeschichte* 34, no. 12 (December 1903): 176–80.
      In his *Geschichte der Kunst aller Zeiten und Völker,* vol. 1 (Leipzig: Bibliog-
      raphisches Institut, 1900), 606, Karl Woermann takes a cautious stance
      when it comes to supposing an artistic dependence on Asia. Incidentally,
      even Seler admits an "infiltration of Asian cultural elements, perhaps a
      downright blending of peoples," for the American Northwest ("Über den
      Ursprung der mittelamerikanischen Kulturen," 18), as well as an intru-
      sion of cultural elements or an exchange (only prompted by the Europe-
      ans?) of such elements from the South Seas (19), such as "knot strings"
      in ancient Peru and on the Marquesas Islands, incidentally also in India,
      in the Malayan Archipelago, and in ancient China—where the mythical
      Emperor Fuxi, around 3000 BC, is associated with them as well as with
      inventing their replacement, character writing (see Stephen W. Bushell,
      Chinese Art, vol. 1 [London: H. M. Stationary Office, 1904], 12–13; and
      Edouard Chavannes, "Les livres chinois avant l'invention du papier,"
      Journal asiatique, 10th ser., 5 [1905]: 5–75, here 47)—and in the time of
      the Sui Dynasty in the land of the "Wo" (Japan) (see August Pfizmaier,
      "Die fremdländischen Reiche zu den Zeiten der Sui," *Sitzungsberichte der
      philosophisch-historischen Classe der Kaiserlichen Akademie der Wissenschaften*
      97 [1880]: 411–90, here 426); compare also Augustin Krämer, "Der Wert
      der Südseekeulen für Völkerbeziehungen," *Globus* 86, no. 7 (August 18,

1904): 125–28, which discusses the occurrence of South Seas clubs in America; on that point, see further Adolf Bernhard Meyer, "Alte Süd-seegegenstände in Südamerika," *Globus* 86, no. 12 (September 22, 1904): 202–3.

142. Franz Heger went in an entirely different direction ten years ago in "Die Zukunft der ethnographischen Museen," in *Festschrift für Adolf Bastian* (1896), 583–94.

143. [This notice preceded Richter, *Museumskunde* 4 (1908): 92–93.]

144. Woldemar von Seidlitz, *Vaterland, Wochenblatt für das Sächsische Volk*, no. 17 (1902): 288a, following Karl Koetschau's interpretation in *Jahrbücher der bildenden Kunst* 2 (1903): 94b (or in *Museumskunde* 1 [1905]: 196).

145. Bode, *Museumskunde* 1 (1905): 9, 12.

146. See Klemm, *Zur Geschichte der Sammlungen*, 196ff.

147. See Klemm, *Zur Geschichte der Sammlungen*, 153ff.

148. Klemm, *Zur Geschichte der Sammlungen*, 156, 166.

149. For Bastian's views on the practice of collecting, see "Über Ethnologische Sammlungen," in *Zeitschrift für Ethnologie* 17 (1885): 38–42. As J. D. E. Schmeltz has already rightly remarked in *Verslag . . . Rijks Ethnographisch Museum te Leiden* (1904/5, 1906), 57, the presentation of Wossidlo titled "Über die Technik des Sammelns," which deals mainly with ethnology, contains valuable hints for ethnographers on research trips.

150. Grosse, *Museumskunde* 1 (1905): 127.

151. Woldemar von Seidlitz explicitly pointed out that it is high time to expand the Asian collections, since Asian artifacts are becoming increasingly rare and more valuable with each passing year (cf. *Museumskunde* 1 [1905]: 181–97).

152. The Horniman Free Museum in London provides a unique and exemplary method of support for ethnographic study. Frederick John Horniman, a private citizen, had been collecting for over forty years while traveling the world. He did not limit himself to the normal forms of patronage—donation—and instead left his house in order to convert it entirely into a public museum. Later he created an impressive new structure for his collection, all at his own expense, in which he could combine his individual passions: a high, beneficial sense of beauty and order, and service for the general good. On this museum, see Adolf Bernhard Meyer, *Eur. Mus.*, 9f. A similar example of an individual effort made for the public good is the Museum Folkwang for Art and Science in Hagen i. W., which Karl Ernst Osthaus founded with his own means and his own tastes (see Koetschau, *Jahrbücher der bildenden Kunst*, 2:93a).

153. Research trips for ethnographic purposes have been ongoing since James Cook's accidental ethnographic discoveries during his first expedition to Tahiti in 1769 to observe the expected transit of Venus across the sun. Gustav Friedrich Klemm (in *Zur Geschichte der Sammlungen*, 239) emphasized how, as early as the beginning of the prior century, ethnographic material collected on such trips reached German museums in noticeable quantities—in many cases artifacts particularly from the South Sea region are finally entering museums today after being held in private (frequently English) collections: "Many travelers funded in part by

the government, in part privately, and in part on their own, carried both natural treasures and antiquities from faraway locales back to Europe and filled cabinets with these valuables. At the time, interest was primarily in items from South America, Egypt, China, and Japan."

154. In *Festschrift für Adolf Bastian* (1896), 600, Grosse rightly claims that the lack of thorough ethnographic education "can by no means be replaced by the 'instruction' experienced by the traveler; for no matter how in depth or well developed a questionnaire given to the traveler might be, it will never fit the particularities of the real situation. Compare, for example, Felix von Luschan's *Anleitung für ethnographische Beobachtungen und Sammlungen in Afrika und Ozeanien*, distributed by the Königliches Museum für Völkerkunde in Berlin, 3rd ed. (Berlin, 1904), and Joseph Halkin's *Enquête ethnographique et sociologique sur les peuples de civilization inférieure: Questionnaire général*, distributed by the Société Belge de Sociologie (Brussels, 1905).

155. Cf., for example, Albert Grünwedel on the fragmentation and removal of Gandharan sculpture in *Sitzungsberichte der Königlich Preußischen Akademie der Wissenschaften zu Berlin* 9 (1901): 8 [209].

156. In this regard, modern Japanese reproduction technique is helpful; the images in the great art periodical *Kokka* are excellent.

157. Krämer, "Der Neubau des Berliner Museums," 24a.

158. It is self-evident that when museums are asked for photographs and are prepared to provide them, they must provide good shots with the correct balance of light and shadow to adequately represent the artifact. The photographs must be scientifically useful and publishable, if necessary. It may appear strange to voice this demand, but the author himself had the experience of a museum providing pictures that, even though large in format, were inadequately lit with poorly positioned objects (the objects were overlapping or touching each other) and therefore not academically useful.

159. In addition, the Royal Museums in Berlin share a plaster-casting studio. On its history, see J. Dielitz in *Zur Geschichte der Königlichen Museen in Berlin: Festschrift* (1880), 167–70.

160. There (of all places), an archaeological museum was founded under the scientific leadership of the École française d'Extrème Orient. See *Museumskunde* 2 (1906): 110.

161. Hans Dedekam, *Museumskunde* 1 (1905): 84.

162. [From Richter, *Museumskunde* 4 (1908): 224ff.]

163. Arguments against such "interiors" in art and applied arts museums, which strive to transport the viewer into the milieu and mood of a past era but thereby deviate from historical accuracy, have been voiced recently by Lehmann in *Die Museen als Volksbildungsstätten* (1904), 38; Augustus Pitt in *Museumskunde* 1 (1905): 72, 74; and Dedekam, ibid., 1:79ff.

164. The views of the author on the "furnishing of museum rooms" are aligned with those of Grosse, Pitt, and Dedekam; see *Museumskunde* 1 (1905): 138f. and 67ff.; 2 (1906): 92f.

165. The builder of the museum recognized a particularly advantageous décor; Adolf Bernhard Meyer (in *Eur. Mus.* 4n2) wrote: "The museum is the

largest, if not the only, modern building that exclusively uses terracotta for the exterior and interior revetment of the walls. This medium allows for a wide range of different ornamentation. On the west side where the zoological collection is located, the terracotta ornamentation (which frequently appears outside and inside) exclusively depicts living beings. On the eastern side where the geological and paleological departments are located, the ornamentation depicts extinct forms."

166. Pictured in Meyer, *Eur. Mus.* 52, fig. 32. Meyer's opinion on the trellis concurs with that given above.

167. For some worthwhile insights garnered from his experiences exhibiting Far Eastern art, see Grosse, *Museumskunde* 1 (1905): 132ff.

168. In one of the largest museums in Germany, the author observed that the most valuable objects of the collection, or at least part of them, were stored in cabinets of which the front glass pane was covered on the interior with paper. This made the contents invisible. It was of great pleasure to the director of the museum to reveal the contents to the extremely surprised author, who had assumed nothing worthwhile was hidden within.

169. Krämer, "Der Neubau des Berliner Museums," 24a.

170. Ernst Grosse, "Über den Ausbau und die Aufstellung öffentlicher Sammlungen von ostasiatischen Kunstwerken," *Museumskunde* 1 (1905): 133, 135.

171. [From Richter, *Museumskunde* 5 (1909): 166ff.]

172. Holmes, *Annual Report of the United States National Museum for 1901*, 264.

173. Cf. *Publikationen aus dem Kgl. Ethnographischen Museum zu Dresden* 14 (1903): 139b f.

174. Heinrich Schurtz, *Urgeschichte der Kultur* (Leipzig, 1900), 450.

175. See *Meyers Konversations-Lexikon* 2, 5 (1893), 361b.

176. Bahnson, *Über ethnographische Museen*, 56a.

177. Pitt, *Museumskunde* 1 (1905): 72.

178. Holmes, *Annual Report of the United States National Museum for 1901*, 275). The thoughts informing this statement are also expressed in the "group label" of the "Synopsis of the Art of Sculptures," 276.

179. The founder of the Copenhagen Museum, Thomsen, was "the first and, for a long time, the only one who was able to bring the idea of a general ethnographic museum into reality." He organized the museum according to "cultural groups" and "groups of peoples." This method is recommended by Holmes, *Annual Report of the United States National Museum for 1901*, 264ff.

180. On the first, see Meyer, *Eur. Mus.*, 10ff. Ibid., 13f., Meyer provides the system of categories according to which the Oxford Museum is arranged. Particularly on p. 11 he argues for this type of organizational system, although on p. 12 he adds, "While such a system is tremendously captivating and stimulating, it should not occur without an accompanying collection that is arranged geographically. . . . Only a large ethnographic museum, such as that in Berlin, is able to achieve both of these."

181. This is similarly valid for exhibitions of prehistoric materials organized by the cultural periods of Stone Age, (Copper) Bronze Age, and Iron Age. (This method is used in the Swiss National Museum in Zurich and

discussed by Franz Heger in *Festschrift für Adolf Bastian* [1896], 589.)
Instead, organization according to discovery site would be preferable.
Museums of applied arts were in earlier times also exclusively arranged
according to the categories of materials—and in many cases remain so.
Glass, enamel, porcelain, wrought iron, and wood carving can "in this
way be studied in its historical, stylistic, and technical development and
multiplicity" (Dedekam, *Museumskunde* 1 [1905]: 78).

182. See also Holmes, *Annual Report of the United States National Museum for
      1901*, 260: "The order and relative position of the separate exhibits in
      each exhibition unit should be approximately uniform."

183. In the Dresden Museum, for example, the Javanese section separates
      from each other Stone Age materials, antiquities from the Hindu period,
      and modern artifacts, and the New Zealand section the cultural remains
      of the so-called Moa hunters and Maori objects. Such an exhibition of
      (prehistoric and) archaeological materials immediately next to modern
      ethnographic objects (even if these are grouped together) is, according
      to older reports, recommended only as long as the entire (prehistoric or)
      archaeological material of an ethnographic museum or department of
      this type is not of such a scope that it can be divided into a geographically
      ordered section separate from the ethnographic material. As a postulate
      for the future, William Henry Holmes proposes that archaeological
      monuments in principle be added to the geographically ordered display
      of modern ethnographica: "Along with the ordinary ethnological
      exhibits should go exhibits of the archaeology of the area, showing the
      prehistoric cultural relics and remains, and carrying the story back to the
      earliest times" (*Annual Report of the United States National Museum for 1901*,
      259, 272).

184. In this way, for example, in the Dresden Museum, the previously
      mentioned Maori objects can without any particular difficulty be
      separated from examples (which in this particular museum are
      nevertheless in proportionately lower number) of items from the period
      of decline of the old pure style of Maori art brought about through an
      awareness of the Europeans.

185. On the trade with New Guinea and New Pomerania involving these bowls,
      cf. Willy Foy, *Abhandlungen und Berichte des Königlichen Zoologischen und
      Anthropologisch-Ethnographischen Museums zu Dresden* VIII (*Festschrift für
      Adolf Bernhard Meyer*), no. 5 (1899): 9. Among others "the Tami people go
      to Bilibili with their wood carvings and tortoise shell handicrafts in order
      to trade for ceramics there" (Maximilian Krieger, *Neu-Guinea* [1899], 224;
      cf. the following note).

186. Ceramics from Bilibili were distributed from the coasts of New Guinea
      and Cape Croisilles all the way to Cape Rigny and even into the region
      of Finschhafen; Krieger, *Neu-Guinea*, 162. The island of Teste created
      pots that are found in the entire area into the South Cape and the
      d'Entrecasteaux Islands, and maybe even into the Louisiade Archipelago;
      Otto Finsch, *Ethnologische Erfahrungen* (= *Annalen K. K. Naturhistorischen
      Hofmuseum: Vienna* VI, 1891), 26; and Krieger, *Neu-Guinea*, 292. On other

centers of pottery in New Guinea, see Krieger, *Neu-Guinea,* 162 (on German New Guinea), 292 and 346 (on British New Guinea), and 382 and 432 (on Dutch New Guinea).

187. Cf. *Publikationen aus dem Kgl. Ethnographischen Museum zu Dresden,* 102b f. See also ibid., 33b f., on trade with dammar resin in bundle (or torch) form in the East Indian Archipelago.

188. The principle of classification is set out for the ethnography of Celebes in the fourteenth volume of the *Publikationen aus dem Kgl. Ethnographischen Museum zu Dresden* of 1903 (Richter and Meyer, "Anhang: Die Bogen-, Strich-, Punkt- und Spiralornamentik von Celebes," *Celebes* I: *Sammlung der Herren Dr. Paul und Dr. Fritz Sarasin aus den Jahren 1893–1896*).

189. [From Richter, "Über die idealen und praktischen Aufgaben der ethnographischen Museen," *Museumskunde* 6 (1910): 40ff.]

190. Educational wall tablets for anthropology, ethnography, and geography, published by Dr. Rudolf Martin, small ed. with 8, large ed. with 24 plates (Zurich: Art. Institut Orell Füssli, 1902). Hölzel, *Rassentypen des Menschen,* with the cooperation of the state councilman Franz Hege, chosen and edited by Prof. Franz Heiderich, painted by Friedrich Beck, 4 pp. (Vienna: Hölzels, 1903). (One plate of European heads is intended to complete the collection.)

191. Hehn, *Kulturpflanze und Hausthiere,* 504.

192. Holmes, *Report of the United States National Museum for 1901,* 259, wants to expand the use of purely anthropological materials as explanatory aids in ethnographic collections to such an extent that the resulting museum would be a fusion of anthropology and ethnography. On p. 259 he states that "it would prove instructive to add to each of these ethnic exhibits illustrations of the physical characteristics of the peoples of the area. These may comprise casts of the face or even of the entire figure; the skeleton or parts of it, and especially the skull, which presents wide and significant variations; examples of artificial deformation and mutilation; and collections of such remains of fossil man as are found in the area. This exhibit may also include pictures, diagrams, and maps, completing a synopsis of the somatic characters." Alfred Cort Haddon concurs in *Nature* 70 (May 5, 1904): 8. Such an undertaking does not only make the overview of both groups of materials more difficult and compromise their particular effect; it also lacks merit in its inversion of concepts: race and culture are separate things that do not subsume each other. The development and expansion of culture does not coincide with those of physical types.

193. According to Holmes, *Report of the United States National Museum for 1901,* 271, "This is the key to the exhibit, the most essential idea, the feature from which the most casual observer can get a definite conception of the people and their culture." Cf. also 258, where he says, "So, since we cannot display the people themselves, we should begin each of our ethnic exhibits by building a lay-figure group." Similarly, Haddon (*Nature,* 7b), writes: "The pleasure and instruction afforded by the realistic mounting of groups of animals are undoubtedly very great, and not less so are

those caused by analogous ethnological groups. The present writer had his first interest in ethnology awakened by the excellent modeled groups of natives in the Crystal Palace, and the wonder and delight these gave to the small boy have never been forgotten." Cf. also the end of note 2 on 244a. Holmes exaggerates the essentially correct principle of explanation through costume mannequins. By demanding a separate group of mannequins for each of his "geo-ethnic units," of which, for example, he identifies nineteen types in North America alone on 268f. (from alternative viewpoints, of course, this number is too low; see §102), he is asking for more than museums are able to provide. Leaving aside the costs of creating these groups of mannequins, even if the groups' authenticity should stand up to criticism (see above), it would be impossible to universally produce them owing to a dearth of material that is suitable as accoutrements. This remains the case even if one happens to possess so great an amount of material from one region that the visualization provided by the group would present a welcome addition.

194.   In *Reisen in Celebes* II (1905), 103.

195.   Awareness of the educational importance of animal groups and the push for their inclusion have advanced so far that the collection of higher animal forms in the zoological museum in Altona, apart from the department of instructive anatomy, already consists solely of such groups.

196.   See Haddon, *Nature*, 7f. "It is . . . to the United States that we have to turn for the most effective development of this art. There are several first class groups of American natives in the American Museum of Natural History [in New York], others are to be found in the Field Columbian Museum [in Chicago]; especially noteworthy in the latter museum are the groups illustrating the rituals of the Hopi Pueblo Indians . . . and a wonderful case illustrating the domestic industries of the Hopi. It was once the writer's good fortune to be in the company of a couple of Navaho Indians who saw these models for the first time; they could not mask the interest they felt in seeing these representations of their neighbors, and great was their delight in noticing that the model of a particular woman, whose face they recognized, had, like her original, an amputated finger. The high-water mark at present reached in this direction is in the dozen groups of lay figures designed by Prof. W. H. Holmes [in Washington]. . . . No one who has seen these splendid groups can doubt that this is the best way of illustrating the more salient features of ethnology." The museum in Chicago also "supplies reproductions to other museums," according to Paul Ehrenreich, *Zeitschrift für Ethnologie* 32 (1900): 21.

197.   For the Pueblo Indians (see Ehrenreich, *Zeitschrift für Ethnologie*). But not in the National Museum in Washington, as Ehrenreich presumes (ibid., 12). Cf. Haddon, *Nature*, 8a: "There are two methods of constructing the lay figures of ethnological groups. The one is to make casts of actual individuals, and the other is to have effigies made by a sculptor. The Chicago groups are examples of the former method, but the Washington groups were made in the following manner: —'The sculptors were required to reproduce the physical type in each instance as accurately as

the available drawing[s] and photographs would permit. Especial effort was made to give a correct impression of the group as a whole, rather than to present portraits of individuals, which can be better presented in other ways. Life masks, as ordinarily taken, convey no clear notion of the people; the mask serves chiefly to misrepresent the native countenance and disposition; besides, the individual face is not necessarily a good type of a group. Good types may, however, be worked out by the skillful artist and sculptor, who alone can adequately present these little-understood people as they really are and with reasonable unity in pose and expression.'"

198. The group lasted from 1885 to 1902. The only true practical consequence to draw from this experience is to exhibit the group behind glass. The report of the museum from 1902 makes no mention in this regard.

199. Holmes, *Report of the United States National Museum for 1901*, 259, specifies different purposes for the groups of costumed mannequins and of model figurines: "Following the family group [the group of life-sized figures, 271], the next most important cultural unit is the dwelling group, which may be modeled in miniature (say one-twelfth or one-twenty-fourth actual size) and illustrates the houses and associated constructions of all kinds, as well as something of the home arts and life of the people. Miniature figures of men, women, and children may be added to the dwelling group to graphically illustrate the practice of the culinary arts, the manufacture of basketry, weaving, pottery, the use of domestic animals, and other arts."

200. See, for example, copies of Chinese bronzes and jade objects, Japanese paintings, Japanese monumental sculptures, Japanese lacquer work and sword decoration, and so on. Copies of masterworks, especially among objects of the latter sort, cannot be compared to the originals in terms of refinement. Yet these copies, in addition to the masterly reproductions of modern Japanese illustration techniques (see §54), are vital for our museums, since the originals are in general no longer available for acquisition. This drawback has recently been stressed by Grosse, *Museumskunde* 1 (1905): 124–29.

201. By the way, this of course includes models that can give the viewer incorrect impressions of scale, form, and materials.

202. Very similar exhortations to those of the present author have recently been voiced by Krämer, "Der Neubau des Berliner Museums," 24a. Cf. also Holmes, *Report of the United States National Museum for 1901*, 258f.

PART II

Reflections on Reading Lauffer and Richter Today

Youth and Arrogance

Julien Chapuis

The first decade of the twentieth century was a period of rapid expansion for museums in Germany. In 1904, the Kaiser-Friedrich-Museum, the present-day Bode Museum, opened on Berlin's Museum Island to house European painting and sculpture collections. Taking advantage of good diplomatic and trade relations between Emperor Wilhelm II and Sultan Abdul Hamid II, German archaeologists conducted excavations in the Ottoman Empire, particularly in Asia Minor and Mesopotamia, and returned to Berlin with monumental treasures, such as the Pergamon Altar from present-day western Turkey and the Ishtar Gate from Babylon. These finds had to be displayed in suitable buildings, and the colossal Pergamon Museum that currently houses them was first envisioned in 1907 and opened in 1930. What museums should be and what they should look like were the subject of heated discussions among professionals. It is for them in particular—these specialists—and not for a general audience that the two essays under discussion were written.

Although Otto Lauffer and Oswald Richter address different fields of museology—historical and ethnographic museums, respectively—it is striking how much the writers have in common. Both present themselves as standard-bearers for areas they consider marginalized by art museums, which draw the lion's share of public funding and whose organizational systems threaten to take over other areas of museology. This imbalance results from a lack of agreement among curators of historical and ethnographic museums on such key issues as function, scope, nomenclature, structure, areas of collecting, and display. The essays are in effect manifestos, road maps aimed at achieving greater coherence among museum specialists. To quote Lauffer: "If our plans are implemented, then perhaps the country will take a significant step toward the desired greater unity of its historical museums" (78). This would strengthen the position of historical and ethnographic museums as they jockey for resources and public recognition.

The authors burn with the fire of conviction, confident in their rightness of purpose—a trait perhaps attributable to youth, as both men were in their early thirties at the time of writing—and their desire to spell out in laborious detail (Richter's 131 sections!) a museum's raison d'être and modus operandi makes for an arduous read. Both acknowledge that collections of historical and ethnographic museums can present an aesthetic interest but that this is secondary to their scientific purpose— sensuality has little place here. Both advocate a tighter focus in areas of collecting and scholarship to counter the lack of consensus on what these museums should be. They demonstrate dogmatism instead of pragmatism in matters of acquisition. For Lauffer, a new acquisition must remain in storage if it does not fit within the organizational principles of the museum; for Richter, the museum should not even accept an object whose place of discovery is undocumented. They differ on one significant point in the presentation of collections, however. Lauffer pleads for displays arranged according to function (e.g., all spoons across time in one vitrine), whereas Richter favors a geographic display that conveys a broader picture of a culture.

Both authors identify the main function of historical and ethnographic museums as the betterment of their visitors. For Richter, "the general task of ethnographic museums can only be this: to contribute to the knowledge and understanding of ourselves" (99–100). Lauffer, who sees an uninterrupted continuum in Europe from late antiquity to the present, understands historical collections as witnesses to a group's historical past. Accordingly, visitors to historical museums should feel an "increase of pride in their homeland" (87).

Richter's conception of what ethnographic museums encompass is extremely broad: "Ethnographic museums provide safe houses for both the beginnings and the culminations of human culture, as well as its manifestations in the present and the past—in particular, where cultures that do not rest upon a Mediterranean heritage are concerned" (142). Objects to be collected by ethnographic museums should be "free of European interference" (144). For Richter, *Naturvölker*—translated here as "primitive people"—exist outside history, for "to enter world history implies achieving continual contact with European history" (175n89). This cliché ignores the fact that eastern Africa, for example, has traded with both Europe and Asia since late antiquity. Richter further states that ethnographic museums teach European (i.e., superior) audiences about themselves by providing "insight into the earliest stages in the development of cultural assets . . . by comparing . . . our mostly high culture with . . . lower cultures" (101). However disturbing, Richter's notion of *Naturvölker* as living outside history while illustrating an early step in the development of which Westerners are the crowning achievement, is an improvement on the conception of ethnography as a branch of zoology and natural history (95). The presentation of "natives" in zoos was practiced well into the twentieth century both in Europe and the United States, while museums in Brussels (Royal Museum for Central Africa) New York (American Museum of Natural History), and Chicago (Field Museum) to this day combine ethnographic and zoological displays.

For Richter, the secondary function of ethnographic museums is clearly tied to the state: to support the colonial enterprise. "The words [of Emperor Wilhelm II] remind us to think differently about ourselves so that 'our grandchildren can have free rein to conquer the globe' (K. Lamprecht), and also to defend and retain our colonial possessions so that no one will one day take our crown. We must recognize that we have a national obligation to expand our trade horizon, which encompasses— as a result of the great discoveries of the eighteenth century, and modern transportation and technology—the entire globe" (105). Phrases such as "national obligation" send chills down the spine, as they have been used repeatedly to justify aggression. While Richter never questions the justness of colonialism, he sees a role for ethnographic museums in promoting a better understanding of "the lands where we want to obtain raw products and sell our fabricated items" (here quoting Kurt Hassert; 110) in order to avoid "brutal colonial wars, which have made other nations vast and rich, [but] do not fit with our *Furor teutonicus*. Brutal egotism in colonial matters is not the German way" (112). This is despite the Herero uprising in present-day Namibia in 1904–8, now recognized as the first genocide of the twentieth century, in which thousands died at the hands of German soldiers—a point left unmentioned by the author.

It is difficult, in Berlin in 2020, to read these essays without thinking of the decades of German history that would follow. Occupying the chair of *Volkskunde* (folklore) at Hamburg University, Lauffer signed, on November 11, 1933, the Oath of Allegiance of German Professors to Adolf Hitler. Whether Richter would have sympathized with National

Socialism remains a matter of conjecture, as he died in 1908 at the age of thirty-four after cutting himself on a poisoned arrow in storage at the ethnographic museum in Dresden. This put an untimely end to a "lonely and serious life [that] knew no pleasure—none at all—save for work and the fulfillment of duty," according to his obituary (137). Richter was, however, fully convinced of the righteousness of colonialism and of the superiority of Europeans. He praised Germans who "accelerate[d] the spread of civilization" (104). It is safe to assume that none of the contributors to the present volume aspire to this.

Oswald Richter and the "Purity of the Specific Local Culture"

Edward S. Cooke, Jr.

Writing just after the zenith of the grand international exhibitions of the second half of the nineteenth century, Oswald Richter sought to distinguish the purpose of the scientifically based national ethnographic museum from the commercial nationalism on display at the fairs. While he recognized the link between cultural education and commercial expansion—evident in the voyeuristic objectification of the colonial other and the display of colonial raw materials and products in those exhibitions—he stressed that ethnographically aware businessmen would be the most effective representatives of a national endeavor. Well-conceived exhibitions of ethnographic materials would educate these secular missionaries, who could then optimize their commercial work throughout the world and contribute to the power of their home nation-states. Overseas trade and politics thus merged in the concept of the ethnographic museum.

In countering promotional exhibition culture, Richter criticized the tendency to group objects by type, as was typical in manufacturers' booths, the density of artistic display in the artistic assemblages, and the appeal to psycho-aesthetic comfort that such vignettes were designed to evoke. He argued instead for a Saussurian geographic approach that focused largely on a synchronic analysis of functionally related objects from a specific region, with a background sense of diachronic development within that locale. By linking objects with common geographic origins and interrelated functions, and by weeding out objects without firm links to that place, the proper ethnographic exhibition would present a clear snapshot of a culture based on scientific observation and taxonomic sorting. Isolating ethnographic identity would affirm the high status of those undertaking the work.

Key to Richter's museological philosophy of a "geographic exhibition" was an unwavering commitment to the "area of creation." The privileging of making was characteristic of the late nineteenth century, when the British design theorist William Morris drew attention to the craftsman's nobility and to the moral importance of craftsmanship. The designer and cultural attaché Hermann Muthesius spread Morrisian principles to Germany, and museum directors such as Justus Brinckmann followed Morris's lead by stressing the importance of local materials and vernacular styles to develop an awareness of national cultural taproots. The context of production, the morality of craftwork, and the search for national styles underscored Morris's writings, as well as the writings of German museum leaders such as Richter. The most authentic object remained just as it emerged from the maker's shop.

In emphasizing where something was made Richter zeroed in on the purity of a location and the stability of an object. He believed that it was possible to isolate a local vernacular and that the best ethnographers would use observational fieldwork to understand native objects and functions, thereby identifying special traits or characteristics of that material culture. Such a tautological pursuit—looking for formal, technological, and functional commonalities that would then be used as evidence for the existence of regional identity—underlies many material culture studies of the twentieth century, including the diffusionist folklore studies of Fred Kniffen and Henry Glassie and the regional furniture studies of John Kirk and Brock Jobe.

The belief in distinct isolation denied the possible influence of interchange or entanglement among trading peoples. Richter admitted that objects move, but he seemed to ignore or discount those outliers even if they were used in that geographic area. Instead he emphasized the importance of "purity." The goal of demonstrating a distinct look and use thus reveals how scientific means of observation and recording were employed to unscientific ends, to develop racialized prejudice or invent nationalized mythologies. Recent scholarship has embraced the messiness of the material culture and, in a world characterized by global commodity chains and intertwined commercial networks, embraced its complexity as well. In emphasizing hybridity and creolization, this new work seeks to understand the editing and translation that each culture undertook. Such an approach emphasizes blending over purity.

The concept of stable purity also precludes the idea that an object can have multiple uses, depending on different groups or points of view, and can change over time. Richter was not interested in what Clifford Geertz would describe as interpretive ambiguity or what Arjun Appadurai would characterize as the social life of the object. Rather, Richter viewed the objects as scientific specimens that provided a single narrative about discrete identity.

While Richter argued about the scientific method of fieldwork, his ultimate goal, revealingly, was not a "factual cultural image of the way things actually were" but rather the creation of "images of cultures as they should be" (155). The projection of an idealized culture, couched in the apparent scientific rigor of the research, continues to plague decorative arts museums right up to the present. Exhibitions of objects continue to be used in the service of nationalistic myths and racial agendas, but the public is led to believe that they are seeing the documented truth, the way life used to be in a specific place at a specific time. In this way museums played a valuable role in the development of romantic nationalism. The writings of Richter on the ethnographic museum and of Otto Lauffer on the historical-archaeological museum help us better understand the roots of the mixed messages inherent in most material culture exhibitions of the past decade.

"Certain Secondary Tasks of Ethnographic Museums": Richter's Writings and the Role of Ethnographic Museums in Germany's Colonial Period

Viola König

I have read the essays in the German original, those complex texts with their interminable footnotes, their rich content, and their cross-references. Oswald Richter died, as a consequence of his fieldwork, at only thirty-four. When did he have time to read all the works he refers to? When did he make notes on them, without a computer? How was he able to combine fieldwork, work in the museum, and writing in the decade and a half he was active?

At the time Richter was working, my grandfather had completed his studies at Friedrich Wilhelm University in Berlin (which became Humboldt University) to become a high school teacher of German, Latin, Greek, history, geography, and philosophy. But Grandfather's real interests were ethnology (*Völkerkunde*), archaeology, and prehistory. Surely he knew Richter's writings. Perhaps they inspired him?

In the 1920s and 1930s, Grandfather's family of six visited the Berlin museums—and the Völkerkundemuseum on Potsdamer Platz in particular, because new acquisitions were on display every weekend. Although Germany, according to the Treaty of Versailles, had had to cede its colonies in 1919, the collections were far from fully surveyed, and researchers continued traveling to all corners of the world and returning with new collections. The exhibits were constantly growing, the display cases overflowing.

The stories my grandmother told about family visits to the Berlin Völkerkundemuseum would influence the way I conceived of exhibitions as the director of that museum (now named Ethnologisches Museum) and the Übersee-Museum in Bremen (in 1907 still called Städtisches Museum für Natur-, Völker- und Handelskunde). It was the controversies about the old "human zoos" (or ethnological exhibitions for *Völkerschauen*) and the criticism of presentations of human beings and cultures in museums that led me to be critical of staged exhibitions— what Richter calls *geschmackvolle Aufstellung* (tasteful exhibition) (146). That is why I conceived and implemented the visible storage *Übermaxx* for the Übersee-Museum (1999). And in the exhibition concept for the new Humboldt Forum, in the reconstructed Berlin Palace on the former Palace Square in the historic center of Berlin, I have planned four large complexes of display cases, like transparent storerooms.

In the years during which we have been preparing the Humboldt Forum, criticism concerning the alleged "loot" and accusations of inadequate research on the provenance of collections from colonial contexts has not come as a surprise to us in the chronically understaffed and underfinanced museum. There is a long record of publications to document our awareness. The criticism, though, finally put an end to the disinterest on the part of German politicians.[1]

Now, however, as I'm reading Lauffer's and Richter's texts, things are moving very quickly: conferences, workshops, podium discussions, newspaper articles, and social media posts are popping up rapidly and are critically engaging with the topics of "Collections from a Colonial Context" and "Treatment of 'Human Remains'" related to restitution and the move to the Humboldt Forum. It has never been more important to make the writings from the colonial era accessible and to situate them within today's context. Picking up these current debates, I will limit my comments to two aspects of Richter's texts: provenance research and colonial context.

Richter and Provenance Research

In his posthumously published essay "On the Ideal and Practical Tasks of Ethnographic Museums," Richter devotes much space to the way collections are stored. Regarding labels, he stresses a precise description of those objects and their functions in particular that "are foreign in our culture," calling for "a short proper name [*Sachbezeichnung*], a notation of the local name in reliable form, and the precise (approximate) geographic origin, if such there be, possibly also the acquisition source (that is, the donor, not the source of purchase, and the collector, if known)."[2] Thus, the demand for details about the exact provenance of objects was indeed made a hundred years ago, but even then it was not always possible to live up to it.[3] Even now, as we are writing the texts for the Humboldt Forum exhibitions, just how much detailed information visitors can handle in object descriptions can be a matter of debate, and there is a sense that the space available for it is insufficient: "One thing, though, must be avoided in all these cases of explanation, namely becoming too erudite. Thus, for example, in the Berlin Museum the local names of objects from countries that possess their own writing system are given on the labels, not only in transcription but also in the local alphabets, partly even only in these latter without any transcription."[4] Richter writes with indignation and thereby gets at the core of our discussions today.

Richter's emphatic call for provenance research and his detailed acquisitions policy remain highly topical:

> Today we demand to know the precise find spot of an object. This find spot needs to be distinguished from the provenance of an object, which must be given greater prominence in the descriptions of objects by those collecting the artifacts. Objects that arrive at a museum without information on their find spot and without an identifiable provenance should not even be accepted. In addition to the provenance, the indigenous name of the object should be noted, as well as the purpose of its ornamentation, its use, its method of creation, and its material. For objects obtained either through sales from dealers or through gifts from donors, these specifications are, as a rule, rarely and insufficiently met. The missing information can be uncovered only through a comparative or arduous and time-consuming literary study. However, a critical traveler, such as one trained by a museum, can obtain the necessary information prior to acquisition with far greater ease. (141–42)

The problematic absence of information on the provenance of ethnographic collections thus already characterized the acquisitions in the colonial era and before. The problem was known and a solution was urged. The dilemma of gifts of unknown origin, too, was an issue in museums, then as now. In addition, collections have become "numerous . . . they have also become so all-encompassing that they are now challenges for their public authorities" (99).

The most problematic demand of Richter's from today's perspective is summarized in the "Discussion of the Study of Race": The German term *Rasse* has a different meaning than the English word *race*. It also means "breed." The term is considered obsolete today because of its misuse during the Nazi era.

> Laypeople must be made aware of the racial distinctions within humankind—or at least of the assumed affiliation of a certain people with a certain race. With circumspection, they can also learn of assumptions about racial correlations and about racial stratification of the population in a certain area, as well as the reasons behind these assumptions. Above all, these viewpoints must be supported by visual representation, since a vibrant understanding of a culture necessitates a conceptualization of what its indigenous members looked like. (158–59)

A current counterposition is staked out in the volume that accompanied the exhibition *Racism: The Invention of Human Races* at the Deutsches Hygiene Museum in Dresden: "Many of the contributions focus on the question: to what extent does the thoughtless reproduction of racist images in science, politics, and everyday life—or in exhibitions—contribute to their enduring efficacy? Would it not make sense not to show such images in the first place? At what point does an object become racist? Already when physical differences between people are depicted? Are there other images, never seen before, to counter them?"[5]

The European Commission Against Racism and Intolerance rejects theories that are founded on the existence of different "races" because all human beings belong to the same species. It defines racism as "the belief that characteristics such as race, colour, language, religion, nationality or national or ethnic origin justify contempt for a person or a group of persons, or the notion of superiority of a person or a group of persons." This includes ascribing cultural and psychological characteristics on the basis of certain external traits such as skin color. European museums today follow this standard without exception.[6] The complex of exhibition media that are no longer acceptable also includes the "figural depictions of indigenous people," such as "facial casts" in the museum (161, 162).

Richter and Colonialism

The most critical part, from today's perspective, is what Richter calls "certain secondary tasks" of ethnographic museums, namely national, political, and commercial tasks (104). Much research has been conducted on the attitudes of ethnologists and curators working in the colonial era, which ranged from enthusiastic to rather disinterested to skeptical. Richter quotes Adolf Bastian, the founding director of the Berlin Völkerkundemuseum: "Brutal colonial wars, which have made other nations vast and rich, do not fit with our *Furor teutonicus*. Brutal egotism in colonial matters is not the German way" (112). Yet Richter himself is unambiguously among the enthusiastic ones and devotes himself to the zeitgeist and the national task, "in consideration of the general world-wide expansion of German national interests; . . . in consideration of the need for protection, which every part of our population requires and today includes those representing German interests abroad; and . . . in consideration of a firm bond between all Germans who have emigrated as bearers and propagators of European civilization, and who are linked both to each other and to their fatherland" (104).

At the center of the national task he sees economic interests as "nations suddenly appear on the horizon and enter into competition with other peoples" and "accordingly, the tasks for our German Empire and people have grown to a mighty scale" (105–6). Therefore "our great history obligates us to participate in the second, still unfinished, fearsome and final expansion of the economic horizon, if we do not want to lose our economic standing and drift toward decline" (106).

When Richter supports the protection and promotion of the colonies, he at the same time demands making "a certain degree of ethnographic and colonial knowledge part of the public domain of our nation," and he sees this task to fall under the purview of the ethnological museums, which "should become places to cultivate knowledge through lectures, discussions, and other means" (106).

In addition, there is the political task.

Ethnographic museums should enable an understanding of the characteristics of people abroad in the light of modern European culture, particularly for the diplomat, the officer, and the mariner, who are all in charge of colonial politics and administration of the colonial state overseas, as well as for the missionary, who works in the service of Christian civilization. The museums should provide education so that political errors and unfortunate circumstances can be avoided and so that irregularities in the course of colonial relationships can be resolved swiftly. (106)

Accordingly, the commercial task of ethnographical museums consists in the education of overseas merchants via the "systematic acquisition of knowledge that has practical value for global trade" (109).

Richter makes no secret of the indispensable connection between national, political, and commercial interests and colonial policy. To defend global market shares, transnational penetration and the exploitation of labor are practiced with comparable methods in the twentieth and twenty-first centuries as well; concepts like colonization, though, are being avoided. A company that seeks to establish its products and brands on other continents and in specific cultural areas must be thoroughly familiar with local consumer habits. A current example for export and import is China; for the practice of identity-instituting gestures, the French president Emmanuel Macron.

Then as now, young and ambitious ethnologists and curators hoping for rapid career advancement have allowed their (political) attitudes to become biased. Someone assuming an anticolonialist attitude in 1907 certainly had no chance of rising in the profession. True conviction and opportunism may have gone hand in hand. Today's political starting point is the opposite. Ethnologists and curators are expected to assume emphatically anticolonialist positions if they want to advance their careers—and I can't help but wonder: What would Oswald Richter's attitude be today? In 2018, the Museum für Völkerkunde in Hamburg changed its name to MARKK:

> The term *Völkerkunde* no longer accords with the identity, contents, and goals of a museum concerned with the world's cultural diversity that seeks to cooperate on equal terms and as partners with provenance societies and diaspora communities. . . . Rather than dealing with clearly delimited "peoples" or "ethnicities," ethnographic museums today focus on cultures and the relationships among them and address the social anchoring of the human being.[7]

A great contrast with 1907? Or just an apparent one? Richter begins his text as follows:

> The museum ethnographer should not be primarily interested in the discovery of new truths. Rather, he should be devoted to furthering an education that deepens our understanding of the

world. This education should guide and prepare individuals to focus their efforts on service to the nation. Ethnographic museums should emphasize this final point in particular. The Germany of the future will be increasingly oriented toward foreign countries, and ethnographic museums should strive to awaken interest in and understanding of their character! (114)

The new Humboldt Forum—in the very center of power of the German capital with its ethnographic collections—pursues a clear political task. Cultures and the thriving of their relationships with each other, as well as the social anchoring of citizens in a global world beyond xenophobia, are preconditions for economic prosperity if, in Richter's words, "we do not want to lose our economic standing and drift toward decline" (106).

Translated by Nils F. Schott

1.   Viola König, "Am rechten Platz? Materielles und immaterielles Kulturerbe aus außereuropäischen Kulturen in europäischen Museen," *Museumskunde* 73, no. 1 (2008): 65–73.
2.   Oswald Richter, "Über die idealen und praktischen Aufgaben der ethnographsichen Museen," *Museumskunde* 6 (1910): 45.
3.   From today's perspective, recording "source of purchase" is significant as well.
4.   Richter, "Idealen und praktischen Aufgaben," 45.
5.   Susanne Wernsing, Christian Geulen, and Klaus Vogel, eds., *Rassismus: Die Erfindung von Menschenrassen*, catalogue for the exhibition at the Deutsches Hygiene-Museum Dresden, May 18, 2018, to January 7, 2019 (Göttingen: Wallstein, 2018). From the publisher's website: https://www .wallstein-verlag.de/9783835332263-rassismus.html.
6.   European Commission Against Racism and Intolerance, *ECRI General Policy Recommendation No. 7 (Revised) on National Legislation to Combat Racism and Racial Discrimination* (adopted on December 13, 2002, and revised on December 7, 2017), https://rm.coe.int/ecri-general -policy-recommendation-no-7-revised-on-national-legislatio/16808b5aae.
7.   "Neuer Name für das Museum für Völkerkunde Hamburg," *Stadtkultur Hamburg*, May 24, 2018, https://www.stadtkultur-hh.de/2018/05/neuer -name-fuer-das-museum-fuer-voelkerkunde-hamburg.

Perfecting the Past: Period Rooms Between Disneyland and the White Box

Deborah L. Krohn

On a hike I stepped into a farmhouse. In the twilight of the great hall, the farmer's wife worked in her colorful folk dress between shimmering brass basins that reflected the flickering hearth fire—an unforgettable image! Today the colorful garb of the woman has become an object of interest, the basins are considered artistic hammered ware, a colorfully painted trunk is newly discovered, and the stonework is of a sought-after type. Suppose that a whole array of these objects can be procured through many nice words plus a little something more and find their way into a museum. Now the hammered basins stand in a cabinet with maybe twenty others. They are of high art historical value. The earthenware is displayed elsewhere. The trunk is set up somewhere else to fill a noticeable gap in the historical development of woodwork. Such a result is actually barbaric. The entire scene is rent apart and ruined, perhaps never to be reunited.[1]

At the heart of Otto Lauffer's 1907 extended panegyric dissecting the historical museum—a relatively new kind of institution gaining popularity and seemingly still in need of intellectual validation at the close of the nineteenth century—he cites a passage from Otto Lehmann that describes the way such a museum might come to possess "domestic antiquities." The question of how to display such objects, including local dress, brass basins, and a trunk, depends on the type of information the public demands and what exactly is communicated, whether through a contextual setting such as a period room or an analytic gallery that presents related artifacts by type. This reflection addresses the phenomenon of period rooms in late modern museums and their role on an experiential continuum that has come to encompass extremes that were not yet part of museum culture when Lehmann and Lauffer were writing.

Period rooms enact history through a theatrical device, the removal of the fourth wall, which is accomplished on the stage through the presence of the proscenium arch, already a familiar strategy in antiquity. Lauffer's discussion is shot through with the importance of the role of local history, or folklore, for nurturing a reverence for the "homeland" through the collecting and display of "domestic antiquities." Lauffer believes that localness is the key to a successful historical museum, distinguishing it from the more general aesthetic or qualitative values of the applied or decorative arts museum. But it seems to me now, from the perspective of the twenty-first century, that, to paraphrase the popular justification for drinking alcohol at any hour of the day, "it's local somewhere." I would argue that the power of a period room, then as now, is created not solely by its rational appeal to the patriotism or personal nostalgia of its beholders but also through the suspension of disbelief to which viewers unwittingly succumb. This is evident in the role that imagination plays in the consumption of the period room, which wields suggestive power precisely because it feeds the imagination, allowing an embodied materialism to color the experience.

Fast-forward to the 1960s in America. In a beloved children's book by E. L. Konigsburg, *From the Mixed-Up Files of Mrs. Basil E. Frankweiler*, Claudia Kincaid and her younger brother Jamie run away from home and hide out in the Metropolitan Museum of Art for several days, where they sleep in an English Renaissance bed and scavenge coins from a fountain. Still for sale in the museum's gift shop, this original "night at the museum," written in 1967, captured the imagination of generations of children long before the Hollywood blockbuster film *Night at the Museum* (2006) and its two sequels, which feature the antics of a feckless security guard in an enchanted Museum of Natural History, where the exhibits come to life, including Native Americans, Egyptian mummies, and Teddy Roosevelt. (The sequels take the enchantment to the Smithsonian Institution and to the British Museum as well.) *Mixed-Up Files* has also been the basis of two films of its own, starring no less than Ingrid Bergman and Lauren Bacall. What these stories share is a fascination with the museum after hours, when the carefully defined boundaries between the forbidden and the permitted dissolve with the darkness and silence. Konigsburg, in framing the children's adventure, which ultimately revolves around solving an art historical mystery, draws on the transgressive fantasy of sleeping in a period bedroom or sitting in a period drawing-room chair, a fantasy that is both created and suppressed by museum curators, who strive to present a simulacrum of the past that is at once enticing yet insulated from the disruptive flow of reality. Claudia and Jamie's experience encapsulates this perfectly: "They wandered back to the rooms of fine French and English furniture. It was here Claudia knew for sure that she had chosen the most elegant place in the world to hide. She wanted to sit on the lounge chair that had been made for Marie Antoinette or at least sit at her writing table. But signs everywhere said not to step on the platform. And some of the chairs had silken ropes strung across the arms to keep you from even trying to sit down. She would have to wait until after lights out to be Marie Antoinette."

Period rooms both attract and repel, distilling the essence of the museum experience for visitors of all ages by drawing the viewer in but discouraging tactile apprehension: look but don't touch. As opposed to the early twentieth century, when Lauffer was taking stock of the first wave of historical museum display, still very much a novelty and spurred, inevitably, by the nationalism that gripped Europe during the nineteenth century, period rooms are now often disparaged by museum curators and are thus increasingly endangered. They occupy a precarious place on the continuum between Disneyland and the "white box" that defines the range of visitor experience today. As museums of all kinds inevitably reevaluate and renovate, reorganizing their permanent collections to reflect prevailing notions of authenticity and new paradigms for display, the period room is often a casualty.

This was the case in the protracted renovation of the Rijksmuseum in Amsterdam, which housed some of the first period rooms in museum settings, installed in the 1870s. When the museum reopened in 2013, all but one of the once-celebrated rooms had vanished. And at the Victoria and Albert Museum in London, some of the period rooms acquired from the late nineteenth century through the early 1980s were dismantled to make way for the British Galleries, a more didactic installation that forefronts the history of design and narratives of manufacture and enterprise; it opened in 2004.[2] Though the space allotted to period rooms at the V&A has contracted, the curators stated in the publication that accompanied the new galleries that the rooms "provide a powerful experience of historical architecture in three dimensions. . . . For those who find abstracted museum objects dry or distant, such rooms can evoke a different atmosphere from that found in museum galleries, suggesting aspects of the lives of previous occupants and connecting with the visitor's own experience of domestic life."[3] In the suite of galleries at the V&A devoted to Europe from 1600 to 1800, the period rooms that survived the long renovation (these galleries opened in 2015) foreground authentic paneling and architectural decor rather than furnishings installed in situ.

In 2014, the Louvre opened a suite of period rooms in the Cour Carrée to display its holdings of French decorative arts from the eras of Louis XIV, XV, and XVI. Though the individual objects are of high quality and distinguished provenance, the settings are fanciful, such as a Turkish seraglio designed by Jacques Garcia, a leading society decorator who was the chief designer for the period rooms, known in French as *period rooms*—they don't even have a French word for them! Here, transparency is the word, with the label confessing that the fabric and trimmings were "inspired by a drawing of the Comte d'Artois Bedroom in the Bagatelle Pavilion." Another room features this label: "The two decorative piers, six wood panels, door leaves and fireplace in this room, from the Dangé residence, have been complemented by wainscoting, a mirror, frames and a cornice, all re-created from period photographs of the room before it was dismantled. The overdoor panels are also modern. The green silk damask is a reweaving of an 18th-century fabric." The honesty of these labels makes one puzzle over the lasting appeal of the period rooms, which have retained the rubric despite their evident and public "deconstruction."

John Harris believes that the earliest period rooms were created in England essentially as backdrops for the display of furniture in "semi-private" houses, but the origin of the phenomenon is impossible to pinpoint.[4] I would argue that the impulse for re-creating historic environments dates from at least the early seventeenth century, sparked by interest in the ancient world among antiquarians in late Renaissance Rome who envisioned the past in architectural settings informed by the nascent practice of archaeology—at least on paper if not in bricks and mortar—and as the setting of festive entertainments that do not survive.

If this more expansive view of the phenomenon is admitted, I would count the earliest surviving examples of period rooms to be dollhouses. These complex and layered objects re-created entire domestic settings in miniature. Complete with furniture, soft furnishings such as curtains and bedcoverings, dishes, pots and pans, and even sometimes the inhabitants themselves in period costume, they provide a wealth of information about daily life in early modern Europe. The earliest recorded dollhouse dates to 1558. It was commissioned by Duke Albrecht V of Bavaria, and though it does not survive, it appears in a 1598 inventory of his *Kunstkammer*, with its own detailed inventory.[5] The Dutch dollhouses now at the Rijksmuseum are perhaps better known than the huge collection in the Germanisches Nationalmuseum in Nürnberg. Heidi Mueller, author of a recent catalogue of the Nürnberg collection, argues that the houses were not accurate representations of households but "merely interpretations of an ideal domestic reality that were intended, in the context of contemporary epistemological discourse, as instructional models or—as we would say today—teaching aids." However, the fact that they were collected almost from their creation indicates that they were valued as more than mere three-dimensional versions of the household organization and management texts that proliferated in the seventeenth century, and perhaps were considered valuable family heirlooms.[6] The earliest four dollhouses, including one from 1639, were acquired in the 1870s following museum director August Essenwein's interest in promoting what he called *Hausaltertümer*, or domestic antiquities, at the beginning of the period discussed by Otto Lauffer and Oswald Richter in this volume. The idea was that presenting these items in context would instruct visitors about daily life in the past. He was intent on creating a series of what he called *Lokalitaten*, or locales, that would represent the "best possible picture of a particular time, place, and social class, so that visitors strolling through such a sequence will re-experience, virtually, the development of domestic culture," to paraphrase Essenwein.[7] Though these period rooms were never created, the museum retains its outstanding collection of domestic and agricultural tools, implements, costumes, and furnishings.

Essenwein's interest in period rooms, like that of Lauffer, Heyne, and Richter, should be seen against the backdrop of rising European nationalism, which together with the Industrial Revolution led to a variety of attempts to preserve artifacts of vanishing rural life and to the birth of folklore, or the "historical core of national culture," as defined by Dorothy Noyes. She writes, "The very compilation of the great anthologies, archives and ethnographic museums was a process of nation-building, fostering ongoing interaction between provincial intellectuals."[8] For ethnographic museums such as the Germanisches Nationalmuseum, as well as museums of applied arts and design like the V&A (which Lauffer does not mention—perhaps he did not know it?), historicism was the dominant paradigm for collection and display of interiors and decoration, with furnishings becoming metonymic markers of idealized domestic life.

Architecture and decoration, both exterior and interior, became powerful symbolic vectors for a variety of collective sentiments. In both Europe and the United States, architectural replicas and interior tableaux of the vanishing built environment were popular destinations. Arthur Hazelius created an open-air museum of traditional architecture and craft, called Skansen, in Stockholm in 1891, following on the success of the Nordiska Museet, or Museum of Cultural History, which he had founded in 1872.[9] As in the Germanisches Nationalmuseum, Skansen's displays include vernacular architecture and furnishings, as well as living history displays. It is today still possible to dine in a traditional Swedish farmhouse, served by costumed waiters.

With the growth of public museums from the end of the nineteenth century, period rooms served as keys to a vanished past or a distant present that most visitors had never seen. The paradigm of contextual display and living history extended beyond the art or folklore museum to so-called life groups at the natural history museums, which were often situated in domestic settings far removed from the viewer's experience, as in the miniature Kwakwaka'wakw village from Franz Boas's 1900 historic Northwest Coast installation, a dollhouse from the far north. These simulacra helped visitors to imagine domestic life in prehistory or among the first peoples. Humans, like the animals nearby, were displayed in their natural habitat, wherever that was. In the natural history museum, localness is subsumed by a greater universal ideal of the origin of the species.

It is in comparison with this kind of period room that the phenomenon in the art museum is brought into sharper focus. The categories of domestic life that were enacted in displays of first peoples at the American Museum of Natural History in New York, the Field Museum in Chicago, and the Peabody Museum in Cambridge, Massachusetts, to name a few, came directly from templates established in early modern Europe. The model of the "godly" household, as Tara Hamling has recently called it in a study of domestic decoration in Protestant England, became the basis for the ethnographic reconstruction of the non-European domestic interior in an attempt to create a conceptual link between self and other.[10] As early European travelers portrayed the peoples they encountered as carrying out such familiar tasks as cooking over an open fire, so the curators of the American Museum of Natural History sought to domesticate their installations on various culture groups by including familiar activities such as cooking, eating, childcare, and sleeping. It is no accident that the creation of period rooms took place at the same moment that ethnographic displays and life groups emerged in other contexts of public spectacle, many less formal than the art museum, such as at the world's fairs or international expositions, popular forms of entertainment in the second half of the nineteenth century.

Period rooms implicitly connect us with an idealized collective past, whether local or global. The so-called Louis XIV Bedroom in the Metropolitan Museum is a good example of this—and Claudia Kincaid's fantasy about Marie Antoinette reinforces this message. Created with furnishings from various sources, and including many replica details to fill in and create symmetry, the Louis XIV bedroom is more stage set than period room, playing to what may be the American fascination with monarchy. But the hut where the shaman performs his exorcist ritual in the Hall of Asian Peoples at the American Museum of Natural History is also a period room. In its deployment of costumed mannequins, it is strikingly similar to display strategies from the 2004 Metropolitan Museum of Art exhibition called *Dangerous Liaisons*, which peopled the otherwise sterile eighteenth-century French period rooms with mannequins in medias res.[11] Both the hut and eighteenth-century salon demonstrate the way people inhabited space and how their dress was adapted to or determined by their environment, and suggest their relationships to one another through the body language and gesture. The period rooms at the Met represent archaic and more splendid but fundamentally familiar versions of the way we live today; the dioramas at the American Museum of Natural History edify through their strangeness: tent flaps rather than boiseries redolent with centuries of polish, the scent of domestic order; clothes of fur and skin rather than the delicate silks and brocades. Dioramas present the other; period rooms show us our better selves.

It may be that the current academic shift from an appositional ethnographic understanding of other cultures to one that stresses globalism and hybridity is behind the demise, or at least the critique, of the period room in the art museum as well. At the beginning of the history of period rooms Lauffer wrote:

Let us now say a word about the display of re-created living spaces, which most museums love to include. Although we also like this type of exhibit very much, two considerations must always be kept in mind. First, such interiors must be created with the local environment in mind, so that they accurately portray local domestic culture. At the same time, these rooms not only must be historically correct in terms of the stylistic assembly of the individual pieces, but they must also reflect the domestic economy of the time and the history of economics and customs. Accordingly, such rooms may not be used as museological "showrooms." (81)

The period room enacts the inherent inconsistencies of the museum itself, in microcosm. The frame created by walls, carpets, curtains, and light streaming through windows seduces us into imagining other times—whether we like it or not. A historically constructed medium, the period room perfects the past, ironing out its creases and cleansing its stains.

1.   Otto Lehmann, "Das Altonaer Museum," in *Die Museen als Volksbildungsstätten: Ergebnisse der 12. Konferenz der Centralstelle für Arbeiter-Wohlfahrtseinrichtungen* (Berlin: Carl Heymann, 1904), 36–38.

2.   Christopher Wilk and Nick Humphrey, eds., *Creating the British Galleries at the V&A: A Study in Museology* (London: V&A Publications, 2004), 167.

3.   Wilk and Humphrey, *Creating the British Galleries*, 165.

4.   John Harris, *Moving Rooms: The Trade in Architectural Salvages* (New Haven, CT: Yale University Press, 2007), 119ff.

5.   Peter Dierner et al., eds., *Johann Baptist Fickler, das inventar der Münchner herzoglichen kunstkammer von 1598: Editionsband: Transkription der Inventarhandschrift cgm 2133* (Munich: Verlag der Bayerischen Akademie der Wissenschaften, 2004).

6.   Heidi A. Mueller, *Good Housekeeping: A Domestic Ideal in Miniature* (Nürnberg: Germanisches Nationalmuseum, 2007), 14.

7.   Mueller, *Good Housekeeping*, 10.

8.   Dorothy Noyes, "Folklore," in *Social Science Encyclopedia*, ed. Adam Kuper and Jessica Kuper, 3rd ed. vol. 1, *A–K* (Abingdon: Routledge, 2004), 416–17.

9.   See Daniel Alan DeGroff, "Artur Hazelius and the Ethnographic Display of the Scandinavian Peasantry: A Study in Context and Appropriation," *European Review of History* 19, no. 2 (2012): 229–48.

10.   Tara Hamling, *Decorating the Godly Household: Religious Art in Protestant Britain, c. 1560–c. 1660* (New Haven, CT: Yale University Press, 2010).

11.   On this, see Ivan Gaskell, "Costume, Period Rooms, and Donors: Dangerous Liaisons in the Art Museum," *Antioch Review* 62, no. 4 (2004): 615–23.

Categories with Consequences

Alisa LaGamma

With the exception of twentieth- and twenty-first-century art created for the art gallery, virtually all museological approaches decontextualize the material culture of other times or places. Museums constitute physical sites and conceptual frameworks for their interpretation that are invariably distinct from those in which they were originally experienced. In *The Order of Things,* Michel Foucault observes of such approaches that "all knowledge is rooted in a life, a society, and a language that have a history."[1] Otto Lauffer's and Oswald Richter's museological texts, "The Historical Museum" and "On the Ideal and Practical Tasks of Ethnographic Museums," afford a sense of those developed by nineteenth-century German museum professionals. That historical moment was an especially consequential one in which the preponderance of works from many non-European societies, including sub-Saharan Africa, were avidly collected for new European institutions. In fact, that flood of unfamiliar material culture in large part informed the new methodologies for its cataloguing and presentation within a museum structure. Read more than a century later, the obsessive and self-reflexive prescriptions Lauffer and Richter provide with such authority come across as a highly contrived classificatory approach that has not withstood the test of time or place.

My recent reading of these two treatises coincides with visits to two contemporaneous museum installations that feature African works, in Dakar, Senegal, and on Berlin's Museum Island. Accordingly, my response to the texts focuses on how the ideas promoted in these museums reflect a European paradigm that has continued to define certain contemporary museum experiences.

It is striking that the authors of both texts articulate approaches to presenting and interpreting material culture that are antidotes to the "art museums" of their day. Lauffer underscores that "if not for this lack [on the part of art museums], then historical associations and ethnological organizations would never have set up collections" (87). In the twenty-first century, the idea that the approach of an art museum is anathema to that of a history museum is less self-evident. While fine arts institutions do prioritize the intrinsic aesthetic value of the works they collect, the significance of these works is related to both artistic movements and historical events. Not only is historical contextualization uncontested, but curators, conservators, and scientists ideally investigate artistic landmarks as primary sources that may reveal insights into the cultures of those who created them at specific moments in time.

In contrast, a greater dissonance inheres between the art museum and the ethnological, or ethnographic, museum. While during the nineteenth century non-Western traditions were absent from Western historical and art museums, over the course of the twentieth century many such institutions broadened their scope beyond a Western canon. The ethnographic museum has by definition, however, remained a self-contained category comprising, as Richter said, "current and former cultures of people whose ancestors were 'not included in the framework of world history that revolved around the ancient cultures of the Mediterranean'" (100). Not only does the ethnographic segregate the exotic "other" from a Western notion of civilization at large, but it is emphatically ahistorical: "Ethnology . . . is traditionally the knowledge we have of peoples without histories; in any case, it studies (both by systematic choice and because of the lack of documents) the structural invariables of cultures rather than the succession of events."[2]

Whereas Western material culture might be presented in either the art or historical museum context, Richter and his fellow European museum professionals conceived of a single variety of institution—that is neither of these—as the appropriate framework for considering the creative output of the entire non-Western world. That separate category of the ethnographic museum mixes the superlative with the simply representative. Richter is explicit about positioning such ethnographic museums as a nineteenth-century extension of the earlier cabinet of curiosities and as instruments of colonial enterprise that would contribute to awareness of an expanding array of beliefs and cultural practices (104–10). His treatise, written when German institutions were in the vanguard of acquiring enormous quantities of cultural artifacts from a diverse array of sources, makes claims for scientific research in the face of the reality that the vast numbers of works assembled by German ethnographic museums are minimally documented: "Today we demand to know the precise find spot of an object. . . . Objects that arrive at a museum without information on their find spot and without an identifiable provenance should not even be accepted. In addition to the provenance, the indigenous name of the object should be noted, as well as the purpose of its ornamentation, its use, its method of creation, and its material. For objects obtained either through sales from dealers or through gifts from donors, these specifications are, as a rule, rarely and insufficiently met. . . . A critical traveler, such as one trained by a museum, can obtain the necessary information prior to acquisition with far greater ease" (141–42). At one time the window of opportunity existed to record the names of authors, the identity of patrons, the specifics of iconography, and related historical events, but that kind of specificity is for the most part absent from the documentation that accompanies African works in such ethnographic collections. While it has sometimes been possible to reconstruct a more rigorous historical understanding of major African landmarks preserved since the nineteenth century among such vast ethnographic holdings, both the lack of precolonial indigenous written sources and the dearth of archival documentation reflect the fact that these works were being assembled for institutions whose concerns were counter to those of the history or art museum.

In May 2018, the Musée de l'Institut Fondamental d'Afrique Noire, known since 2007 as the Musée Théodore Monod d'Art Africain, in Dakar, Senegal, hosted the opening colloquium that accompanied the launch of the thirteenth edition of Dak'art, or the Dakar Biennale. The museum building located at Place Soweto is a public branch of the Institut Fondamental d'Afrique Noire (IFAN). For generations this has been Dakar's one public museum, open year round, where material culture from the region is on display. In 1936, IFAN (originally Institut Français d'Afrique Noire) was conceived as an institute for research relating to France's West African colonies. Its collections were envisioned as "representative" of the material culture of what became French-speaking West Africa. During the 1940s and 1950s, IFAN became the repository for major archaeological discoveries across Mali, Mauritania, Senegal, and Niger that extended back to the earliest Neolithic cultures and to discoveries and historical landmarks ranging from Islamic lithic inscriptions from the medieval cemetery of Gao in present-day Mali to precious gold ornaments unearthed in burial tumuli at the site of Rao near

Saint Louis in Senegal dating between 1250 and 1350. IFAN researchers assembled nineteenth- and twentieth-century artifacts, including masks and figurative sculpture identified with major traditions within the prescribed territory. Since 1959, IFAN has been overseen by Cheikh Anta Diop University.

A bifurcation developed almost as soon as the collection was formed. The archaeological displays and collections on the university campus have been accessible only to researchers in prehistory and archaeology, while the museum is limited to IFAN's nineteenth- and twentieth-century holdings. Titled *Arts et traditions artisanales en Afrique de l'Ouest*, the public display put in place in 1961 has undergone only minor renovations since (in 1992). This curious inconsistent split recalls Richter's prescription regarding archaeological holdings: "We recommend segregating those holdings to a designated space (such as a special room) away from the general ethnographic material and arranging them according to temporal and geographic criteria" (132). The practical effect of this has been the invisibility of IFAN's significant archaeological holdings, which continue to expand through new discoveries, and the increasing irrelevance of the museum.

During Senegal's earliest chapter as an independent nation-state, its president, the poet-statesman Léopold Sédar Senghor, took pride in this museum as a showcase connecting his people to the region at large and to its distinctive forms of creative expression. Frozen in time, however, its holdings have not expanded to include contemporary forms of artistic expression or commentary that might make them pertinent to local or international visitors. The museum installation devoted to artifacts identified with former colonial frontiers, from traditions unfamiliar to Senegalese and foreigners alike, is a timeless and static display devoid of a sense of their dynamism as forms of expression. Not only is there an absence of history; there is no hint of the many-layered past that preceded European colonialism made concrete through the archaeological collections. The exception is a rugged monumental megalith in the form of a lyre, dated to before the sixteenth century, from a first-millennium open-air ceremonial site in central Senegal. Displaced from what has since become a World Heritage site, this impressive landmark was recovered from a private residence and transferred to the museum grounds in the 1990s. Its imposing presence offers a statement concerning the highly distinctive cultural legacy represented within. However, in the absence of any explanation, it appears incongruous or is simply unnoticed. Housed within a colonial structure surrounded by a garden built as the French governor's residence, the IFAN museum exists as an anachronism at the heart of Dakar's dynamic urban center. Apart from serving as a venue for sub-Saharan Africa's major biennale of contemporary art exhibitions, it is generally in search of an audience. Host to an event devoted to vanguard displays, IFAN is prevented from developing its own narrative and voice by the weight of an imported museological approach.

Back in Europe, the exhibition *Beyond Compare* at Berlin's Bode Museum introduced new life into its galleries of European medieval and Renaissance sculpture. This initiative developed during the planning of Berlin's Humboldt Forum. As a counterpoint to the institutions of Museum Island, which subdivide much of humankind's achievements within the distinct Altes, Pergamon, Neues, Alte Nationalgalerie, and Bode museums, the collections of both the Ethnologisches Museum and the Museum für Asiatische Kunst are being distilled and are to be reintroduced in a more centrally located structure. In this new non-Western block, they will stand apart from but face Museum Island.

Collaboration between Bode's Julien Chapuis and the curators of Berlin's African collection of the Ethnologisches Museum, Jonathan Fine and Paola Ivanov, sought to bridge the divide between Berlin's European art and non-Western ethnographic museum collections by positioning major landmarks of African art in dialogue with those in Bode's permanent collection.[3] This temporary intervention unfolds as an exercise in cross-cultural comparison across the museum. Some of the face-to-face confrontations between European and African works were conceived in purely formal terms. Others provide a juxtaposition of parallel idioms of expression that posed comparable demands upon their African and European authors addressed in radically different ways.

A striking example of this was the confrontation between two potent sculptural elements conceived as reliquaries: a nineteenth-century Mahongwe work from Gabon or the Republic of the Congo and the sixteenth-century bust of a bishop from Brussels. In both works sacred matter was the point of departure for the creation of portable altars whose power was amplified through idealized representations of influential ancestors seen as effective intercessors with the divine. The intense realism of the life-size European saint underscores the furrows of the subject's brow, the glow of his complexion, and his rich vestments and attributes of office. Precious relics from the Cologne-based cult of Saint Ursula given by Charles V after his visit to the Rhineland remain intact—a skull fragment in its head and a splinter of a rib in the chest. The radically pared-down Mahongwe representation takes the form of a wood understructure wrapped in an armature of costly applied metalwork. Here too the focus is on the head, but it takes a slightly concave form with minimal applied features that project from the surface in the form of circular eyes and a beaklike nose. The summit and base of the head are extended by cylindrical forms that denote an elite coiffure and neck. The sculpture's simple openwork terminus was the site for the attachment of a now-missing bundle of relics drawn from the crania of lineage founders. The work was given to Berlin in 1875 by the Leipzig-born explorer and geologist Oscar Lenz, who acquired it on one of several trips along the upper Ogooué River between 1874 and 1876. This element from a portable altar is the earliest example of a major equatorial African devotional art form that has been preserved, though Lenz simply identifies it as a "fetish-idol of the Aduma and Oschebo peoples."[4] Although it was field-collected by a man of science, our knowledge of it is thus based on a general understanding of what is a relatively poorly documented tradition.

The opportunity to move beyond segregating what have historically been classified as "ethnographic" collections from those of art museums is a necessary paradigm-shifting precedent. It establishes the arbitrariness of these categories and underscores the decontextualization of both traditions. Long-term challenges for museums, whether in Dakar, Berlin, or New York, will be to evoke the dynamic performative and ritual dimensions of both European and non-Western forms of expression through evocative display that moves beyond labeling and digital media. Where the legacy of ethnographic institutions has not dominated, the cultural heritage of non-Western societies has encountered fewer impediments to its presentation within global museum contexts that consider it in historical terms. In centers where it remains in large part positioned within ethnographic institutions, the Bode intervention is to date a rare remedy for that status quo. While this translation of Lauffer and Richter is my introduction to their writings, the positions they espouse are ones that have defined the predominant taxonomies obsessively applied to non-Western material culture in Europe and beyond for over a century. The prescriptions pronounced so authoritatively by Lauffer, Richter, and their nineteenth-century peers constitute approaches that continue to have an outsize impact on our sense of what museums might be.

1.   Michel Foucault, *The Order of Things: An Archaeology of the Human Sciences* (New York: Pantheon, 1973), 372.

2.   Foucault, *Order of Things*, 373.

3.   Julien Chapuis, Jonathan Fine, and Paola Ivanov, eds., *Beyond Compare: Art from Africa in the Bode Museum* (Berlin: Staatliche Museen zu Berlin, 2017).

4.   Alisa LaGamma, ed., *Eternal Ancestors: The Art of the Central African Reliquary* (New York: Metropolitan Museum of Art; New Haven, CT: Yale University Press, 2007), 212.

Visions of Juxtaposition: Peiresc/Bataille, Monuments/Documents

Peter N. Miller

Georges Bataille's work as the *sécretaire-général* (generally treated as "managing editor") of *Documents*, a magazine that was published in fifteen parts in 1929 and 1930, has attracted a substantial body of scholarly attention. It is generally seen as a milestone in the history of surrealism and in the context of Bataille's feud with André Breton.[1] It has also been placed in the history of ethnography, captured most succinctly by James Clifford's "ethnographic surrealism."[2] In recent years, the role of Bataille's collaborator Carl Einstein has been seen as a bridge to the world of German scholarship.[3] The recently recovered relationship of *Documents* to the scholars grouped around Aby Warburg has complicated simple genealogies of the modern.[4] I would like to point to its relationship to the seventeenth-century's cabinet of curiosities, but by way of a more immediate predecessor.

In 1843, the first volume of Gustav Friedrich Klemm's *Allgemeine Kultur-geschichte* was published.[5] Nine more volumes were to come over the next decade. In the appendix to volume 1, Klemm added to his developmental account of human culture a "Fantasy for a Museum of Culture History." In it, he imagined a museum in which each gallery room documented a different stage of that development (roughly one room per volume). The imagining was not too far-fetched, either, as the fantasy museum's items were drawn largely from his own burgeoning collection. Klemm had begun his career as a curator in the Saxon porcelain collection before becoming a librarian in the royal collection, and his landmark *History of Collections in Germany* (1837) traced the early modern *Kunst- und Wunderkammern* of Germany into their present-day incarnations. His "fantasy" can be seen as a re-presentation of the *Wunderkammer*'s synthesis of historical, ethnographic, and natural objects. As a theorist of cultural history—and as *the* pioneering writer on cultural science (*Kulturwissenschaft*)—he provided an important model for Hans von und zu Aufseß, whose national cultural history museum opened in Nürnberg in 1853.[6] Otto Lauffer and Oswald Richter (especially Lauffer), in turn, learned from Aufseß to think about the museum as a research vehicle for studying world culture. Their emphasis on "purpose" as a path to connect collecting and display provided a scientific basis for the universal museum.

But what of the *Wunderkammer*'s unmediated juxtapositions that Klemm studied so carefully in order to overcome them in his own fantasy of organization? This is where *Documents* belongs to the history of the museum, and thus of the object. Seen from this perspective, the magazine's juxtaposition of archaeology and ethnography and Beaux-Arts (the three constants in its subtitle) carries over much of the content and spirit of the early modern treasure house. The cultural critique implied by this kind of juxtaposition—using the archaeological and the ethnographic, as well as a concentration on the contemporary avant-garde, to undermine the overdetermined cultural preferences loaded into the uppercase, and upper-class, History of Art—was totally of its time.[7] Yet it also shaped the way scholars and artists of the turn of the twenty-first century have taught us to view the early modern *Wunderkammer*.[8] After Bataille, but still deeply touched by surrealism, there is Joseph Cornell, and through him—on to the erudite reassemblers David Wilson, Mark Dion, and Arseny Zhilyaev. Another line descending from Bataille emphasizes more the objects of daily life as uncanny knowledge (this might take us from Harold Szeemann to the Museum der unerhörten Dinge in Berlin) or as sites of political intervention, as with Fred Wilson and Thomas Hirschhorn.

One way to make this argument would be to survey the historical topics published in *Documents*—Sumerian sculptures, Viking ships, Siberian metalwork, cubism, Ingres, numismatics, ethnographic museums, and so forth—and those published alongside them on contemporary topics, especially by Bataille. These interventions make for a constantly jarring juxtaposition. This targeting of contemporary conventions marks the distance-taking from Klemm, as well as from Lauffer and Richter and Bode.

A more economical, more precise, and perhaps even more jarring way of capturing this moment of the breaking—or renewing—of the

Wunderkammer tradition might be to juxtapose the juxtaposer, Bataille, with an arch-embodiment of the world of the early modern *Wunderkammer*: Nicolas Fabri de Peiresc (1580–1637).[9] On the surface, the two could hardly seem more different. But Bataille was trained at the École des Chartes, the institution whose founding in 1821 sought to systematize the idiosyncratic collection of evidentiary skills that Peiresc and his friends had developed and mastered two centuries earlier, and what the Germans had systematized half a century before as the auxiliary sciences of history (*historische Hilfswissenschaften*). After graduation, Bataille got a job at the Bibliothèque Nationale, first as a curator in the prints department and then in the Cabinet des Médailles—a modern department of the library that was, effectively, a *Wunderkammer*, and whose collection incorporated objects from early modern French *Wunderkammern*, including that of Peiresc. At this early stage of his career Bataille published on numismatics in learned journals, and two of his collaborators in the founding of *Documents* were colleagues in the Cabinet des Médailles, Pierre d'Espezel and Jean Babelon.[10]

Let us be more specific. Of Bataille's most important contributions to the magazine, we may single out two, each of which was published in the first number of the year: "Le cheval académique" in 1929 and "Le bas matérialisme" in 1930.[11] The former analogized pre-conquest Gaul to contemporary Central Africa.[12] Bataille presented the depictions of horses on pre-Roman Gallic coins as "representing, from a social point of view, a veritable antithesis of classical civilization."[13] That the depictions of horses were so different enabled Bataille to use them to argue that the "absurdities of the barbarians contradict the scientific arrogances, the nightmares with geometric lines, monster horses imagined in Gaul with the academic horse."[14] The attack on the Greek cultural exemplar was bound up in that final term. "Académique" invoked the Academy, which referred to Plato and his theory of the "Forms" or "Ideas." This dominant piece of Western metaphysics was the real target of the article.

The second article, published a year later, picked up where the previous one had left off, declaring that the "variants of this metaphysical scaffolding are of no more interest than are the different styles of architecture." What passed as the materialist critique, Marx's "dialectical materialism," Bataille identified as just another kind of Hegelian idealism, and thus still trapped by the terms it was trying to oust. For a materialism that was the negation of idealism—"which amounts to saying, finally, of the very basis of *all* philosophy," one had to go still lower.[15]

For this "bas matérialisme" Bataille turned to gnosticism. And, since its texts had all been destroyed by the Christian heresiarchs who led its persecution in late antiquity, men such as Marcion (85–160) and Epiphanius (310–403), the modern inquirer had to turn to the documents of gnosticism that had survived, namely the strange intaglio stones that combined Greek, Egyptian, and Jewish imagery and alphabets. Referring to "modern interpretation," Bataille identified in gnosticism a notion of "active matter" that rejected the "profoundly monistic Hellenistic spirit, whose dominant tendency saw matter and evil as degradations of superior principles." Bataille saw in gnosticism something not so different from contemporary materialism, by which he meant "a materialism not implying an ontology, not implying that matter is the thing-in-itself."[16] The consequences of this were clear to him: "it was a question of disconcerting the human spirit and idealism before something base, to the extent that one recognized the helplessness of superior principles," that in turn "permits the intellect to escape from the constraints of idealism."[17]

Peiresc had worked on these very subjects: the iconography of Gallic coins, and gnostic gems.[18] He, too, began from the hypothesis of a possible connection between Central Africa and Gaul, drawing from the similar types of extreme hairdressing described by contemporary travelers to Africa and found on Gallic coins. Peiresc framed his discussion by providing a possible Greek (Macedonian) influence on Gallic numismatics. He devoted his most careful attention, however, to the iconography. His main focus was on the hairstyles, but he commented specifically on the equally elaborate and strange horses on these coins.[19]

Peiresc's formidable research on gnostic gems began during his trip to Italy before he reached the age of twenty, and his interest in the subject lasted long into adulthood. His scholarly communication on Epiphanius with Natalitio Beneditti and with Jean L'Heureux Macarius, and his literary executor Philips van Winghe, became part of Macarius's posthumous *Abraxas Proteus* (1657), the foundation of the "modern interpretation" of gnosticism referred to by Bataille.[20] And Peiresc saw gnosticism as a historical phenomenon that continued through the Cathars of the Middle Ages and on to the "Alombrados" in contemporary Spain, whom he described to Peter-Paul Rubens as the "Basilidiani di Seviglia."[21]

As a *Chartiste* and curator in the Cabinet des Médailles, Bataille would definitely have known of Peiresc. The essays and volumes of letters edited and published by Tamizey de Larroque would have been available to him. But Bataille could even more easily have walked down the short flight of stairs separating the Cabinet des Médailles from the Western Manuscripts Reading Room and there sat with fifteen volumes of Peiresc manuscripts—correspondence, reading notes, memoranda, sketches, excerpts—including his notes on gnostic gems, all catalogued in the preceding decade by Léopold Delisle. In the print room, where he had been curator, there were two other volumes of Peiresceana, drawings of objects once in his possession. Whether there are surviving Bataille papers that further document this encounter I do not yet know.

Contrasting Peiresc and Bataille helps pinpoint the difference between the early modern *Wunderkammer* as an engine of research and Bataille's *Wunderkammer* as a vehicle of critique. There is one further, even more precise way of marking the difference between these two visions of juxtaposition: that between the words "monument" and "document." The former was used frequently by antiquaries like Peiresc ("un des plus belles monuments de l'antiquité") and then modernized by Montfaucon (*Les monuments de la monarchie française*) and nationalized after the French Revolution by Lenoir (*La musée des monuments français*). With the birth of archaeology in nineteenth-century Germany, "monument" became *Denkmal*, and its scholarly treatment *Denkmalkunde*.[22] In his *Archaeology of Knowledge*, Foucault made the monument-document axis a foundation of the new history. But it was Bataille who first deployed this rhetorical weapon, and he wielded it against the contemporary idea of archaeology.[23]

Waldemar Deonna was a professor of archaeology at Geneva and a commentator on the art of the avant-garde who published books on futurism and surrealism and wrote a posthumously published study of one of Bataille's key subjects, the symbolism of the eye (*Le symbolisme de l'oeil*, 1965).[24] In 1922 he published *Archéologie: Son domaine, son but*, a French updating of the German *Handbuch* tradition, and especially of the *Handbuch der Archäologie der Kunst*, whose landmarks were by Karl Otfried Müller (1830) and Karl Bernhard Stark (1880).

"Monument" is all over Deonna's text. A history of archaeology would be a history of the matter of archaeology (i.e., "the discovery of monuments"), of the history of "the study of monuments," and a history of the methods developed "for understanding these monuments." All in all, he wrote, archaeology is "l'histoire des monuments." Material monuments were, he wrote, the most important of the "exteriorized documents of history." He also refers to objects as "monuments matériels des arts" and as "documents matériels." Genealogically, he notes that Raoul Rochette, whose 1828 lectures on archaeology were the first course of lectures delivered on that subject in France, referred to "monuments figurées" to distinguish them from "monuments littéraires." Salomon Reinach defined archaeology as the "explication of the past through man-made monuments." Studying these "monuments ouvrés," Deonna wrote, meant studying "art." More to the point, Deonna adds, "texts, medals, monuments allow for reconstituting the skeleton of the past, but one who does not know how to determine the sentiments and ideas from which they derive cannot know history." And, a page later: "What I want to know, and above all, are the ideas that are realized in these statues, beliefs, [and] the individual, psychological, physiological, geographical, economic, social conditions of all sorts to which they respond."[25] This is precisely what Bataille was rejecting. If "documents" meant anything, it meant a resistance to synthesis, an effort to interrupt the process of building from the many "externalized documents of the past" to the already overdetermined monument and so prevent the erection of ever greater ideological construction. His goal is the fragment, not the narrative; the archive, not the museum.[26]

Bataille read Deonna in 1928.[27] The very next year he replaced "monument" with "document" as the object of archaeology in the title of the new magazine. And while it has been more common to note the use of ethnography in *Documents* to disrupt conventional hierarchies, it might be this new notion of "archaeology" that provoked the greatest disruption. Here it is not Bataille so much as his partner, Carl Einstein, who was most destructive. For if Bataille's target was the grand narrative, it was Einstein who realized that it rested upon a world of clearly defined and unthinkingly accepted objects. His praise of the cubist revolution exploded all that.

Einstein began his "Aphorismes méthodiques" by describing painting as a "defense against the passage of time, and thus a defense against death." What the antiquaries would have described as *tempus edax rerum*, he identifies with Euclidean space and rigid objects ("the receptacles of conventions"). Changing the view of space means questioning the stability of objects and thus the painting itself. "The object," he writes, "is an ensemble of varied experiences, and it is because of this that one can trigger a number of varied reactions." The representational realism of the Renaissance was, therefore, "a kind of utopian literature," a "teleological optimism," a "heroization corresponding to ancient mythology." All this rested upon a very simple structure: "a static psychology from an objective content and not from psychological processes." The Renaissance viewed the world as a work of art conformable to physical laws and at the same time to human reason. Einstein described this as a "scientific fetishism" that established the identity of the human being with the natural world.[28] With cubism, the "limits of objects have disappeared." There is no longer a direct correspondence between the natural world and the human. Now humans "live in the orbit of objects that have become psychological functions. Optical simultaneity is replaced by analogies. One could speak of a mystical anatomy."[29]

With this attack on the autonomous existence of the object and its implication in a series of psychological processes that might exceed the capacity of any given person to identify them, we have laid bare the gulf between Peiresc and Bataille, between the monument, which is, after all, a way of talking about the world of objects, and the document, which is the datum shorn of any particular telos or idea.

Recognizing that so much here was at stake, and that contemporaries were aware of all that hung on the autonomy of the object, is the only way to read the unhinged response of Wilhelm von Bode to analytical cubism, published in 1913 but republished in *Documents* in 1930 in an issue devoted to Picasso. For Bode, it was no less than the end of civilization as he knew it.

> In this new art is made manifest in a particularly repugnant way the tendency of our democratic era toward the destruction of the barriers protecting religion and morality, toward a leveling more and more complete, toward a suppression of originality and independent character, toward the disappearance of a sense of quality that is replaced by the triumph of mediocrity and brutality. The aesthetic is rejected. The search for beauty in art is declared ridiculous. A new kind of beauty is discovered in ugliness and vulgarity. One goes so far as to make a new religion in which the new art would be the highest expression of art and morality.[30]

When Arnaldo Momigliano described twentieth-century sociologists as "armed antiquarians" (*antiquari armati*), he would surely not have had this battle in mind, nor Georges Bataille.[31] And yet it would seem to fit his work in *Documents* at least as well as it does Max Weber, the actual object of Momigliano's observation. And when Momigliano opined in 1950 that "France remained traditionally the best home for the antiquaries until not so many years ago," he did not indicate that he had Bataille or *Documents* in mind.[32] And yet Bataille and Einstein's magazine has had a crucial role in the return to the "*Wunderkammer* aesthetic" in the later twentieth-century history of installation art and the museological retreat from the universal.[33] It occupies an important place in a backward-facing history of antiquarianism and played an important role in the forward-facing reshaping of a kind of contemporary antiquarianism. How these two lines intertwined in the second half of the twentieth century would be the subject of a separate study.

1.   We can begin with the special issue of *Critique* (1963): 195–96: "Hommage à Georges Bataille"; Dawn Ades and Simon Baker, eds., *Undercover Surrealism: Georges Bataille and DOCUMENTS* (London: Hayward Gallery; Cambridge, MA: MIT Press, 2006); Thomas Augais, "Trait pour trait: Alberto Giacometti et les écrivains par voltes et faces d'ateliers" (PhD diss., University of Lyons, 2009), "4. Le Projet de Bataille," http://theses.univ-lyon2.fr/documents/getpart.php?id=lyon2.2009. augais_t&part=158159; Marja Warehime, "'Vision sauvage' and Images of Culture: Georges Bataille, Editor of *Documents*," *French Review* 60 (1986): 39–45; Jean-Michel Besnier, "Georges Bataille et la modernité: La politique de l'impossible," *Revue du MAUSS*, no. 25 (2005): 190–206, https://doi.org/10.3917/rdm.025.0190; Georges Bataille, *Visions of Excess: Selected Writings, 1927–1939*, ed. Alan Stoekl (Minneapolis: University of Minnesota Press, 1985).

2.   James Clifford, "On Ethnographic Surrealism," *Comparative Study of Society and History* (1981): 539–64; Clifford, "Documents: A *Decomposition*," *Visual Anthropology Review* 7 (1991): 62–83; K. H. Kiefer, "Die Ethnologisierung des kunstkritischen Diskurses—Carl Einstein's Beitrag zu 'Documents,'" in *Elan vital oder das Auge des Eros*, ed. H. Gassner (Munich: Haus der Kunst, 1994), 90–103; Gaetano Ciarcia, "'L'impossible' etnografia di un'avanguardia: Il case di 'Documents,'" *La ricerca folklorica* 35 (1997): 129–39.

3.   Einstein studied with Wölfflin and Giedion. Rainer Rumold, "'Painting as a Language: Why Not?' Carl Einstein in 'Documents,'" *October* 107 (2004): 75–94. This special issue is devoted to Einstein. See also Conor Joyce, *Carl Einstein in "Documents" and His Collaboration with Georges Bataille* (Bloomington, IN: Xlibris, 2003); and Lillian Meffre, *Carl Einstein 1885–1940: Itinéraires d'une pensée moderne* (Paris: PUF, 2002).

4.   Spyros Papapetros, "Between the Academy and the Avant-Garde: Carl Einstein and Fritz Saxl Correspond," *October* 139 (2012): 77–96; Joyce, *Carl Einstein*, 38–39. On the wider connections between the Warburg circle and surrealism, see Georges Didi-Huberman, *L'image survivante: Histoire de l'art et temps des fantômes selon Aby Warburg* (Paris: Minuit, 2002), 482; Benjamin Buchloh, "Gerhard Richter's Atlas: The Anomic Archive," *October* 88 (1999): 128.

5.   This paragraph draws on my *History and Its Objects: Antiquarianism and Material Culture Since 1500* (Ithaca, NY: Cornell University Press, 2017), ch. 7.

6.   See Peter N. Miller, *History and Its Objects,* ch. 7; "Kulturwissenschaft Before Warburg," in *Aby Warburg 150: Work, Legacy, and Promise,* ed. David Freedberg and Claudia Wedepohl (Berlin: De Gruyter, forthcoming).

7.   C. F. B. Miller, "Archaeology," in Ades and Baker, *Undercover Surrealism,* 42–50; Rainer Rumold, "Archeologies of Modernity in *Transition* and *Documents,* 1929/30," *Comparative Literature Studies* 37 (2000): 15 77. The approach to archaeology could have been inspired by an article written the previous year by a contributor to *Documents,* Georges-Henri Rivière: "Archéologismes," *Cahiers d'art* 1 (1927): 177.

8.   Clifford, "On Ethnographic Surrealism," 134: "This odd museum merely documents, juxtaposes, relativizes—a perverse collection."

9.   See the author's *Peiresc's Europe* (2000), *Peiresc's Orient* (2012), and *Peiresc's Mediterranean World* (2015).

10.   "Sur le séjour en Espagne de Georges Bataille (1922): Quelques documents nouveaux," *Bibliothèque de l'École des chartes* 146 (1988): 179–90, only glancingly deals with what Bataille would have studied at the École and what, precisely, he did as curator at the Bibliothèque Nationale de France. In summer 1928 Bataille wrote an article on coins from Central Asia published in *Aréthuse* and also contributed to the issue of the *Cahiers de la République des lettres,* edited by Alfred Métraux, on a show of ancient American arts that Georges-Henri Rivière, another contributor to *Documents,* curated the same year in the Musée des Arts Décoratifs (Ades, "Beaux-Arts," 64).

11.   Jean-Philippe Antoine, "'Le cheval académique': Georges Bataille, *Documents* et le classique," *L'immagine del "classico" negli anni venti e trenta del Novecento,* May 2006, Pisa, Italy; Deborah L. Stein, "The Theft of the Goddess Amba Mata: Ontological Location and Georges Bataille's *bas matérialisme,*" *RES: Anthropology and Aesthetics* 57/58 (2010): 264–82. All citations will be from the two-volume edition of *Documents,* with preface by Denis Hollier, in *Les cahiers de Gradhiva* ([Paris]: JeanMichelPlace, 1991).

12.   On the importance of Africa in *Documents,* see Coline Bidault, "La présentation des objets africains dans DOCUMENTS (1929/1930), magazine illustré," *Les cahiers de l'École du Louvre,* DOI: 10.4000/cel.500.

13.   "Le cheval académique," *Documents* 1 (1929): 27.

14.   "Le cheval académique," *Documents* 1 (1929): 29.

15.   Bataille, "Base Materialism and Gnosticism," in *Visions of Excess,* 45.

16.   Bataille, "Base Materialism and Gnosticism," 47.

17.   Bataille, "Base Materialism and Gnosticism," 51.

18.   These were also the only two articles from *Documents* that found their way into Warburg's library. See Papapetros, "Between the Academy and the Avant-Garde," 94.

19.   Peter N. Miller, "History of Religion Becomes Ethnology: Some Evidence from Peiresc's Africa," *Journal of the History of Ideas* 4 (2006): 678–81.

20.   Peter N. Miller, "The Antiquary's Art of Comparison: Peiresc and Abraxas," in *Philologie und Erkenntnis,* ed. Ralph Häfner (Tübingen: Max Niemeyer, 2001), 70–84.

21.   Cited in Peter N. Miller, "Antiquary's Art of Comparison," 89.

22.   See Peter N. Miller, *History and Its Objects*, ch. 5; Françoise Choay, *The Invention of the Historic Monument* (1992), trans. Lauren M. O'Connell (Cambridge: Cambridge University Press, 2001), esp. chs. 2, 4.

23.   Sophia Berrebi, *The Shape of Evidence: Contemporary Art and the Document* (Amsterdam: Valiz, 2014), esp. 36–44.

24.   *Futuristes d'autrefois et d'aujourd'hui* (1912); *De la planète Mars en Terre sainte: Art et subconscient; Un médium peintre; Hélène Smith* (1932).

25.   Waldemar Deonna, *Archéologie: Son domaine, son but* (Paris: Flammarion, 1922), 8, 11, 20–21, 42, 47, 185–86.

26.   See, for instance, Berrebi, *Shape of Evidence*, 90.

27.   C. F. B. Miller, *Archaeology*, 43.

28.   Carl Einstein, "Aphorismes méthodiques," *Documents* 1 (1929): 32–34.

29.   Carl Einstein, "André Masson, étude ethnologique," *Documents* 2 (1929): 102. The novelty of Einstein's psychological approach is clear when compared, for example, with Roger Allard, "Die Kennzeichen der Erneuerung in der Malerei," in *Der Blaue Reiter*, ed. F. Marc and W. Kandinsky, 2nd ed. (Munich: Piper, 1914), 36.

30.   "Dans cet art nouveau se manifeste d'une façon particulièrement répugnante la tendance de notre époque démocratique vers la destruction des barrières gênantes de la religion et de la morale, vers le nivellement de plus en plus complet, vers la suppression de l'originalité et des caractères indépendantes, vers la disparition du sens de la qualité qu'on remplace par le triomphe de la médiocrité et de la brutalité. L'esthétique est écartée. On déclare ridicule la recherche de la beauté dans l'art. On construit une beauté nouvelle qu'on veut avoir découvrire dans la laideur et la vulgarité. On va jusqu'à en faire une religion nouvelle dont l'art nouveau veut être l'expression la plus haute au point de vue artistique et morale" (*Documents* 3 [1930]: 183).

31.   Arnaldo Momigliano, "Prospettiva 1967 della storia greca," in *Quarto contributo alla storia degli studi classici e del mondo antico* (Rome: Storia e letteratura, 1969), 51.

32.   Arnaldo Momigliano, "Ancient History and the Antiquarian," in *Contributo alla storia degli studi classici* (Rome: Storia e letteratura, 1955), 102.

33.   Clifford, "On Ethnographic Surrealism," 553.

The Future in the Past

H. Glenn Penny

These essays from the past have much to teach us about the future. Otto Lauffer and Oswald Richter produced them during a period of formative debates about museums' potential. At that time, museums were meant to be much more than places of civic self-promotion, entertainment, or edification. The research potential of museums was still assumed, still eagerly pursued. The connections between ethnological museums and universities, for example, as Richter knew very well, were strengthening. Today, those connections are largely gone. None of the people debating museums' potential in *Museumskunde* during the first decade of the twentieth century thought much about espresso bars, gift shops, or *Gastronomie*. Museums' boards and directors were not preparing to hire people to coordinate events, figure out where the wedding parties would take place, or take charge of advertising campaigns and promotional ventures. Instead, they still thought first and foremost about exhibition as part of intellectual exploration and research. They thought about museums as places that produced knowledge.

Yet trends away from knowledge production and toward entertainment or a kind of packaged edification—perfect for school classes or the middle-class families on weekend visits—were well under way. Both Lauffer and Richter were inadvertently taking part in them, even as they were pushing back against the homogenizing power of the art museum, which came to dominate museum spaces and dictate modes of display in Berlin, and most everywhere else. Both argue about the "character" of history and ethnological museums. They want that character to be determined by intellectual foundations and intellectual visions, not simply the contents of their collections, naming fashions, or the emerging trend toward displays made comestible for general audiences.

Lauffer, in particular, is focused on designations and differentiations. For him, names are a serious matter. Things are much the same a hundred years later, and Lauffer sounds rather timely when asking readers: What does cultural history even mean? He is concerned with the imprecision of the term. Too many kinds of museums had adopted it, and it had lost its descriptive and analytical power. In the twenty-first century, Lauffer's lament would have been quickly absorbed into the debates about branding. In the German-speaking countries of Europe during the last decades, for example, many *Völkerkunde* (ethnological) museums were faced with the same question: What's in a name? Many are still struggling with that problem.

During the last decade of the twentieth century, directors and board members began worrying about how the term *Völkerkunde* was used and abused. They fretted over how people working in their museums, as well as their visitors, understood it. Many determined that this brand/label/name was bad, undermined by the trappings of the past, especially negative associations with anything tied to notions of *Volk*, a term tainted by the Nazis. So they set out to develop new terms that would capture the trends in globalization and a pluralistic appreciation for the multiplicities of cultures. Hence, many *Völkerkunde* museum directors and their boards adopted names such as Museum of Cultures (Basel), Museum of Five Continents (Munich), World Cultural Museum (Frankfurt), and World Museum (Vienna). The Deutsche Gesellschaft für Völkerkunde (German Association for Ethnology) followed suit, changing its name to the Deutsche Gesellschaft für Sozial- und Kulturanthropologie (German Association for Social and Cultural Anthropology). The irony is that an appreciation for the multiplicity of cultures and global trends that these name changes were meant to evoke is precisely what the *Völkerkunde* museums of the late nineteenth and early twentieth centuries were focused on—except that, as Richter underscores in his essay, their first goal remained the production of knowledge, not merely its dissemination. A large number of critics have also made precisely this point about the name change of the German Association for Ethnology.

At the same time, while the renaming trend is general, not all these newly branded ethnological museums can be the same. Their collections are different; they have different histories; and they serve different communities. This too is an age-old concern. Lauffer grapples with it in his essay on historical museums. He emphasizes that the local importance of any museum is critical for its self-articulation, for its mission. Limited means, he reminds his readers, require an even more precise understanding of an institution's goals. Quite right. In the case of the archaeological and historical museums he champions, that means thinking about the larger trends in archaeology, and thus ancient history, and their meaning for local geographies. In many ways, that neat articulation immediately globalizes local artifacts, placing them into broader conceptual schematics while also offering better understandings of local history.

As he also argues, historical and ethnographic museums should not uncritically follow trends in display, led overwhelmingly by art museums, especially not their emphasis on the unique characteristics and the aesthetics of individual items in their displays. He contended that such aesthetics, championed by Berlin art historian Wilhelm von Bode and others, should not be allowed to undermine the specific academic or museological agendas of local institutions. Local archaeological and historical museums, for example, were more akin to the intellectual mission of archives. Such museums were meant to deal with objects as much as texts. That required a different kind of spatial organization, but the mission was comparable.

In the end, neither Lauffer nor Richter was able to resolve the inherent tensions between serving a public and serving a science. Lauffer hoped to lay out a set of guidelines that would create a kind of conformity among historical museums, encouraging them to focus on local histories and collections, yet urging them to follow consistent principles of organization and display. Those would necessarily be different from art museums' principles yet consistent across history museums. In that way, the various museums could manage their individual collections, focus on local audiences, and participate in a joint project. Who, precisely, might oversee this centralization was left to memberships in associations. There was no need for state intervention or a redistribution of resources or artifacts. Still, Lauffer was convinced that all successful museums inevitably would run out of space and be forced to divide their collections between those used for public display and those used for research. Here he was on the same page as Bode, sharing a position against which the ethnologists in Berlin's *Völkerkunde* museum argued vociferously until they too succumbed to that principle in the 1920s.

For Berlin's ethnologists, the problem, much as Lauffer argued, was not only the lack of space. Their commitment to research over public edification set them at odds with the hegemonic power of art museums generated by bureaucratic structures that placed scientific museums under the auspices of museum administrations headed by art historians. Bode had his own ideas about how to organize *Völkerkunde* museums: dividing the collections into small, aesthetically pleasing exhibits for the general public and placing the rest in storage or separate research facilities. He also advocated more radical reorganizations: for example, he recommended removing all the collections from Asia and combining them with the Asian art collections in another museum.

Such moves were anathema for the ethnologists in the *Völkerkunde* museum. Their science was founded on a principle of using displays of objects for studying humanity across time and space, and globalizing that study through an emphasis on objects, not just written texts. Moreover, it was essential to their purpose that no part of the world, such as Asia, be singled out. It also made no sense to their mission to set out aesthetically arresting or particularly interesting objects for special attention. That would only undermine their goal of seeing the intersections between the general and the particular and narrating a total history of humanity. For, as Richter argues and then twice illustrates by citing Goethe, the mission of these museums was all about the interconnections. As Goethe put it: "He who knows himself and others will also recognize that: Orient and Occident may no longer be divided."

Contemporary discussions of ethnological museums or those formerly known as *Völkerkunde* museums often make the mistake of assuming that the museums' purpose was to put objectified others on display for the delight, and perhaps also the edification, of Europeans. One reads this far too often in contemporary debates about the Humboldt Forum, which only illustrates how little the pundits who utter those statements understand about the history of the collections and the museums. In the German context, few statements could be further from the truth. The entire point of creating these museums was to pursue a global history of humanity in all its variations and through that pursuit gain a deeper self-understanding. In that sense, Richter's essay remains timely as well. That is precisely what is being reclaimed in the newly styled ethnological museums and museums of world culture. Attempts to distance these institutes from an imagined past are bringing them closer to their original purposes. It is ironic, but for the good.

Richter too began his extensive essay with basic questions: What is ethnography? What is in a name? And what practices hide behind it? He answered those questions by emphasizing the analytic, comparative, and most of all, inductive methods on which the science was based. To provide those answers, he captured the positions of his mentors, and to legitimate those positions and underscore the value of the museums, Richter, like many others, engaged in a Faustian bargain by tying the virtues of the science into the practical needs of the present, particularly those of the state. Thus, while he repeatedly underscored that ethnology emerged before either the modern German nation-state or its colonies, he argued that it could offer something to both. Most notably, he followed Felix von Luschan, who had long been the director of the Berlin Museum's African and Oceanic sections, in arguing that German colonies would be much better run, more humane, and more profitable if ethnology and particularly the *Völkerkunde* museum were to be used to educate all Germans who sought to live and work abroad, particularly those who were heading to Germany's colonial territories. "Error in judgment," Richter argued, citing Adolf Bastian, the founder of the Berlin Museum, "stems from error in understanding" (112). So much violence and so many misdeeds, they all argued, could be avoided with knowledge.

Underscoring the practical uses of these intellectually driven museums was both foolhardy and wise. Richter embraced those arguments without recognizing that tying the museums to contemporary concerns also condemned them to their fates as times changed. In the postcolonial world, the call to decolonize museums, which Richter explains were never set up with the colonies in mind, has become ubiquitous. People have since forgotten that, as Richter put it, "the ultimate objective of all ethnographic work, which is thus the general task of ethnographic museums, can only be this: to contribute to the knowledge and understanding of ourselves" (99–100). That is a globally inclusive "we." As they seek to reclaim that goal without understanding its long history, many contemporary actors risk making similar errors—all the more reason to read these debates from the past.

Triangulating Art/Artifact: Indigenous Studies as the Third Term

Ruth B. Phillips

To read, in the present, the fine-grained analyses of history and ethnography museums set out by Otto Lauffer and Oswald Richter in the German museology journal *Museumskunde* over a century ago is to experience an uncomfortable sense of recognition. On one level, their writings manifest the rigor with which earlier generations of museologists explored questions that scholars and curators have continued to revisit. On another, they lay bare the nationalist and imperialist politics that have been formative of the modern, discipline-based museum typology.

Each writer argues with logic and passion for the value and intellectual parameters of his museological sector, urging the need to clarify its mandate, systematize and expand its collecting practices, and prioritize popular education and scholarly research. Both maintain that only in this way—rather than by trying to compete with art museums—will their respective museums earn the prominence they deserve within the hierarchy of museum types.[1] Their insistence on the necessity of clearly bounded domains is a textbook case of the purification of disciplinary knowledges identified as a quintessentially modern project by actor-network theorists.[2]

For Lauffer, the effective local history museum helps its visitors to develop what we would today call strong identities. Quoting his mentor and teacher Moriz Heyne, he urges the importance of claiming one's own history: "Through its local character, a collection creates a warm atmosphere for its visitors," allowing them to "witness their predecessors' achievements and their memorials, so many of which still shape their

238

homeland." In this way, "as they learn of ancient accomplishments from which they still benefit, modern visitors may sense a continuity in their people's thoughts and feelings within themselves, perhaps more than they ever realized" (53).

Richter, in contrast, refrains from offering rose-colored glasses to his visitors, but rather foregrounds the ethnographic museum's ability to convey the imperialist ideologies and economic and political "realities" of the modern world. Its strategic value would have been evident to citizens of a nation trying to catch up with other European powers in the creation of a colonial empire. According to his logic, "the need to participate in economic expansion and to protect our colonies . . . demands our systematic attention to the peoples of the globe and to our colonies in particular." Logically, he concludes, "the role . . . of imparting a lively and impressive perspective on the cultures of many peoples of the globe, particularly in our colonies, will be played by our ethnographic museums" (106).

It would be hard to find a more naked affirmation of the ties between colonialism and ethnography compellingly analyzed by postcolonial theorists—Johannes Fabian, for example, in *Time and the Other*, or Thomas Richards in *The Imperial Archive*, Nicholas Thomas in *Entangled Objects* and *Colonialism's Cultures*, and Tony Bennett in *The Birth of the Museum* and *Pasts Beyond Memory*.[3] These and other analyses reveal the integral connection between the two streams of argument presented in the *Museumskunde* essays—disciplinary rigor and imperialist ideological inscription. Although discursive deconstruction has not dismantled the colonizing legacies of the modern museum typology, it has prepared the ground for activist projects of institutional decolonization. Together, these forces have led to significant shifts of power within institutions and introduced innovative museum practices ranging from collaboration with source-community members to the ritually correct handling of culturally sensitive collections.

These new modes work to destabilize *both* art and artifact as exclusive paradigms of the object, and intervene in the tense relationship between them that lies at the heart of the *Museumskunde* essays. Before exploring this contemporary dynamic more fully it will be helpful to briefly review the subsequent unfolding of the art/artifact debates. Three now classic formulations must stand in for a much larger literature. Anthropologist Robert Redfield's 1959 essay "Art and Icon," first delivered as a lecture at New York's Museum of Primitive Art, worries much the same questions of aesthetic versus cognitive meaning that preoccupied Lauffer and Richter.

"The aesthetic and the iconic are two worlds of thought," Redfield wrote. "In the case of works of art they are bound one to the other by the physical object, the artifact, which is, as it were, a body in which two souls dwell."[4] His conclusion replaces Richter's overt imperialism with a softer, universalist humanism: "Whether we come to see the artifact as a creative mastery of form, or see it as a sign or symbol of a traditional way of life, we are discovering, for ourselves, new territory of our common humanity."[5]

At the heart of philosopher Arthur Danto's 1989 "Artifact and Art" is a concern with the legacy of modernist primitivism in light of expanded late modernist definitions of art. Danto takes an ontological approach, exploring the way art and meaning are constructed and consumed across cultures by makers, users, and museum visitors according to the play of the conceptual, the formal, and the contextual.[6] Stephen Greenblatt, in contrast, confronts the challenges of ethics, cultural relativism, and postimperial politics in his 1991 "Resonance and Wonder" and recasts the art/artifact dialectic in terms of viewer responses. Resonance, for him, signifies "the power of the displayed object to reach out beyond its formal boundaries to a larger world," while the aesthetic response is "a form of wondering and admiring and knowing."[7] Of particular relevance to this discussion is Greenblatt's conclusion that the two responses cannot— and perhaps should not—be wrenched apart. "I think that the impact of most exhibitions is likely to be enhanced if there is a strong initial appeal to wonder, a wonder that then leads to the desire for resonance," he writes, "for it is generally easier in our culture to pass from wonder to resonance than from resonance to wonder. In either case the goal— difficult but not utopian—should be to press beyond the limits of the models, cross boundaries, create strong hybrids. For both the poetics and the politics of representation are most completely fulfilled in the experience of wonderful resonance and resonant wonder."[8]

The approaches to visual and material culture of the mother disciplines have also been the focus of dialogue and debate. In 2003, the Clark Art Institute devoted its annual conference to "Anthropologies of Art." The convenor, Mariët Westermann, invited speakers who had been exploring "intersections and divergences" to "engage in a sustained exchange about their disciplinary motivations, protocols, and boundaries."[9] A parallel engagement with a more specific museological focus was staged in 2006, when the Harvard Art Museums collaborated with the Peabody Museum of Archaeology and Ethnography to organize a symposium titled "Crossing Boundaries: Art and Anthropology Museums in Search of Common Ground." As organizers Ivan Gaskell and Jeffrey Quilter wrote, the conference was "part of a long-term project to promote scholarly collaboration among the collecting entities of the university to address world cultures."[10] A third conference took place in Paris a year later at the recently opened Musée du quai Branly. Art historian Thierry Dufrêne and anthropologist Anne-Christine Taylor titled it simply "Histoire de l'art et anthropologie," while the title of the conference book, *Cannibalismes disciplinaires: Quand l'histoire de l'art et l'anthropologie se rencontrent* (inspired by Montaigne), evokes a kind of Darwinian struggle for survival. I came away from these conferences with a strong sense of ongoing disciplinary disconnects. By and large, speakers stuck to the problems central to their respective disciplines, while key issues around the authority of source-community protocols, epistemologies, and ontologies were ignored or unevenly addressed.

More recently, consortia of major European ethnography museums have organized RIME and SWICH, two successive multiyear projects of research and experimental exhibition funded by the European Union.[11] They transpose key questions asked by Lauffer and Richter into the de-colonial and pluralist context created by immigration, refugees, and diaspora. In 2018, another round of discussions took place in London at a massive conference titled "Art, Materiality, Representation," organized by Britain's Royal Anthropological Institute, the British Museum, and the University of London's School of Oriental and African Studies.[12] After more than a century, then, the questions put by Lauffer and Richter remain open. Each generation, it would seem, has recognized the same overlaps and internal contradictions, yet Western constructs of art and artifact, visuality and materiality, aesthetics and social meaning have resisted all attempts to be pulled apart or mapped onto each other.

Given this stalemate, are we ready to invite another perspective, one that positions itself *outside* the modern Western knowledge system? I answer as a settler Canadian currently living through a period of unprecedented national consciousness-raising regarding the destructive impacts of colonization on Indigenous peoples.[13] As in other settler societies, our current phase of museum development is being inflected by an alternative approach that I will call—provisionally—Indigenous studies. As a field of theory and practice, Indigenous studies emerged from the reflexive critical discourses of the last decades of the twentieth century. In a recent edited volume, Chris Andersen and Jean O'Brien provide a helpful survey of its sources and methods. The subtitle of their introduction—"An Appeal for Methodological Promiscuity"—clearly signals Indigenous studies scholars' refusal of disciplinarity.[14] Rather, the field embraces a constellation of methods, theories, practices, and ethical positions. It promotes research on and preservation of Indigenous knowledge and affirms its authority, but it also insists on the need for ongoing critical evaluation of colonial systems and their impacts on Indigenous societies and cultural traditions. An Indigenous studies orientation fosters a holistic approach to knowledge, the recognition of collective as opposed to individual identities, the fundamental relationship of these identities to land and place, nonlinear trajectories of time, reciprocal relationships with the "natural" world, and the primary responsibility of researchers to contribute to the revitalization and health of Indigenous societies.[15] As noted earlier, the *absence* of bounded disciplinary spaces in Indigenous studies—its *a*-disciplinarity— is conceptually resonant with Western postdisciplinary approaches such as actor-network theory.[16]

As a third term intruded into the art/artifact debates, Indigenous studies identifies *both* the art *and* the artifact paradigms as colonial impositions. Its effect is to telescope the disciplinary dualism that has preoccupied Western scholars for so long, while, in another sense, creating a new triangulation with older aesthetic and cognitive approaches. In both senses, however, I would argue that it renders the art/artifact and art history / anthropology dualism moot: "open to argument, debatable; uncertain, doubtful; unable to be firmly resolved," as the *Oxford English Dictionary* defines the term. When an issue is declared moot, furthermore, we are authorized to move past it even though it remains unresolved. The triangulation of current museum practices is an inevitable product of colonialism's long sway. In this context, James Clifford has written of the "profound shift of power relations and discursive locations" that has been in progress during the late twentieth and early twenty-first centuries, while also recognizing that "decentering doesn't mean abolition, defeat, disappearance, or transcendence of 'the West'—that still-potent zone of power. But a change, uneven and incomplete, has been under way. The ground has shifted under our feet."[17]

At present, it is easiest to observe the impact of the Indigenous studies orientation on museum representation in exhibitions that foster, through collaborative or Indigenous curation, the articulation of distinctive approaches to space, place, and narrative. The Royal Ontario Museum's 2017 exhibition *Anishinaabeg: Art & Power*, curated by Arni Brownstone, Alan Corbiere, and Saul Williams in 2017, is an excellent example because it exemplified the hybridity inherent in the triangulation I am describing.

In combining installations of contemporary art, modern easel paintings and prints, examples of aesthetically enriched historic material culture, archaeologically studied rock paintings, and historical narratives, it affirmed the holism of Indigenous knowledge and expressive culture. The exhibition was, furthermore, structured according to Indigenous principles of directionality, spatial orientation, and temporality.[18]

The success of the exhibition in promoting a new way of viewing Anishinaabe art, history, and culture was in part produced by the ability of Indigenous scholars and curators like Corbiere and Williams to transform Western paradigms from within. Like other members of modern societies, they are trained in Western disciplines and constructs of art and artifact and draw on them in their decolonial work while also bringing forward the ancient worldviews and intellectual cultures to which they are heir. Two images seem to me to capture such historical and present realities. In one, made around 1913, an unnamed Sioux schoolchild drew a past battle scene in a traditional but Westernized graphic style. At the top of the page, definitions of anthropology and zoology are penned in clear cursive script, probably by a settler teacher (fig. 1). In a second image, titled *Dominion*, made by Kwakwaka'wakw artist Mary Anne Barkhouse, a wolf moves forward determinedly despite the overwritten biblical text declaring man's absolute domination over nature (fig. 2). Both images instantiate the irreversible process of colonial inscription and the equally long history of Indigenous survivance. The child and the professionally trained artist use Western modes of representation to affirm, respectively, Indigenous historical memory and a nonbinary concept of nature. The new museum paradigm, I have no doubt, will inhabit and resist modern modes of museological inscription in much this way.

Not everyone, of course, will agree that this is the desired paradigm shift. Indigenous scholars have mounted sharp and important critiques of the processes that are moving it forward—Glen Coulthard denounces "inclusivity" and the "politics of recognition" as neoliberal solutions; Zoe Todd argues that the "ontological turn" is yet another appropriative strategy; and Eve Tuck and K. Wayne Yang write that decolonization in the cultural sphere assuages white guilt and evades actual returns of stolen lands.[19] While their arguments remind us of real dangers entailed by the work of decolonization, they are, if read literally, defeatist. We cannot undo the historical fact of colonization but we *can* transfer power in meaningful ways that allow us to work together as equal partners and to share responsibility for the creation of representational modes that best serve a new era.

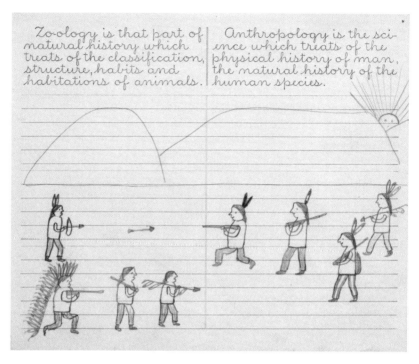

Fig. 1. Drawing by Sioux child, collected by Episcopalian missionary
A. McGreevey Beede, 1913–14, at Fort Yates, North Dakota (Edward
Ayer collection, Newberry Library, Chicago).

Fig. 2. Mary Anne Barkhouse, *Dominion* (2011), from the Resilience
digital billboard project (2018).

1.   I have explored this typology in "How Museums Marginalize: Naming
      Domains of Inclusion and Exclusion," in *Museum Pieces: Toward the
      Indigenization of Canadian Museums* (Montreal: McGill-Queen's University
      Press, 2011).
2.   The classic statement of this theory is Bruno Latour, *We Have Never Been
      Modern*, trans. Catherine Porter (Cambridge, MA: Harvard University
      Press, 1991).
3.   Johannes Fabian, *Time and the Other: How Anthropology Makes Its Object*
      (New York: Columbia University Press, 1983); Thomas Richards, *The
      Imperial Archive: Knowledge and the Fantasy of Empire* (New York: Verso,
      1993); Nicholas Thomas, *Entangled Objects: Exchange, Material Culture and
      Colonialism in the Pacific* (Cambridge, MA: Harvard University Press, 1991),
      and *Colonialism's Culture: Anthropology, Travel, and Government* (Princeton,
      NJ: Princeton University Press, 1994); and Tony Bennett, *The Birth of the
      Museum: History, Theory, Politics* (New York: Routledge, 1995), and *Pasts
      Beyond Memory: Evolution, Museums, Colonialism* (New York: Routledge,
      2004).
4.   Robert Redfield, "Art and Icon," in *Aspects of Primitive Art*, by Robert Red-
      field, Melville J. Herskovits, and Gordon F. Ekholm (New York: Museum
      of Primitive Art, 1959), 37.
5.   Redfield, "Art and Icon," 38.
6.   Arthur Danto, "Artifact and Art," in *Art/Artifact: African Art in Anthropol-
      ogy Collections*, ed. Susan Vogel (New York: Center for African Art, 1989),
      18–32.
7.   Stephen Greenblatt, "Resonance and Wonder," in *Exhibiting Cultures: The
      Poetics and Politics of Museum Display*, ed. Ivan Karp and Steven D. Lavine
      (Washington, DC: Smithsonian Institution Press, 1991), 42, 53.
8.   Greenblatt, "Resonance and Wonder," 54.
9.   Mariët Westermann, "Introduction: The Objects of Art History and
      Anthropology," in *Anthropologies of Art*, ed. Westermann (New Haven, CT:
      Yale University Press, 2005).
10.   Ivan Gaskell and Jeffrey Quilter, "Museums—Crossing Boundaries,"
      special issue, *RES* 52 (Autumn 2007): 5.
11.   The RIME-INEM project (Reseau Internationale du Musées d'Ethno-
      graphie / International Network of Ethnographic Museums) ran from
      2008 to 2014 and brought together ten leading European ethnography
      museums under the affirmation that "in an ever more globalizing and
      multicultural world, it is necessary to redefine the place and the role of
      ethnography museums" (https://culturelab.be/archive/rime/). SWICH
      (Sharing a World of Innovation, Creativity, and Heritage), which ran from
      2014 to 2018, was a project that focused on "the role of ethnographic
      museums within an increasingly differentiated European society." It built
      on the work done by RIME using a further premise: "The focus now lies
      on central concerns of visionary ethnographic museum practice within

the context of a post-migrant society" (http://www.swich-project.eu
/about/).

12. Parts of this chapter are based on my presentation at that conference,
"The Issue Is Moot: Old Disciplinary Debates in an Age of
Decolonization."

13. The 2015 report of the Truth and Reconciliation Commission on
Residential Schools (TRC) and the 150th anniversary of the Canadian
Confederation in 2016 were the immediate catalysts. Institutions across
Canada, including museums and universities, have been called upon to
respond to the TRC's "Calls to Action," markedly hastening the process of
change that was already in progress. Number 68 is directed at museums:
"We call upon the federal government to provide funding to the Canadian Museums Association to undertake, in collaboration with Aborigi-
nal peoples, a national review of museum policies and best practices to
determine the level of compliance with the *United Nations Declaration on
the Rights of Indigenous Peoples* [*UNDRIP*] and to make recommendations"
(http://nctr.ca/assets/reports/Calls_to_Action_English2.pdf). *UNDRIP*
affirms the rights of Indigenous peoples to reclaim and live in accordance
with their own cultural knowledges and ontological beliefs (www.un.org/
esa/socdev/unpfii/documents/DRIPS
_en.pdf).

14. Chris Andersen and Jean M. O'Brien, "Introduction—Indigenous Studies: An Appeal for Methodological Promiscuity," in *Sources and Methods
in Indigenous Studies*, ed. Andersen and O'Brien (New York: Routledge,
2016), 2.

15. This agenda is not new. Rather, Indigenous artists and others have been
promoting it for many years. In a 1974 essay, for example, artist Jimmie
Durham wrote: "When new things come into our circle, it expands. When
new things come into Western society another square is added."

16. See Jessica L. Horton, *Art for an Undivided Earth: The American Indian
Movement Generation* (Durham, NC: Duke University Press, 2016).

17. James Clifford "Feeling Historical," *Cultural Anthropology* 27, no. 3
(August 2012), 419.

18. And see, in particular, Laura Peers's insightful review of the exhibition in
the *Journal of Museum Ethnography* 31 (March 2018): 239–44.

19. See Charles Taylor, "The Politics of Recognition," in *Multiculturalism
and the Politics of Recognition*, ed. Amy Gutman (Princeton, NJ: Princeton
University Press, 1992), 25–74; Glen Sean Coulthard, *Red Skin, White
Masks: Rejecting the Colonial Politics of Recognition* (Minneapolis: University
of Minnesota Press, 2014); Zoe Todd, "An Indigenous Feminist's Take on
the Ontological Turn: Ontology Is Just Another Word for Colonialism,"
Journal of Historical Sociology 29, no. 1 (March 2016): 4–22; and Eve Tuck
and K. Wayne Yang, "Decolonization Is Not a Metaphor," *Decolonization:
Indigeneity, Education & Society* 1, no. 1 (2012): 1–40.

Richter and Us

Jeffrey Quilter

The *Museumskunde* articles by Otto Lauffer and Oswald Richter transport me to the Europe of my early youth, in the mid-1950s to early 1960s. It was a world in which the Great War was not that of the 1940s but the earlier one, which resulted in a noticeable lack of men of a certain age. It was a world in which antimacassars still graced the top of thickly upholstered chairs, and neighbors who had been through the Blitz together still addressed one another as "Mr." and "Mrs." Chamber pots remained a common household item, and Americans and Brits were warned not to drink the water on the Continent. And so, although my oldest close relatives were born in the late 1890s, coming of age in the Edwardian era and not the Victorian one, I nevertheless can identify with the *Weltanschauung* from which Lauffer and Richter wrote.

It is perhaps too easy to point out the striving for a sense of German ethnic identity especially in Lauffer's discussion of historical museums in *Museumskunde*. The goal is for every town of any size or of any account to have its own historical museum. Thus, both difference and commonality will be expressed as each burgh establishes its historical particulars within an overarching national identity. If each town has a museum, then each region should too, with a national museum uniting all.

And how apparently simple and straightforward is Richter's vision! Consider his clear-eyed methodology based on a rationalized, ordered world in which each unit fits neatly into a larger whole. Consider how this contrasts so sharply with the opening pages of Foucault's *Archaeology of Knowledge*, in which the author points to the "sedimentary strata" of the past and those who have attempted to understand it. Only six decades separate Richter and Foucault, and so, indeed, we take note once again that the long, great war that stretched through most of the twentieth century shook the colonial powers and rocked the world.

In Richter's day, ethnography was new, lacking a "unifying and firmly grounded methodology and a developed professional criticism" (99). And while ethnography was only coming into being, at least in the author's view, the ethnographic museum was newer still. Because of this, writes Richter, "ethnographic museums have no root in the consciousness of the people—or even in the consciousness of a specific discipline—[which] means that there is simply no general public understanding of the museums' content and purpose" (99).

And so, while the learnedness of the author is without doubt and his ability to draw upon many diverse scholars is impressive, we still might take pause. Richter is up on the latest theoretical writings of Bastian and Virchow, still considered foundational scholars, but he cites Lamprecht too, a cultural historian and follower of Wundt's ethnopsychology, and who was criticized in his own day by none other than Max Weber. Nevertheless, what comes through in *Museumskunde* is a commitment to learning and understanding, as well as a broadmindedness lacking today in many quarters of both academic and general culture.

Richter repeatedly makes the point that the ethnographic project is to study the "other" in order to better understand ourselves. This view is wedded to a benign and generous view of imperialism and colonialism. I could not help but smile and wince, at the same time, in reading, "The Kaiser's words were surely not influenced by thoughts of colonial expansion" (104), and then to read a "White Man's Burden" manifesto, in which the salesman, priest, and soldier all do their jobs in lifting up the primitive while at the same time making a tidy profit of one form or another, be it in sales, salvation, or standard-bearing.

We all know—or, perhaps, in these troubled times, I might say that most of us *should* know—that even in its heyday there were sharp critics of colonial expansion, including Mark Twain. At the same time, however, it is worth keeping in mind that there were many complicated, inconsistent, and confused views of colonial enterprises in the nineteenth century and earlier, just as there are similar views of what is going on in the world today.

As the former director of the second-largest anthropological museum in the United States, I am particularly sensitive, these days, to the drubbing that old-fashioned anthropology has gotten. It is neither my job nor my intention to defend its existence or its purpose here, but I find a generosity of spirit in Richter's writings, even if he was rather naive about what the Kaiser had in mind for Germany overseas.

Reading this document was salutary for me inasmuch as it underscored how we all too easily view the world through our own cultural lenses in our own particulars of time, place, and associations. We may take pause at what will be written about our viewpoints sixty years hence.

An Attempt at Order
in a Time of Flux

Matthew Rampley

The extended discussions of the taxonomy of museums offered by Otto Lauffer and Oswald Richter occurred at a time of considerable change. While they could refer to centuries-old traditions of collecting—Richter identifies the Renaissance *Wunderkammer* as the origin of the ethnographic museum—they were in fact describing a very recent museological landscape. Inherited practices were being transformed and new kinds of museums were coming into existence, and these shifts were due to the professionalization of the museum world as well as to the emergence of the new academic (or "scientific") disciplines of ethnography and anthropology. Lauffer and Richter were trying to navigate their way through this terrain, in which the very purpose of certain types of museums was coming into question. At the heart of their deliberations, however, was the question as to the meaning of material artifacts, the meaning that could be attached to their display, and the objective of the institutions devoted to them. The museum of applied arts is not the subject of a separate essay in the pages of *Museumskunde*, but it is a constant referent for both authors. For if Richter and Lauffer were concerned that material objects of historical and ethnographic significance were sometimes falsely viewed on account of their aesthetic qualities, then, equally, museums of applied arts were undergoing a kind of crisis at the turn of the nineteenth and twentieth centuries because they were losing their distinctive identity. The fascination with folk art and issues of cultural and national identity across Europe from the 1890s onward meant that the applied arts were increasingly coming to be valorized for their function of cultural representation.

250

Following the model of the South Kensington Museum and then, in mainland Europe, the Museum for Art and Industry in Vienna, the museums of applied art proliferated in the 1870s and 1880s across Germany and Austria-Hungary as a means of improving design quality and competitiveness, based on the idea that the finest examples of design practice, drawn from any location and from any historical era, might provide inspiration in the present. This conception drew on the Kantian doctrine of emulation; in the *Critique of the Power of Judgment* Kant had stressed that the artist-genius did not slavishly *copy* the art of the past, but rather inferred the principles at work and used those as the basis for further creative production.

Coupled with this was Gottfried Semper's argument that the most fundamental issues of all involved the relation between material and formal design. This view, often equated with historicism, has been much derided, yet it was potentially radical, for it rejected classical aesthetic norms. Japanese and Chinese art, for example, was collected avidly for its understanding of basic design principles, which outshone that of much European art. Yet by the mid-1890s, historicism, for all its potential, had degenerated into imitation of the past, and the museums of applied arts held diminishing relevance for contemporary design practice, which often had to meet economic and social demands that had no precedents. Hence, in 1895, Alfred Lichtwark could dismiss the whole program as an outmoded relic that confused historical study with genuine creative work.[1] Two years later, the Museum for Art and Industry in Vienna was thrown into turmoil when the newly appointed director, Alfred von Scala, repudiated its historicist orientation and embraced contemporary design, particularly from England.

Museums of applied art thus faced a dilemma, in that they housed historical collections that seemed to have been overtaken by events; no longer relevant to contemporary practice, they became indices of cultural history. This may have solved a crisis in terms of the legitimation of museums of applied arts, but as Lauffer indicated in his discussion of the embrace of the idea by such leading museum figures as Wilhelm von Bode, Justus Brinckmann, and Julius Lessing, it was a threat to the separate identity of historical museums. There was no small irony in this, since museums of applied arts had in part functioned as important instruments of modernization and professionalization. Rudolf Eitelberger, founder of the Vienna Museum for Art and Industry, had regarded them as "scientific" successors to the older regional museums, in which material objects had been collected for merely local topographical or antiquarian interest. As part of his plan for museum reform in the 1870s, the museums of applied arts had integrated the objects into a coherent intellectual and aesthetic program, where they could receive proper scholarly treatment.[2]

Writing in 1906, Lauffer was implicitly rebutting that view and making a claim for the distinctive function of material objects in historical museums. In addition, he recognized that redefining museums of applied arts as instruments of cultural history was less straightforward than Lichtwark and his peers may have imagined. In keeping with their aims, the applied arts museums had collected artifacts for their individual exemplary status, whereas, Lauffer asserts, "cultural history should focus on the manifestations that are typical and commonly repeated" (43). Although he is not mentioned in this article, this formulation bears more than a passing resemblance to the notion of "ideal types" that was central to Max Weber's recently published account of social-historical method.[3] The collections of *atypical* objects in the museums of applied arts would hardly be appropriate for this task. Furthermore, the meaning of the term "cultural history" was open to question. The field was still struggling to gain legitimacy in the early twentieth century, but one of its more prominent representatives, Karl Lamprecht, understood it to be the history of mentalities.[4] Yet how, argues Lauffer, can this be represented through material artifacts? Even the curators of historical museums seem uncertain, he acknowledges, with poorly considered displays of artifacts that often appear to have no clear purpose. Lauffer's solution to the danger of conflation of the two types of institution is to argue for a focus on the *function* of artifacts, yet this is hardly adequate, even on his own terms, since he readily acknowledges the rich semantic dimension of material objects. This can hardly be conveyed by the purely functional approach, but the difficulty he has in devising a satisfactory alternative says much about the uncertainties and ambiguities involved in the interpretation and presentation of objects.

The crisis in applied arts museums may have threatened to blur boundaries with historical museums, but it also emphasized the need for sharpened reflection on the meaning of the term "cultural history." As Richter's essay reveals, it had comparable implications for ethnography and ethnographic museums. Anthropology and ethnography were still young disciplines at the time Richter wrote on the topic: Rudolf Virchow, one of the pioneers, had founded the German Anthropological Association in 1869, and the understanding of the subject was still a matter of discussion and debate. For Richter it is clear that the purpose of ethnography is "to contribute to the knowledge and understanding of ourselves" (99–100). It is a comparative science, and the study of other cultures reveals something about human nature in general. Analysis of the particular provides a route to understanding the universal, and the most instructive comparisons are with those cultures rooted outside the ancient civilizations of the Mediterranean. The objects in ethnographic museums had been collected on the basis of their indicative function and of their role as "historical effects of the social psyches of different human communities." Yet Richter struggles to articulate in further depth *how* they fulfill this role, and it is this that makes ethnographic collections vulnerable to conflation with collections of applied arts. As he notes, they exert an aesthetic appeal. This may be incidental to their cultural and social function, hence he terms it an "aesthetic secondary effect" (113). Yet he also admits this attracts audiences, and therefore museums have to *facilitate* reception of their artistic quality, sometimes just through simple measures such as the relative placement of objects in the exhibition space. His position is nevertheless contradictory, since he commends as entirely understandable the exclusion of the art of South and East Asia from ethnographic museums on the grounds that it has already taken on an exemplary function for European art—a perfect illustration, one might have thought, of the comparative and cross-cultural interests of ethnography.

Critical analysis of ethnographic museums has frequently focused on their role in the wider apparatus of ethnographic study and its implication in the European and North American colonial project. Richter is startlingly frank in his admission of this, and he also celebrates the fact. Ethnographic museums will have fulfilled their function, he argues, if they have contributed to more enlightened colonial policies based on a greater understanding of the cultures of the colonized. Moreover, the civilizing mission of the colonial powers is deeply enmeshed in the global spread of capitalism: "The trader is the pioneer of civilization," as he states (104).

The attempts by Richter and Lauffer at a taxonomic ordering of museums are themselves exercises in the construction of ideal types, but as Weber emphasized, such types are merely heuristic devices that are as often as not contradicted by empirical and historical particulars. Lauffer stipulates that historical museums should collect and display only those items that can be connected directly to their locality, either because they were produced there or because they played some part in its social and cultural life, even if produced elsewhere. This stands at odds with the practices of the leading applied arts museums, which went out of their way to collect objects from across the world. Whereas the displays in the museums of applied arts sought to illustrate certain techniques or media *across* cultures, those in historical museums, he argued, staged ensembles of objects that helped visualize the culture and history of a particular place and time. Yet practice in museums of fine and applied arts already was converging on this model. Bode is known for introducing the idea of the period room, widely copied throughout Europe, in which diverse objects were brought together as material evidence of a specific culture (though his own thinking was a bit more nuanced). For Richter, the ethnographic artifacts end up having the kind of exemplary status that Eitelberger had originally envisioned for the Museum for Art and Industry. Regarding the example of batik, he states, "When our culture once again prioritizes love and sentiment over reason and knowledge, and when artistic sense is a greater guide than the taste of the parvenu, then we will witness new textile techniques (such as batik) and the rebirth of old art forms (such as wood carving), which has been devalued through mechanization" (114).

The analyses and programs offered by Lauffer and Richter are products of their time, and the museological landscape has changed massively from that of a century ago. Yet even if we no longer find their answers compelling, the questions they asked still have pertinence for the present, primarily because they touch on issues that remain unresolved. The identity of historical museums may no longer be a matter of controversy—although *individual* museums will always be a focus of debate—but the identity and purpose of museums of ethnography and applied arts are as contested as the meaning of the collections they house.

1.   Alfred Lichtwark, "Kunst und Gewerbe," *Das Kunstgewerbe* 5, nos. 7–8 (1895): 25–26.
2.   Rudolf Eitelberger, "Zur Reform der Landesmuseen in Österreich," in *Gesammelte kunsthistorische Schriften* II (Vienna, 1897), 241–52.
3.   Max Weber, "Die 'Objektivität' sozialwissenschaftlicher und sozialpolitischer Erkenntnis," *Archiv für Sozialwissenschaft und Sozialpolitik* N. F. 1 (1904): 22–87.
4.   See Roger Chickering, *Karl Lamprecht: A German Academic Life, 1856–1915* (Atlantic Highlands, NJ: Humanities Press, 1993).

Words and Things

Anke te Heesen

At the end of the nineteenth century, Wilhelm Dilthey presented a project for establishing a special kind of archive. In his lecture "Archives for Literature" he impressed on his listeners that so far, not much had been done for the permanent conservation of the manuscripts and documents of scholars and authors. Large investments were being made in natural history collections but not in collections in the history of literature.[1] He is less concerned, he says, with the printed books of the great minds—with regard to these materials, libraries have made great strides—than with handwritten sources, whose significance has not been sufficiently appreciated. What is special about them, he writes, is this: every time we read a book, we look for the person and the "effective forces" behind the book, but these cannot be found in the books— they are found in the manuscripts. Here, in the "drafts, letters, notes," an atmosphere is expressed and "source-like evidence" for the "color, warmth, and realities of life" and the "innumerable effective forces that have been active here" are found. The things that thereby allow for a look into the "workshop" of the mind of the author, Dilthey says, become available especially when they are collected in the so-called *Nachlaß*, now known as the estate or papers. At the time of his lecture, there was no settled concept of the literary archive yet, no developed concept of the *Nachlaß*. Such collections were in the possession of the family or were preserved by chance. Dilthey sketches an agenda for building up and organizing such institutions. This requires trained staff, appropriate ways of storing materials, and focused state funding. Such archives must be left not to private collectors but to institutions that outlast individual human lives and can make materials permanently accessible for the benefit of the general public.

A few years later, the texts by Otto Lauffer and Oswald Richter presented in this volume go in a similar direction. Wider in scope and richer in detail, they seek to give an overview based on the everyday work in museums, they compare existing museums, and they provide a history of these establishments in order to sketch a comprehensive project for the "historical" or the "ethnographic" museum. In so doing, they do not shy away from describing the bases on which such museums are to be built or from examining the practical aspects, such as layouts of rooms and the arrangement of objects. Dilthey does not go that far, but all three proposals appeared at the time, following the foundation of the Reich, during which German museums and archives were being restructured and the capital, Berlin, had become a central site for debates and memoranda about what significance collections had for the very idea of a nation-state. Archives and museums alike were caught in the crossfire of this public debate and struggled with similar problems of funding and perception. And finally, they had to confront the old emphases of collecting: the historical museum cannot be subsumed under art or decorative arts, nor can the objects of scholarly creative processes be preserved in just any library. That is why, around 1900, there arose projects for an institutional differentiation of autonomous branches and disciplines, whose systematization of object domains we are still dealing with today. At issue in all cases are the realia of history.

Dilthey's lecture has garnered a measure of fame and is considered to mark the beginning of institutional literary archives (even if its practical effects—that is, precisely, the founding of these central archives—would have to wait another few decades). The collecting of manuscripts and objects from estates was placed under the newly articulated category of the humanities (*Geisteswissenschaften*). The texts by Lauffer and Richter do not assume so prominent a place in museum historiography. This may be due to the authors' lesser renown, or to the texts' lengthiness and redundancies. But they lay out an entire panorama that points far beyond the concerns of cultural history and of ethnography/ethnology. When we bring the three texts together, we see central lines of development that gain importance around 1900 and make a comparative reading rewarding, including the science developed in and through the museum, which is an applied science because it results from the collections, and the significance of the objects, which contemporaries referred to as "realia."

Applied Science

While we today are used to perceiving museums especially under the aspect of viewing, of transmitting contents to a public, Lauffer and Richter show how around 1900, in the midst of the reorganization of the German museums, the science developed in and out of museums was just as important. In fact, an "urge," to use Stifter's term (*Drang*), had arisen from the many objects, from the accumulation of things, calling for order and systematicity. In the case of the ethnological museum, Richter cites the emerging science of ethnology: because there was a need for teaching via objects (to provide information about foreign peoples for missionary activity or colonial administration), accumulations evolved into collections and formed the basis of "comparative ethnography." This ethnography, Richter writes, features a "relevance" that allows for connections with different humanities disciplines, and it must be pursued as an anthropology or cultural history for the sake of the human being's self-conception (100). In the case of the historical museum, Lauffer was concerned with creating a reliable order for all the objects hitherto subsumed under the broad category "German antiquities." They were the precondition for an ethnologically oriented history of everyday life, a history that ennobled the Grimm brothers' "pious pondering of the insignificant" and made writing a history of culture possible. Provenance research, materials science, training the comparative gaze, and quality control were techniques developed in the museum on which the new science was based: "Research begins with observation and critical contemplation," as Lauffer quoted Alexander Cartellieri (45). Dilthey, Richter, and Lauffer were equally concerned with "material evidences of culture," although the three men were well aware that objects in the museums and archives would not yield exhaustive information about the human being as a whole (103). But at the very least the objects represented a necessary basis for humanities research, and for that reason they were worth being collected and studied. The collections of museums were to be presented in such a way as to instruct the public, but they were primarily to serve an applied science growing out of them.

Realia

The discussion about the objects collected brings out just how much, read together, the three texts bundle the strands of museum history around 1900. The name these objects shared was "realia," defined in contemporary dictionaries as hard facts, undeniably visible and impossible to reject, the opposite of empty talk. Around 1900, we learn from these texts, realia are revalued; special attention is being paid to the things and nonbooks in the collections. Their home is no longer the realm of local historians fussing about, of retired colonial officials or family heirs. Realia enter into the modern system of the specialized institution (museum/archive). They are being professionalized and tied to modern life, and they must live up to progress and at the same time resist the "restlessness of modern life."[2] Historically significant realia can no longer be claimed as art or decorative art (Lauffer), teaching material (Richter), or family possessions (Dilthey) but must enter into a well-justified, scientifically, and historically valid order. As Lauffer's "witnesses of the past" and "visual material," and as Cartellieri's "traces" (31, 55, 45), they are not to be used for "considerations of form" or "stylistics"; instead, they constitute central "material sources of history" and count among the decisive "material evidences of culture."

While the late eighteenth and early nineteenth centuries may be called the time of the founding and opening of museums, the time around 1900 is characterized by the comprehensive (re)structuring of the museum as a scientific and public institution. Today, we should bear in mind that—all the work of transmission and the number of visitors notwithstanding—museums, thanks to the expertise of curators who keep and expand collections, are institutions of research. This is not something easily conveyed to policy makers, which is why (even) closer and more prominent cooperation of universities with museums is desirable, to prove the necessity of museums once more. Today, there is a need to explain why those parts of the museums that by necessity remain closed and largely inaccessible to the public require funding. The two texts published here can support and reinvigorate this discussion; there is more in the "words and things" than we have so far got out of them.

Translated by Nils F. Schott

---

1.   Wilhelm Dilthey, "Archive für Literatur," in *Gesammelte Schriften*, vol. 15, ed. Ulrich Hermann (Göttingen: Vandenhoeck & Ruprecht, 1970), 1–16.
2.   Dilthey, "Archive für Literatur," 8, 9.

Mix It Up: Five Observations on Collections and Museums

Nicholas Thomas

The remarkable texts by Otto Lauffer and Oswald Richter stand as fascinating counterpoints to contemporaneous, better-known writings by Franz Boas and A. C. Haddon, among others, on the purposes of anthropological and other museums. They reflect a moment of ambition and of disciplinary definition. New forms of knowledge required specification and separation: the identification of proper objects, and the values, concepts, methods, institutions, and organization appropriate to them. For those who associate "museum studies" primarily with the proliferating university programs and textbooks of the last thirty to forty years, these texts are arresting. Some of Lauffer's and Richter's propositions reflect the epoch—the high-water mark of imperialism— and are as embedded in evolutionary and Eurocentric thinking as we would expect. Other questions, surprisingly, are not so different from those that curators and exhibition-makers ask of themselves today. The texts remind us that museum theory has a deep history and that it embraces many strands of national and more cosmopolitan debate.

I am in no sense an expert in late nineteenth- and early twentieth-century histories of knowledge and cultural institutions, so I leave it to others to comment on Lauffer and Richter in detail. I am struck by the sense in which our own moment is different. Like the early 1900s, it is a moment of ambition, and of museological ambition in particular. But the locus of creativity now appears characterized not by specialization and separation but by mixing things up, by which I mean an affirmation of the mixed identities of museum artifacts and of cross-disciplinary curatorial experimentation. This may sound like an epistemological anarchism, a scholarly or curatorial version of Fluxus. It is not. It is, rather, a considered approach that follows from serious reflection on museums and what they contain. These comments draw on more extended discussions; in the interests of brevity I offer five propositions here.

Artifacts Are Portable, Durable, and Mutable

It is worth reflecting on precisely what objects fill museums. They are, of course, extraordinarily diverse if we consider those held by museums of every kind—they range from large-scale works of art to coins and pottery fragments, from specimens of insects to the skeletons of whales and dinosaurs. It may be impossible to generalize usefully about the entire range, given that works of contemporary art now include digital files and installations that consist in part of physical components but are more importantly "made" of intricately detailed instructions for their realization and presentation. Yet archaeological, anthropological, and historical museums typically hold objects that were portable, hence susceptible to being acquired, removed from sites of origin, brought back to homes or institutions, circulated via markets, and managed within museums. These forms were, moreover, durable, some naturally more so than others; they thus had the capacity to be not only transported across space but preserved over time in an institutional setting. These were also qualities of so-called natural specimens, in fact prepared forms treated or mounted in conformity with one procedure or another; museum specimens have commonly been supported, cleaned, painted, conserved, or otherwise materially modified. Portability and durability are conducive to mutability, not necessarily in the sense that an object is susceptible to physical adaptation but in the sense that the meanings, values, and narrative it bears or is associated with may be more or less profoundly changed—in the directions both of impoverishment and of enhancement. The relative physical stability that makes it possible for something to be a museum artifact thus makes it inevitable that its identity is not stable, that it outlives the character and significance that it started with.

Collections Are Made of Relations, Not Just of Things

Perhaps notoriously, the most arresting feature of the major museum collection is its sheer number of works and specimens. While this may be most striking in the case of archaeological and natural history collections, art museums may also hold tens of thousands of coins and medals or quantities of prints of a similar order. This makes it appear as though the identity of a collection is in the mass of things: it is like an artifactual library. I have suggested elsewhere that this is like seeing a nation as a mass of individual people. A nation is evidently a formation of principles of inclusion and exclusion, such as of the legal order of citizenship and many forms of quasi-citizenship (permanent residence, working visas, etc.), institutions, symbolic expressions such as flags, and treaties with wider bodies, as well a typically contested national narrative. Far-fetched as the analogy may appear, I suggest that the museum collection is made up of relations in suggestively similar ways: artifacts are included or excluded on a variety of grounds. There are liminal states (e.g., objects that are on long-term loan or deposit, or are part of a "handling" collection); there are items that form subsets and series, that may be parts of collections, other parts of which are held by other museums, and that are rendered meaningful by relations with, for example, labels and documentary records. Much of this information may be more or less visible, accessible, present, or actively employed at varying times; connections may be lost or obscured, only to resurface. The relational assemblage that is the collection is thus almost organic: it is susceptible to activation and reactivation that bring its significance and social effect into view in new ways.

Collections Are Not What They Were

It is a correlate of these propositions that collections such as those which Lauffer and Richter sought to order and curate now possess different qualities from those they had at the time of their formation, even if the artifacts themselves are the same. Collections, such as those made by the ethnologists of the famous Hamburg Südsee expedition of 1908–10, were assembled for reasons that differ from the reasons that those collections are significant today. In one sense the former values and the present ones are sharply distinct: a material archive of ethnographic documentation can be seen to be profoundly different from a body of Indigenous heritage. One is a rationalist and colonialist formation, the other a resource for the self-representation, understanding, and affirmation of heritage and cultural knowledge on the part of Indigenous peoples, among others. But overlaps and ambiguities blur the distinctions between these seemingly contrasting, epoch-specific values: some early ethnologists were, for example, often deeply interested in and empathetic toward Indigenous knowledge. In any case, collections are singularly versatile as cultural and research resources. The same artifacts are "disposable" for varied exhibitionary, educational, social, and political purposes. Collections may lapse into obscurity and "hibernate" for protracted periods, as ethnographic collections have surely done. But they are then susceptible to novel and abrupt illumination in the context of debates about decolonization and other issues.

Museums Have Separated Things That Belong Together

Collecting has an ancient history, and the making of collections has been, if not absolutely pervasive, a widespread phenomenon in societies of many kinds over many epochs. But the systematic collecting of specimens from the field—ethnographic, natural historical, archaeological—is a practice of modern science, which could specifically be associated with the activities and legacies of followers of Linnaeus and their successors. While ethnographic collecting has many antecedents, the gathering of material in the field from native peoples on an extensive scale, followed by documentation and the deposit of collections in educational institutions, amounts to a historically distinctive endeavor, one apparently inaugurated by Joseph Banks, James Cook, and others on Cook's first voyage in the *Endeavour*. The practice was soon taken up by people traveling to many regions of the world. Such collections were commonly made in parallel with natural history acquisitions by the same people, at the same time, often with the same local assistants, who procured shells, plants, birds, fish, and other fauna, as well as artifacts of diverse sorts.

In many cases the donations of travelers initially went to encompassing collections, which embraced the natural and the artificial. Institutions like the Australian Museum in Sydney, the American Museum of Natural History in New York, and the Übersee-Museum in Bremen continue to hold both natural history and ethnography collections. More typically, the emergence of the modern disciplines that stimulated the Lauffer and Richter essays saw collections differentiated into specialist museums, or (in the case of the Hunterian in Glasgow) the holdings of what nominally remained a single museum distributed across what in practice became separate museums located within the relevant university departments.

Mix Them Up

In recent decades an awareness has developed of the extent to which material culture is not merely peripheral or expressive in social life but is also constitutive. Things and the movements of things generate social relations and forms. We have become aware of the extent to which material methodologies are not ancillary or specialist but can lead to understandings that could not be reached otherwise. Hence collections encompassing scientific specimens, archival objects, artworks, and images offer a proliferation of possibilities for inquiry. They also speak to a plethora of more or less contentious questions in public culture and politics: Which histories should be commemorated, and how? Where do artifacts of exceptional significance belong? And so on.

Collections can stimulate and advance both scholarly knowledge and public debate through activation. In inert and stable form, they are what they are, but through mobilization, re-curation, and fresh juxtaposition they bring into view new relations and potentially provocative combinations. The efforts of nineteenth-century and subsequent scholars and institutions to establish specific fields with their provinces bore fruit in a variety of ways. Today it seems vital that we de-install some of those divisions and, in particular, that we connect the environmental and the cultural. At one time, a question of what type of wood was used to make an artifact might have appeared banal. Now it may speak volumes concerning place, knowledge, craft, and sustainability: the substance of the many lives, reflected obliquely but richly in museum collections.

Life and Death in the Museum

Céline Trautmann-Waller

Although Germany was not the first country to boast a public museum, the development of museums there in the nineteenth century was impressive, not least because of its micro-territorial and federal structure. Otto Lauffer and Oswald Richter document this development with numerous German examples: the museums in Jena, Hamburg, Bremen, Dresden, Leipzig, Frankfort, Göttingen, Nürnberg, Breslau, and of course Berlin's topologically suggestive Museum Island. The international perspective of Richter's panorama is striking. This is certainly due to his numerous *Studienreisen*, mentioned in the obituary by Oskar Nuoffer introducing the article published after Richter's death in 1908 (136–37). Following his interest in Indonesia, the museums Richter uses as examples or counterexamples often are ethnographic institutions in the Netherlands (Leiden, Haarlem, Rotterdam), but he extends his comparisons to museums in England, France, and the United States. According to Richter, there was only one German museum capable of showing cultures in a large ethnographic panorama. In fact, given the scale of the German Empire, one such museum was enough, in his view. To him it was the Ethnological Museum in Berlin, where he began working in 1904 after training in Dresden.

The rise of public museums of different kinds was accompanied by the will and the need to foster professionalization and critical exchange. This led not only to the creation of a specific bulletin in most of the museums (for example, *Zeitschrift des nordböhmischen Gewerbemuseums* and *Mitteilungen aus dem germanischen Nationalmuseum*, both quoted by Lauffer) but also to the launching, in 1905, of *Museumskunde*, a review dedicated to the administration and techniques of public and private collections. The growing number of museums allowed, or perhaps demanded, an inner differentiation (see, for example, Richter's discussion about the emergence of Indian archaeology in the realm of ethnology) and establish ment of a taxonomy or typology. The types distinguished by our authors are the museum for applied arts (*Kunstgewerbemuseum*), the art collection (*Kunstsammlung*), the historical museum (*historisches Museum*), the ethnographic museum (*ethnologisches Museum* or *Völkerkundemuseum*). Unsurprisingly, each defends the value of the type of museum he experienced every day: Lauffer as director of the Historical Museum in Frankfurt am Main and Richter as an employee of the Ethnological Museum in Berlin. But the aim of their publications was also a general rationalization of museum collections, a delimitation of the areas of collecting for each museum type (*Grenzlinien ihrer Sammlungsbereiche*, as Richter calls these limits). In Lauffer's reaction to a polemic by his colleague Schwedeler-Meyer, the importance of these taxonomic questions sometimes seems to be exaggerated: for instance, when he discusses whether hunting can be counted among the "monuments of social life" or whether antiquities of the guilds (*Zunftaltertümer*) belong to the same group as artisans' tools (*Handwerksgerät*).

Still, this territorial perspective is legitimized by an epistemological argument, the areas of collecting being defined in accordance with the corresponding sciences. In the series by Richter the epistemological and theoretical considerations take a strange form, as they are developed in footnotes that run from one page to the next, overwhelming the text in some cases. One wonders whether this is the expression of a theoretical urge somehow repressed by the practical Richter, but the assurance of his arguments seems to contradict this interpretation.

In Lauffer's articles the scientific referent for the historical museum is not in fact history but *Altertumskunde*—as a twin of *Germanistik*, which was his own field. Lauffer revives here the debates about words and things (*Wörter und Sachen*), going back to the polemic between August Boeckh and Gottfried Herrmann about the extension of philology to material (and not only textual) objects, but also to Grimm and his research on German antiquities. As shown in an obituary written by Lauffer in 1906, this is linked partly to Lauffer's *Doktorvater* Moriz Heyne, professor and museum director, first in Basel and then in Göttingen, who, according to Lauffer, didn't develop the two fields, material culture and texts, in parallel but united them in his work. In this sense Heyne is described as representing a branch of science Lauffer calls German archaeology, in the same sense as we speak of classical archaeology. According to Lauffer, the best a historical museum can give us is "insight into the connection between things" (Einblick in den Zusammenhang der Dinge) or evidence of the "cultural-historical connections" (kulturgeschichtliche Zusammenhänge), with reference to the cultural historian Karl Lamprecht, among others, even if he refuses to consider historical museums as authentic historico-cultural collections (*kulturhistorische Sammlungen*). Richter, too, frequently quotes Lamprecht because of his contribution to the study of cultural history (*Kulturgeschichte*) and material culture. But he may refer as well to ethnologists—for example, to Adolf Bastian, the founder of German anthropology and of the Ethnological Museum in Berlin—or to the German emperor. For both Richter and Lauffer, the museum is also a political institution fostering the national identity of Germany. If Lauffer insists on the sense of home (*Heimatgefühl*) that the historical museums, centered on local collections, can support, Richter sometimes aligns ethnographic and colonial knowledge, even if he counts political needs among the "subsidiary tasks" (*Nebenaufgaben*) of ethnographic museums and defends a striking interpretation of the *Furor teutonicus* to differentiate it from English and German imperialism.

Although they defend quite different views, Richter and Lauffer both insist on differentiating their museum type from art collections, which to them constitute the main threat to the scientific character of historical or ethnographic museums. Even if we know that museum directors were sometimes competing for the same objects, it is unclear why there should be any danger of confusing the historical museum with the *Kunstgewerbemuseum*, which is the main point of Lauffer's article. Because the category of *Kunstgewerbe* mixes artistic and technical criteria, the museum of decorative arts appears as a rival in their eyes, troubling the geographical, historical, and cultural classification of the two other museum types. Richter himself cites the museum in Dresden as an ethnographic museum in which concern for the artistic dimension of the artifacts was prominent. And the reader may be puzzled by his rejection of artistic criteria regarding ethnographic collections, as in other passages he writes at length about the artistic value of such collections (ornaments from New Zealand, sculptures from Benin, lacquers or textiles from South Asia).

Both authors show contempt for modes of collecting and exhibiting that they find unsystematic, unprofessional, and nonscientific. They blame these lapses on the public, who want to be entertained rather than educated; on authorities who give insufficient financial support; on the world market, which transforms the collections into objects of speculation; and on the museums themselves. Richter, for example, looks forward to a time when ethnographic museums will see their "role . . . as more than the mere compiling and housing of ethnographic artifacts" (115). One author who is quoted in this respect by both museum specialists is Gustav Klemm. His book *Zur Geschichte der Sammlungen für Wissenschaft und Kunst in Deutschland* (1836/37) is used to remind the reader that if the public museums are an institution of a new kind, the collecting and the collections are of course much older. As Richter explains, the ethnographic collections stem from the *Raritäten- and Curiositäten-Kabinetten* and originated, in a somehow contingent way, from the accumulation of material in other collections. Very few emerged from the practical necessities of teaching and research. Some were created to answer colonial or missionary needs, like the one in Rotterdam. Only the ethnological museum in Breslau was created according to a clear plan and is, in this sense, a modern museum.

The rational and systematic discourse thus is quite often contradicted by the heterogeneity of the collections. Richter suggests that museums are full of undesired objects—for example, duplicates (*Dubletten*)—so that the question of space (*Raumfrage*) becomes a vital one. But he also defends what he calls the "rights of objects," once they are "apt to enter a museum" (*museumsfähig*), to be preserved, treated with respect, and exhibited with good taste and scientific accuracy. On the other hand, some of the examples he and Lauffer cite evince a resistance of collections to any reorganization. This resistance could be defined as a historical weight or even as a certain autonomy of the objects. Richter's death, the result of handling poisoned arrows at the Dresden Museum, and his final martyrdom as described by Nuoffer, could then be seen as a strange story of rebellious objects, imported en masse from distant lands, apparently neutralized through their integration into museum collections but finally reassuming their original function.

Today, the Humboldt Forum is also facing the challenge to make a new museum with old collections and, partly because of its central location, reveals the lines along which runs the discussion about museums in the twenty-first century. The articles by Richter and Lauffer show that these lines are not so different from those of the nineteenth century: between politics, market, education, and entertainment;

exhibiting and doing research; the "rights of objects" and the rights of people; the necessity of making a selection among locally existing collections and the ambition to reflect a part or all of the world; the museum as a deadly place or as a place where objects come to life, in other ways than murderously.

Photographs, Showcases, and Multiple Agencies: Modes of Representation and Directions of Gaze

Eva-Maria Troelenberg

A bit more than a century ago, Dresden counted itself among the best places in the world to learn about the arts and material cultures of the Southeast Asian Archipelago and the so-called Südsee. Anyone interested in this would only have had to go downtown to the historic Zwinger building, which housed the Ethnographic Museum. Founded in 1873, this collection was shaped by the interests of the Darwinist scholar Adolph Bernhard Meyer, whose field trips had focused on Celebes, the Philippines, and parts of New Guinea.[1] This focus coincided very much with one of the main geographic directions of the indirect imperialist strategies adopted by the German Empire after 1871.[2]

One of the more practical sections of Oswald Richter's *Museumskunde* essay contains a series of photographs from contemporary ethnographic collections, illustrating a range of bad, better, and best practices of museum display. The gold standard, as it were, is represented by a photograph that must have been taken literally at the threshold of one of the halls of the Dresden collection: the "Hall of the East Indian Archipelago and the South Seas," according to the caption (fig. 1). Crossing this threshold, visitors would be guided along a carefully arranged, regular sequence of showcases, all of them head-high, tailored to the scale of the individual beholder's contemplation.

It is the typical setting of a *Vitrinenmuseum* (museum of vitrines, a term coined by Barbara Mundt,[3] which offers a unifying framework for an array of diverse historical and geographical objects: textiles, arms, tools, small pieces of furniture, sacred and secular artifacts, and very

Fig. 1. Hall of the East
Indian Archipelago
and the South Seas
in the Ethnographic
Museum of Dresden.
From Richter, "Über
die idealen und
praktischen Aufgaben,"
Museumskunde 4
(1908): 224.

likely even human remains—all brought together in the representational regime of the showcase, which creates a clear binary between the
visitor and the exhibit. This seems to be designed as if to confirm the
notions of both the ideal and the practical, which feature so prominently
in Richter's overall argument. It is interesting that he chooses a gallery
view of an ethnographic museum for the illustration of this ideal and
practical standard: the juxtaposition of the beholder's rational gaze and
the passive otherness of the object-domain emphasizes the museum's
claim to order, overview, and teleological fulfillment. It is a constellation
that tames the "noise" of the objects' histories and prepares them for the
seemingly objective scholarship that was regarded as the ultimate historical vantage point.[4]

   The showcases are not the only representational regime at play. The
perspective of the photograph as such is precisely attuned to the visual
and spatial statement of the display. Obviously, the camera had been
placed to evoke a linear perspective, slightly off center, to provide space
for the sequence of showcases to the left. A dark line on the floor, possibly

Fig. 2. Koloniaal Museum of Haarlem. From Richter, "Über die idealen und praktischen Aufgaben," *Museumskunde* 4 (1908): 225.

a coincidental element of the pavement, and the rectangular squares of the coffered ceiling support the direction of gaze from the foreground to the background. Altogether, this creates an illusion of stepping into a room, moving forward, capturing space. The strength of this visual message becomes even more obvious in contrast with a photograph from the Koloniaal Museum in Haarlem, presented as an example of bad practice (fig. 2). This museum had been founded as part of the Royal Dutch Tropical Institute in the 1860s. Its collections largely reflected the Dutch colonial enterprise in the East Indies[5]—so the range of objects on display was probably similar to the range in Dresden. However, the objects are presented in a completely different manner. A set of tabletop glass cases holds smaller items, partly covering or serving as provisional shelves for a muddle of weapons, cloths, pots, drums, and other items that cover every inch of wall surface. These exhibits are combined with what appear to be framed documents or paintings, which probably serve as comments or sources loosely related to the contents of the collection. Altogether, it is the exact opposite of the tamed and rigid order of things in Dresden.

Again, the staging of the photograph seems to support the impression of chaos and disorder. Much like the Dresden gallery view, it evokes the moment of the first gaze into a room that is to be discovered by the visitor, but the wide angle of the photograph provides little focus, scale, or orientation. Moreover, this panoramic view of the room and its contents is cropped on all sides, resulting in an almost claustrophobic atmosphere, almost as if the objects were crawling onto the beholder. There is a hint of perspective, as the collection is arranged in an enfilade—but the view into the next hall only heralds further disarray. A uniformed museum guard who happens to stand in the doorway, hands folded tightly behind his back, is obviously little help in "taming" or disciplining this rampant object-scape.

From today's point of view, both examples show outdated styles of museum display. However, their juxtaposition remains epistemically productive on several levels. We can assume that neither of these photographs was taken explicitly for the purpose of illustrating Richter's essay but that they were selected and combined for the sake of his argument. Keeping this in mind, it is striking that the Dresden Museum seems to have applied not only a more orderly display strategy but also a more intentional and self-aware mode of photography. The institution was, obviously, well prepared to circulate its image, in the truest sense of the word.

The combination of these images also testifies to the sharp transnational competition that marked many museum debates in Europe during the decades leading up to World War I. Those debates were often particularly fierce when intertwined with questions of a colonial or imperial dimension.[6] In this perspective, these two photographic gallery shots became an instrument for a rather typically German argument, as the Kaiserreich sought to make up for its relatively smaller role in the "Great Game" of colonialism by emphasizing its superiority in terms of academic and cultural penetration of territories and appropriation of world cultures.

It has been argued that, in general, "the work of photographs in the museum space remains remarkably under-analysed,"[7] and this may be particularly true for the genre of the photographic gallery view, which often seems to remain outside the relational triangle between the museum exhibit, the object or documentary photograph, and the photograph as object.[8]

However, it may be considered more than just a lateral movement to the emergence of a critical "new museology" that artists first started to discover the epistemic value of the image-histories of museum settings, and some of them also invested in or triggered a theoretical and historical discourse that has been ongoing over several decades.[9]

Klaus Wehner (alias Museum Clausum), for instance, asks what happens if we treat the "museum itself as the subject of photographs."[10]

Working with the concept of the "posed object," his artistic work presents and questions the museum space as an image that is by no means neutral but always reflects curatorial decisions—and hence also represents underlying politics or anthropological preconditions, or reveals seemingly invisible traces of labor and agency in museums and collections. This artistic gaze reveals and questions the object on display as a "posed object," caught in a static moment and thus trapped, as it were. With such an approach in mind, we become even more sharply aware of the teleological order of the museum, with its clear patterns of active versus passive, historical versus contemporary positions.

At the same time, such approaches reveal that if we consider the image-archives of museum history not just as casual illustration material but as playing a substantial part in the history and prehistory of today's museum theory, they may "offer nothing less than a visual anthropology of the changing forms of public museums."[11] An expanded understanding of the history of museums as intertwined with a history of its own images and image-making policies will thus be a productive endeavor, not only in historical perspectives but in contemporary and future perspectives.[12] More than a century after the ethnographic museums in Dresden and elsewhere started photographing their collections, the challenge of cross-cultural representation of arts and material cultures is still a virulent question.

Our close reading of two exemplary photo documents and their historical background has revealed why time has passed by Richter's categories of the ideal and practical display. In the multifaceted postcolonial or even postglobal condition, museum visitors from all geographic and cultural backgrounds or social walks of life have become much more active as co-owners, commentators, or agents in the museum, thus creating a network of complex and multidirected interrelations among image, object, and beholder.[13]

The most recent wave of this development is in no small part related to the democratization of the medium of photography, in recent years accelerated by the spread and use of smartphones and image-based social media apps such as Instagram. We are now witnessing a moment when the image politics of museums, as well as the aesthetic practices of museum visitors and other agents in the field, lead to crucial shifts bearing on the control, accessibility, and possibly also commercial or political exploitation of museums and their holdings.

With the historical perspective in mind, it should be clear that these are not only questions of practical image policies or technical availability. Rather, they will inform how museums and the narratives attached to them will be perceived and written for the present, and how our present will be epistemically unpacked by future historians.

1.   Petra Martin, "Meyer, Adolph Bernhard," in *Sächsische Biografie*, ed. Institut für Sächsische Geschichte und Volkskunde e.V. (2005), http://www.isgv.de/saebi/.

2.   Suzanne Marchand, *German Orientalism in the Age of Empire: Religion, Race, and Scholarship* (Washington, DC: German Historical Institute, 2009).

3.   Barbara Mundt, *Die deutschen Kunstgewerbemuseen im 19. Jahrhundert* (Munich: Prestel, 1974).

4.   Elizabeth Edwards, *Raw Histories: Photographs, Anthropology, and Museums* (Oxford: Berg, 2001).

5.   Harrie Leyten and Bibi Damen, eds., *Art, Anthropology, and the Modes of Re-presentation* (Amsterdam: KIT, 1993).

6.   On a parallel debate on the display of Islamic art, see, e.g., Eva-Maria Troelenberg, "Berlin, Munich, Paris: Une rivalité salutaire." *Qantara* 82 (2012): 43–46.

7.   Elizabeth Edwards and Sigrid Lien, *Uncertain Images: Museums and the Work of Photographs* (Farnham, UK: Ashgate, 2014), 3.

8.   See, e.g., Costanza Caraffa, "Documentary Photographs as Objects and Originals," in *The Challenge of the Object, CIHA Congress Proceedings*, ed. Ulrich Großmann and Petra Krutisch (Nürnberg: Anzeiger des Germanischen Nationalmuseums, 2013), 3:824–27.

9.   See, e.g., Georgina Born, "Public Museums, Museum Photography, and the Limits of Reflexivity: An Essay on the Exhibition Camera Obscured; Photographic Documentation and the Public Museum," *Journal of Material Culture* 3, no. 2 (1998): 223–54; Klaus Wehner, "Photography—Museum: On Posing, Imageness, and the *Punctum*," in *The Thing About Museums: Objects and Experience, Representation and Contestation*, ed. Sandra Dudley et al. (Abingdon, UK: Routledge, 2012), 79–94.

10.   Wehner, "Photography—Museum," 79.

11.   Born, "Public Museums," 224.

12.   Eva-Maria Troelenberg and Melania Savino, eds., *Images of the Art Museum: Connecting Gaze and Discourse in the History of Museology* (Berlin: De Gruyter, 2017).

13.   See, e.g., Nina Simon, "The Participatory Museum," Museum 2.0 (blog), 2010, http:// museumtwo.blogspot.com/.

The Museum Beyond Walls

Mariët Westermann

What can the museum do to become a multidirectional portal between its culture and the cultures of its visitor communities?

It is popular nowadays to say that a good museum is one without walls, but of course there is not really any such thing. If you are thinking about the sort of museum that Martin Roth led so brilliantly in Dresden and London—the great Enlightenment institutions that gathered all human knowledge they found worth keeping in the form of the world's objects—you realize that these encyclopedic museums cannot do without walls. There may be partial exceptions, like the great botanical gardens of the world, though even they need walls to contain the tropical plants or climate-controlled herbaria that keep the world's vegetal life in taxonomic order.

And walls are not bad: they support a roof to shelter your collections, let you hang things to look at, even give you places to draw. So when we talk about museums without walls, we really are asking how museums can make their walls more porous to the public for whom these museums were created, and on whose support they depend. We are asking how museums can go beyond their walls to serve the public better.

The New York Botanical Garden has become good at this. While it still presents rare plants as museum objects, it also lets kids touch and even eat them, with its wonderful Edible Academy. This historically white institution is located in the Bronx, a very diverse borough, and now radiates such programs out to the many community gardens there. The staff learn what families, teachers, and business owners are interested in, and conversely help the communities care for their plants. The logic that connects these programs to the garden's mission goes like this: Kids like to touch things—kids like to eat—and so do lots of adults—plants are critical to our food security and pleasure—ergo, communities have a large stake in the garden, and the garden in them, even if none of these visitors ever learns the Latin name of any plant.

If museums want to understand what a user might want from them, they have to change the way they think of themselves, to shift from being owners of knowledge that gets pushed out to the public to becoming knowledge institutions that meet potential users where they are. They cannot assume that their carefully curated offer is of interest to most people in society but must find a way to provide museum knowledge and objects to enhance people's experiences in meaningful ways. This requires listening to what people are telling you, but it doesn't mean you simply "give people what they want," as curators often fear.

There is a lot to learn from libraries in this regard. In the digital age they have transformed themselves from places to borrow books to hubs that connect users to knowledge, primarily through the internet. And they offer places for people to connect with each other for study and conversation, for storytelling and spoken-word events, even for making music. They have expanded their opening hours and found themselves to be critical resources for today's users, in ways they could not have imagined when their primary function was lending works in print.

Museums have not quite made the same adjustments: ten to five is still a standard opening time for all but the largest museums. But museum education departments have been leading the way back to the public user. At the Metropolitan Museum of Art in New York, on any weekday morning the education spaces are abuzz with kids, parents, and nannies in storytelling activities—or so it was before COVID-19. The point is not to talk only about art but to use art and ideas associated with it as inspiration for talk and play. The socialization part is a major draw, with toddlers and kindergarteners learning to take turns, or parents observing how teachers coax their kids to try new things. Here the museum literally has taken a page out of the new library's book.

The largest per-minute visitor draw to the Metropolitan Museum, however, is not its elementary school programs or even its 2017 Michelangelo exhibition: it is a semiannual evening called "Teens Take the MET," when five thousand young people ages thirteen to nineteen invade the Met to go anywhere they want, make art or music, enjoy performances, learn art history if they so choose, socialize, dance, and eat. It is free, and you don't have to register—you just show up. Many teens become repeat visitors or return for regular programming. The museum organizes the event with forty community-based organizations, many in areas of social disadvantage and exclusion. As some of these areas are quite far from the museum, the Met creates other programs with the organizations that the youths can access in their neighborhoods regardless of whether they come to the Met event.

Other museums are addressing needs and interests of America's new immigrants. The New-York Historical Society, for example, realized that many immigrants struggle to pass the US citizenship test, which is drawn from one hundred questions that you may be asked—many of them about arcane historical facts. (I know—I had to take it.) The Historical Society has incredibly rich collections related to history and government in the United States. Several years ago they began to offer courses around objects and documents in their collections to help candidates master the material and grasp connections among the questions. Almost a thousand students took the course in the first year, and of those, 201 from 59 different countries became citizens in April 2018. They were sworn in at the Historical Society itself by a very special official, Supreme Court Justice Ruth Bader Ginsburg, who had heard about the program and asked to conduct the ceremony. In her remarks, she recalled her poor immigrant father from Odessa who spoke no English, and she stressed how important it was that American citizens exercise their democratic rights and duties. The Historical Society gave the new citizens a family membership to go along with their naturalization certificates. I don't often cry in museums, but that was one of those times.

The success of these programs, which do not fundamentally depend on curatorial research, raises the question of the curator's role in relation to the museum user. Historically, it is the collections and curators that have stood at the heart of museums, not the educators or visitors. For much of the twentieth century, the museum's core business was acquiring the finest objects, presenting them in galleries and exhibitions, and conserving them for the future. That collections-focused mission depended on cadres of expert curators and conservators who conduct research, maintain a certain distance from the public, and often refer to collections, galleries, and conservation labs as "theirs."

It's not a great recipe for imagining the museum beyond walls, unless you rethink the mandate of the curator, whose name has its root in the

Latin *cura,* or "care." Some museum curators now think of themselves as carers not just for objects but for objects that were made by people like us. By extension they consider it their task to care for the relationships people today can have with those objects, and with each other through them. Doing this means caring for one's community and, moreover, for curators to think of themselves as part of the community, rather than to think of the community as something outside the museum's walls. The Los Angeles County Museum of Art has transformed itself in this way from a decent, sleepy collection visited by the well-to-do into a vibrant public space that thinks of the city's demographic diversity as its greatest asset. It opened up its grounds by having an artist, Chris Burden, bring in the city with *Urban Light,* an installation of historic streetlamps from the West Coast. It is the most exhilarating front door to a museum I know.

But realizing that many residents in Los Angeles never make it to the museum, maybe because it is far away but more likely because they don't feel the museum is for them, LACMA is taking the museum to the diverse communities of Los Angeles and into spaces that are their spaces, where the museum gives up some measure of control. These include LACMA's satellite gallery in the Charles White Elementary School in a largely Hispanic-Latino neighborhood. One recent show, on art by Latino artists addressing loss and resilience, was curated by Vincent Ramos, an artist and educator.

What these examples suggest is that a museum can meet users where they are without losing its noble commitment to preserving stunning works of human design and manufacture so that all can enjoy them. Much of that work should continue within the museum's walls, but the energies gathered outside can help transform the museum's interior from a detailed art history lesson for the few into a place for all those who want to be with art, one of humanity's finest inventions.

This essay is adapted from remarks made at "What Can Culture Do? Memorial Symposium for Martin Roth," Kraftwerk, Berlin, June 23, 2018.

Conclusion: Max Weber
in the Museum

Peter N. Miller

Oswald Richter's arguments in his long article in *Museumskunde* find their widest significance when read alongside Max Weber's exactly contemporary essays. This exercise, in turn, can help us read Weber as a museum theorist—an identity he does not yet have and that could be of use for museum thinking today.

First, the acknowledgment: it is not easy to find Max Weber in a museum. His travel diaries report scant visits. So, in Montpellier: "This morning I saw paintings by Courbet in the museum, the best in France next to the ones in Paris and Lille." But what made the one in Montpellier so good, and what made the ones in Paris and Lille "the best," or, indeed, which museums was he referring to? The subject seemed not important enough for Weber to mention. Or, writing to his mother in 1911: "Spent a week in Munich: galleries, art exhibitions, architecture, *Meistersinger*." Again, nothing on what he saw, or where.[1]

Second: it is not easy to find museums in Max Weber's scholarly writings, either. For instance, though he announced that he would write a "sociology of 'cultural contents' (art, literature, and worldview)," such a work was never finished, and its incomplete strands do not include discussion of museums or cultural heritage institutions more broadly.[2] That he wrote nothing at all about museums, despite their growing role in society, and despite the presence of culture and its institutions in his work, suggests not an accidental miss but a real and profound blind spot. This may make our effort to turn Weber into a museum thinker appear counterintuitive. On top of that, we have to do it by implication and analogy. But there is no other way, and, I would argue, the potential payoff is enormous.[3]

Weber, around 1900, was responding to the crisis of historicism in the discourse formulated by the neo-Kantians—that is, through analysis of the logic of the cultural sciences. Between 1903 and 1908, around the same time that the *Museumskunde* essays were published, Weber wrote three methodologically rich pieces provoked by this "crisis" but leading fruitfully away in different directions. The first investigated the premises of history as understood and practiced by the economic historians Wilhelm Roscher and Friedrich Knies. The second was devoted to the possibility of objectivity in the cultural sciences. The third focused on history as a cultural science.[4] In this first decade of the twentieth century Weber did not see himself as doing "sociology"—according to Günther Roth he did not claim this term for himself until 1910—and instead placed the analysis of society within the "cultural sciences."[5] In what follows, inspired by Richter's aspirational philosophical language, we will focus on Weber's effort "to spell out the logic behind our actual research practices." With this we will then be able to discern the full-blown implications for a museum science in the *Museumskunde* essays.[6]

How We Know

In his 1903 essay on Roscher and historical economics, Weber talked about the importance of comparison as "one of many possible tools for constructing *individual* concepts." Eventually this would make it possible to reduce the ungraspable limitlessness of reality to graspable "individual concepts."[7] Concept formation was a topic dear to the neo-Kantians because only the existence of a concept made knowledge, strictly speaking, possible. For Weber, the concept worked to make sense of the concrete by effecting some kind of reduction—otherwise, all subjects would be needed to cast light on every other. Facts alone did not create meaning. And yet, for Weber, the particularity of the concrete could never be sacrificed.

In his "Objectivity" essay of the following year he turned this idea into the basis of his new science. "The social science that *we* want to pursue is a *science of reality*. We want to understand *the distinctive character* of the reality of the life in which we are placed and which surrounds us—on the one hand: the interrelation and the cultural *significance and importance* of its individual elements as they manifest themselves today; and, on the other: the reason why [these elements] historically developed as they did and not otherwise."[8]

The challenge, as Weber saw it, was how to select from out of the infinite welter of particularity, and from the indeterminacy of description— "each sees what is in his own heart"—the smaller sample that could be analyzed with the historical tools available to human beings. What could not be corralled into a category of greater interest to more people was to be left for the antiquarians. The temptation to emphasize lawlike predictability tempted even good historians. But at the limit, he wrote, empirical evidence "cannot tell someone what he *ought to* do, but only what he *can* do and—possibly—what he *wants to* do."[9]

Weber saw this gap as a necessary but not necessarily melancholy condition. The extraordinary and much commented-upon passage at the end of the "Objectivity" essay reads like a kind of eulogy for a past *episteme*. What Weber seems to be acknowledging is that the early modern project of amassing information in the belief that it would add up to a coherent map of knowledge that would in turn point to the transcendent was over.

> The fate of a cultural epoch that has eaten from the tree of knowledge is that it must realize that we cannot read off the meaning of events in this world from the results—however complete they may be—of our scrutiny of those events, but that we ourselves must be able to create that meaning. We have to realize that the advance of empirical knowledge can never produce "world views," and that consequently, the most lofty ideals, those that move us most profoundly, will forever only be realized in a struggle against other ideals, [ideals] that are just as holy for others as ours are for us.[10]

Weber's melancholy seems directly to invoke an extraordinary passage in Hegel's *Phenomenology of Spirit* that discusses the different kind of knowledge of the past that is available to those who come after.

> So Fate does not restore their world to us along with the works of antique art. It gives not the spring and summer of the ethical life in which they blossomed and ripened but only the veiled recollection of that actual world. Our active enjoyment of them is therefore not an act of divine worship through which our consciousness might come to its perfect truth and fulfillment; it is an external activity— the wiping-off of some drops of rain or specks of dust from these

fruits, so to speak—one which erects an intricate scaffolding of the dead elements of their outward existence—the language, the historical circumstances, etc. in place of the inner elements of the ethical life which environed, created, and inspired them. And all this we do, not in order to enter into their very life but only to possess an idea of them in our imagination.[11]

Gadamer put exactly this passage at the heart of his rejection of historicist hermeneutics.[12] Weber, like Hegel before him and Gadamer after, remained confident that knowledge was still possible, but not within the older paradigm of heaping up more and more things in the belief that quantity would eventually trigger quality—imaginatively reentering the life of the past as the hermeneuticists from Schleiermacher through Droysen and Dilthey believed possible. Rather, Weber argued that knowledge came only from the aggregating work of the "concept." "The fields of inquiry of scientific disciplines are based not on '*concrete*' relations between '*things*,' but on '*theoretical*' relations between '*problems*.'"[13] It was the way they were constellated that created meaning.[14] Weber's example was astronomy. Knowing what was happening on any given planet did not make it part of "an enlarged and improved future science of astronomy."[15] This could be achieved only with generalizing concepts, not just with more and more information about goings-on in discrete locations in the universe. In terms of knowledge, Weber's insistence on problems rather than facts marked the decisive step away from antiquarianism—this was how he showed a way beyond Hegel's closing the door on history-as-reconstruction.

If we were now to apply Weber's argument to the world of collections, we would conclude that collecting more and more was not the way to knowledge, to some kind of "new and improved" museum studies of the future. It would be arch to talk about a "neo-Kantian theory of museum display," because these philosophers themselves paid no attention to museums and their questions. And yet the role they assigned to the "concept," as a means of stepping back from the welter of particularities in order to allow information to be organized into knowledge, does seem to provide a philosophical structure for the curator's artisan-like practice of pulling particular objects out of storage and putting them on display in order to demonstrate, through embodiment, thoughts, practices, or belief systems.

Weber highlighted Roscher's internally inconsistent embrace of both a philosophical method that is "generalizing abstraction" and a historical one focused on "the *descriptive* representation of reality in its full actuality." Weber read this against the backdrop of Windelband's distinction between the nomological and the ideographic. The philosophical, generalizing sciences purged content as they became more universal—in order to *become* more universal—and thus became increasingly removed from empirical reality. Concepts, by which we might understand any piece of intellectual apparatus "that is formed by logical processing of a perceptual multiplicity [of phenomena] with the aim of *acquiring knowledge of what is important*,"[16] had to empty out some amount of content in order to do their work, and thus widened the gap between them at one end and concrete experience at the other. How could Roscher claim both for "the historical"?

We might see in Weber's challenge to Roscher—which was explicitly framed as a challenge to the German historical profession more generally—a challenge to museum professionals as well. There was an unbridgeable gap between the heaping up of more and more things and the argument (by implication) that what was collected demonstrated higher-level theoretical claims: that is, the history of the earth or art or human life. The problem for collecting institutions implicit in the terms of Weber's critique of Roscher stemmed from the claim that "it is impossible to conceive of a description of even the smallest section of reality that could ever be exhaustive." Because of the individuality of all phenomena, no one artifact could be subsumed under law as a representative case. Having lots of objects only meant having lots of objects.[17] However, Weber did allow for "imputation": a single object could speak to the "individual constellation to which it should be imputed as a result." And, furthermore, this could even be a "causal imputation" moving from their particularity to the general—that is, the concept. The work of all "past lovers," whether curators or historians or novelists or reenactors, was performed on this very spot. "To what extent the historian (in the widest sense of the term) is able to perform that [causal] imputation reliably by bringing his method[olog]ically schooled imagination, enriched by the experiences of his personal life, to bear, and what extent he will need help from specialized disciplines, that will depend on the individual case."[18] Reading this in the context of museum thinking, "imputation" seems to be a perfect word for capturing the work curators do in arraying artifacts. We will return to the other key terms in this sentence, "imagination" and "personal life."

Weber's great innovation in the "Objectivity" essay was the "ideal type," which he then explored at greater length the next year in his *Protestant Ethic and the Spirit of Capitalism* (1905). It was his way of improving upon "imputation" as the only way to bridge the distance between the individual artifact, or concrete historical experience, and the meaning-giving concept. "This possibility can be important, and even essential, both for heuristic purposes and as an aid to exposition. In *research* the ideal type seeks to render the scholar's judgment concerning causal imputation more acute: it *is not* a 'hypothesis,' but it seeks to guide the formulation of hypotheses. It *is not* a *depiction* of reality, but it seeks to provide [the scientific] account with unambiguous means of expression." But how did the "ideal type" provide a more "acute" way of keeping connected to content than imputation? Here is how Weber explained it in 1904:

> It [the ideal type] is obtained by means of a one-sided accentuation of one or a number of viewpoints and through the synthesis of a great many diffuse and discrete individual phenomena (more present in one place, fewer in another, and occasionally completely absent), which are in conformity with those one-sided, accentuated viewpoints, into an internally consistent mental image. In its conceptual purity, this mental image cannot be found empirically anywhere in reality. It is a utopia, and the task of the historian then becomes that of establishing, in each individual case, how close reality is to, or how distant from, that ideal image.[19]

The ideal type is the "attempt, on the basis of the state of our knowledge and by means of the conceptual construct at our disposal, to bring order to the chaos of those facts that we have in a given case chosen to include within the field of our *interest.*" The state of our knowledge, especially in the area of culture, is a result of the constant struggle of the concepts to accommodate new data.

Though Weber was not intending it, this discussion of "concept" and "ideal type" could be helpful in considering how museums argue. Richter wanted us to recognize that in museum work the crystallization of bigger truths out of a profusion of objects involved a degree of abstracting. The number of items collected, even in the biggest museums, would always be tiny relative to the totality of objects produced by a culture in its time and place, making doubtful the representative status of those collected objects. An exhibition checklist was never metonymy for the reality it gestured at because the ratio of known to unknown was too high. Richter's abstracting was Weber's ideal type. The exhibition is, to use

Weber's term, a "utopia" in exactly the way he uses it to describe the ideal type. Moreover, just as the displayed object performed by "imputation," rethinking it in terms of the ideal type would be a way to give exhibiting a rigorous argumentative structure while acknowledging that it reflects the viewpoint of the curator (values), and the limits of a given checklist or collection (values, again).

For Weber, the ideal type was an essential piece in the construction of a cultural science. For a curator, the displayed object was essential in the creation of a museum science. But before we can come back to this idea of museum science as cultural science, we need to see how Weber revises his view of history.

How We Know the Past

Weber understood his own practice to be historical. For instance, he concluded the "Objectivity" essay by identifying himself with the "Historical School" ("of which we ourselves are pupils"). But he was far from being an uncritical member of this tribe: its view of slow progress in the purification of concepts "through the observation of empirical regularities" reflected a hopelessly flawed understanding of the logic of the cultural sciences. He described as "classical-scholastic" the epistemology "assumed by the majority of the research workers" associated with academic history in Germany. The flaw was the same as noted by Simmel: there was no simple correspondence between what happened out there in the world and what the historian described or reconstructed.

The false god of "Realism," cousin to description and born of a correspondence theory of truth, could not easily accommodate the practice of cultural history because there was no pre-given "there" that could plausibly be pronounced the externally abiding object of inquiry. All cultural history was a creation of the historian. But by attacking the epistemic foundations of the German Historical School in the "Objectivity" essay Weber was implying—at this point only implying—that *all* history, even of battles or kings, was written under the conditions previously ascribed to cultural history only, which is to say that all historical stories were crafted by the historian and did not exist "out there" in the world. Therefore, the importance of the debate about cultural history was that arguments for its establishment would a fortiori work to legitimate the other cultural sciences. But what made a cultural phenomenon out of discrete facts? Weber's friend Heinrich Rickert called this the "problem of constitution." For Weber the question took a "transcendental" shape: What kind of knowledge was cultural knowledge?[20]

In 1906, Weber tackled this question through a critique of the methodological presuppositions of the historian Eduard Meyer. Meyer was one of the sharpest-tongued foes of Karl Lamprecht's attempt to write a German history that was a cultural history. Weber nevertheless called his own essay "Critical Studies in the Logic of the Cultural Sciences"— subsuming history within the cultural sciences, as had Rickert. He began by dispensing with the facile assumption that history was all about collecting, verifying, and describing sources. Rather, "the 'really' scientific work" was done only after fact-gathering had been completed.[21]

Weber saw in Meyer's blind spot a typical example of the Historical School in action. This was not Roscher, oblivious to his own contradiction in terms. Nor was it the popular view that saw history as "being 'purely' the description of given realities, or the simple reproduction of 'facts.'"[22] Meyer's error was more sophisticated. He took Goethe's maxim about the ineffability of the individual and made of it a credo, such that not sharing it meant that you were a bad historian. Meyer emphasized the individual as a way of arguing "that a certain (anti-deterministic) philosophical condition is the precondition of the validity of historical method"—and thus blocking any parallel to the natural sciences.[23] If Rickert and the neo-Kantians were troubled by the *hiatus irrationalis*— how to get from the randomness of particularity to the meaningfulness of the concept—Weber was accusing Meyer, and the Historical School more broadly, of pronouncing the irrational the measure of good history.[24] This, for Weber, was getting it all wrong. Yes, history was a science of reality precisely because "individual, particular components of reality are relevant not only as a *heuristic instrument* but [also] purely and simply as the *object* of that knowledge; and . . . concrete causal relationships are relevant not as causes of *knowledge* but as *real* causes."[25] But fetishizing the concrete particularities meant ignoring the scientific possibilities that could be accessed only at a second order.

What Meyer was missing with his narrow emphasis on historical individuals and their non-lawlike behavior (irrationality) was illustrated by Weber in a blindingly brilliant set piece unpacking Goethe's letters to his lover, Frau von Stein, so instructive that it should be force-fed to anyone training to work on the human past. The first possibility was that the letters actually shed light on Goethe's creative work. This, Weber wrote, would be important for literary history. But even if the letters did not shed light on his creative production, they could still be interesting heuristically, illustrating something characteristic of Goethe's "distinctive historical qualities." And even if not bearing on the interpretation of a work, the letters could still provide background insights, Weber wrote, "into a conduct of life and an outlook on life that were peculiar to Goethe throughout his whole life, at least for a considerable length of time." Or perhaps the letters told us nothing at all unique to Goethe. Yet they might tell us some details about German life at the time: "the 'historical' *fact* inserted as a real link into the causal context of his 'life.'" But even if they did not tell us anything specific about Goethe or Germany, the letters could still be evidence for German cultural psychology or social psychology—that is, something at the collective level. Finally, even if the letters failed to provide the slightest bit of useful historical data, "it is conceivable" that a psychiatrist interested in the human condition could use the data in Goethe's love letters as typical illustrations "of certain ascetic 'aberrations,' just as, for instance, Rousseau's *Confessions* are of interest to the specialist in nervous diseases."[26] For Meyer, with his limited view of what constituted the historical, almost none of this would have been accessible. For us, a century later, Weber's analysis previews many of the varieties of approaches to the past that would flourish in the twentieth century, from history to cultural history to cultural anthropology to social psychology to psychohistory.

The tools Weber employed to crack open the Goethe correspondence were two: "value interpretation" and "value analysis." The former, he wrote, "teaches us to 'understand' the spiritual content of that correspondence."[27] *Verstehen,* as we have noted, was the key term in Schleiermacher's hermeneutical theory and came to Weber via August Boeckh, Johann Gustav Droysen, and Wilhelm Dilthey.[28] It defined the work done in the human as opposed to the natural sciences. "Value" came to Weber via Rickert and denoted the sphere of human meaning creation, or culture. For Weber, "value" represented the individual's particular combination of commitments and priorities that structured the encounter with the welter of the world's particularities. When he writes that "value interpretation" is the precondition of any good historical work, what he means is that the historian must have awareness of the reasons why, out of the multiplicity of facts, she focuses on some things and not on others. Moreover, Weber did not see this solely as a defensive operation, acknowledging "the 'creative' influence the historian's own strong value judgments can exert towards the successful attainment of historical knowledge. . . . Value judgments serve the cause of interpretation."[29] These motives may be political, professional, or deeply personal. For this reason, Weber wrote, when doing value interpretation we reach right up to "the outermost limit of what can still be termed 'intellectual treatment of empirical [material].'" For instance, in the last of the five contexts in which Goethe's letters could be read there is no longer, he writes, a concern with "'historical work' in the logical sense of the term." When we contemplate performing psychological-universal readings of Goethe's letters, we are at the heliopause of the historical.

Value analysis is more complicated. Weber describes it as a kind of interpretation that is distinct from the "causal" type of interpretation used in unpacking the first four Goethean contexts. When Meyer spoke of a "philological consideration of the past," he was, according to Weber, talking about the aspects of historical study that were "static" or could be treated as unchanging. These included literature and art but also "state and religious institutions, . . . manners and customs, . . . attitudes," and even the "whole culture of an epoch treated as a unity." Weber insisted that this type of study was not to be considered "an 'auxiliary science' for history, as its approach to its objects is indeed quite different from that of history." Though it was "static," and static because the late eighteenth century was viewed as distinct from history, Weber was not so sure. He thought there could be a kind of research on the past that was historical but descriptive rather than causal. Weber gave as an example an account of the Athenian *ecclesia* provided by Boeckh in his study of Athenian household finance, which even Meyer recognized as historical.[30]

Weber's distinctions here were not sharp—value *analysis* was part of value *interpretation* but also separate from it; value analysis was not history but was historical. The landmarks by which he is navigating here all come from the antiquarian cosmos (philology, auxiliary sciences, manners, customs, religion). We could see Weber, in forging his new category, following in the footsteps of Ludwig August von Schlözer (1735–1809), who had described history as structural analysis set in motion and structural analysis as history made static.[31] A century later, Hans von und zu Aufseß divided the Nürnberg museum's collections into objects bearing witness to "history" and those to static "conditions," or *Zustände*. Weber used this very word to describe the realm of value analysis (*zuständlich*). The main point, for Weber, is that value analysis sometimes encountered facts that were historical without having any connection to anything causal— exactly how Momigliano described the antiquary: "the type of man who is interested in historical facts without being interested in history."[32]

Looking ahead to the next decade of Weber's career, we can see that what we have just described in terms of history and antiquarianism could perfectly well be described in terms of sociology.

Getting the interpretation of Goethe's letters just right required "a *historical* investigation into the conditions under which those letters came into existence, an examination of all the most minute, as well as the most comprehensive, relationships, both in Goethe's purely personal and 'domestic' life in the cultural life of the total 'environment' (in the widest sense of the term) of those days, [to the extent that they] had causal importance." The facts give us an "insight into those constellations of [Goethe's] mind against the background of which they were composed and thus [teach] us to truly 'understand' the letters themselves."[33] Value analysis *and* value interpretation were required in order to give the "most comprehensive" account. The historian as cultural scientist— and remember that at this point Weber did not identify himself as a sociologist—explored the everyday event of "'understanding' individual human action in terms of its motivation."[34]

"Understanding" (*Verstehen*) appealed to both Droysen and Dilthey as historians because it could refer to understanding a statement, as well as to understanding a person.[35] This made it possible not only to narrate what happened, as if from the outside, but also to get inside the historical actor's head. However, the peril of such empathic "understanding" lay in the way it opened the door to the irrational or the incommensurable. Droysen, who seems to have been the first to build this term into his understanding of the historian's craft, looked back to Wilhelm von Humboldt for inspiration.[36]

Weber's analysis of this problem began with the difficulty of achieving successful empathy and ended with the difficulty produced by having successfully achieved empathy. When thinking about the experience of a historical figure, he wrote, the historian switched from first-person to third-person experiences. This distancing had the effect of turning people into "objects" of study. Empathy, or "inner participation" in the experience of a living person, was real, but could it extend to a person who had become an object?[37]

At this point in his analysis of empathy Weber turned to his great Italian contemporary Benedetto Croce in order to clarify, against a different kind of target, what he understood by understanding.[38] Croce had maintained that this thing the Germans called understanding (knowledge through empathy) was impossible because the objects of study—facts—stood at such a remove from us that we could grasp them only through intuition. Knowledge came from concepts—he clearly shared this assumption with the neo-Kantians—and concepts operated at a second order: they were based on "relations between objects." The concept had a general nature, while objects were particularities. But— not convinced by the neo-Kantians' solutions—Croce believed that history had no concepts. Or, as Weber put it, "Whether a fact in our life 'was [a] real [fact]'—the only question that history is concerned with— cannot be found out by means of any conceptual analysis." For Croce, according to Weber, the most one could do was the "reproduction of intuitions," and he thus concluded that "history is memory."[39]

But even history-as-memory-grasped-through-intuition was too much for Weber. He argued that "it is quite erroneous to believe—as so many laymen do, and Croce accepts—that history is a 'reproduction of (empirical) perception' or a depiction of previous 'immediate experiencing.'" "As soon as it [experience] becomes an object of *thought*," Weber wrote, it instead becomes "another 'experience' of the earlier experience." Empathy with the historical figure was, therefore, possible, but it could not take you all the way back to that figure's past.

This decoupling of concept from object pitched history perilously close to phenomenology. Weber was too much the historian to allow this. And, in any case, an experience of an inner experience was simply a new experience "that includes the 'feeling' . . . of having once already 'immediately experienced' 'this'—['this'] being a part, which remains indeterminate, of what is given in the present 'immediate experience.'"[40] Psychological self-evidence of this sort belonged to phenomenology and not history.

For Weber, history lived in the space between "the categorical, mathematical evidentness of spatial relations, and the phenomenolog-ically conditioned evidentness of the life of the mind, which can be [an] object of 'empathy.'"[41] *Pace* Simmel, history did not happen solely inside the historian's head; it referred to the world and communicated an interpretation to other people.[42] The empirical mattered. Weber was not prepared to write off the world, and with it the possibility of explanation, by limiting the cultural sciences to interpretation (understanding) alone. Nor was he willing to fall back upon the certainties of the phenomenological.

What about a history of feelings? Surely here, Weber muses, was a place for the historian's empathy. Some argued that it was especially nec-essary for the understanding of cultural products. "When a historian, an archaeologist, a philologist, 'enters into the spirit of' 'personalities,'

'artistic epochs' [or] 'languages,' this takes the form of certain 'feelings of commonality,' 'feelings for language,' etc., and it has even been
claimed that those feelings are the most reliable 'canon' for the historical determination of, for instance, the provenance of a document or a
work of art, or for the interpretation of the reasons behind, and the
meaning of, a historical act." But, try as he might, Weber could not
convince himself of this. While feelings were important, the acquisition
of feeling for a past feeling could be obtained only through "constant
intellectual occupation with the 'material,'—that is to say: practice, and
therefore, 'empirical experience.'" Nothing could be claimed on the
basis of shared feelings alone. "Every conscious scholar," Weber wrote,
"must categorically deny that references to 'feelings of totality' . . .
can claim to have any sort of value, unless [those references] can be
translated into precisely articulated, demonstrable judgments . . . and
can therefore be tested." Weber rejected the inevitable vagueness that
comes with divining by feeling, writing, "Each one sees what he carries
in his heart."[43]

Yes, a historical appeal to "feelings" could be a shorthand description. Or it could be a way of helping the audience grasp a character or
time or place. In all this the historian used words to evoke feeling. Still,
Weber remained cautious. "As long as [the reexperiencing of an experi-
ence] remains at the stage of what is 'felt,' [the historian's value feelings]
will always and unavoidably be non-articulated." The problem was that
the appeal to emotion was all about the emotional life of the observer,
and "not the 'life' of the epoch or the personality in question, or of the
concrete work of art."

Weber gives as an example the encounter with a foreign town,
which can produce in us a "feeling of totality" through our response
to things like the angle of the chimneys, the shape of the roof cornices,
and the like, all of which "are absolutely incidental, that is to say: of no
causal importance" for the people who live there. "The same is true,"
he concludes, "of all non-articulated historical 'intuitions'"—Croce's
term again, though now explicitly connected to objects that are material
forms. These claims cannot be "valid" because they have not been
analytically articulated. (Croce, we recall, described these "intuitions" as
feeding "memory," not history.) And, deeper within Weber's response,
was a fear of totalizing. The search for a "total character" that responded
to a "feeling of totality"—this aestheticizing was what Weber saw as
an "enormous danger." The danger came in the distance between
this aspiration and the "empirical historical knowledge of actual

interconnections (causal interpretations)." The gap between empathy and the empirical was where Weber made his stand.

Croce was not interested in real objects. But can we apply Weber's discussion of historical subjects as *objects* of inquiry, conducted via Croce, to real, three-dimensional objects? Weber's discussion of objects, at least on the surface, seems not so different from Husserl's call in those same years to return "zu den Sachen selbst"—"to the things themselves"—another comment that had little to do with specific objects yet did refer to the world at large and thus indirectly to objects as well. In just the same way that it is not implausible to treat Husserl's "Sachen" as real things, building on his premises but moving in a direction he did not himself go, or even license, it is possible to take Croce's objects as Weber read them, and to treat them as real objects for the purpose of seeing exactly where this might take us.

Weber's discussion of the way a city makes a psychic impact through its physical form, and his difficulty with precisely this form of purely sentimental presentation, suggests that he would have difficulty with today's knowledge projects based on empathy, such as *The Hare with Amber Eyes* or a Neil MacGregor–like hundred stories book. But, we might wonder, is this a rejection of objects as knowledge? Or just a rejection of them insofar as they were being activated *only* through empathy?

It was in 1906, after writing about the "Spirit" of Protestantism and capitalism that Weber explicitly turned to the methodological issues at stake in writing cultural history. He does not speak in terms of cultural history but rather of cultural science, perhaps wary of too close an association with Lamprecht. The values studied by the cultural sciences, Weber wrote, do not occur on their own but as embodied in something else. "The 'interpretation' of 'Faust' or of 'Puritanism' or of some specific aspect of 'Greek culture,'" he writes, "in *this* sense is an inquiry into those 'values' which 'we' *can* find 'embodied' in these objects." The discovery and establishment of these values was the task of empirical scholarship.[44] But it could only be accomplished with the assistance of that "methodologically schooled imagination" Weber placed at the core of value interpretation.

As with his discussion of "objects" in Croce, Weber's discussion of cultural "objects" like *Faust* can, I think, be extended to museum objects. They, too, are "embodied values" whose meaning can be unlocked only by the empirical research of individual scholars. But getting from individual facts to their embodiment, whether as concept or ideal type or museum object, requires an act of interpretation.

And every act of interpretation, according to Weber, is a more or less implicit statement of philosophy of history. What this means is that the "validity" of the values involved in the choice of historical material can never be established in the same way as the validity of empirical facts. And this means that the objects of historical scholarship, like the objects of museum scholarship, have a validity that their interpretation, whether arrayed on a page or displayed in a gallery, does not. "Instead," Weber writes, "it is an interpretation of the values that 'we' 'can' find in the object—or maybe even 'should' [find in the object]." If we say that interpretation *should* find these values, then we are inside a "normative discipline," he writes, such as aesthetics. If we say that interpretation *can* find these values in the object, we are within "value relations of the object." Weber does not explain what this means, but I think we can say that it refers to the information we discover by doing historical research that is conditioned by the historian's particular framing of the question. This work, he argues, is "the only way in which one can leave behind the complete impreciseness of [what has been grasped by] 'empathy' and reach that kind of precision that knowledge of individual spiritual and intellectual conceptions is capable of attaining."[45] With this, Weber seems confident that he had found both a way to the embodiment of values in particular objects as well as access to their emotional dimension, all without yielding to the temptation of totalizing or empathic gestures.

While the historian might think that he can explain the facts of daily life with ironclad certainty, as soon as he tries to make a broader statement about the "character" of a time, place, or person, he is doing no differently than the interpreter of *Faust*—that is, operating in the murky ways of the cultural historian. Eduard Meyer, Weber writes, one-sidedly saw the "'static,' 'systematic' treatment of a [given] material as constituting the difference of principle from the historical." Rickert, too, saw the "systematic" as closer to the natural sciences than to the cultural sciences.[46] But Weber objected to this. All complex historical work, he wrote, involved a "process of *abstraction*" as it "transforms the given 'reality' in order to make it into a historical 'fact.'" In Goethe's words, Weber wrote in conclusion, "there is 'theory' in 'facts.'"[47] It wasn't just that Weber was defending the status of the structural, the static, the cultural, even the antiquarian, as historical. He was also saying that political or military history—the more familiar forms of history—was no different from cultural history in being shaped by the values of the historian and not simply transcribed from nature.

Returning, at the end, to the question of the differences between the human and natural sciences, Weber returned also to the role of the "imagination." Even Ranke, for all his work in archives, was a "diviner" of the past, according to Weber. Without imagination the historian "will remain a sort of junior clerk of history." This was no different, Weber continued, in the work of mathematicians or biologists. Their discoveries "all flash 'intuitively' through the imagination as hypotheses and are subsequently 'verified' by confrontation with facts; that is to say: the question of their 'validity' is examined in the light of the already existing empirical knowledge, and they are formulated in a logically correct way."[48] If the historian's use of her imagination is not run through evidence, or if she suggests the course of events without documenting it, "surely that account would be a historical novel and not a [set of] scientific findings." There can be artfulness of style and design, but there had always to be "a firm framework of causal imputation" to enable us to use the word "true" for a historical work. This is Weber's fundamental claim.

In the passage in the 1904 essay on objectivity that we have cited before, Weber made a subtle and impassioned and precise argument about the complexity of history as a science of concrete reality (*Wirklichkeitswissenschaft*): "To what extent the historian (in the widest sense of the term) is able to perform that [causal] imputation reliably by bringing his method[olog]ically schooled imagination, enriched by the experiences of his personal life, to bear, and to what extent he will need help from specialized disciplines, that will depend on the individual case."[49] Research, precision, detail—all were necessary. But so too was an imagination informed by that research and further nurtured by a similarly methodologically schooled reading of the historian's own life. And even with all this, exactly how the "imputation," or extrapolation, worked could be assessed only on a case-by-case basis. This was more hedged than anything offered by Dilthey or Rickert or even Simmel, but also much truer to the actual experience of doing history. It is important to emphasize Weber's commitment to scholarly rigor. Even the "experiences of his personal life" were not an alternative to scholarship, as in Nietzsche's critique of philology from the 1870s, but immanent through the mechanism of value interpretation. By acknowledging that the historian's starting point and interests are a function of personal experience Weber has integrated the self and the scholar even as he then insists that beyond values there lay only the rigor of science.[50]

In 1913, Weber was still writing about interpretation and *Verstehen*. Human behavior had to be "understood," and understanding was obtained by interpretation, only now that his leading category was "sociology" rather than "cultural science," he called it *verstehende Soziologie*—"interpretive sociology"—rather than *historische Kulturwissenschaft*.[51] But when Weber talked about sociology as interpretive, "he meant to affirm that in history only men act, not social organisms or reified collectivities," and that we were to seek out the "ideas and intentions of historical actors rather than search for 'scientific' laws."[52]

Arnaldo Momigliano read and thought about Weber all through his career.[53] Coming back to his dichotomizing "Ancient History and the Antiquarian" after reading Weber can help us understand the foundation of the lifelong conversation Momigliano had with him. Both were trying to understand how historical scholarship worked, one via metatheory and the other via the history of history. Momigliano may not have written much about the theory of history, and Weber not much about the history of history. But when Momigliano returned to Weber in the 1960s he was able to draw the conclusion that sociologists were but "antiquarians armed with modern methods for fighting the follies—juvenile and senile—of absolute historicism."[54] Weber, for his part, was aware that detailed, preparatory scholarship in an age of big-question social science would appear "utterly stale and tedious, or at least very secondary—and indeed, if it is carried out for its own sake, completely pointless."[55] But, as we have seen, he was also committed to the historical character of scholarship on the past that was noncausal (value analysis), muddying any simple dichotomy between history and antiquarianism.

Finally, because the cultural sciences were historical, and because history in Germany was shaped by the Historical School, it made sense to Weber to review its principles—much as he had done already in his article on Roscher. He also offered a justification for this methodological reflection. It raised implicit assumptions "to the level of explicit consciousness." "On the whole," he wrote, "I can agree with this: methodology can never be more than a self-reflection on the means that have proved useful in [scientific] practice; and one does not need to be made explicitly aware of those means in order to produce useful work." Metatheory was not a precondition for good work, just as knowledge of anatomy was not needed in order to walk. It was only if someone was having a problem walking and needed treatment that knowledge of anatomy became essential. "But this," Weber wrote, "is undeniably the situation in which history finds itself in the present." Knowledge of the epistemic preconditions of historical research was now something that historians needed to know.[56] It still is. And if we want to take seriously the possibility of a *Museumswissenschaft*, then knowledge of these epistemic foundations is necessary as well.

Museumswissenschaft as *Kulturwissenschaft*, ca. 1900

Philosophically speaking, the first decade of the twentieth century may be said to have begun with Edmund Husserl's *Philosophical Investigations* (vol. 1, 1900; vol. 2, 1901) and his phenomenological appeal to return "to the things themselves." Husserl was not referring to things so much as principles, or "objects of thought," though Heidegger followed the implications of Husserl's language toward the world of "equipment." An editorial on the first page of the first volume of the journal *Wörter und Sachen*, which appeared at the very end of that decade (1909), saw the need to proclaim the very opposite—that is, to stay truer to Husserl, and that by "things" they did not intend merely objects possessing extension but also "thoughts, ideas and institutions" given verbal expression. The editorial declared the study of language as comprising only one part of "Kulturwissenschaft." "The future of *Kulturgeschichte*," the anonymous editor wrote, "lies in the uniting of *Sprachwissenschaft* and *Sachwissenschaft*."[57] At the time of writing, "the history of 'things'" was not fully built out, and basic etymological work remained necessary. The project of the reciprocal illumination of words by things and things by words was fully comparative and required the broadest scope. Hence the framing of this project in terms of *Kulturwissenschaft*.

The view from Glasgow was very similar. David Murray in 1904 had proposed a special commission—he noted that in Hamburg it had taken the form of a "Culturhistorisches Museum"—which he translated as historical-culture—"to take charge of and enlarge the museums of Ethnography, Archaeology, and Applied Arts." These three museums referred to "the lower forms of civilization of the present time," "the life, the thought and culture of prehistoric peoples," and "the manners and customs of our own day." Together they functioned through the mechanism of comparison.[58] It was widely accepted, Murray wrote, that picture galleries and libraries were central components of modern institutionalized culture. Museums were not so central. And yet without them certain kinds of knowledge work could not occur:

> History, as now pursued, is founded upon the study not only of original documents, but of all the objects of public and private life that are accessible. The novelist is not satisfied unless he portrays the times he describes with the accuracy of an archaeologist, and the stage depicts the scene it presents as faithfully as possible. The materials for such study and equipment are to be found principally in museums.[59]

Museum knowledge, as such, was inseparable from the question of display. This is where Lauffer and Richter, with their focus on the empirical encounter, on archaeology, and on purpose, offered a clear picture. But when they were writing, and more important, when Koetschau was publishing them in *Museumskunde*, the question of display was a topic of public discussion. In fact, just a year before Lauffer began publishing on the historical museum, *Museumskunde* had published Wilhelm von Bode's address on the opening of the new Friedrich-Wilhelm-Museum in Berlin.

If we recall the rigor with which Lauffer and Richter treated display, we might be shocked by Bode's approach. For example,

> The corners of the halls are left as empty as possible, so that each wall represents a calmly closed picture. Moreover, we have not left too much space between the pictures, because otherwise the wall fabric as such asserted itself too strongly. Rounding off all the pictures hung on a wall to create a harmonious overall picture through the multiplicity and symmetry of opposites in format, subject, color, and tone, as well as isolating each individual picture through the diverging neighboring pictures, are the main principles according to which the paintings are set up in all departments.[60]

The quest for simplicity and symmetry extended so far that Bode rejected the idea of displaying sculptures with the paintings as too "busy" (*unruhig*), and he saw the display of paintings along with their corresponding drawings as impractical. Richter even cited this in his discussion of display.[61] Some period objects could, however, be displayed near the paintings, Bode wrote, but the gallery was under no circumstances to follow the model of the decorative arts museum (he cites Zurich's in particular).[62] The original space in which the painting lived was deemed important for the modern viewer to experience, but it was to be evoked through lighting and architecture rather than decoration. This is what Malcolm Baker has described as a "period style" room, rather than a period room.[63] Overcrowding was what Bode feared, and so he proposed limiting the contents of rooms to give the works the "greatest possible isolation."[64] But Bode also worried about coherence on the macro scale, as did Lauffer and Richter. Bode warned that decorative arts museums that mixed rooms from different religions, peoples, and periods ran the risk of crossing the line distinguishing them from ethnography museums—a telling comment, however unintended.[65]

Bode's discussion of the display of decorative objects is unscientific in a different way: a "tastefully arranged installation of only selected pieces," he writes, was the best way "to capture the interest of the public." Even where he does invoke cultural-historical display principles—presumably the putting together of objects in context—he argues that it is for the improvement of artisanal work, effectively blurring the difference between the founding principles of the South Kensington and Germanic national museums.[66]

Moreover, when Bode gives examples of cultural-historical installations for the purpose of artistic improvement, he is still operating, as a curator, with the principles of a decorator rather than a scientist.

> The cultural-historical arrangement in separate rooms, and in large museums a few rooms, completes the space, consistently, in quite modern decor. Here, however, the by no means occasional mass acquisitions from world exhibitions may be piled up (one sees what has happened in the largest museums!). But a room should be a harmonious whole from the hand of a single or a very few similarly and singularly talented people; for example, a chapel by Louis Tiffany, a living room by one of the English decorators— best of all a room by the few German artists, who have gradually been influenced by Japan, and, inspired by a Whistler-like fruitful direction, pursue a naturalistically perceived and musically tuned decorative approach, but formed of their own imagination and on national foundations.[67]

Bode, in short, may have established a model for curatorial practice, but he does not give us anything that we would need for our project of establishing the content of a "Museumswissenschaft."

By contrast, Lauffer and Richter insisted on "empirical" research and would have agreed that both ethnography and history were "sciences of reality" (*Wirklichkeitswissenschaften*). If "objects" in Croce, as in Husserl, may have hovered on the edge of metaphor, the route from Richter to Weber gives us a clear sense that the real reality is the object, and so—moving now from Weber back to Richter—*Museumswissenschaft* must be a *Wirklichkeitswissenschaft*, for the museum is the place of concreteness par excellence. What we do in a museum is entirely the Weberian project of imputation from the concrete to the general—we create ideal types in the form of exhibitions and use them to understand past worlds.

Aby Warburg, Weber's exact contemporary, described his practice as an art historical cultural science ("kunstgeschichtliche Kulturwissenschaft"). But he aimed to move the world not into the museum but onto the writing table (as in his famous remark about the tortuous path of enlightenment from the mountaintops of Sils-Maria to the lowlands of the scholar's study, for example). If we want a *museumswissenschaftliche Kulturwissenschaft*, we will need Lauffer and Richter *and* Weber. Weber saw that Rickert's problem of constitution was crucial: only if we can agree that there is such a thing as the cultural sciences can we then specify what kind of knowledge was theirs. By the same token, if we want to know what kind of knowledge is museum knowledge, then we need works like Richter's and Lauffer's, which establish *Museumswissenschaft* as a field of knowledge.

Weber's commitment to the empirical was his way of resisting the perils of sentimentalization, what he called "totalization." Had he known of Warburg's associative thinking, he might have expressed some concern about it for just this reason. Warburg, for his part, seemed to have been paying attention to Weber; in the introduction to his lecture in January 1929 in Rome he proclaimed his belief in "the close points of contact between Archaeology, Art History and sociologically exact Historical Science."[68]

Weber seemed to worry about the loss of a common platform for argumentation once empirical research was swapped out for feeling or feeling operated free from the claims of evidence. He would have been very uncomfortable with the twentieth-century turn launched by Georges Bataille and the surrealists, which found in the premodern museum collection an aesthetic source for a philosophical critique of modernity's taxonomic categories. To the extent that we can imagine Weber as a museums thinker, we would see him struggling with the associative logic of the *Wunderkammer*.

To really appreciate what Weber, or Richter through Weber, brought to thinking about museums, we need to go back to the ancestor of *Museumskunde*, the Dresden-based pioneer publication of the previous generation, Johann Georg Theodor Grässe's *Zeitschrift für Museologie und Antiquitätenkunde*. In 1883 Grässe published an article titled "Die Museologie als Fachwissenschaft." In it, he argued that up to that point there was no agreed-upon formation for the museum professional akin to Friedrich Ebert's *Die Bildung des Bibliothekars* (1820). He insisted on the importance of academic training—no moonlighting artists any longer— but also of specific knowledge: philosophy, philology, history, languages.

Broad culture, yes, but also detailed knowledge of "mythology, symbolism, heraldry, sigillography, paleography, numismatics, ethnography, ceramics."[69] What Grässe was enumerating was none other than the contents of the *historische Hilfswissenschaften*, or auxiliary sciences of history, the corpus of knowledge that developed out of seventeenth-century antiquarian scholarship and shaped early nineteenth-century regional cultural history in Germany.[70] Grässe focused on the qualifications of museum professionals and their evaluation. This was discipline defined in terms of individuals and training. What Richter and Weber give us a generation later is discipline defined in terms of a way of thinking. That is what the turn to metatheory produced: an epistemic view of museum studies, something that did not exist at that point and which, a generation later, had been lost, even among those still reading Lauffer and Richter, to the process Gadamer later called "effective history" (*Wirkungsgeschichte*).[71] Weber's epistemological essays had been collected and republished, but to an audience that saw him as a founder of sociology and no longer a theorist of *Kulturwissenschaft*.[72]

By inserting ourselves into this ongoing process of meaning-making we can ask what a Weberian *Museumswissenschaft* might look like. It would be a science of the "concrete" or "empirical" (a *Wirklichkeitswissenschaft*). It would move from "imputation" of argument to the greater rigor of the "ideal type." It would put research at the heart of museum activity. At Weber's insistence, those putting exhibitions together would examine the way they used individual objects to stand for larger categories, acknowledging that there will always be a gap between the displayed object and the "concept" being argued for. And those putting exhibitions together would also have to acknowledge the way their "methodologically schooled imagination" and "life experience" affected their interpretations. He would have us remember that the exhibition space was, just like the ideal type, a "utopia," and not the past "as it actually was." And he would have us bear in mind that the seriousness of display as an intellectual venture means recognizing the "inalienable right" of objects. But, following Goethe's idea of "morphology," one would also acknowledge that the constellating of objects in an exhibition could give new meaning, from the outside, to those objects and that this would change over time with changing states of knowledge.[73] Most important, museum collection and display would create knowledge that otherwise would not have come into existence.[74]

This museology never came to be. What stood in the way, aside from the difficulty of these texts and the mismatch between their creators and their readers, and aside from the bad timing of unfolding during the *Lamprechtstreit*, and aside from the asymmetrical power relationship between art museums and all other museums, and aside from the intervening catastrophe of Nazism, was the vexed relationship between humanities disciplines and applied learning. Treating museum learning as a discipline now, in the twenty-first century, means accepting that applied learning has a place in the humanities. This is still a difficult sell, though the increasingly powerful pull of data may make things easier for other kinds of applications. But, even more, accepting the applied means acknowledging that today's current, proud disciplines could be the *Hilfswissenschaften* of tomorrow—bodies of knowledge that we use as needed to solve real-world questions.

The challenge of the world beyond the cloister, court, or quad is something with which the disciplines have always struggled. The core of the conflict between basic and applied research is that the world is not cut up into disciplines. But if we see the future as posing questions, and if we acknowledge that there is a positive value in being able to answer them well, then a museums science could be much more central to the endeavor of humanistic education. We need history, art history, archaeology, and anthropology—and that's just for the "historical museum," to use Lauffer's term—but also botany, materials science, chemistry, physics, and zoology, among others, if we are to imagine the problem-solving horizon of the future. And if we believe in democracy, then the museum's value as a place where citizens can learn not just facts but how to evaluate them and to argue with them, is no trivial consideration. Maybe, in that future, the museum will take its place at the center of the university campus, not as the passive storehouse on which the disciplines occasionally draw for their more prestigious higher-order theorizing but the reverse: the experimental place where approaches to the object are taken from various helping disciplines and then collaboratively applied to the world.[75]

1.   Marianne Weber, *Max Weber: A Biography*, trans. Harry Zohn (New Brunswick, NJ: Transaction, 1988), 485, 499.

2.   Mentioned in a letter to Paul Siebeck of December 30, 1913, cited in *The Max Weber Dictionary*, 2nd ed., ed. Richard Swedberg and Ola Agevall (Stanford, CA: Stanford University Press, 2016), 327.

3.   Swedberg and Agevall present furthering the project of theorizing with Weber as a goal of their *Max Weber Dictionary*.

4.   "Roscher and Knies and the Logical Problems of Historical Economics" (3 parts: 1903, 1905, 1906); "The 'Objectivity' of Knowledge in Social

Science and Social Policy" (1904); "Critical Studies in the Logic of the Cultural Sciences" (1906). These essays were gathered and published posthumously as Max Weber, *Wissenschaftslehre* (Tübingen: J. C. B. Mohr, 1922).

5.   Richard Bendix and Guenther Roth, *Scholarship and Partisanship: Essays on Max Weber* (Berkeley: University of California Press, 1971), 37; *Max Weber Dictionary*, 76.

6.   Ola Agevall, "A Science of Unique Events: Max Weber's Methodology of the Cultural Sciences" (Ph.D. diss., Uppsala University, 1999), 112. The broader implications of Weber's work on the cultural sciences have been discussed carefully by Fritz Ringer, *Max Weber's Methodology: The Unification of the Cultural and Social Sciences* (Cambridge, MA: Harvard University Press, 1997).

7.   Max Weber, "Roscher's 'Historical Method,'" in *Max Weber: Collected Methodological Writings*, ed. Hans Henrik Bruun and Sam Whimster, trans. Hans Henrik Bruun (New York: Routledge, 2014), 11. On comparison, see Renaud Gagné, Simon Goldhill, and Geoffrey E. R. Lloyd, eds., *Regimes of Comparatism: Frameworks of Comparison in History, Religion and Anthropology* (Leiden: Brill, 2019), esp. 447–58.

8.   Max Weber, "The 'Objectivity' of Knowledge in Social Science and Social Policy," in *Collected Methodological Writings*, 115.

9.   Weber, "'Objectivity' of Knowledge," in *Collected Methodological Writings*, 103.

10.   Weber, "'Objectivity' of Knowledge," in *Collected Methodological Writings*, 104–5.

11.   G. W. F. Hegel, *Phenomenology of Spirit*, trans. A. V. Miller (Oxford: Oxford University Press, 1977), para. 753, 455–56.

12.   See Hans-Georg Gadamer, *Truth and Method* (1960; New York: Crossroad, 1985), pts. I, II, 2(d), 149.

13.   Weber, "'Objectivity' of Knowledge," in *Collected Methodological Writings*, 111.

14.   *Max Weber Dictionary*, 69.

15.   Weber, "'Objectivity' of Knowledge," in *Collected Methodological Writings*, 111.

16.   Weber, "Roscher's 'Historical Method,'" in *Collected Methodological Writings*, 4–5, 6n6.

17.   Weber, "Knies and the Problem of Irrationality," in *Collected Methodological Writings*, 136: "The decisive point, however, is the following: history is simply not confined to the domain of 'mental life.' On the contrary, it 'conceives' the entire historical constellation of the 'external' world both as a motive and as a product of the 'mental life' of the bearers of historical action. That is to say: things which, in their concrete multiplicity, have no place in a psychological laboratory."

18.   Weber, "'Objectivity' of Knowledge," in *Collected Methodological Writings*, 117–18.

19.   Weber, "'Objectivity' of Knowledge," in *Collected Methodological Writings*, 125.

20.   See Guy Oakes, *Weber and Rickert: Concept Formation in the Cultural Sciences*, (Cambridge, MA: MIT Press, 1988), 24–26.

21.   Weber, "Critical Studies in the Logic of the Cultural Sciences," in *Collected Methodological Writings*, 140

22.   Weber, "Critical Studies in the Logic of the Cultural Sciences," in *Collected Methodological Writings*, 152.

23.   Weber, "Critical Studies in the Logic of the Cultural Sciences," in *Collected Methodological Writings*, 146.

24.   Guy Oakes, "Rickert's Value Theory and the Foundations of Weber's Methodology," *Sociological Theory* 6 (1988): 39.

25.   Weber, "Critical Studies in the Logic of the Cultural Sciences," in *Collected Methodological Writings*, 152.

26.   Weber, "Critical Studies in the Logic of the Cultural Sciences," in *Collected Methodological Writings*, 155–56.

27.   Weber, "Critical Studies in the Logic of the Cultural Sciences," in *Collected Methodological Writings*, 157. See also Hans Henrik Bruun, *Science, Values and Politics in Max Weber's Methodology* (2007; London: Routledge, 2016), ch. 2.

28.   J. Wach, *Das Verstehen: Grundzüge einer Geschichte der hemeneutischen Theorie im 19. Jahrhundert* (Tübingen, 1926); Manfred Riedel, *Verstehen oder Erklären? Zur Theorie und Geschichte der hermeneutischen Wissenschaften* (Stuttgart: Klett-Cotta, 1978).

29.   Weber, "Knies and the Problem of Irrationality," in *Collected Methodological Writings*, 65n1.

30.   Weber, "Critical Studies in the Logic of the Cultural Sciences," in *Collected Methodological Writings*, 158–59.

31.   "Geschichte ist eine fortlaufende Statistik; und Statistik ist eine stillstehende Geschichte." See Miller, *History and Its Objects*, 86–89.

32.   Weber, "Critical Studies in the Logic of the Cultural Sciences," in *Collected Methodological Writings*, 158–59; Arnaldo Momigliano, "The Rise of Antiquarian Research," in *The Classical Foundations of Modern Historiography* (Berkeley: University of California Press, 1990), 54.

33.   Weber, "Critical Studies in the Logic of the Cultural Sciences," in *Collected Methodological Writings*, 160.

34.   Weber, "Knies and the Problem of Irrationality (Continued)," in *Collected Methodological Writings*, 87–88.

35.   Hans Henrik Bruun, "Weber's Sociology—'Verstehend' or 'Deutend'?," *Max Weber Studies* 16 (2016): 43.

36.   See Fulvio Tessitore, "L'istorica' di Droysen tra Humboldt e Hegel," *Storicismo e pensiero politico* (Milan: Riccardo Ricciardi, 1974), 63–117.

37.   Weber, "Knies and the Problem of Irrationality (Continued)," in *Collected Methodological Writings*, 69.

38.   In 1905, through the intermediation of their mutual friend Karl Vossler, Croce sent Weber a copy of his *Logic*, and in the next year Weber sent Croce the third part of his essay on "Knies and the Problem of Irrationality." For a direct engagement with this exchange, see Fulvio Tessitore, "Croce e Weber," in his *Contributi alla storia e alla teoria dello*

storicismo (Rome: Storia e Letteratura, 1997), 395–403; and Edoardo Massimilla, "La 'commedia degli equivoci' di 'uno dei più belli intelletti dei nostri tempi': Benedetto Croce critico di Max Weber," in *Croce e la modernità tedesca*, ed. Santi Di Bella and Francesca Rizzo (Canterrano: Aracne, 2017), 131–40.

39.   Weber, "Knies and the Problem of Irrationality (Continued)," in *Collected Methodological Writings*, 70.

40.   Weber, "Knies and the Problem of Irrationality (Continued)," in *Collected Methodological Writings*, 70–71.

41.   Weber, "Knies and the Problem of Irrationality (Continued)," in *Collected Methodological Writings*, 74–75.

42.   Georg Simmel, *The Problems of the Philosophy of History: An Epistemological Essay*, trans., ed., and intro. Guy Oakes (New York: Free Press, 1977), 75–82.

43.   Weber, "Knies and the Problem of Irrationality (Continued)," in *Collected Methodological Writings*, 76.

44.   Weber, "Knies and the Problem of Irrationality (Continued)," in *Collected Methodological Writings*, 78–79.

45.   Weber, "Knies and the Problem of Irrationality (Continued)," in *Collected Methodological Writings*, 79.

46.   Weber, "Critical Studies in the Logic of the Cultural Sciences," in *Collected Methodological Writings*, 168.

47.   Weber, "Critical Studies in the Logic of the Cultural Sciences," in *Collected Methodological Writings*, 175. The quote from Goethe also served as the motto of chapter 1 of Rickert's *Die Grenzen der naturwissenschaftlichen Begriffsbildung*: "Das höchtste wäre, zu begreifen, dass alles Faktische schon Theorie ist." On this, see Arthur G. Zajonc, "Facts as Theory: Aspects of Goethe's Philosophy of Science," in *Goethe and the Sciences: A Reappraisal*, ed. Frederick Amrine, Francis J. Zucker, and Harvey Wheeler (Dordrecht: D. Reidel, 1987), 219–45.

48.   Weber, "Critical Studies in the Logic of the Cultural Sciences," in *Collected Methodological Writings*, 175–77.

49.   Weber, "'Objectivity' of Knowledge," in *Collected Methodological Writings*, 118.

50.   Weber believed that the personal side of scholarship was to be kept as far away as possible from the public side of scholarship. As late as 1919, in "Science as a Vocation," where Weber rebutted the view that scholarship was a kind of training in wisdom and professors surrogate sages, he did not even address the question of how—or whether—life was a preparation for scholarship. Weber, "Science as a Profession and Vocation," in *Collected Methodological Writings*, 348–49.

51.   Weber, "On Some Categories of Interpretive Sociology," in *Collected Methodological Writings*, 273–74.

52.   Guenther Roth and Wolfgang Schluchter, *Max Weber's Vision of History: Ethics and Methods* (Berkeley: University of California Press, 1979), 205.

53.   See *L'Archivio Arnaldo Momigliano: Inventario analitico*, ed. Giovanna Granata, preface by Riccardo di Donato (Rome: Storia e Letteratura,

2006), Notebooks N-b 1 (1939–42); P-c 7 (July, December 1961); N-f 165 (August 1976), 169 (1977), 176 (1979); P-i 3 (1982).

54. "I sociologi, come ho tante volte avvertito, non sono che gli antiquari armati di metodi moderni per combattere le folle giovanili o senili dello storicismo assoluto." "Prospettiva 1967 della storia greca" (1967), in *Quarto contributo alla storia degli studi classici e del mondo antico* (Rome: Storia e Letteratura, 1969), 51. See also the very important linkage between antiquarianism and sociology in the conclusion to the Sather Lecture devoted to antiquarianism (Momigliano, *Classical Foundations of Modern Historiography*, 78–79), composed in the second half of 1961.

55. Weber, "Critical Studies in the Logic of the Cultural Sciences," in *Collected Methodological Writings*, 161.

56. Weber, "Critical Studies in the Logic of the Cultural Sciences," in *Collected Methodological Writings*, 140–41.

57. "Vorwort," *Wörter und Sachen* 1 (1909): 1.

58. David Murray, *Museums: Their History and Their Use* (Glasgow, 1904), 235, 254.

59. Murray, *Museums*, 278.

60. "Die Ecken der Säle sind möglichst frei gelassen, damit sich jede Wand als ruhig geschlossenes Bild darstellt. Im übrigen haben wir nicht zuviel Zwischenraum zwischen den Bildern gelassen, weil sich sonst der Wandstoff als solcher zu stark geltend macht. Abrundung sämtlicher auf einer Wand aufgehängter Bilder zu einem harmonischen Gesamtbild durch Mannigfaltigkeit und Symmetrie der Gegensätze in Format, Gegenstand, Farbe und Ton, und daneben Isolierung jedes einzelnen Bildes durch die abweichenden Nachbarbilder, sind die Hauptprinzipien, nach denen die Gemälde in allen Abteilungen aufgestellt sind." Wilhelm von Bode, "Das Kaiser-Friedrich-Museum in Berlin: Zur Eröffnung am 18.Oktober 1904," *Museumskunde* 1 (1905): 8–9.

61. Bode, "Das Kaiser-Friedrich-Museum in Berlin," 9.

62. From 1904 and the preparations of the Kaiser-Wilhelm-Museum (Wilhelm von Bode, *Mein Leben*, ed. Thomas W. Gaehtgens and Barbara Paul [Berlin: Nicolaische, 1997], 300–301).

63. Malcolm Baker, "Bode and Museum Display: The Arrangement of the Kaiser-Friedrich-Museum and the South Kensington Response," *Jahrbuch der Berliner Museen* 38 (1996): 145 [= Beiheft "Kennerschaft." Kolloquium zum 150sten Geburtstag von Wilhelm von Bode].

64. Wilhelm von Bode, "The Renaissance Museum," *Fortnightly Review* 56 (1891): 511. Bode did allow for the creation of full-scale apartments, though in these the display of paintings would be the secondary feature, and even then the number of pieces of furniture would be limited (512).

65. Wilhelm von Bode, *Kunst und Kunstgewerbe am Ende des Neunzehnten Jahrhunderts* (Berlin: Bruno und Paul Cassirer, 1901): "Ob es bei der Einrichtung solcher zeitlich und national beschränkter Räume richtig ist, so weit zu gehen, alte Wohnräume der verschiedensten Zeiten und Völker nachzubilden und mit deren künstlerischem Hausrat auszuschmücken, die Kulträume der verschiedenen Religionen und Zeiten in ähnlicher

Weise in ihrer Dekoration vorzuführen, möchte ich bezweifeln. Dies birgt die Gefahr in sich, den Völkermuseen, die in der Art der Anordnung den Kunstgewerbemuseen gegenüber entschieden den richtigen Weg einschlagen, Konkurrenz zu machen" (65–66).

66.   Bode, "Die Aufgaben der Kunstgewerbemuseen," 124.

67.   Bode, "Die Aufgaben der Kunstgewerbemuseen," 126–27.

68.   "engeren Fühlungnahme zwischen Archäeologie, Kunstgeschichte und soziologischer exacter Geschichtswissenschaft." Quoted in Dieter Wuttke, *Cosmopolis der Wissenschaft: E. R. Curtius und das Warburg Institute; Briefe 1928 bis 1953 und andere Dokumente* (Baden-Baden, 1989), 231.

69.   Johann Georg Theodor Grässe, "Die Museologie als Fachwissenschaft," *Zeitschrift für Museologie und Antiquitätenkunde* 6 (1883): 113–15, 129–31.

70.   Miller, *History and Its Objects*, chs. 3, 4, 6.

71.   Note the handful of references to Lauffer (4) and Richter (4), and Thurnwald rather than Richter (8) in Pessler, "Die Forschungsaufgaben der kulturgeschichtlichen Museen," in *Forschungsinstitute: Ihre Geschichte, Organisation und Ziele*, ed. Ludolph Brauer, Albrecht Mendelssohn Bartholdy, and Adolf Meyer, 2 vols. (Hamburg: Paul Hartung, 1930), 1:260–79.

72.   For the precise fate of this term in the years 1929–33, see Peter N. Miller, "Kulturwissenschaft before Warburg," in *Aby Warburg 150: Work, Legacy, and Promise*, ed. David Freedberg and Claudia Wedepohl (Berlin: De Gruyter, forthcoming).

73.   For cultural history as fundamentally morphological, see Johan Huizinga, "The Task of Cultural History," in *Men and Ideas: History, the Middle Ages, the Renaissance*, trans. James S. Holmes and Hans van Marle (New York: Meridian, 1959), 59, 64.

74.   Hans-Jörg Rheinberger's provocative but only gestured-at suggestion that specific visualization techniques—he names compression/dilation, enhancement, and schematization—could be borrowed from the life sciences and used as exhibition display practices hints at a parallel project having deep affinities with the Weberian vision of the exhibition as a utopic form of model-building. See "Visualization in the Sciences—and in Exhibitions?," in *The Exhibition as Product and Generator of Scholarship*, ed. Susanne Lehmann-Brauns, Christian Sichau, and Helmuth Trischler (Berlin: Max-Planck-Institut für Wissenschaftsgeschichte, 2010), Preprint 399, 9–24.

75.   In this I follow André Leroi-Gourhan, "L'ethnologie et la muséographie," *Revue de synthèse* 2 (1936): 27–30, trans. in *André Leroi-Gourhan on Technology, Evolution, and Social Life: A Selection of Writings from the 1930s to the 1970s*, ed. and intro. Nathan Schlanger (New York: Bard Graduate Center, 2022).

Contributors

Julien Chapuis is deputy director of the Bode Museum, Berlin. From 1997 to 2007 he was curator of medieval art at the Metropolitan Museum of Art, New York.

Edward S. Cooke, Jr., is the Charles F. Montgomery Professor of the History of Art at Yale University.

Viola König is professor of pre-Columbian studies and cultural anthropology at Freie Universität Berlin. She was director of the Ethnologisches Museum Berlin (2001–17) and Übersee-Museum Bremen (1992–2001).

Deborah L. Krohn is associate professor and chair of academic programs at Bard Graduate Center. Her research and teaching areas include early modern European art and cultural history, history and theory of museums, culinary history, and book history.

Alisa LaGamma is the Ceil and Michael E. Pulitzer Curator in charge of the Department of the Arts of Africa, Oceania, and the Americas at the Metropolitan Museum of Art. Her most recent exhibition and publication is *Sahel: Art and Power on the Shores of the Sahara* (2020).

Peter N. Miller is dean and professor at Bard Graduate Center.

H. Glenn Penny is professor of history, University of Iowa. He is the author of *Im Schatten Humboldts: Eine tragische Geschichte der deutschen Ethnologie* (2019).

Ruth B. Phillips is Canada Research Professor and Professor of Art History emerita at Carleton University in Ottawa. She researches and publishes on Native American art and critical museology.

Jeffrey Quilter is an archaeologist and the former director of the Peabody Museum of Archaeology & Ethnology at Harvard University (2007–19).

Matthew Rampley is principal research investigator at Masaryk University Brno, focusing on art and cultural politics in central Europe. His latest book is *Liberalism, Nationalism and Design Reform in the Habsburg Empire* (2020).

Anke te Heesen is professor of the history of science at Humboldt University of Berlin.

Nicholas Thomas has written extensively on encounters, empire, and art in the Pacific, and on museum histories and futures. He is director of the Museum of Archaeology and Anthropology in Cambridge.

Céline Trautmann-Waller has written about the history of human sciences (philology, ethnology, anthropology, aesthetics) and is currently working on a book about applied arts.

Eva-Maria Troelenberg is professor of modern and contemporary art history at Utrecht University. Her research focuses on exchange processes between the Islamic world and Europe in the arts and material culture, and on cross-cultural museum histories.

Mariët Westermann is the vice chancellor of NYU Abu Dhabi. Previously, she led major initiatives for the humanities, museums, and diversity at the Mellon Foundation.

Index